BEYOND CRIMEA

AGNIA GRIGAS

Beyond Crimea

THE NEW RUSSIAN EMPIRE

Yale UNIVERSITY PRESS

NEW HAVEN AND LONDON

Published with assistance from the Mary Cady Tew Memorial Fund.

Yale University Press books may be purchased in quantity for educational, business, or promotional use. For information, please e-mail sales.press@yale.edu (U.S. office) or sales@yaleup.co.uk (U.K. office).

Set in Scala and Scala Sans type by Westchester Publishing Services, Danbury, Connecticut.
Printed in the United States of America.

Library of Congress Control Number: 2015944595
ISBN 978-0-300-21450-5 (cloth : alk. paper)

A catalogue record for this book is available from the British Library.

This paper meets the requirements of ANSI/NISO Z39.48-1992 (Permanence of Paper).

10 9 8 7 6 5 4 3 2 1

For Julius

CONTENTS

ACKNOWLEDGMENTS

THIS WORK, WHICH COVERS fifteen different states and another half-dozen breakaway territories composed of numerous nationalities and ethnic groups, has been made possible only by the insights, comments, and research assistance of regional experts as well as scholars of Russia. Here I would like to acknowledge in-country scholars, experts, and event participants who provided local language skills and insights for the country case studies or helped conduct interviews in remote places and frozen-conflict zones. In my work on Ukraine I am grateful for the assistance of Dmytro Kondratenko and the insights of Dmytro Levus and Lilia Muslimova. For research on Georgia, I would like to acknowledge the help of my research assistant Tengiz Sultanishvili, and the comments of Elguja Gvazava, Vytis Jurkonis, and Tengiz Pkhaladze. For contributing to this book's analysis of Moldova, I appreciate the assistance and insights of Iuliana Marcinschi, Victor Chirilă, and Dmitri Gavrilov. For contributing to my understanding of the Baltic States, I am grateful to my research assistant Lukas Trakimavičius and to Juljan Jachovič, Laurynas Kasčiūnas, Andis Kudors, Ivan Lavrentjev, Nerijus Maliukevičius, and Raivo Vetik. For assistance with material related to Central Asia, I would like to first thank my research assistant Dinara Pisareva and in addition to acknowledge the input of Fabio Belafatti, Alexander Cooley, Nargis Kassenova, Askar Nursha, Sebastian Peyrouse, Otto Pohl, and Charles E. Ziegler.

For information related to Belarus I am indebted to the assistance of Vytis Jurkonis and the comments of Pavel Usov and Roman Yakovlevsky, and regarding Armenia, I am grateful for the help of Hovhannes Nikoghosyan and the insights of Emil Sanamyan. For work on Russian compatriot policies I would like to acknowledge my research assistant Sabina Karmazinaitė and the insights of Ammon Cheskin.

I would also like to thank colleagues and mentors from the political science and international relations community, including Alexander Motyl, Jack Snyder, Daniel Treisman, and Douglas Becker for their comments and suggestions. I would also like to express my gratitude to my thoughtful and insightful copy editor Gavin Lewis and to academic writing coach Amy Benson Brown, who encouraged me to make this book accessible to a wide audience. My editor at Yale University Press, Jaya Aninda Chatterjee, deserves special mention for her enthusiasm for and dedication to this project from the start.

I am most grateful to nearly one hundred Russian speakers residing from the Baltic States to Central Asia, in cities and small towns, some enjoying peaceful conditions and others suffering in areas of conflict and war: protected only by their anonymity, they agreed to be interviewed for this book and offer their voices while their very presence is politicized and often exploited both by their countries of residence and by the Russian government. Finally, I alone take responsibility for all of the book's content and any unintended errors or shortcomings.

CIS	Commonwealth of Independent States
CSTO	Collective Security Treaty Organization
DDoS	Distributed denial of service
EU	European Union
FSB	Federal Security Service
GDP	Gross domestic product
IDC	Institute for Democracy and Cooperation
KGB	Committee for State Security
LNG	Liquefied natural gas
NATO	North Atlantic Treaty Organization
NGO	Nongovernmental organization
OSCE	Organization for Security and Co-operation in Europe
RSFSR	Russian Soviet Federative Socialist Republic
SVR	Federal Intelligence Service
UN	United Nations
USSR	Union of Soviet Socialist Republics

BEYOND CRIMEA

CHAPTER ONE

The Return to Empire

RUSSIA'S ANNEXATION OF CRIMEA in March of 2014 and the subsequent war in eastern Ukraine have alarmed European powers and the United States and raised the specter of further aggression. Just a year before the takeover of Crimea, while many Russia experts anticipated an active Russian foreign economic policy vis-à-vis its neighboring states and a tug-of-war over Ukraine, none expected a military threat reminiscent of the twentieth-century conflicts or the Cold War era.[1] In fact, before Russia's annexation of Crimea, a consistent threat to the post-Soviet space seemed implausible. After Crimea, Donetsk, Luhansk, and Mariupol, however, Russia's ability to redraw Europe's map and incite wars is evident. Following upon the pro-Russian separatism and conflict in South Ossetia, Abkhazia, and Transnistria in the 1990s and 2000s, the Ukrainian conflict suggests a continuing and worrying trajectory. Revanchist and resurgent, Russia appears ready to challenge the current post–Cold War order. By 2015 most scholars, analysts, and Western leaders concurred that the Russian government led by Vladimir Putin has emerged as a challenger rather than a partner to Europe and the United States.[2] Regardless of how the ongoing Russo-Ukrainian war unfolds in the coming years, the tensions between Russia and the West are unlikely to subside because the fundamental sources of conflict will persist. Over the next decade the questions on every Russia scholar's, policymaker's, and

military strategist's mind will remain: Will Russia seek additional territorial expansion in Eastern Europe and the post-Soviet states? Will Russia
try to redraw its boundaries with the former Soviet republics? Russia's
annexation of Crimea and waging a shadow war in eastern Ukraine on the
pretext of protecting the so-called Russian compatriots demonstrates
that a reassessment of the Kremlin's territorial objectives vis-à-vis its diaspora residing in the former Soviet republics is imperative. Who is at risk?
What military, humanitarian, propaganda, and soft power tools will Moscow utilize? Where is Russia likely to succeed in achieving its aims? Where
will the Kremlin likely fail? This book addresses these questions head-on.

Since the early 2000s Russia has consistently sought to maintain and
regain influence as well as has reinvigorated its efforts to expand its territory in the former Soviet Union republics. There have been a number
of explanations of the driving factors of such policies. Russia's ongoing
influence on the foreign policy, economy, political systems, and energy
sectors of the post-Soviet space and Europe has already been studied.
Here, however, I will tell a story that has been overlooked, but one that
Moscow has persistently pursued—the story of Russian "compatriots."
This loosely defined term that the Kremlin adopted in the early 1990s
refers to a wide range of approximately 25 to 150 million people living outside of the borders of the Russian Federation. Broadly the "compatriots"
belong to two groups, which will be necessary to distinguish in the following discussion. First, in the narrowest sense they include actual
ethnic Russians residing abroad, whom I will refer to as such, or simply
as Russians. Second, and in a broader sense, they include both ethnic Russians and non–ethnic Russians who nevertheless use the Russian language
significantly or exclusively in daily life, whom I will call "Russian speakers"
or "Russophones." In the broadest sense the Russian government has
sometimes even applied the term "compatriots" to descendants of citizens
of the Soviet Union in general, including other individuals and ethnic
groups who may not be Russian speakers but who hold various cultural,
political, and spiritual affiliations with the Russian Federation, the historical Russian Empire, and the "Russian world." In discussing these three
groups together in the context of Moscow's policies, I too will often call
these groups "Russian compatriots" or just "compatriots"; however, many
post-Soviet states resist the use of this term, as do many of the people to
whom Moscow applies it. I will therefore also use more neutral terms like

"Russian diaspora," "Russian minority/minorities," and "Russian-speaking minority/minorities," and the like to refer to ethnic Russians and Russian speakers residing abroad.

Many ethnic Russians came to live outside the Russian Federation and in the former Soviet republics when they migrated for work or were forcibly relocated during the Soviet era and even in tsarist times. Following the disintegration of the Soviet Union, most remained and became citizens of the newly independent states. Over time, this Russian diaspora, reconstructed politically by Moscow as Russian compatriots, has become the instrument of Russian neo-imperial aims. In this book I will show how since the 1990s and particularly since the 2000s, Moscow's policies have leveraged the existence of Russian compatriots, particularly ethnic Russians and Russian speakers residing abroad, to gain influence over and challenge the sovereignty of foreign states and at times even take over territories. This book will demonstrate that Moscow's hold on these groups serves as an effective pretext for and instrument of much of Russia's expansionist foreign policy. While Moscow has been using its diaspora as a means of influence since the 1990s, the Russo-Georgian conflict of 2008 was the first full-fledged war between Russia and a post-Soviet state fought largely over Russian compatriots. However, since that time not many discerned a connection between the seemingly disparate Russian policies of compatriot support, humanitarian agendas, handing out Russian citizenship, and information warfare in remote parts of the former Soviet space. Nonetheless, the territorial implications of Moscow's policies toward its compatriots have been demonstrated in Ukraine's Crimea and eastern territories, in Georgia's South Ossetia and Abkhazia, and Moldova's Transnistria. The distribution of Russian speakers and ethnic Russians across the former Soviet Union countries and current separatist areas and conflict zones is shown in Map 1. Russia's compatriot policies have raised tensions in Moldova's Gagauzia, Estonia's Ida-Viru county, Latvia's Latgale region, northern Kazakhstan, Armenia, and elsewhere in the post-Soviet space. The developments in Ukraine, Georgia, and beyond have shown that Russia's compatriot policies are inextricably tied to its expansionist ambitions and neo-imperial aims. For Moscow, compatriot policies perform an integrative function—a unification of the Russian peoples combined with potential to unify with the motherland the territories where they reside.

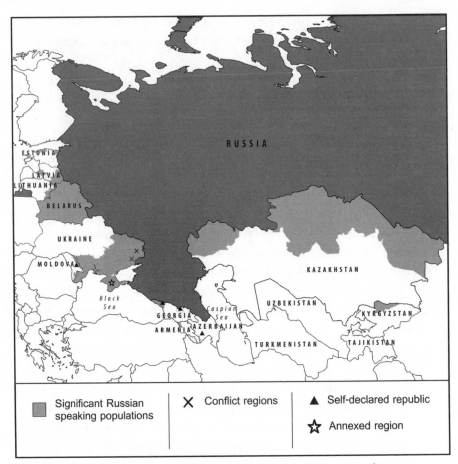

MAP 1. Distribution of Russian speakers and disputed territories across the post-Soviet states. Map drawn by Giedrė Tamašauskaitė

While neo-imperialism has been a prominent trend in Putin's era, it is in fact rooted in the history of the Russian Empire. There is an undeniable historical continuity between present Russian imperial projects and past projects of the Romanovs and the Soviets. The Russian Federation has in many respects followed in the footsteps of its historical predecessors and will continue to do so, because of the similar ideological, cultural, security, and geopolitical drivers that have been rooted in the centuries-long imperial experience of the three empires—the Russian Federation, the Soviet Union, and the Russian Empire—that have occupied the same Russian political space and territories. The Grand Duchy of Moscow (Muscovy) started out as a landlocked principality in the late thirteenth century and expanded aggressively to acquire new lands and peoples, as well as access to waterways. The subsequent expansion of the Romanov empire in the seventeenth and eighteenth centuries under Peter the Great and Catherine the Great was driven by a desire for new lands, the taming of bordering nations, and the quest for warm-water ports on the Baltic Sea, in Crimea, and in the Caucasus.

Russia's policies toward the inhabitants of its imperial space have also been consistent for centuries. Historically, Moscow's imperial quest has created sizable pockets of ethnic Russians, Russian speakers, and other displaced minorities in the territories that constituted the Russian Empire. The tsars imposed Russification policies that made the Russian language and the Cyrillic alphabet official while banning native ones on most of the subjugated territories. Other policies included ethnic cleansing, resettlement and deportations of locals, and colonization by Russians to create multiethnic populations in newly acquired lands.[3] During the Soviet empire, Stalin's ethnic policies continued the tsarist trajectory. Russification was pursued during the entire Soviet period despite the official proclamations of equal rights for all nations. Soviet-era immigration policies sought to increase the percentage of Russians while diminishing the percentage of local ethnicities in every Soviet republic excluding Russia. The purpose was threefold. First, targeted immigration supported industrialization in the Soviet republics by enlarging the local labor force. Second, immigrations and the creation of multi-ethnic societies helped establish a new identity, a "Soviet nationality." The third goal was to enmesh and intertwine the fifteen Soviet republics within the Union ethnically, culturally, politically, and economically.[4] As a result of these ethnic policies and Soviet imperial rule, following the fall of the USSR the boundaries of its successor states did not always reflect the ethnic, political, or economic realities on the ground for many Russians and non-Russians alike.[5] As a result, the legacies of Russia's historical imperial projects, and specifically tsarist and Stalinist ethnic policies, have created the means, causes, and conditions for Russia's imperial revival. Since the 2000s this revival has been facilitated and driven by the pretext of protecting Russian compatriots in the former Soviet republics.

POST–COLD WAR NARRATIVES AND DEBATES

The analysis of Russian foreign policy has been greatly influenced by the times and their geopolitical context. The end of the Cold War and the perceived triumph of democracy and capitalism marked a decline of interest in Russia and the former Soviet space. In 1989 American political scientist Francis Fukuyama argued that "what we may be witnessing is not just the end of the Cold War, or the passing of a particular period of post-war history, but the end of history as such: that is, the end point of mankind's ideological evolution and the universalization of Western liberal democracy as the final form of human government."[6] The concept of "the end of history" gained popularity among international relations scholars and policymakers and influenced the study of Russia and the post-Soviet space. The fledgling Russian democracy under President Boris Yeltsin and the enlargement of NATO and the EU to include Central and Eastern European states in the late 1990s and 2000s bolstered this hopeful concept of the "end of history." The Cold War seemed an element of the past safely confined to history books. Yeltsin pulled out Soviet troops from Eastern Europe, dramatically cut Russia's military spending, and agreed to let Ukraine keep part of the Soviet Black Sea Fleet—all while not stoking separatism in Crimea. Neither Yeltsin's regime nor the incoming Putin regime recognized the independence of Georgia's South Ossetia or Abkhazia. Moscow still has not recognized Moldova's breakaway territory of Transnistria. Under Yeltsin and Putin, Russia also accepted two rounds of NATO enlargement by the adhesion of former Warsaw Pact states and the former Soviet republics of Estonia, Latvia, and Lithuania in 1999 and 2004. In the 2000s, Putin closed Russia's military bases in Cuba and Vietnam, while the United States opened military bases in Central Asia. Since 1991 Russia and the United States continued to collaborate on disarmament of weapons of mass destruction, and post-9/11 on the fight against global terrorism. Russia looked like a potential partner for the West. Where did this story of East meets West go wrong? Was this narrative of cooperation between Russia and the West ever really true? Some ask today if the West pushed the weak and humiliated Russia too far and failed to understand its strategic national interests and security concerns. Or was there an alternative narrative all along?

As political scientist Alexander Motyl observed in 2001, "[c]ommunities of people do not become nations simply because we wish to imagine them as such; regimes do not become democratic just because we use the modifier; and political entities do not become—or stop being—empires merely because terminological fashion says so."[7] By the mid-2000s it was increasingly clear that Russia had not become a democratic state, nor had its aspirations for empire been squashed by the "end of history." Tensions over the post–Cold War order and post-Soviet borders reemerged. NATO and EU expansion reached Russia's borders and the borders of its so-called near abroad states that Moscow viewed as its inherent sphere of influence. In the same period Russia went to war for the first time outside its borders in the Russo-Georgian conflict of 2008.

Nonetheless, Russia's imperial revival appeared like a marginal idea in the broader context of Russian foreign policy for most of the 1990s and 2000s. Neo-imperialism was embraced mostly rhetorically and superficially by a handful of radical Russian politicians like Vladimir Zhirinovsky or alluded to by Putin and his entourage for rhetorical flourish and to drum up nationalism among the domestic audience. Some attributed this nascent imperialism to Russia's growing wealth and confidence driven by high oil prices of the mid-2000s.[8] Some pointed again to the natural need to correct the alleged "humiliation" of Russia after the collapse of the USSR.[9] Following the global economic downturn of 2008 and the domestic protests of 2011–13 against Putin's regime, some saw Russia as isolated, embattled, and defensive and hence pushing back against these constraining international conditions.[10] Some suggested that the rising nationalism and aggression was Putin's response to his weakening popularity and growing opposition at home and an attempt to rally the country behind the Russian flag.[11] But few took the rising signs of Russia's vaulting imperial ambitions seriously. Indeed over the past five years, most scholars have justified this indifference by alleging that Russia was a shadow of its former self and its military presented no challenge to the European continent or international order.[12] For instance, in 2011, scholar of Russia and at the time director of the Carnegie Moscow Center, Dmitri Trenin, echoed a common sentiment at the time: "Russia's remarkable disinterest in its former empire has been paralleled by the other former Soviet republics distancing themselves from the former imperial center."[13] With the Georgian war already forgotten, the signs of Russian neo-imperialism were not all that evident.

Some scholars and commentators—especially those closer to the part of the world in question—did foresee Russia's expansionist drive all along. In 1994, Norwegian academic and founder of peace and conflict studies Johan Galtung stated that Russia is expansionist and likely to base its agenda "on Slavic culture and religious orthodoxy, building a Soviet Union II based on Russia, Belarus, eastern Ukraine and northern Kazakhstan."[14] In 2001 Ukrainian-American Motyl argued that Russia is pursuing "creeping reimperialization."[15] In 2008, without much support at the time, British commentator and *Economist* editor Edward Lucas argued that Putin's Russia has waged a "new cold war" on the West.[16] In 2009, Kiev-born, Moscow-based political scientist and former Yeltsin adviser Emil Pain concluded, rather anticlimactically but nonetheless in dramatic counterpoint to the established view, that Russia demonstrates an "imperial syndrome" and seeks "maintaining territories" while preserving or re-creating an empire.[17] Days ahead of the annexation of Crimea in March 2014, I argued that we are witnessing an expansionist strategy in action—Moscow's efforts to grab land in the former Soviet space under the guise of protecting Russian compatriots.[18]

Following the annexation of Crimea, there has been much debate on how to respond to Russia's revanchism, but the debate has not been new. Since the 2000s, there has been disagreement about whether Russia can be a true partner to the West or whether it will remain a potential threat. The United States under the leadership of George W. Bush supported NATO expansion to Ukraine and Georgia and installing a missile defense system for Central and Eastern Europe. President Barack Obama sought to "reset" relations with Moscow and some progress was made before the initiative fizzled. Following Russia's aggression in eastern Ukraine, head of the Senate Foreign Relations Committee Robert Menendez and other senators argued for arming Ukraine to fight Russia.[19] In December 2014 the U.S. Congress voted for another round of tougher sanctions.[20] In early 2015, after rocket attacks from Russian-supported separatist regions on the Ukrainian city of Mariupol, the EU extended its sanctions on Russia. Motyl has argued in *Foreign Affairs* that George F. Kennan's Cold War policy of "containment," formulated in regard to the Soviet Union, should be applied to contemporary Russia to thwart its expansionism in Ukraine and the post-Soviet space.[21] However, before a long-term response to Russia's neo-imperial strategy can be launched, an understanding of

Russia's policies as well as their drivers and aims is imperative. At the center of Moscow's expansionist policies lies the question of the Russian "compatriots."

THE REIMPERIALIZATION POLICY TRAJECTORY

The central argument of this book is that since the 1990s and particularly since the 2000s there has been an increasing tendency in Russian foreign policy toward reimperialization of the post-Soviet space, especially in regard to the territories where Russian compatriots reside. Under Putin's leadership, Moscow's policies demonstrate an increasingly orchestrated effort to utilize its Russian compatriots in neighboring states in order to opportunistically grab land and gradually rebuild its historic empire when domestic and international conditions are favorable. Over the past decade, Moscow has sought influence over the Russian and Russian-speaking diaspora by offering them Russian citizenship and passports and eventually calling for their military and legal protection. This has resulted in de facto or de jure annexation of territories where Russian compatriots reside, as demonstrated in Ukraine, Georgia, and Moldova. Indeed, Putin's request to the Russian Senate to approve military intervention in Ukraine in order to "protect the interests of Russian citizens and compatriots"[22] on 1 March 2014 highlighted once seemingly innocuous compatriot policies that had been formulated two decades ago. These policies, whose origins and development will be explained in detail in Chapter 3, were ostensibly meant to protect and support ethnic Russians and Russian speakers living in the near abroad. These policies could appear to be part of Moscow's harmless soft power and cultural efforts. Instead, these compatriot efforts should be understood as part of Russia's and the Putin regime's consistent policy trajectory that seeks territorial gains in the former Soviet republics, especially where three factors are present: (1) a large and concentrated population of Russian speakers or ethnic Russians; (2) that population resides in territories bordering Russia; (3) the population is receptive to Russia's influence.

Throughout this book, I will demonstrate how Russia employs soft power, compatriot and humanitarian policies, information warfare, and "passportization" (systematic distribution of Russian citizenship) to prepare for more aggressive military policies under the guise of separatism, civil conflict, peacekeeping, and support for compatriots. The outcome may be hybrid warfare—or a military strategy that seamlessly blends conventional military tactics with irregular ones that can include civilian participation, guerilla warfare, and modern technology to achieve an advantage both on land and in cyberspace. These methods help Russia's foreign policy to achieve its expansionist and territorial ambitions. I propose that there is a consistent trajectory in Russia's policies toward the former Soviet republics and their populations, and particularly their territories where Russian compatriots reside that follows seven stages. What I term the "Russian reimperialization policy trajectory" starts with (1) soft power and continues to (2) humanitarian policies, (3) compatriot policies, (4) information warfare, (5) "passportization," (6) protection, and finally (7) annexation.

In this book I will demonstrate how the reimperialization trajectory is employed in action through case studies of nearly all of the post-Soviet states. Countries will be grouped and analyzed not always by their geographic proximity but rather by where they fall on this trajectory. The analysis will group states like Ukraine, Georgia, and Moldova that have demonstrated the full spectrum of Russia's reimperialization policies including de facto or de jure annexation of their territories. The Baltic States will be viewed together because with significant ethnic Russian and Russian-speaking populations they demonstrate the extent, limits, and risks of Russia's compatriot policies in EU and NATO member states. The Central Asian states have demonstrated relative success in repelling Moscow's measures including efforts at passportization of ethnic Russian and Russian-speaking minorities. The focus will be on Kazakhstan, which also faces the greatest risk of separatism and conflict due to its vast territories bordering Russia that are populated by a large Russian minority. Russia's dependent allies, Belarus and Armenia, will be discussed together because they offer alternative lessons as the seemingly least likely sites of Russia's aggression. Azerbaijan and a few of the Central Asian countries will be awarded less attention as they do not significantly add new insights on Moscow's reimperialization efforts and in the latter cases, publicly available information is limited.

To offset the facts and figures of historical and contemporary realities of Moscow's compatriot policies and the Russian diaspora, I will rely on the warmth of human voices of this largely misunderstood but highly politicized group of people. Each country study will present portraits of ethnic Russians and Russian speakers selected from nearly a hundred interviews. I have specifically reached out to younger Russians and Russophones born following the dissolution of the Soviet Union. They represent the future generation of a population that Russia would like to claim as its compatriots and they will likely impact their countries' relations with Moscow in the years to come. Russian speakers rather than solely ethnic Russians have been selected because in most of the analyzed countries, language, identity, ethnicity, and citizenship do not always go hand in hand. Furthermore, Russia often opportunistically counts among its compatriots those who are Russian-language speakers, whatever their relationship to these other categories, or simply those who have a cultural or spiritual connection with Russia or the Orthodox Church. Certainly this is no scientific survey, as I could not gather a representative sample from every ethnic, age, or socio-economic group. Likewise, only the voices of those who were willing to be interviewed will be heard here. In many (though not all) cases they represent a more Westernized, open, and perhaps bold group than their peers. Some, residing in remote corners of autocratic countries and frozen-conflict territories, were often too fearful to participate in my survey, or simply unreachable. The purpose of letting these voices be heard is thus, not to offer a scientific portrait of the Russian compatriot, but rather to humanize the issues at stake and to illustrate more vividly the complexity of the feelings within and across different people. Likewise, this is a story of countries, peoples, and issues that until recently have not received much attention from mainstream scholars and analysts. As such I have sought to tell this story as authentically as possible, supplementing my research of documents, policies, media reports, and academic studies with the insights of local experts and scholars. My approach is likewise driven by my goal of shedding light on the complex and multidimensional issues at stake in Moscow's efforts to engage and co-opt its compatriots. Many of Russia's policies follow the now widely accepted paradigm of "winning the hearts and minds"[23] of target peoples, albeit with a mix of coercion, information warfare, and the threat of military aggression. As the case studies will demonstrate, Moscow has outmatched the target countries in their own efforts to engage their Russian minorities. However, an effective response to Moscow's policies in the form of counterengagement strategies can be launched only with a deeper understanding of these target "compatriot" populations. This book will offer insight into a group of people spread across Ukraine, Georgia, Moldova, the Baltic States, Kazakhstan, Kyrgyzstan, and elsewhere that Moscow has tried to claim but both their home countries and the West would also be wise to engage.

RUSSIAN "EMPIRE": THE EVOLUTION OF A CONCEPT

In addition to being a study of Russian compatriots this book is also a study of the Russian reimperialization project. The use of terms such as "empire" and "reimperialization" may appear dramatic and archaic. Nonetheless, scholars are talking more of empire today than they did twenty-five years ago. What do these terms mean? Reimperialization means the reemergence, revival, or reconstitution of empire.[24] International relations scholar Michael Doyle defines empire as "a relationship, formal or informal, in which one state controls the effective political sovereignty of another political society. It can be achieved by force, by political collaboration, by economic, social, or cultural dependence."[25] For Motyl, empire is more about the funneling of resources from the periphery to the core. He characterizes empire "as a hierarchically organized political system with a hub-like structure—a rimless wheel—within which a core elite and state dominate peripheral elites and societies by serving as intermediaries for their significant interactions and by channeling resource flows from the periphery to the core and back to the periphery."[26] For the purposes of the argument of this book, I consider the contemporary Russian Federation as an "empire" and the successor of the historical Soviet and Romanov empires—a concept that requires some explanation, especially as regards the Soviet Union.

Russian history is a history of empire. The Russian Empire was officially proclaimed by Tsar Peter the Great in 1721 and lasted until Russia's first (February) revolution in 1917. At its peak it stretched over Europe and Asia to North America and included colonies in Alaska and northern California. In landmass it was one of the largest empires in history, surpassed only by the British and Mongol empires. However, the Russian Empire's origins date even earlier—it grew from the Muscovite Russia in the fifteenth century, particularly after Ivan the Terrible was proclaimed tsar in 1547. An important feature of the Russian Empire was serfdom—landless peasants who belonged to the feudal landlord. The concept was almost the equivalent of slavery, as the master could do as he pleased with his serfs and their families, who in 1857 included nearly 40 percent of the empire's population.[27] Established as early as the eleventh century, the system was abolished by decree in 1861 (the same year the American Civil War broke out to end slavery) but many conditions of serfdom persisted.

Indeed, in Russian history, the ideas of empire, tsars, and serfdom are dominant threads that have contributed to present-day Russia and its foreign policy. The culture of a strong leader (a tsar) and of vast masses in bondage (serfs) continues to influence Russian society and identity, and also, as I will demonstrate in Chapter 3, Moscow's top-down policies toward its "compatriots." Motyl's idea of empire as a mechanism of funneling resources from the periphery to the center is also related to unique conditions of the Russian empire. The system of serfdom was introduced by Moscow into newly acquired territories, which increasingly were colonized by Russian or loyal landlords, and thus facilitated the extraction of resources from the periphery to the center.

While tsarist Russia was undoubtedly an "empire"—there is some disagreement whether the term can be applied to the Soviet Union. During the Cold War, the liberal academic establishment did not perceive the Soviet Union as an empire even though it was multinational and hypercentralized. Likewise, the fact that some poorer Soviet republics received more resources than they contributed also challenged the notion of empire. In general, the seemingly pejorative label was perceived as "rabid anticommunism" and "cold war messianism," among the academic establishment, in line with President Ronald Reagan's characterization of the Soviet Union as an "evil empire."[28] Economists John A. Hobson and Rudolf Hilferding, as well as Lenin himself, all maintained that only capitalism produced imperialism, and by this logic the Soviet Union could not be an empire. Indeed, to the uproar of many Sovietologists, French scholar Hélène Carrère d'Encausse was among the first academicians to suggest that "empire" was the correct scholarly designation for the Soviet Union in her 1979 seminal work that predicted the fall of the Soviet regime.[29] It was only after the Soviet Union collapsed that its labeling as an empire became widely accepted—in part because that was how the non-Russian popular fronts as well as Soviet Russian analysts widely described it during the late years of perestroika in the late 1980s.[30]

In what ways is the contemporary Russian Federation linked to the historical empires of the Soviet Union and the tsars? The Russian Federation is the successor state of both the Russian Soviet Federative Socialist Republic (RSFSR) and the Soviet Union, and it inherited the financial obligations and nuclear privileges of the USSR. The RSFSR itself was no nation-state but rather a collection of different administrative regions organized by ethnicity.[31] Like a Russian *matryoshka* doll that has a set of wooden dolls of decreasing size placed one inside the other, so was the RSFSR a smaller empire within the larger USSR, which in turn was part of the larger Soviet empire that included satellite states like the Central and Eastern European Warsaw Pact states and Mongolia. Yet in fact, the RSFSR, the USSR, and the Soviet bloc were not three distinct empires at all. They were all one and the same Russian empire ruled largely by Russians from Moscow and apart from much of East-Central Europe, having much the same borders as the tsarist empire. The Soviet Union occupied almost the identical territory of the tsarist empire, while today the Russian Federation coincides with the borders of the RSFSR. The Russian Federation's proclaimed special sphere of interest is broader and follows the borders of the Soviet Union. Outside the communist ideology, there was very little difference in the imperial project of the Soviets versus that of the Romanovs and increasingly little difference from that of Putin's Russia, which seemingly has adopted imperialism as its ideology. Moscow has always been the core and the other states and territories were the vassals in this centuries-long imperial project.

While the history of Russia as an empire is generally little disputed, the question that remains is whether Russia's history determines its present. In other words, does Russia's historical past necessitate imperial ideology or foreign policy or a reimperialization drive, as this book argues? Political scientist and scholar of Russia Daniel Treisman argued otherwise: "Of course, the past matters; but the footprints do not control the walker. Countries are always both reliving and escaping from their histories, and those histories are not single narratives but albums of distinct and often mutually contradictory stories that offer multiple possibilities for development."[32] Yet tsarist and Soviet policies have created the conditions of a Russian diaspora and Russified minorities across the Eurasian continent that persist until the present day, and which offer a path to Russian imperial ambitions. This is coupled with the fact that Russia views itself as a nation-state rather than a civic state. In Moscow's eyes the Russian nation remains divided by post-Soviet state borders following the collapse of the Soviet Union.[33] As Putin declared in his speech on March 18, 2014, following the annexation of Crimea, "Millions of people went to bed in one country and awoke in different ones, overnight becoming ethnic minorities in former Union republics, while the Russian nation became one of the biggest, if not the biggest ethnic group in the world to be divided by borders."[34] Regardless of the fact that these people have been settled for generations in territories that are now independent states, Moscow seems intent on uniting the Russian diaspora and the territories where they reside under the flag of the Russian Federation.

The Russian government would, however, shun the label of an empire or a reimperializing power. In the case of Crimea's annexation, Moscow argued that it was righting a historic wrong by taking back Russian land that was unfairly given to Ukraine by Soviet leader Nikita Khrushchev in 1954. In the case of Georgia or the Commonwealth of Independent States (CIS) countries, Moscow (with its supporters) has argued that Russia was simply trying to protect its sphere of influence and interests that were under threat from NATO and EU expansion. For instance, following the Russo-Georgian war in August of 2008 then-President Dmitry Medvedev stated that "As is the case of other countries, there are regions in which Russia has privileged interests."[35] In 2014, Secretary of the Security Council of Russia Nikolai Patrushev was quick to emphasize Russia's "assets," all the while arguing that the United States seeks expansion at the expense of Russian interests. According to Patrushev, in the 1990s "Russia unilaterally surrendered its assets on the world stage without being compensated at all."[36] Yet, underneath all of these arguments regarding spheres of influence and inherently Russian lands and "assets" is the same tone of an imperial power seeking to maintain its empire or reimperialize. Indeed, as Motyl states: "Important as historical reality, conceptual category, and analytical device, empires refuse to go away."[37] In the case of Russia, compatriots become a pretext and sometimes an ideological driver in this broader quest for empire that provides a mission, (at times) greater economic and population resources, and most often, a sense of greater security and a distraction from domestic problems.

In the analysis of the driving forces of a state's foreign policy, it is helpful to assess their nature. Are these forces primarily structural? Are they fostered by agents of history? Are they driven by personalities? To apply these competing views to Russia's situation, one might ask: Is Russia's reimperialization driven by structural factors like the global balance of power and the balance of power and resources between Russia and its near abroad states? Or has the figure of Vladimir Putin been central in policies of reimperialization? Certainly, Putin has been an important architect in the political reconstruction of the Russian diaspora into Russian compatriots and in launching the policy of their military protection during the 2000s on the principle of protecting the "legitimate rights and interests" of Russian citizens abroad.[38] On the other hand, the Russian diaspora and Russia's quest for empire predate Putin by centuries and will likely remain issues long after Putin retires from power. Putin's policies reflect in many ways the ambitions of the Russian society and state, as demonstrated by his 85 percent approval rating in late 2014.[39] For the purposes of this analysis, I will not aim to unpack the Kremlin's decision-making apparatus, but will take note of the different actors in Russian foreign policy such as the executive leadership, the Foreign Ministry, and the Russian military, and will pay particular attention to individuals like Putin and even to the legacies of Joseph Stalin. In the end, I hold that Russia's structural and historical predilections have played the key role in its quest for reimperialization, while Putin's leadership and the related domestic political circumstances have been strongly contributing rather than central factors. Throughout this book the focus will fall on the potential structural, ideological-historical, economic, and political drivers of Russia's reimperialization regarding each set of states discussed.

DRIVERS OF IMPERIAL REVIVAL

Simply put, this book will argue that reimperialization—either by regaining lost territories or by maintaining influence and sometimes regaining it where it has been lost—is the end-goal of Moscow's policies. The politically constructed Russian compatriots are one of the means. In some regards this claim of reimperialization is less controversial than it sounds, since one of the seminal theories of international relations, realism, assumes that a state's primary interest lies in maximizing its power and resources. Nonetheless, a number of questions remain about why, weighing its abilities and constraints as well as the costs and benefits, Russia would seek reimperialization. What are the drivers that lead the Russian elite and the government of Vladimir Putin to rebuild the Russian empire? The ideological-historical, structural, political, and economic drivers of Russian motives and interests are sometimes the same and sometimes vary in regard to the different post-Soviet states. Putin's regime has emphasized the ideological themes of uniting the divided Russian nation and of Russia's mission in the world stemming from its unique cultural identity as the home of Slavic and Orthodox Christian civilization. Russia's self-perception is one of empire, and this ideology has been created over the centuries of Russia's history as a multiethnic imperial state where the Russian nation held a privileged position. As the Russian empire is strongly wedded to the Russian national psyche so Russian imperialism is wedded to Russian nationalism.[40] Opinion polls show that from 1996 to 2012 among the primary expectations of the Russian public from their president has been to restore or maintain "Russia's superpower status."[41] The Russian civilization, nation, and in turn the compatriots figure prominently in Moscow's ideological, historical, and cultural rationales for reimperialization. In this unique blend of nationalist and imperialist ideology, the compatriots are parts of the "body" of Russia and of Russian civilization.

The Russian empire has also historically served as means to Moscow's security. The Muscovites were under siege from both Europe and Asia: from the Mongol hordes in the thirteenth century to Napoleonic armies in 1812. The states of the Caucasus and Central Asia and their territories served as a buffer zone for Russia in the south against Islamic civilizations of the Middle East. Ukraine, Belarus, and Moldova continue to serve as buffer zones against Europe and now NATO, while the Baltic States (now NATO members) are sorely missed from Moscow's zone of influence. At the same time Russia and all former Soviet republics (excluding the Baltic States) are now members of NATO's Partnership for Peace program. Nonetheless, recurring talks for NATO membership for, say, Georgia or Ukraine have caused a violent reaction (both metaphorically and literally speaking) in Moscow. Despite Tbilisi's or Kiev's right to choose its foreign policy, Moscow still perceives these states as part of its neo-imperial project.

When assessing Russia's foreign policy priorities vis-à-vis the former Soviet republics, one could question if rather than reimperialization,

Moscow's agenda is solely one of limiting the foreign policy options of the former Soviet republics—preventing their integration into the EU and NATO and instead ensuring their deep integration into Moscow-led economic and political institutions. This would guarantee "good-neighborly relations" between Russia and the post-Soviet world.[42] Yet, this perspective stems from the notion that Russia is entitled to special interests within a sphere of influence or in the words of Doyle, that "one state controls the effective political sovereignty of another political society."[43] One could also conclude that Moscow is seeking to create a new and alternative order in the post-Soviet space. At a minimum, this would entail the Eurasian Economic Union—a Moscow-led political and economic union between Russia, Armenia, Belarus, Kazakhstan, and Kyrgyzstan established in 2015, replacing the Eurasian Customs Union of 2010 and the prior Eurasian Economic Community of 2000. At a maximum, Moscow's plans for the post-Soviet space would entail a new political entity that would include within its borders Russia, Ukraine, Belarus, and Kazakhstan.[44]

Within the security rationale for reimperialization, the Russian compatriots also play an important role. By taking over territories inhabited by compatriots, Moscow is able to establish stronger defenses and borders than if it were to take over potentially less loyal territories. Furthermore, national security and power are in no small part a function of size. Russia's population is less than half that of the United States, about one-third that of the European Union, and only one-eighth that of China. Russia's compatriot policy coupled with reimperialization enlarges Russia's population and territories.

There are also domestic electoral factors stoking Putin's expansionist drive. Russia's military exploits—taming Chechnya's rebellion, victory in the Russo-Georgian war, taking back Crimea, "protecting" Russians in southeastern Ukraine—have all boded well for Putin's personal popularity. Putin first made a name for himself as Russia's new president elect when he sent troops to Chechnya in January of 2000, gaining an 84 percent approval rating.[45] In 2014 pending Crimea's annexation, Putin's approval rating was 72 percent, marking a three-year high after several years of decline, which continued to increase to 85 percent by the end of 2014, almost as high as in 2008 following the Georgian war when his approval rating was 88 percent.[46] Compatriots also feed into in the domestic motives for reimperialization because their incorporation into the Russian Federation appeals to the strong ethnic and cultural dimensions of Russian national rather than civic identity. Finally, another domestic factor in Russia's drive for reimperialization, or perhaps more precisely an effort to hold on to its sphere of influence, is driven by the fear of and desire to contain the success of popular movements calling for regime change that have swept the post-Soviet space. The "colored" popular revolutions started with Georgia's Rose Revolution in 2003, Ukraine's Orange Revolution in 2004, Kyrgyzstan's Tulip Revolution of 2005, Moldova's Grape or Twitter Revolution in 2009, and Ukraine's Maidan of 2013–14. The overturning of stagnant and corrupt regimes could only serve as an example to the Russian people, and Moscow's massive public protests in 2011–13 only reinforced this potential threat to the Putin regime.

There are also economic motives behind Russia's imperial hold on the post-Soviet space. Russia has worked hard to maintain the post-Soviet states in its economic fold by its Eurasian Customs Union and Eurasian Economic Union projects. However, the alternative of EU membership also held appeal for a number of CIS states, including Georgia, Moldova, Ukraine, Armenia, and Azerbaijan, which defied Moscow and started negotiating association agreements and working to meet the conditionality requirements. It is no coincidence that flashpoints between Russia on the one hand and Moldova, Georgia, Armenia, and Ukraine on the other occurred when these countries were seeking closer ties to the EU. The resulting conflicts and challenges to Moldova's, Georgia's, and Ukraine's territorial integrity will serve as a significant hindrance to these states' aspirations to join the EU in the future.

When assessing Moscow's economic interests and motives for reimperialization, it is imperative to understand that the Russian economy is driven by natural resources. Countries that either possess such resources or provide land and sea routes to export them to other markets are and historically have been potential targets of Russia's expansion. Through the territories of Ukraine and Belarus, pipelines export Russian energy sources to European markets. The pipeline crossing Ukraine transports up to half of Russian gas exports to Europe, while the ports of Crimea offer quick access to the eastern Mediterranean, the Balkans, and the Middle East. The ports of the Baltic States have historically served to transport Russia's oil and oil products to European markets until the mid-2000s.

Kazakhstan, Uzbekistan, and Turkmenistan themselves possess vast resources of coal, oil, and gas. Through Georgian territory runs the competing Baku-Tbilisi-Ceyhan oil pipeline, the second longest of the former Soviet Union, which brings Caspian (instead of Russian) oil to Turkey and the Mediterranean.[47] Russia's own vast energy resources have served as powerful means of influence in the near abroad. Members of the Russian diaspora have played their part in this great game of energy influence. Looking across the CIS states, the Baltic States, and beyond, politicians and businessmen loyal to Moscow (often but not always ethnically Russian and with connections to the Kremlin) have benefited from lucrative energy contracts and advantageous deals.[48] Corrupt deal-making has allowed Moscow to put in its pocket a number of politicians not only from its near abroad but increasingly from the EU.[49]

This raises the question why Moscow would opt for potentially more costly and challenging militarized and territorially acquisitive neo-imperialism, when its own energy levers have enabled it to maintain an economic imperial project in neighboring countries. The answer here probably lies in the fact that Europe and even some former Soviet states have been increasingly pursuing strategies of energy diversification. Since 2009, EU regulation has constrained Russia's gas monopoly in member states through its Third Energy Package, which has already resulted in splitting up some of Gazprom's European assets. In 2015, after a three-year investigation, the European Commission released its antitrust charges against Gazprom's practices. The Baltic States and Ukraine among others are looking to liquefied natural gas (LNG) terminals to gain access to alternative sources of gas, while Central Asian and Caucasus states have seen some success in leveraging their own energy resources and exporting them via non–Russian-controlled pipelines to China and Europe. Meanwhile, in North America, the U.S. shale boom has made the United States into a leading global producer of oil and gas in the 2010s. American LNG export and import technologies will make it possible for countries to import gas from almost anywhere in the world, which in the future could reduce dependence on old Russian-controlled gas pipelines. Finally, while Moscow has still been able to maintain the loyalty of some post-Soviet regimes with sweetened energy or economic deals struck with the elites and Kremlin-friendly interest groups, today the publics of a number of post-Soviet states are increasingly (though not always consistently) calling for transparency, reforms, and change. In some regards, Putin's regime has less leverage over the post-Soviet space than that of Yeltsin, but rather than peacefully withdrawing, it raises the specter of further aggression via the remaining lever of Russian compatriots.

Moscow's efforts at imperial revival will certainly incur economic costs. While Russia's ongoing energy stranglehold has somewhat curtailed the West's ability to impose biting economic sanctions following Crimea's annexation in 2014, even moderate sanctions made a significant impact in less than a year. Throughout 2014, Russia's economic and fiscal numbers took a beating with the ruble trading at record lows, while inflation soared and the Central Bank raised interest rates. In 2014 official capital flight from Russia totaled more than $130 billion, but unofficial estimates were much higher.[50] Collapsing global oil prices of 2014 brought more woes, since oil and gas revenues are the backbone of Russia's economy, contributing to more than half of its revenues. The year closed with global oil prices trading at a five-year low of $60 per barrel, in strong contrast to the Russo-Georgian war when in July 2008 oil was trading at its record peak of $147 per barrel. According to the Russian Finance Ministry in 2014, Russia is poised to lose some $140 billion a year due to declining oil prices and Western sanctions.[51] Indeed, the re-imperialization trajectory is easier for Moscow to implement when oil prices are high and Europe is energy vulnerable, but as the case of Crimea demonstrates, economic costs do not deter aggression.

These costs notwithstanding, there has been no sign that either economic pressure or international isolation has deterred Russia's expansionist strategy post-Crimea. This suggests that historical-ideological, domestic political, and security issues, rather than economic drivers, have been paramount in Putin's efforts to challenge the borders of the former Soviet republics. As the seemingly more liberal President Medvedev stated in August 2008 after the Georgian war, "We are not afraid of anything, including the prospect of a new Cold War."[52] Likewise, both policy developments of 2014 and 2015 suggest (and Kremlin insiders confirm) that Putin is less interested in the economy than in great power politics, and most of all interested in remaining in power.[53] Since Crimea, Moscow has been increasingly bolder in sending its troops and weapons to eastern Ukraine despite NATO's pressure, the tragedy of the downing of

Flight MH17 by Russian-supported militias, the Minsk I cease-fire agreement, the rocket attack on civilian targets in Ukraine's southern city of Mariupol, and even the Minsk II agreement of February 2015. Moreover, the intensity and gravity of incidents involving Russian and Western militaries and security agencies visibly increased. In 2014 there were over forty incidents from the Baltic Sea to the High North and Canada, which involved violations of national airspace, emergency scrambles, narrowly avoided midair collisions, close encounters at sea, simulated attack runs, and other dangerous actions occurring on a regular basis.[54] In October 2014, NATO reported that it had intercepted more than one hundred Russian aircraft, three times more than in 2013—many of them intruders into the airspace of the Baltic States.[55] Indeed, there are no signs to suggest that high economic and diplomatic costs will lead Putin to abandon his imperial revival project in the years to come.

OVERVIEW

The next chapter sets out my proposed seven phases of the reimperialization policy trajectory. The discussion will highlight the tight connection between Russia's softer means of influence and its hard power tactics that may result in territorial annexation. The proposed trajectory should be viewed as an explanatory tool rather than a timetable for further Russian adventurism or expansionism.

Chapter 3 examines Moscow's policies and legal framework regarding its diaspora from the 1990s to 2015, demonstrating how over time ethnic Russians, Russian speakers, and other minorities abroad have been politically conceptualized as "compatriots." The chapter highlights the development of Moscow's policies in the 2000s from perceiving compatriots as a problem to seeing them as a potential resource to be employed for Russia's geopolitical aspirations. The origins of the term "compatriot" are reviewed, as well as Stalin's ethnic policies that created the present-day conditions of the Russian diaspora and ethnically mixed states.

In Chapter 4, case studies are presented where Moscow's policies have completed the full progression of the reimperialization policy trajectory from soft power to compatriot protection to separatism and finally to annexation. Analysis of Ukraine places the 2014–15 war in a broader framework of Russia's policies, demonstrating how the annexation of Crimea as well as the ongoing separatist conflict in eastern Ukraine were gradually achieved with soft power, passportization, and information warfare policies. The case of Ukraine is contrasted to Moscow's policies toward Georgia's South Ossetia and Abkhazia, and Moldova's Transnistria and Gagauzia.

The unique case of the Baltic States as EU and NATO members is discussed in Chapter 5. The implications of Russia's compatriot policies in Estonia, Latvia, and Lithuania are assessed, particularly how these policies are evolving beyond soft power tools toward passportization and information warfare. The chapter evaluates the successes and failures of Russia's policies and the likelihood of future conflict by drawing on past examples such as Moscow-incited tensions in Tallinn in the 2000s, and comparison with the conflicts in eastern Ukraine, Georgia, Moldova, and beyond.

Chapter 6 considers the Central Asian countries of Kazakhstan, Kyrgyzstan, Tajikistan, Turkmenistan, and Uzbekistan in regard to Russian compatriot policies, showing that Kazakhstan bears the most risk for the long-term expansionist implications of these policies because of the large numbers of ethnic Russians and Russian speakers residing in territories on Russia's border. The chapter traces the variations in Russia's pursuit of reimperialization in the Central Asian states, demonstrating that in Kazakhstan, Uzbekistan, and Turkmenistan Russia had difficulty moving beyond soft power and humanitarian and compatriot support in the face of the authoritarian nature of these regimes and their nation-building policies.

The last set of country case studies, Belarus and Armenia, is dealt with in Chapter 7. These states have been among Russia's closest allies since their independence and offer a unique perspective on how Moscow's compatriot-driven reimperialization policies can be pursued in highly cooperative, dependent, and vulnerable post-Soviet states. The analysis demonstrates that such states are less able to resist both Russia's softer and its more coercive means of influence, so that they are maintained de facto in Russia's imperial project without the need to resort to outright aggression.

The conclusion summarizes the progression of Moscow's compatriot-driven expansionism from the most clear and current examples to future risk cases in Russia's neighborhood. I argue that Moscow has succeeded in implementing its reimperialization trajectory in Ukraine, Georgia,

Moldova; made notable progress in the Baltic States; reaped many benefits in Armenia and Belarus; and largely fallen short in Central Asia. I also assess the long-term consequences of Russia's neo-imperialist policies, including frozen conflicts and the muted ability of the territorially jeopardized countries to lead independent foreign policies. Finally I consider the implications of the book's findings for Western policy toward Russia and Russian compatriots as well as focus on near abroad countries' policies toward their Russophone and other minorities.

CHAPTER TWO

Russian Reimperialization

FROM SOFT POWER TO ANNEXATION

[Putin] talks about the need to rebuild the world order, about
Russia's birthright to its own sphere of influence, about the
necessity of protecting the Russian minorities abroad. The Kremlin
uses minorities, language and cultural issues to blow up the
neighboring countries from the inside.

—*Boris Nemtsov, February 2015*

THE COLLAPSE OF THE SOVIET UNION was a joyous occasion for
many people from the fourteen subjugated Soviet republics, including
many Russians who sought to transform the Russian Federation into a
civic state out of the rubble of an empire. However, for some of the old
guard of the Kremlin, the dissolution of the Union was a disaster that in
a fortnight wiped out a superpower of some 293 million Soviet citizens
and some eight and a half million square miles that stretched from the
European continent to China. The early years of the fledgling Russian
democracy under President Boris Yeltsin were marked by painful reforms
and an economic slump that was in no small part due to the low global
oil prices of the 1990s.[1] Under the leadership of Yeltsin and his first foreign minister, Andrey Kozyrev (1991–96), there was an effort to leave
behind Russia's imperial ambitions—demonstrated by the withdrawal
of Russian troops from Eastern Europe in the early 1990s, cuts in military spending, recognition of the borders of Russia's neighbors, and in
the case of Ukraine, letting Kiev keep part of the Black Sea Fleet while
not encouraging Crimea's separatists. However, the emergence of strongman President Vladimir Putin in 1999 and growing wealth from rising
global oil prices reignited Moscow's drive to rebuild Russia's lost power

and influence based on the historical legacies of the Soviet Union and even the Romanov empire. Indeed, there was an effort to extend Moscow's sphere of influence (if not its actual territory) to match the borders of the historical Russian empire. As Putin noted in January 2012, the Soviet Union "actually was Great Russia whose base formed back in the 18th century."[2]

This chapter sets forth the central argument of this book, proposing that the Russian government, especially during the regime of Vladimir Putin, has consistently used ethnic Russians and Russian speakers residing abroad to extend its influence and expand its borders at opportune domestic and international moments with the aim of reimperialization of the former Soviet space. Reimperialization is the end of Moscow's policies. The Russian diaspora—reconstructed politically as compatriots— has been the means. Since the early 1990s, and particularly the mid-2000s, Moscow has wooed the Russian diaspora, conceptualized it as Russian compatriots, and sought to unite it in a "Russian World" and provide it with Russian passports. Rhetorical, diplomatic, and even military protection of the Russian compatriots and the newly minted citizens has followed. Eventually, on a number of occasions, compatriots were exploited to achieve Russia's territorial ambitions in the post-Soviet space. In the cases of eastern Ukraine and Crimea as well as Georgia's South Ossetia and Abkhazia, this has resulted in outright or de facto annexation of territories where Russian compatriots and Russian speakers reside. To a lesser extent, the same is true for Moldova's Transnistria. Many similar processes vis-à-vis Russian compatriots are under way in Estonia, Latvia, Lithuania, Belarus, Kazakhstan, and other states in Russia's near abroad.

I propose that Moscow has pursued an increasingly consistent seven-stage reimperialization policy trajectory toward its compatriots, moving from (1) soft power to (2) humanitarian policies, (3) compatriot policies, (4) passportization, (5) information warfare, (6) protection, and (7) informal control or formal annexation of the territories where the compatriots reside. This trajectory starts with Russia's cultural, economic, and linguistic influence over compatriot populations and their target states. Subsequently or simultaneously, Moscow pursues humanitarian policies of aid and support for the various rights of Russian speakers in foreign states unilaterally, bilaterally, and via multilateral institutions. Then the politically reconstructed diaspora community of compatriots is institutionalized and formalized through various policies, including laws, programs, and organizations, such as the Russian state–funded Russkiy Mir (Russian World) Foundation and the Russkiy Dom (Russia House) network. Policies of passportization—offering Russian citizenship to ethnic Russians, Russian speakers, and other minorities residing in specific territories of the former Soviet republics—create concentrated groups of Russian citizens outside Russia's borders. Then the conditions are set for Moscow's information warfare campaign targeted at domestic, foreign, and compatriot audiences that proclaims an "urgent" need for the protection of Russian compatriots and citizens in foreign territories. The final stage is fueling of separatism that results in Moscow's outright annexation or control of the territories where the compatriots reside. Some of the seven stages of this reimperialization trajectory can overlap, occur simultaneously, or occur in a slightly different order. The general trajectory, however, moves from co-optation of ethnic Russians and Russian speakers to territorial expansion under the guise of compatriot or minority protection, all under the veil of a blitz of information warfare.

Rather than a timetable or a formalized set of policies, the proposed seven-phase scenario reveals the aims of and provides context for the seemingly disparate Russian policies that until now have been under the radar. This is not a timetable to predict if and when Moscow will seek military protection of Russian compatriots and territorial annexation in, say, Kazakhstan or Estonia. However, the scenario signals that if a state has already been a target of the previous five phases of soft power, humanitarian, compatriot, passportization, and information policies, then the groundwork has been laid for potentially more aggressive tactics in the future. Across all former Soviet republics, Russia has already achieved various degrees of success with these policies from country to country. Still, annexation is far from a certain outcome but rather a possibility. Likewise, despite consistent policies to lay the groundwork for influence and control over territories where Russian compatriots reside, Moscow's specific policy outcomes cannot be predicted or guaranteed.

Some may argue that Moscow's policies in Ukraine, Georgia, Moldova, and beyond have been haphazard rather than planned, and that there is no consistent discernable trajectory in Russian government policies. Indeed, as the next chapter will show, the evolution of Moscow's policies toward compatriots has taken time to develop and demonstrated inconsistencies and even initial incoherency. However, the some twenty different Russian policies and laws related to compatriots enacted from 1994 to 2015 and outlined in the next chapter clearly demonstrate that the Kremlin has awarded increasing attention to its diaspora as a tool of foreign policy. It is also reasonable to conclude that Putin's actions and particularly their timing have been driven by opportunism. Certainly, the 2014 Ukraine's Maidan movement, which sought to bring the country closer to the West and resulted in bloody clashes between pro-Russia and pro-West groups in Kiev, and in the deposition of Ukrainian President Viktor Yanukovych, created instability in Ukraine and in turn a ripe moment for Moscow to take back Crimea and stoke conflict in the eastern part of the country.[3] Likewise, the Georgian military operation to retake its breakaway territory of South Ossetia in 2008, where Russian peacekeepers were stationed, was another opportune moment for Russia to officially move its troops into South Ossetia and Abkhazia. On a much smaller scale, the Estonian government's 2007 decision to relocate Tallinn's Soviet-era war memorial also proved opportune for Moscow to stoke riots by Estonia's Russian minority. Nonetheless, opportunism can go hand in hand with careful planning. "Fortune favors the bold" says a Latin proverb, but Louis Pasteur said that "fortune favors the prepared." The reimperialization trajectory fits well with both maxims.

In the following sections, I will detail the seven phases of the reimperialization trajectory as a road map of Russian foreign policy toward post-Soviet states with large ethnic Russian and Russian-speaking minorities, providing the framework for the later country case study chapters that will locate states like Ukraine, Georgia, Moldova, Estonia, Latvia, Lithuania, Belarus, Armenia, Kazakhstan, and others on the trajectory. It will be in the case study chapters rather than here that extensive examples of reimperialization policies will be provided. Those chapters will also demonstrate an element of common timing when the reimperialization trajectory turns from softer to more aggressive policies. This has generally been when countries like Moldova, Georgia, Ukraine, and Armenia turned Westward and sought closer relations with NATO or the EU. The states in question then generally experienced a rapid progression from Russia's soft power policies to intensified information warfare, arming and training of separatist groups, and passportization.

STAGE 1: SOFT POWER

According to American political scientist and leading scholar of soft power, Joseph Nye, that form of power is a state's ability to wield influence based on its culture, political values, and foreign policies, which must be perceived as legitimate and having moral authority. Soft power facilitates a state's public diplomacy by building long-term relationships that influence the context for government policymaking.[4] Over the past decades there has been debate over whether Russia even has any soft power and, if so, what sets Russia's soft power apart from that of other states. Russia scholar James Sherr has demonstrated that Russia's influence is based on "hard diplomacy" and "soft coercion." The latter is an "influence that is indirectly coercive, resting on covert methods (penetration, bribery, blackmail)."[5] He also argues that Russia uses co-optation of various business, political, and private groups through the establishment of networks bonded by mutual interest to promote its objectives.[6]

Russia's objectives and the means used to achieve them raise concerns for the target states. Russia's discourse and policies demonstrate its resolve to maintain a "zone of privileged interest" in the post-Soviet states and postcommunist Europe often irrespective of the wishes of these countries. To achieve these objectives Moscow uses a combination of hard and soft power. Disentangling Russia's soft power from hard power is difficult because it often takes forms that are covert, implicitly coercive, or of dubious legality.[7] For this reason, and because Moscow often interlinks different issue areas, in this book softer methods like cultural, religious, and linguistic appeals will be discussed together with harder methods that usually fall outside the scope of soft power like economic coercion and sanctions. Furthermore, as the country case studies demonstrate, Moscow uses soft power not to avoid hard power methods, but in order to pave the way for subsequent use of hard power.[8]

While Russia's instruments of influence have varied from energy exports to culture and business networks, all of these instruments have been greatly securitized. In other words, cultural and business interests have often been conceptualized by the Russian government as being in the same sphere as security and military matters, thus legitimizing Moscow's reliance on extraordinary means to secure against perceived or constructed threats toward Russian language or culture. For instance, Russian culture is defined by the Foreign Policy Review of the Russian

Ministry of Foreign Affairs as "an instrument to ensure Russia's economic and foreign policy interests and positive image in the world."[9] Russian culture is shared by not only ethnic Russians but also Russian speakers and those under Russian influence.[10] Russian compatriots have also served both as a target of Russia's soft power and as Moscow's means to wield soft power over target countries such as Ukraine, Latvia, and Kazakhstan. Lastly, unlike most states where soft power is largely produced by civil society, Russia controls the institutions and individuals that help shape the country's image and thus its soft power, such as the media, NGOs, cultural figures, universities, and the church.[11]

Just as Russian soft and hard power are often intertwined, so too are Russian soft power, and its humanitarian and compatriot policies. Sherr argues that in Russian perception, these three elements are essentially synonymous.[12] For the purposes of this book, Russia's soft power includes its efforts to reinforce linguistic, cultural, economic, and religious affinities with neighboring states as well as to co-opt different interest groups. The Russian language is an important means and pretext for softer and harder methods of influence. Just before the official collapse of the Soviet Union in 1989, some 139 million people from the fourteen former Soviet republics (excluding Russia) knew the Russian language to a greater or lesser extent and shared many cultural, social, political, and economic ties with Russia.[13] Of those people, some 25 million were ethnic Russians with even closer identification with the Russian state.[14] As the next chapter will demonstrate, it took some years before an orchestrated policy and mechanisms to deal with the Russian diaspora developed, though Moscow's efforts to privilege the Russian language in both the government and the education systems of post-Soviet states emerged early on.

Russian high culture, with its classic authors, composers, and choreographers, remains well regarded in most parts of the world and could be a legitimate and effective component of the country's soft power. Indeed, true soft power must attract rather than trick or coerce. Russian popular culture also remains relevant for many countries of the former Soviet Union where the Russian language is widely spoken. As Russia expert Fiona Hill noted at possibly the height of the country's soft power in 2004, Russia offers "a burgeoning popular culture spread through satellite TV, a growing film industry, rock music, Russian popular novels and the revival of the crowning achievements of the Russian artistic tradition."[15] This culture flourishes not only among the older generation but also among the younger set in the post-Soviet space, despite the influx of popular culture from the United States, Europe, and Asia. However, to date it seems that the natural appeal of Russian culture has been insufficient to support the Kremlin's geopolitical aims of imperial revival.[16] Instead, Russia has turned to institutionalized means of soft power and various state-sponsored organizations.

The majority of Russia's soft power instruments operate under the guiding concept and associated organizations that go under the name of the Russian World—a portmanteau term for the common post-Soviet space shared by a presumed special spiritual and civilizational community. Although the term might involve a plethora of interpretations, according to Marek Menkiszak of the Warsaw Centre for Eastern Studies, it is generally defined as "the community of Russian-speaking people centered around Russia, who identify with the Orthodox Christian religion and culture and who cherish the same shared values, irrespective of their citizenship and ethnic background."[17] The Russian World is institutionalized via the Russkiy Mir Foundation, which seeks to attune the Russophone community with Russian soft power and is widely recognized as an instrument of Moscow's geopolitics. The strategic importance that the Russian government has attached to the foundation cannot be underestimated. Established in 2007 by decree of President Putin, it is a joint venture of the Ministry of Foreign Affairs and the Ministry of Education. It seeks to promote the Russian language and culture across the globe. The foundation estimates that some 35 million individuals in over ninety countries, the majority of which are concentrated in the CIS and the Baltic States, make up the Russian World.[18] Since its inception, the chairman of the management board has been Vyacheslav Nikonov. The grandson of Stalin's foreign minister Vyacheslav Molotov (of the famed secret Molotov-Ribbentrop Pact that sought to divide Eastern Europe between the Nazis and the Soviets), Nikonov served on the staff of Gorbachev, Yeltsin, and Putin, and as assistant to the chairman of the KGB in 1991–92. He is also a well-regarded political scientist. Under his guidance, the foundation has grown into a powerful organization. For its promotion of Russian culture, financing of various projects in Russian schools, and provision of Russian language and history courses abroad, the Russkiy Mir has been generally well received by the diaspora population.[19] In some regards it can be compared to the British Council or the International Organisation of La Francophonie. However, the main distinction between Russkiy Mir and other similar organizations is its evident political dimension as exemplified by Nikonov's ties to the Kremlin and the KGB, and its ideology of including in the Russian World only those Russians who maintain loyalty to Russia, thus excluding, for example, Russians who supported the removal of the Soviet monument in Estonia in 2007.[20] Likewise it engages in exaggerated media coverage of various "injustices" suffered by the Russian minorities in their countries of residence—activities that have no parallel in the British Council or La Francophonie.[21]

The Russian Orthodox Church has also become an institution of Russian soft power under the leadership of the Patriarch Kirill I of Moscow. Elected in 2009, Kirill, like Putin, is a native of St. Petersburg. He allegedly shares another feature in common with Putin—he has been reported as having had links to the KGB during the Soviet period as codenamed agent "Mikhailov."[22] The patriarch has also been criticized by the Western media for his unflinching support for Putin's regime, including calling the Putin era "a miracle of God."[23] Likewise, he has endorsed the Russian World policy, explaining in 2014: "the civilization of Russia belongs to something broader than the Russian Federation. This civilization we call the Russian world. . . . To this world can belong people who do not belong to the Slavic world, but who embraced the cultural and spiritual component of this world as their own."[24] Moreover, the head of the Orthodox Church does not shy away from voicing his view of Russia's role in international affairs. In an interview in 2014 he declared that "Russia cannot be a vassal. Because Russia is not only a country, it is a whole civilization, it is a thousand-year story, a cultural melting-pot, of enormous power."[25] The patriarch has even been called "the most effective instrument of Russian soft power in the 'near abroad.'"[26]

The rising influence of the Russian church both domestically and abroad can be attributed to the strong revival of Orthodoxy since the 1990s. Though all religions, including the Russian church, were forcibly oppressed during the Soviet era, from 1991 to 2008 the share of Russian adults identifying as Orthodox Christian rose from 31 percent to 72 percent.[27] Globally there are about 150 million adherents to the Russian Orthodox Church, which though autocephalous (autonomous) is part of the Eastern Orthodox Church with some 250 million followers. The church, headed by the Moscow Patriarchate, exercises jurisdiction over most Eastern Orthodox Christians living in the former republics of the USSR and their diasporas abroad. Out of all Eastern Orthodox churches in the post-Soviet states, only the autocephalous Georgian church is independent from Moscow.[28] Meanwhile, the Armenian Apostolic Church, which is the world's oldest national church and is part of Oriental rather than Eastern Orthodoxy, has historically remained both de jure and de facto free from Moscow's clout. Due to its vast reach and rising influence, however, the Russian church has become an important element of Russia's soft power efforts abroad and an inseparable part of the reimperialization trajectory, as will be seen in the case study chapters.

STAGE 2: HUMANITARIAN POLICIES

The rising prominence of human rights in international law has given rise to a "humanitarian dimension" in Russian foreign policy that constitutes the second stage of the trajectory. To date, this humanitarian dimension has been understudied. The very understanding of "humanitarian" policies differs in the West and Russia, where *gumanitarnoye sotrudnichestvo* (humanitarian cooperation) is used interchangeably with "public diplomacy" and refers to "people to people" policies, "NGO diplomacy," and "cultural diplomacy."[29] The most recent Russian Foreign Policy Review of 2007 noted four aspects of the "humanitarian trend" of foreign policy: consular issues, human rights protection, cultural and scientific cooperation, and compatriot policies.[30] However, to elaborate my proposed reimperialization paradigm, I will examine Russia's humanitarian policies separately from complementary tools like soft power, compatriot policies, and consular efforts like passportization. Instead, I will include here Moscow's escalation of human rights questions of Russian compatriots, assistance to the Russian diaspora abroad, and even peacekeeping operations.

The relationship of the Russian Federation to human rights has been somewhat paradoxical. On the one hand, Moscow has rejected outside criticisms of its own human rights violations. It has called for regional standards of human rights to meet the cultural and historical needs of particular societies, rather than standards imposed from the outside. On the other hand, Moscow still proclaims the universal nature of such rights. In practice, Russia mainly raises the issue of human rights on the international stage in relation to the rights of ethnic Russians, Russian speakers, or Russian citizens residing in the countries of its near abroad. In contrast to the norms of the international humanitarian community that stipulate that humanitarian assistance should be guided by principles of humanity, impartiality, neutrality, and independence from political, economic, military, and other objectives, Russia's efforts to protect human rights are closely intertwined with the notion of assisting and protecting the rights of its compatriots.[31] Most often, humanitarian efforts serve as a pretext to advance Russia's geopolitical aims. Indeed, like Russia's version of soft power, Russia's humanitarian policies are also a unique construct.

Exactly as human rights have increasingly become important in international relations and Russia itself has faced criticism for its domestic human rights record, Moscow has increasingly turned to humanitarian policies as an element of its foreign policy.[32] According to the 2009 study *The "Humanitarian Dimension" of the Russian Foreign Policy Toward Georgia, Moldova, Ukraine, and the Baltic States*, "Russia has chosen an offensive approach to human rights issues as the best form of defense."[33] As a result, Russia has sought out "artificial pseudo-problems" of human rights in the states of its near abroad.[34] This counterattack serves several purposes. First, it distracts the attention of the international community from Russia's own human rights violations. Second, it questions the extent to which states like the Baltics or Ukraine can protect the rights of their minorities, thus challenging the legitimacy of these national governments and seeking to "discredit those countries in eyes of international society."[35] Moscow's vocal campaign over Russian diaspora rights enables it to internationalize and even legitimize the issue. Finally, Russian foreign policy has embraced the protection of human rights at times when it could not use international law to advance its interests. For instance, the evident weakness of Russia's arguments under international law regarding Crimea and eastern Ukraine has resulted in Moscow's decision to defend its actions by broad notions of compatriot protection, legitimacy, justice, and above all national interest.[36]

Certainly, since 1991, various minorities in the post-Soviet space, including ethnic Russians and Russian speakers, have faced occasional and in some cases arguably systemic though not explicit discrimination, potential economic hardships, and cultural integration difficulties. However, since the mid-1990s Moscow has packaged the issues of multicultural, transitional societies as "human rights violations," tying them together with accusations of "fascism" when this suited its foreign policy aims.[37] Moscow's antifascist rhetoric targeting alleged abusers of the Russian compatriots' rights is even more paradoxical when viewed in light of the fact that Putin regime's close ties to Europe's neofascist and extreme right parties are well documented and include floating the French far right National Front with a €9 million loan in 2014.[38] But Moscow's perplexing efforts to "fight fascism" in the former Soviet republics serve a purpose. By seeking to portray its opponents in the Baltic States or in Kiev as "fascists," the Russian government and its proxies by definition appear "antifascist." For instance, Putin compared the 2014 conflict between the Ukrainian army and pro-Russian militias in the Ukrainian city of Donetsk with the heroic antifascist struggle of the Russians during the epic two-year siege of Leningrad in the Second World War.[39] Paradoxically, in early 2015, the supposedly antifascist pro-Russian leader of the self-proclaimed People's Republic of Donetsk, Alexander Zakharchenko, declared that Kiev is actually run by "miserable Jews."[40] Rhetoric aside, present-day Russian "antifascism" has nothing to do with genuine antifascism, which is characterized by adherence to democratic principles, respect for international law, and the protection of human rights.[41]

To date Russia has sought out existing international organizations and created ones of its own to pursue the issue of violations of human rights of Russian compatriots. Among international organizations, Russia raised and faced the issue of human rights violations in the United Nations, the UN Human Rights Council, the OSCE, the Parliamentary Assembly of the Council of Europe, and the European Court of Human Rights.[42] Russia was particularly vocal in denouncing the alleged human rights violations of the Baltic States and also tried to hinder their accession to such international organizations as the Council of Europe and the European Union.[43] However, these attempts were largely unsuccessful as various commissions concluded that the three Baltic countries were in fact complying with all human rights standards.[44] Possibly the most important Russian organization working on human rights is the Institute for Democracy and Cooperation (IDC), established in 2007 and funded by "private donors" who remain absolutely clandestine.[45] Headquartered in New York, this NGO is officially described as a "non-governmental think-tank dedicated to analyzing, defining, and promoting mutual understanding between Russia and the United States."[46] The Institute publishes reports of human rights violations in Western democracies, such as *The State of Human Rights in the U.S.* (October 2013). Its Paris branch focuses on "the relationship between state sovereignty and human rights," "interpretation of human rights and the way they are applied in different countries," and "the way in which historical memory is used in contemporary politics."[47] The organization's research had a geopolitical tone in 2013, 2014, and 2015 with pieces like "The West's Post-Modernism and the New Cultural Cold War," "The Geopolitics of New Multipolarity," "The United Nations Report Is Neither Realistic Nor Credible" (regarding the UN Human Rights Council's Commission of Inquiry on Syria), and "Ideology and Geopolitics in Two Cold Wars."[48] In contrast to Russia's own agenda of criticizing human rights conditions in the United States or the EU, a number of respected, international organizations such as Amnesty International and Human Rights Watch condemn Russia for mistreatment of ethnic minorities within its borders.

Russian humanitarian policies have also taken on military undertones, especially with Russian peacekeeping operations. Especially in the cases of Georgia and arguably Tajikistan, which are discussed in later chapters, these operations have served as a means for Russia to establish its long-term military presence and create military bases in foreign territories under the pretext of protecting Russian compatriots or other minorities.

In summary, Russian humanitarian policies are a means of increasing Russian influence outside the Russian Federation and are closely tied to Russian soft power, compatriot policies, and propaganda campaigns. However, they have generally but mistakenly been viewed as outside the scope of Russian territorial aims and reimperialization efforts. This road map of the reimperialization trajectory demonstrates how these interconnected, softer policies all lead to Moscow's efforts for military protection of Russian compatriots and control of the territories where they reside.

STAGE 3: COMPATRIOT POLICIES

While the word "compatriot" generally refers to a fellow countryman or countrywoman, the equivalent Russian word, *sootechestvennik*, has come to denote the Russian diaspora residing outside the Russian Federation and encompasses ethnic, cultural, linguistic, political, and even spiritual connotations. The term most often refers to ethnic Russians residing in the former states of the Soviet Union, but Moscow has also broadened it by including Russian speakers who may be of various other nationalities such as Ukrainians, Belarusians, Tatars, Abkhazians, Ossetians, and other peoples that were Russified during the Soviet era or even those who are not Russophones but have other cultural, religious, or historical ties to Russia. The origins and evolution of this nebulous "compatriot" category and terminology as well as the development of Russia's compatriot policies since the 1990s will be examined closely in the following chapter. In addition that chapter will demonstrate how under Putin's regime the Russian compatriots have been increasingly conceptualized as a potential resource to be employed in foreign policy. Russia has been described as using its compatriots since the 2000s as a "geopolitical entity," most often with the aim to promote its own national interests rather than those of compatriots.[49] Moscow does so irrespective of the laws and preferences of compatriots' home countries or the compatriots themselves. And while there may be genuine sincerity in Russia's cultural and nationalist efforts to claim its diaspora, these efforts pale in comparison to Moscow's manipulation of compatriots as a tool of influence over and territorial aggression against neighboring states. This section will briefly demonstrate how Moscow's compatriot policies fit with the other items of Russia's tool kit. Indeed, compatriots are the crux of Moscow's reimperialization policies in its near abroad. They are the thread that ties together many other means of Russian influence.

Russian compatriots not only figure in all stages of the reimperialization trajectory, they are the driving force behind it. For instance, Russia's soft power over neighboring states stems in great part from the presence of the sizable Russian and Russian-speaking minorities. At the same time, Moscow's work to maintain soft power over those minorities in some ways precludes their successful integration into their states of residence while the perceived grievances of Russian compatriots enables Russia to engage in human rights efforts. These grievances, termed "human rights abuses" are then used as a pretext in subsequent stages of passportization, support for separatist movements, and finally efforts at protection and usurpation of territories. As the case studies will demonstrate, the human rights abuses endured by Russian compatriots are often blatantly invented, and certainly their claims are disseminated to exacerbate tensions in neighboring states via Russian information warfare campaigns. In the final stages of Moscow's reimperialization trajectory, as in the cases of South Ossetia, Abkhazia, and Crimea, compatriot protection is given as a reason for Russia's military intervention.

The complex interlinkage of the compatriot issue with Russia's other tools and goals of foreign policy can be seen in the various strategic government bodies that oversee and fund the compatriot policy, including the ministries of Foreign Affairs, Culture, and Education. However, possibly the most important federal institution in this area has been the Federal Agency for Commonwealth of Independent States Affairs, Compatriots Living Abroad, and International Humanitarian Cooperation (known for short as Rossotrudnichestvo). This agency was established with the explicit aim of "maintaining Russia's influence in the Commonwealth of Independent States, and to foster friendly ties for the advancement of Russia's political and economic interests in foreign states."[50] Rossotrudnichestvo may well constitute one of the most ambitious instruments to advance Russian interests abroad: since its establishment in 2008 it has rapidly expanded opening 93 branch offices in 80 countries.[51] In 2013 President Putin signed an order to increase the agency's budget from 2 billion rubles (approximately $37 million) to 9.5 billion rubles (approximately $174 million) by 2020, thus making it one of the most expensive instruments of support for compatriots abroad.[52]

Regional, local, and federal government institutions have also worked to execute Russia's compatriot policies. From the late 1990s to late 2000s, the Moscow City Council and Yuri Luzhkov, the longtime mayor of Moscow (1992–2010), were prominent supporters of compatriot policies. During Luzhkov's tenure as mayor, he reportedly spent hundreds of millions of dollars from Moscow's well-padded city budget in the near abroad.[53] Among other initiatives, he founded so-called Luzhkov scholarships for ethnic Russian students from post-Soviet countries (in parallel with scholarships from the Russian Ministry of Education). In 2003, the City of Moscow also launched its own compatriot policy via its Department for Foreign Economic Activity and International Relations.[54] These policies included programs such as political and economic assistance to compatriots in Crimea, while also supporting the populace of the peninsula in gaining greater political autonomy from Kiev.[55]

Funds for various compatriot causes are allocated simultaneously through a large variety of government organizations and programs. For instance, in 2011 the Ministry of Foreign Affairs allocated 400 million rubles (approximately $14 million) annually for the compatriot policy through its embassies.[56] At the same time, the Ministry of Science and Education agreed on a 2011–15 budget for the Russian Language Program of 2.5 billion rubles (approximately $88 million).[57] In May 2011, President Medvedev announced the creation of the Foundation for Supporting and Protecting the Rights of Compatriots Living Abroad, under the auspices of the Foreign Ministry to be a "permanent, systemic and effective system to protect the interests of our compatriots."[58] The Fund's official purpose was to "render legal and organizational assistance to compatriots whose rights are violated abroad. . . . The new organization will also monitor violations of their rights."[59] The foundation has allegedly been involved in helping finance separatist and militia groups in eastern Ukraine. In May 2014 the Ukrainian security services confiscated the bank accounts of a Ukrainian organization *Dar Zhizhni* (Gift of Life) that in April 2014 received 8 million rubles (approximately $250,000) from the foundation, and according to a Ukrainian court decision had been using the funds to provide financial and media support to extremists in the Donbas to advance separatism and pro-Russian propaganda.[60]

Moscow also institutionalizes the compatriots through various other cultural organizations, including the Russkiy Mir Foundation and the Russkiy Dom network. Throughout the 2000s the ideological concept of the "Russian World" gained strength on the back of Russkiy Dom, which was established in 1999 to promote Russian values, language, and culture as well as offering legal protection to Russians.[61] By 2011 Russkiy Dom's annual budget was some $30 million, with over fifty centers across the globe, including such disparate countries as Germany, Latvia, the United States, Switzerland, and Mexico.[62] Likewise, Russia lends support to various transnational movements and organizations of the post-Soviet space that have historical or cultural ties to Russia and are deemed to be part of the Russian World. One example is the Cossacks, an East Slavic people with strong military and Orthodox Christian traditions living across Russia, Ukraine, the Caucasus, Central Asia, and beyond. They have enjoyed Moscow's political, financial, and even military support for their separatist movements and have fought on the Russian side in the wars of Transnistria, Georgia, and most recently Ukraine where they have formed a short-lived and self-proclaimed separatist Cossack People's Republic in the east of the country, which eventually was liquidated and incorporated into the Luhansk People's Republic.[63]

Russia also organizes large-scale events for its compatriots, such as the World Congress of Russian Compatriots, held in Russia every three years since 2003, where representatives from post-Soviet countries meet in a forum with the Russian president and other state leaders. Topics of discussion range from minority rights, resettlement back to Russia, to preservation of cultural and linguistic ties with the motherland.[64] In some ways the congress is reminiscent of the early Soviet Comintern, or Communist International, which in the 1920s and 1930s held World Congresses in Moscow where representatives from international and European communist parties would meet. The Comintern was a tool of Soviet foreign policy, and the Kremlin held a disproportionate power share in the congresses which it used to promote its revolutionary ideals while expecting the foreign participants to declare loyalty to Moscow rather than to their home countries.[65] Likewise, Russian compatriot representatives are expected to agree loyally with the policies outlined in the Kremlin, while they have limited ability to shape compatriot policy.[66] According to participants, Russian embassies, which aid the recruitment processes, provide advance instructions to compatriots on what to do and what not to do at the congresses.[67] It is no surprise that reports have cited a decline in compatriot participation at the World Congress meetings from around a thousand in 2009 to slightly over five hundred in 2012.[68] Nonetheless, what is most concerning for post-Soviet states (and will be outlined in detail in the case study chapters) is the fact that compatriot organizations encourage the diaspora to make political demands such as changes in language and citizenship policies and calls for regional separatism and autonomy, as well as disseminating specific historical interpretations that split societies along ethnic lines.

STAGE 4: PASSPORTIZATION

The idea of providing ethnic Russians, Russian speakers, and others in the post-Soviet states with Russian passports has long appealed to the Russian government. As the next chapter will outline, in the early 1990s Moscow sought to establish the principle of dual citizenship in the post-Soviet space and at the same time sought to "passportize" whole regions outside its borders. In the global context, a number of states accept the principle of dual citizenship, and it could be argued that Moscow's efforts to negotiate the principle with the sovereign post-Soviet states (especially in the case of Central Asia) were not unusual. However, Moscow's passportization policies, which often violate the laws of the foreign states affected, differed significantly from accepted international norms. The policies undermined state sovereignty by encouraging often unlawful activities of handing out passports and by their targeting of specific populations of ethnic Russians and Russian speakers residing in particular foreign territories where Russia sought greater influence. They also targeted other minority populations like Ossetians and Abkhazians that resided in breakaway territories of Georgia. As a result there was fierce opposition from many countries to both Russia's passportization efforts and the related principle of dual citizenship. In 2006, then First Deputy Prime Minister Medvedev argued that while "the international practice of the past several decades" rejects dual citizenship, it could become relevant as the CIS reached a level of integration comparable to that of the EU.[69] Still among the CIS only Tajikistan has a formal agreement with Russia enabling dual citizenship while Kyrgyzstan and Armenia have not formalized the agreement but their citizenship laws could allow for it. Nonetheless, the semilegal practices of obtaining Russian citizenship continue unabated in much of the post-Soviet world since the early 1990s.

In some cases, the fact that residents of the former Soviet republics had not acquired citizenship in the newly independent post-Soviet states (due either to imposed legal constraints or to their own unwillingness) was also used by Moscow as a reason for passportization. The Russian government has maintained that if former citizens of the Soviet Union had not received citizenship in the new states, then "Russia as a legal successor to the Soviet Union was obligated to grant these people citizenship and rights under the Constitution of Russia."[70] This logic has been particularly relevant in Estonia and Latvia, which, as discussed in more detail in the chapter on the Baltic States, did not grant automatic citizenship to Soviet-era migrants who included many Russians and Russian speakers. Tallinn's and Riga's policies and the resulting passportless populations played well into Moscow's hands, providing an arguably justifiable reason for their passportization as well as creating an international grievance. Meanwhile, in Georgia's South Ossetia and Abkhazia and Moldova's Transnistria, while Tbilisi and Chisinau granted automatic citizenship to inhabitants of these territories, separatist movements precluded many from obtaining Georgian or Moldovan passports. In these territories there was ready acceptance of Moscow's passportization policies. However, in most other former Soviet republics, like Ukraine's Crimea or northern Kazakhstan, Moscow was clandestinely and often illegally offering Russian citizenship to foreign citizens. Interestingly, Russian ethnicity was not a prerequisite for passportization in Moldova and Georgia. For instance, in the case of South Ossetia, there were virtually no ethnic Russians or native Russian speakers according to the 1989 census which lists ethnic Ossetians as making up 66 percent of the population and ethnic Georgians as totaling 29 percent.[71] Whether targeting Russians or other nationalities, Russian passportization policies have played an important role in establishing and reinforcing separatism in Transnistria, Abkhazia, South Ossetia, and Crimea.

Indeed, passportization is no simple consular matter. While most countries focus their consular activities on tourism, cultural and educational exchanges, and migration of workers, Russia has made consular activities a means to its security and territorial ambitions. Moscow's policies of protecting its citizens and compatriots abroad have rightfully made most post-Soviet countries suspicious of Russian consular activities.[72] According to anthropologist Florian Mühlfried, passportization is a clear case of "a new form of imperialism by civic means."[73] Its origins have been said to date back to the Cold War, when the notion of socialist international solidarity was used as grounds for intervention throughout the world. In the Putin era it has been replaced by a paternalistic ideology of providing help to fellow citizens and compatriots in need—an ideology formulated in the modern language of human rights.[74]

The main actors in the passportization process, in addition to Russian consulates, have been public organizations, field forces or special door-to-door brigades, and at times even individuals. In Georgia, when the 2002 new Russian Citizenship Law simplified procedures, the Russian government created passport application centers in Abkhazia and South Ossetia.[75] At the same time a public organization, the Congress of Russian Communities, spearheaded the passportization process in Abkhazia and field forces traveled to remote mountain villages to hand out passports.[76] In Crimea, the Russian consulate in Simferopol had been aggressively issuing Russian passports for years leading up to the 2014 conflict.[77] The passportization policies achieved some success. According to the Russian Federal Migration Service, from 2000 to 2009 almost 3 million people living on the territory of the former Soviet Union beyond the Russian Federation had received Russian citizenship.[78] Many among these were dual citizens, especially in countries like Moldova and Ukraine.

Russia has generally not forced its citizenship on its diaspora or other nationals. Russian citizenship has had some appeal for the Russian minority and other nationalities, as seen in South Ossetia, Abkhazia, Transnistria, Estonia, Latvia, and Armenia. First, any citizenship may hold appeal for people without passports as in Estonia and Latvia. Second, there are also economic motives for acquiring Russian citizenship, which makes it easier and less expensive to travel to Russia as it eliminates the need for visas—an attraction, for example, in Moldova, Georgia, and Armenia. Russians may seek frequent travel to Russia to visit their relatives while all nationalities may benefit from visa-free travel if they work in Russia or reside near the border with the Russian Federation and conduct business or trade across the border. Third, Russian citizenship entitles passport holders additional benefits such as education in Russia, child support payments, free health care, support for large families, worker and military pensions, and the right to vote in Russian presidential and Duma elections.[79] Some of these benefits, though, are selectively administered and favor separatist territories. For instance, in 2008 Russian citizens residing in Moldova's Transnistria received supplementary pension payments, while Russian citizens residing elsewhere in Moldova did not receive such payments.[80] Lastly, the appeal of Russian citizenship may reflect the success Russia has achieved in its soft power efforts to maintain the loyalty of ethnic Russians and Russian speakers abroad and attract other nationalities.

STAGE 5: INFORMATION WARFARE

The previous four stages of the neo-imperialist trajectory all pave the way for the blitz of information warfare and mark a pivot point preceding more open aggression from Moscow. Information warfare is the aggressive use of propaganda to destabilize, demoralize, or manipulate the target audience and achieve an advantage over an opponent including by seeking to deny, degrade, corrupt, or destroy the opponent's sources of information. Some use of propaganda, loosely defined as information of a biased or misleading nature used to promote a political cause or point of view, is common among states even during times of peace and is often perceived to be part of soft power efforts. However, a turn to information warfare signals an escalation of tensions and sometimes also a turn to military engagement. In the Russian National Security Concept of 2000, the term "information warfare" was introduced to describe the threats Russia was facing, and rather ambiguously, also as the "improvement and protection of the domestic information infrastructure and integration of Russia into the world information domain."[81] Russian analysts, when referring to the internal and external information warfare threats that the country faces, argue that such warfare also "presumes 'nontraditional occupation,' namely the possibility of controlling territory and making use of its resources without the victor's physical presence on the territory of the vanquished."[82] In my proposed seven-stage trajectory, information warfare is a crucial turning point when an "urgent" need for the "protection" of Russian compatriots and citizens is conceptualized. However, information warfare campaigns are preceded by decades of softer propaganda tactics, spread of pro-Russia historical narratives, and efforts by Russian state-run media companies to capture the audience of post-Soviet states.

The targets of Russian information propaganda are legion: the Russian diaspora, the broader audience of the countries within Russia's sphere of influence, Russian domestic audiences, and the international community. While Russian media sometimes target these different audiences at different stages and in different ways, at times they do so simultaneously. Most generally, the initial target audience tends to be the compatriots residing in any particular former Soviet republic, who are presented with a Moscow-biased version of current events and history. Then, the idea is introduced that the compatriots are at risk from hostile

forces in Europe, America, the titular nationality—the dominant epony-
mous ethnic group in the country—and/or the country's nationalist and
"fascist" groups. The surprisingly high degree to which Russian information warfare and propaganda are accepted both domestically and in
the former Soviet republics is closely related to the fact that Russian state-
controlled media tend to dominate the information space of the entire post-
Soviet region. Local media do not have sufficient resources or are simply
not sufficiently established to compete with Russian state-funded media.
Likewise, due to the prevalence of the Russian language, the vast majority of the audience consistently opts for Russian over English or other
foreign-language media. In November 2014, the Russian state-owned
news agency Rossiya Segodnya announced the launch of a new international media project, Sputnik, that will broadcast in forty-five languages
and have offices in all post-Soviet states with the exception of Turkmenistan.[83] The Russian government also intended to beef up the spending
in 2015 for the Russia Today international TV network and for Rossiya
Segodnya, which also incorporates the Voice of Russia radio station and
the international news agency RIA Novosti, by 40 percent and 200 percent respectively.[84] However, given the enormous fluctuations of the
ruble in the foreign exchange market, which in early 2015 lost nearly
50 percent of its value vis-à-vis the dollar, the combined funding for Russia Today and Rossiya Segodnya actually decreased from $695 million in
2014 to $335 million in 2015.[85]

Information warfare campaigns in the near abroad tend to create divisions in target societies as well as shore up support for Russia's military campaigns among the domestic audience. The campaigns are either
simultaneously or subsequently extended to international audiences in
order to present events with a Kremlin bias and justify Russia's policy
choices. As case study chapters will show, Moscow's information warfare
was exemplified in the Georgian and Ukrainian wars where it was used
strategically to advance Russian military aims. In the case of Kyrgyzstan,
Moscow's targeted propaganda campaign arguably played a contributing
role in toppling a regime.

The Russian propaganda machine is an elaborate industry that dates
back to the Second World War with the purpose of deception and manipulation of information. Russian information warfare theory is derived
directly from *spetspropaganda* (special propaganda) theory, which was first

taught as a separate subject in 1942 at the Russian Military Institute of Foreign Languages. Although the subject was removed from the curriculum after the collapse of the USSR, it was reintroduced after Putin launched the Information Security Doctrine in September 2000. The doctrine was generally interpreted as the state's attempt to take control over mass media and subordinate its functioning to the needs of government and national security.[86] Among its outlined measures for maintenance of information security in domestic politics was the "launching of counterpropaganda activities aimed at prevention of negative outcomes from the dissemination of disinformation about Russian internal politics."[87] At that point the Russian Military Institute was rebranded as the Department of Foreign Military Information of the Military University of the Ministry of Defense of the Russian Federation.[88] According to deputy director of the Warsaw Centre for Eastern Studies, Jolanta Darczewska, in the Department of Foreign Military Information the Russian military trains specialists in "organizing foreign information and military communication," "information analysis," and "monitoring and development of military information."[89] However, information warfare is not limited to this single institution: as of 2014 there were at least 74 research and scientific institutions, forming the Scientific and Methodological Association of Higher Education Facilities of the Russian Federation Covering Information Security, established upon the initiative of the FSB (the former KGB).[90]

The modern Russian information warfare tradition distinguishes itself from its peers in other countries by the extensive use of such concepts as *strategicheskaya maskirovka* (strategic masking) and reflexive control. The highest cadres of Kremlin's leadership have studied this science, including Deputy Prime Minister Dmitry Rogozin, who has been in charge of the Russian defense industry since 2011. Rogozin comes from a family of Soviet military scientists, and was among the first seven persons sanctioned by the U.S. government following Crimea's annexation in March 2014. In his writing he has analyzed the strategic masking concept, which involves the use of deception and manipulation of the enemy.[91] According to Rogozin, strategic masking is devised by the highest politico-military levels and employs various military units to jam radios, spread disinformation via media, and manipulate the enemy into believing false reports of military movements.[92] This has been demonstrated in the Ukrainian and Georgian wars where non-Russian media were immediately blocked in occupied territories and the strategic government and military communications of these countries were breached and impaired. Reflexive control is defined by Rogozin as a means of supplying an opponent with specially prepared information or disinformation to incline him to voluntarily make the predetermined decision desired by the initiator of the action.[93] All this is accomplished while exploiting the moral, psychological, and other factors affecting the target.[94] In practice, these tactics can include lowering the morale of the opponent's military or society and thus making them less likely to resist foreign military aggression.

Along with specialized institutions that focus on training information warfare specialists, Russia also operates institutions that are dedicated to manufacturing and spreading propaganda to mass audiences. In St. Petersburg, Russian businessmen run a bona fide internet comment factory, Internet Research LLC, employing about 250 people working twelve-hour shifts round the clock writing pro-Kremlin blogs. The connection of the comment factory with the Kremlin has not been proven, but then, such links are difficult to establish in many forms of information and cyber warfare.[95] The employees of Internet Research mostly work in the Russian blogging platform LiveJournal and a Facebookesque social network, Vkontakte.[96] Some write the posts, others comment on them. The content always focuses on praising Putin and his policies while condemning the West[97]—for instance, with allegations of Ukraine being run by a pro-American Kiev junta or by pro-American Nazis.[98]

In addition to a blogging factory, there is a perception that the Russian government operates an army of hackers who conduct cyber warfare campaigns supporting its foreign policy and military aims. Cyber warfare relies on computers and other electronic devices for hacking and damaging an enemy's information systems and its strategic or tactical resources for purposes of espionage or sabotage. Indeed, many cyber security experts agree that since the 2000s Russia has acquired the greatest capability in the world for cyber warfare and uses it primarily for foreign policy aims, in contrast to the runner-up, China, which concentrates on economically motivated cyber espionage. Although the Kremlin denies it, Russia was the first in history to coordinate a cyber attack with a military campaign when its hackers reportedly worked alongside Russian military forces in their invasion of Georgia in 2008, targeting Georgian internet infrastructure.[99] Earlier in Estonia, in 2007, pro-Russia hackers carried out a highly similar DDoS (distributed denial of service) campaign against Estonian business and government during a diplomatic spat between Tallinn and Moscow.[100] Likewise, since 2014 pro-Russian hackers have been leading a cyber espionage campaign against the Ukrainian government and even against NATO.[101]

The Russian media are among the main actors disseminating Kremlin propaganda. From about 2004 onward, or essentially since Putin came to power, the Russian media rapidly became a tool controlled by the state. A 2014 book by the Russian-born British writer and television producer Peter Pomerantsev describes Putin's authoritarian-style methods to establish the Kremlin's complete control over the media and thereby to create an alternative reality.[102] The three major Russian channels are owned either directly by the Kremlin or by state-owned companies, and Russia's only independent television channel, TV Rain (Telekanal Dozhd), is facing enormous pressure from the Federal Supervision Agency for Information Technologies and Communications (Roskomnadzor).[103] Freedom House's *Freedom of the Press 2014* survey direly summarizes the situation as follows:

> The media environment in Russia . . . is characterized by the use of a pliant judiciary to prosecute independent journalists, impunity for the physical harassment and murder of journalists, and continued state control or influence over almost all traditional media outlets. In 2013, the Russian government enacted additional legal restrictions on freedom of speech. . . . While bloggers and journalists, as well as radio and television broadcasters, are successfully utilizing the internet to reach audiences interested in alternative and more balanced sources of information, the government has begun to use a combination of the law, the courts, and regulatory pressure to extend its crackdown to online media."[104]

Experts on the Russian media propaganda apparatus even argue that it has become "the central mechanism of a new type of authoritarianism far subtler than 20th-century strains."[105] The Russian political activist and chess grandmaster Garry Kasparov commented on the role of the opposition in the face of state propaganda in 2014: "Unfortunately, we have to reiterate that white is white and black is black. Because today the country is living in complete lies, which are broadcast 24/7 by the state propaganda machine."[106]

Russian propaganda has also been evolving to combine popular culture with information warfare. For example in late 2014, a well-known Russian actor was shown with a machine gun shooting or pretending to shoot at Ukrainian forces during a cease-fire, while wearing a press helmet. This incident was unanimously condemned by the Ukrainian authorities, who described the actor as an "accomplice in terrorist activities" following the incident.[107] He was also criticized at home by Russia's Union of Journalists and the head of the union's Moscow branch.[108] The participation of a popular Russian figure in the Ukrainian war was likely intended to boost morale and support for the war in Russia.

In addition to the state-dominated news media, the Russian government has established organizations to provide a Kremlin-approved view of history. In 2009 the paradoxically named President's Commission to Prevent Falsification of History was established. The organization aims at promulgating history as set out by the Soviet regime if not outright historical revisionism. As with Russkiy Mir, top-level officials from the President's administration, the FSB, the Federal Intelligence Service (SVR), and the Ministry of Foreign Affairs support this organization. The commission has sought both to "explain" history and to "prevent attempts to rewrite history [that] are becoming more and more harsh, depraved and aggressive."[109] Contentious historical topics include Stalinist repressions, Soviet occupation of the Baltic States, and the Molotov-Ribbentrop Pact. In late 2014, Putin himself attempted on several occasions to rehabilitate the previously condemned pact, which sought to carve up Eastern Europe. During a meeting with young historians in Moscow, Putin stated, "The Soviet Union signed a non-aggression treaty with Germany. People say: 'Ach, that's bad.' But what's bad about that if the Soviet Union didn't want to fight, what's bad about it?"[110] Also, in 2008 the Historical Memory Foundation was established in Moscow with the official goal of countering the efforts of European states to "rewrite the history" of the twentieth century, when in reality these states seek greater acknowledgment of Soviet-era atrocities both at home and abroad. The foundation is guided by the controversial figure Alexander Dyukov, who has made a name for himself by seeking to deny or diminish Soviet repressions. He is banned from a number of European Schengen zone countries.[111]

Just as Russia's human rights agenda is focused on the idea of fascism, so too does the issue of fascism color Russia's information warfare and its views of history. Certainly, the struggle against Nazi forces during the Second World War left an indelible imprint on the Soviet and Russian psyche. In the war against the fascists, some 20 to 30 million Soviet citizens of various nationalities died—more deaths than any single country suffered. Since the 2000s, however, the Russian government has increasingly turned the idea of fascism into a political tool and Russian historians are increasingly promoting this Kremlin line.[112] Indeed, fascism has served the Kremlin as a useful label to pin on its opponents—whether the Baltic States, the West in general, or since 2014 the Ukrainian government. This process of manufacturing enemies out of foreign states and peoples via the media has been demonstrated in the case of Latvia by American-Latvian political scientist and Council of Europe Commissioner for Human Rights Nils Muižnieks, but a similar process can be seen vis-à-vis other states as well.[113] These efforts to manufacture "self" versus "other" also serve to unify Russian society with ideological conceptions which are centered on three pillars of Russian national identity: Christian Orthodoxy, victory against fascism in the Second World War, and anti-Americanism.[114]

Two possible motives drive Russia's efforts in the historical sphere. First, Putin's regime has been consciously rehabilitating Soviet-era leaders as symbols as well as returning to a Soviet interpretation of history.[115] Second, Moscow's historical revisionism seeks to counter the efforts of Central and Eastern Europe to study Soviet persecutions and deportations against both the Russian people and other nations. In the EU, there has been a movement to recognize Soviet historical crimes equally with those of the Nazis. In April 2009, with the support of Baltic and Polish members, the European Parliament passed a resolution on the European conscience and totalitarianism that came just short of equating Soviet and Nazi crimes.[116] Likewise, the EU has created Black Ribbon Day or the European Day of Remembrance for Victims of Stalinism and Nazism, and an educational project, the Platform of European Memory and Conscience. However, the regime of Vladimir Putin relies on disinformation and historical reinterpretations not to reassess the past but instead to push forward its foreign policy agenda in the present—particularly when it comes to "protecting" its so-called compatriots and claiming people and territories that are perceived as historically Russian.

STAGE 6: PROTECTION

The previous five stages of the reimperialization trajectory would traditionally represent softer forms of a state's influence. In the case of Russia, however, these soft instruments have been highly securitized, reflecting "soft coercion" rather than traditional soft power. The sixth stage, that of "protecting" Russian compatriots, marks a concrete departure from softer methods toward hard power. This is the stage where military campaigns could commence, though hybrid warfare is possibly more likely to play a role than conventional warfare.

The implicit notion of protecting Russian compatriots is present at nearly all of the five previous stages of the trajectory. Humanitarian policies deal specifically with seeking to ensure and protect the rights of the Russian compatriots. As will be demonstrated in the next chapter, Russia's laws, policies, and strategies on compatriot issues enshrine, institutionalize, and legalize this protection even when such a practice is unusual in international law. An offer of a passport is in its very essence an offer of state protection—both inside and outside Russia's borders. Finally, information warfare often focuses on the alleged violations of Russian human rights, threats of fascism, and even preposterous accusations of genocide of the Russian diaspora, as voiced by the main federal investigative authority, the Russian Investigative Committee, during the Russian-Ukrainian conflict in late 2014.[117] Thus, Moscow-led protection of compatriots becomes the natural extension of earlier Russian policies.

The Russian notion of protection is very broad, as Moscow has reserved for itself almost all its forms in response to various levels of threat. Moscow's earliest conceptualizations of how to defend its compatriots abroad via military intervention were established in a draft military doctrine published in May 1992. It defined one of the basic tasks of the military as defense of the "rights and interests of citizens of Russia and people linked with it ethnically and culturally abroad."[118] While the final text of the military doctrine, published in 1993, narrowed the group to be defended to just citizens, it still defined "the suppression of the rights, freedoms and lawful interests of Russian citizens in foreign states as a source of military danger."[119] In recent times, Russia's policies in Georgia and particularly in Ukraine have established two criteria according to which the Kremlin can use military force to protect Russian compatriots. First, when there is a presumed threat to their security (their lives or physical well-being).[120] Second, when Russian compatriots (but not necessarily their legal representatives) request Russia's assistance.[121] However, the Russian government has declared on more than one occasion that it seeks to protect Russian compatriots and citizens abroad not only in the face of danger but during any infringements of their "dignity" and "honor." For example, during the Russo-Georgian war in August 2008, Medvedev reiterated that "protecting the lives and dignity of our citizens, wherever they may be, is an unquestionable priority for our country."[122] Russia's use of military force in South Ossetia was also justified as defense of "the dignity and honor of the Russian citizens."[123] Finally, as the case of Ukraine demonstrated in 2014, this protection need not be officially requested or even approved by the compatriots. The Kremlin has seemingly called to protect compatriots in eastern Ukraine from the new government in Kiev by its own decision. For instance, a month after the annexation of Crimea, in April 2014, the Gallup Organization conducted polls in Ukraine and found that only 8 percent of the population in eastern Ukraine responded "definitely yes" to wanting protection by the Russian army. In contrast, 52 percent of eastern Ukrainians responded "definitely no." Likewise, 11 percent responded "rather yes" while 17 percent responded "rather no."[124] While the accuracy of the sample in this or any poll can always be questioned, there was no evidence to suggest that (beyond the small number of separatist insurgents supported by Russian militias) eastern Ukrainians sought Moscow's protection.

Ultimately, President Putin has regarded any threat to the supranational concept of the Russian World as a pretext for protection. In the case of Ukraine, on June 24, 2014, Putin argued: "We shall always protect the ethnic Russians in Ukraine, as well as that part of Ukraine's population that feels inseparably linked with Russia ethnically, culturally and linguistically, that feels to be a part of the broader *Russkiy Mir.*"[125] As Russian policy experts such as Marlene Laruelle conclude, the concept of the Russian World "serves as a justification for what Russia considers to be its right to oversee the evolution of its neighbors, and sometimes for an interventionist policy."[126] In addition, Russian state interests and not only

Russian minorities can also warrant protection. For instance, as then president Medvedev reiterated at the end of August 2008 following the Russo-Georgian war: "Russians have special interests in the former Soviet Union and in friendly relations with these states. Intrusions by others into these regions that undermine pro-Russian regimes will be regarded as a threat to Russia's special interests."[127] This statements has been echoed vis-à-vis Armenia, Belarus, and other Russian ally states. However, the protection of Russian minorities or even Russian state interest is not necessarily the end goal of the reimperialization trajectory.

STAGE 7: ANNEXATION

The final stage of the trajectory is either formal or de facto annexation of the territories where compatriots reside. However, Russia's reimperialization of post-Soviet territories and the policies that can result in annexation should be understood as an ongoing, long-term process rather than a final step. In this process human rights violations, protection, and the right to self-determination are evoked. Polls may be conducted and referendums held. Even the rapid referendum in and annexation of Ukraine's Crimea belies the fact that Moscow's policies of passportization had been under way in the peninsula for many years before, as will be demonstrated in Chapter 4. The variation in timing and conditions of Russia's efforts of territorial expansion across the post-Soviet space does not diminish the consistency of Russia's aim of extending its power over or taking over former Soviet territories where Russian compatriots reside. The propaganda for protecting Russian compatriots facilitates Russia's search for a modern-day version of the Anschluss, in which Nazi Germany invaded and incorporated Austria in accordance with its propaganda campaign for uniting ethnic Germans and the territories where they resided in a single state.

To date, Crimea is the sole case of outright annexation. It is a unique case, Moscow's defenders may argue, because fifty years ago, this originally Tatar territory was part of the Russian state. By contrast, Moscow has still not recognized Transnistria's independence nor tried to annex the territory, despite the fact that it declared its independence from Moldova in 1990. Nonetheless, albeit internationally unrecognized (except by South Ossetia and Abkhazia), Transnistria has in effect become Moscow's puppet territory. Georgia's South Ossetia and Abkhazia have declared independence and both are now seeking closer integration with the Russian Federation. Ukraine's militant-run Luhansk and Donetsk, self-proclaimed "people's republics" are likely to follow in the footsteps of South Ossetia, Abkhazia, and Transnistria. The separatist forces in the two conflict zones in Ukraine are largely armed, manned, and supported by Russia (in spite of Moscow's denials), and the separatists' "independence" may in the future even gain Moscow's official recognition, if not lead to annexation.

Despite the Kremlin's assertions of the right to protect compatriots and citizens anywhere in the world, and especially in the near abroad, it has shown some reluctance and caution about officially sending in armed forces for this purpose or for annexation. The Russian military engaged the Georgian forces in South Ossetia and Abkhazia but insisted it did so only after Tbilisi sent in troops to recapture the rebel territories. In Ukraine, Moscow preferred to rely on hybrid warfare. It is very telling that even by mid-2015, despite all evidence to the contrary, the Kremlin has refused to admit both domestically and internationally that Russian armed forces were fighting in eastern Ukraine. Instead, high-ranking Russian officials such as Foreign Minister Sergey Lavrov and Russia's envoy to the UN Vitaly Churkin have argued that the Russian soldiers who were fighting in Ukraine's Donbas region were merely volunteers.[128] Likewise, Russian soldiers on the ground explain that they are simply spending their vacation days in eastern Ukraine and personally support the activities of the separatists.[129] The purpose of such a narrative has been to consistently deny Russian military interference and characterize the war as a conflict between Kiev and a group of local, homegrown rebels rather than Russian forces. Furthermore, in May 2015, Putin issued a decree to the effect that deaths of Russian soldiers or injuries to them occurring in the course of "special operations" can be classified as military secrets, even in peacetime.[130] This effectively blocked any public inquiries regarding the involvement of Russian soldiers in Ukraine and the resulting casualties.

This preference for a covert and shadow war seems to stem from the "Gerasimov Doctrine," published in February 2013 in the Russian *Military-Industrial Courier*. In his article, the Chief of the General Staff of the Russian Federation, General Valery Gerasimov, proposed eight phases of modern hybrid warfare to subvert states and gain control of territories without resorting to conventional military means. General Gerasimov concluded that "The very 'rules of war' have changed," and that today nonmilitary means such as the "use of political, economic, informational, humanitarian, and other non-military measures—applied in coordination with the protest potential of the population" can exceed "the power of force of weapons in their effectiveness" and "that the open use of forces—often under the guise of peacekeeping and crisis regulation—is resorted to only at a certain stage, primarily for the achievement of final success in the conflict."[131] Hybrid warfare rather than traditional military campaigns is crucial to Russia's reimperialization efforts and effectively utilizes, among other tactics, efforts to win the hearts and minds of a civilian population, and information and cyber warfare.

In the long run, Moscow may be increasingly unable to bear the costs of territorial expansion and military campaigns to reimperialize more post-Soviet territories. Though Russia has recently modernized its military, at some point the cost of modernization may become prohibitive. Yet Moscow has demonstrated great ability and success in engaging in low-cost hybrid warfare and creating frozen-conflict zones in Transnistria, South Ossetia, Abkhazia, and potentially Luhansk and Donetsk. Frozen conflicts are defined as conditions where active armed conflict may have ended but no peace treaty or political resolution has resolved the tensions to the satisfaction of the different sides. In a frozen conflict zone internal sovereignty can be achieved on a breakaway territory but at the expense of "external sovereignty" (recognition in the international system).[132] The term "frozen conflict" is almost completely associated with the breakaway post-Soviet territories that emerged as a result of Moscow's efforts to protect its compatriots. While such conflicts do not amount to direct annexation, they permanently remove territories from the states in question, place them under Russia's direct influence, and pave the way for Russia's subsequent territorial expansion. They benefit various local and transnational interest groups (including Russian groups) involved in transportation of commercial goods, money laundering, organized crime, and arms trafficking. After years spent as unrecognized entities in the gray zone of the international community, these territories eventually seek closer ties to Russia or absorption into the Russian Federation rather than independence, as seen in the cases of South Ossetia, Abkhazia, and Transnistria. While frozen conflicts may serve as stepping-stones for annexation by Moscow, they are equally effective in destabilizing target states like Moldova, Georgia, and Ukraine. By challenging the territorial integrity of these states, Moscow is able to thwart their pushes for EU or NATO membership and thus constrain their foreign policies and keep them in its sphere of influence—a key aim of the Russian government and the reimperialization trajectory.

The proposed seven stages of Russia's reimperialization policy trajectory help make sense of the seemingly disparate processes under way in many of the fourteen states of the former Soviet Union. They serve as a lens through which to view the Kremlin's efforts at extending its influence and territory in the former Soviet republics, irrespective of their wishes or the wishes of the so-called compatriots. The seven-stage paradigm is not a timetable for Moscow's imminent annexation. Instead, it outlines how the stage is set for military escalation and how hybrid warfare, annexation, separatism, and frozen conflicts can become possibilities. The more aggressive phases of reimperialization often come into play either at opportune moments or when the target countries are deliberating closer ties with EU or NATO, as in the cases of Ukraine, Georgia, Moldova, and Armenia. EU or NATO membership, as in the case of the Baltic States, does not preclude Russia's use of softer reimperialization tactics, nor does it completely exclude the possibility of separatism and armed conflict.

Russian compatriot policies are both distinct aspects of Russian reimperialization and at the same time underlie all seven stages of the proposed trajectory. Compatriot policies have been little studied before and are in many ways the main focus of this book. As a result, Russian compatriot policies and related foreign policy, national security, and citizenship strategies will be assessed in detail in the next chapter. Having demonstrated the final aims of compatriot policies in the imperial revival project, the following chapter will trace how the Russian diaspora and Russian speakers have been conceptualized, politicized, and securitized as compatriots to become an instrument of Russia's foreign policy since the 1990s.

CHAPTER THREE

The Origins and Development of Russian Compatriot Policies

... the collapse of the Soviet Union was a major geopolitical disaster of the century. And for the Russian nation, it became a genuine drama. Tens of millions of our co-citizens and compatriots found themselves outside Russian territory.

—Vladimir Putin, *State of the Nation Address, 25 April 2005*

THERE IS NO CONCEPT more nebulous but potentially more important for the geopolitics of the former Soviet space than that of "Russian compatriots." Compatriots have served an important role in Russia's quest to reestablish itself as a great power on the world stage. Since the 2000s, compatriot policies have served an integrative function: that of uniting the Russian people and the foreign lands where they reside under the flag of the Russian Federation. Moscow has spent decades trying to define the concept of a "compatriot," despite its geostrategic importance for Russia. While the term "compatriot" generally refers to a "fellow countryman or countrywoman," the Russian word, *sootechestvennik* (literally "those who are with the fatherland"), has come to refer most often to ethnic Russians and Russian speakers residing outside the Russian Federation and encompasses ethnic, cultural, linguistic, political, and even spiritual connotations. Its usage has been broad and mutable. Almost any Russian speaker who resides outside of Russia, or even anyone who was born in the Soviet Union, has been at some point defined by Moscow as a Russian compatriot. Even Russian ethnicity or Russian language is not a prerequisite for belonging to this category. Anyone hailing from some 185 ethnic groups that have historically resided in the territory of the Russian Federation or the Soviet Union could be deemed a compatriot.

A Russian grandfather and veteran, for example, who has lived in Tallinn, Estonia, since the Second World War could be considered a compatriot. But so could a high-school student in Brighton Beach, Brooklyn, whose Jewish grandparents arrived in the 1950s from Odessa, Ukraine, escaping the Soviet regime. An ethnic Ossetian living in a mountain village in the Georgian breakaway territory of South Ossetia who speaks his native Iranian language can also fall under the same category—likewise a Tatar girl who is a Russian speaker and lives in the historic city of Samarkand, Uzbekistan, in the heart of Central Asia. The two things that connect Moscow's so-called compatriots all over the world are being habitual Russian speakers and/or descent from former Soviet or Russian citizens or nations inhabiting former Russian imperial lands. Compatriots are ethnic Russians only in the narrowest sense of Moscow's use of the term. In 1991 there were about 25 million ethnic Russians residing outside the Russian Federation in the former Soviet Republics.[1] They constituted significant percentages of the population in Kazakhstan (38 percent), Latvia (34 percent), Estonia (30 percent), and Ukraine (22 percent).[2] In the 2010s, there were about 30 million native Russian speakers outside the Russian Federation.[3] But taking into account the entire population of the independent former Soviet republics, there is a total of nearly 150 million individuals who are descendants of Soviet citizens and thus have at different times qualified for Moscow's identification as compatriots.[4] While Russia aims to define compatriots based on language or descent, in reality these individuals are highly diverse—geographically, ethnically, linguistically, generationally, and socially. Over the decades, Moscow has tried to but come short of creating a legal status for the compatriots, and their rights and responsibilities notably differ from those of Russian citizens. Nonetheless, the Russian government has called on numerous occasions for support and protection of its compatriots by various means. This protection may entail many things, from supporting language and cultural programs, to appealing to international organizations to address discrimination of Russian minorities, to their military protection, as in both Ukraine and Georgia.

The official usage of the term "compatriot" arose only after the dissolution of the Soviet Union, in early 1993, when it was employed by the Ministry of Foreign Affairs and other government departments.[5] There is no evidence that the term was ever used with the same political connotations during the Russian empire or during the Soviet era. As *Great Soviet Encyclopedia* entries show, until the 1990s the term *sootechestvennik* was nothing more than a Russian version of a French word *compatriote* (fellow countryman/countrywoman).[6] According to the entry in the 1955 edition, which also cited Lenin's use of the term, *sootechestvennik* was used as a translation of the Latin word *patriota* (meaning exactly "compatriot").[7] Joseph Stalin used the word *sootechestvennik* with exactly the same meaning in his Victory Speech following Germany's surrender in 1945.[8] But neither Lenin nor Stalin used the term with the same political connotation that it increasingly gained in the 1990s.

This politicized and securitized concept of "compatriot," and certainly the notion of protecting one's compatriots (rather than one's citizens) who reside or are even citizens of foreign states is somewhat unusual in the global context, but not unprecedented. For instance, while Israel offers citizenship to Jews in general, it encourages them to return to the motherland rather than seeking to protect them abroad. Likewise, during the American invasion of Grenada in 1983, President Ronald Reagan argued that one of the motives of the operation was to protect American medical students on the island. Romania, Hungary, Croatia, Serbia, and other countries have also pursued policies of support toward their diasporas. From the mid-1990s on, these countries offered benefits in various degrees in such areas as education, employment, and welfare not only to their compatriots, but also to passport holders, or in the short-lived case of Hungary, to identity card holders.[9] Though these policies have attracted significant criticism on the grounds that they were intended to undermine the sovereignty of neighboring states, they have largely paled in comparison to the compatriot policies practiced by Russia.[10] The sheer comprehensiveness, consistency, and tenacity of Russia's compatriot policy place it in a league of its own. To be sure, I do not argue that any policy to support one's compatriots is automatically illegitimate. Countries can call for other states to respect the human and civil rights of their conationals or other peoples. Diplomacy can be used to achieve such aims. Financing cultural and educational programs are also commonly used measures. But it is crucial to distinguish different forms that such policies can take—launching cultural television programs cannot be equated to sending in tanks. Using the pretext of compatriot protection to move in troops or refuse to withdraw them falls outside the scope of diplomatic or cultural initiatives. In some regards, Russia's compatriot policies are more reminiscent of postcolonial policies, which suggest the imperial nature of the Soviet Union and the neo-imperial fallout from its collapse. For example, when India gained independence from the British Empire in 1947, Indians remained British subjects until 1950. Subsequently, some individuals who did not obtain Indian citizenship maintained a status of "British subject without citizenship." However, unlike in the case of Russia, these categories were clearly and legally defined by mutual agreement between India and Britain.[11]

In part the uniqueness of Russian compatriot policies in contemporary times stems from the scale of the issue and the nature of the Soviet empire, which had displaced, deported, and colonized sizable populations of different nations. Overnight with the fall of the USSR, Russia lost some 25 million ethnic Russians and additional Russian speakers to foreign states. These people had been citizens of the Soviet Union. Since Russia was the official successor state of the Soviet Union, accepting all of the Soviet Union's former obligations, it made sense that Moscow would also take responsibility for the Soviet-era Russian migrants and deportees of all ethnicities to Soviet territories that stretched from the Baltic Sea to the Central Asian steppes. The situation was complicated by the fact that some newly reestablished states like Estonia and Latvia failed to automatically provide citizenship to Soviet-era migrants, while interethnic conflict emerged in Georgia, and some Central Asian states like Uzbekistan embarked on nation-building that favored their titular majorities. As a result, some members of the Russian diaspora were left without any citizenship. The situation was made more complex by the fact that the Soviet-era Russian or Russian-speaking migrants were a highly diverse and fragmented group, many of whom had no desire to return to the motherland as they had developed strong ties to their countries of residence or had few ties to the Russian Federation. As this chapter will demonstrate, in the 1990s Russia was facing its own economic difficulties, and was not in a position to assist their return. Instead, Moscow cast them as compatriots.

Previously Moscow's compatriot policies have been studied as a form of soft power and the humanitarian dimension of foreign policy.[12] In contrast to coercive power, soft power aims to gain influence through appeals to cultural and historic affinities and shared values.[13] While it has been recognized that Russia uses compatriots for geopolitical influence,[14] the full significance of these policies outside soft power has not been grasped.[15] Likewise, the humanitarian dimension of Russia's foreign policy has been viewed as outside the scope of military or economic sanctions.[16] However, Russian compatriot policies have evolved to be and thus should be understood as a strategic tool of foreign policy and geopolitical ambitions.[17] Compatriots were an important element of Russia's Foreign Policy Concept of 2000 and reiterated in the updated Concept of 2013, and they are at the crux of Russia's reimperialization policy. As noted, the definition and the concept of "compatriots" are not fixed, but they are also linked as much to the individuals themselves as to Russian national identity and Russian foreign policy. In any case, the central proposition of this book is that Russia's humanitarian, compatriot, and soft power policies have become increasingly enmeshed with its territorial aims and military tactics.

This chapter will trace this most important phase and component of reimperialization trajectory. Moscow's policies and legal framework toward its compatriots emerged rather incoherently in the 1990s. By the 2000s, however, the legal and policy framework took a decided turn and compatriot policies were coupled with the Russian government's geopolitical and increasingly revisionist aims. A brief review of Stalin's ethnic policies, which helped create sizable Russian and Russian-speaking minorities in the post-Soviet space, will provide historical context. The evolution of definitions of the term "compatriot," and the development of related policies, will then be traced from the presidency of Boris Yeltsin to the rule of Vladimir Putin.

STALIN'S ETHNIC POLICIES

In the 1930s Joseph Stalin laid the foundations of what would result in large numbers of Russians and Russophones residing in territories from the Baltic Sea to Central Asia. The Georgian-born robber-revolutionary turned leader-dictator spent his life trying to be more Russian than the Russians themselves despite his heavy Georgian accent in Russian and his distinctive appearance betraying his Caucasian roots.[18] He did not trust the loyalty of the different nationalities of the Soviet Union and in the end sought to eliminate or Russify them. Many of his policies resulted in deporting various nationalities from their native countries into other parts of the Soviet Union and importing Russian workers to create ethnically mixed populations. As American historian Timothy Snyder has argued, Stalin took a different course in ethnic policies from his predecessor Lenin and other Bolsheviks.[19] Stalin did not believe in positive discrimination in selecting non-Russians for the project of building the Soviet Union (though he himself had been selected and favored). He was searching for tools to consolidate Soviet society ideologically and find a basis for its common identity. Stalin perceived nationalism, especially in other Soviet nations, to be a threat to Bolshevism.[20] Therefore, promoting the Russian language and culture together with the idea of Russians being "first among equals" in a "friendly Soviet family of nations" was meant to create a sense of unity in the Soviet state.

In his quest to strengthen the Soviet empire and his rule, Stalin ordered mass murder and the deportation of many nations (including the Russians) to Soviet labor camps, or the so-called Gulag.[21] Already by the end of 1930s, Stalin had a quarter of a million Soviet citizens shot, solely on the grounds of their nationalities.[22] Before the Second World War, the labor camps had the dual purpose of providing free labor to contribute to the growth of the Soviet economy and punishing "enemies of the state."[23] As the war approached, Stalin was increasingly concerned with the security of the Soviet Union's borders. Therefore, ethnic cleansings were carried out to relocate minorities from border regions inward into Russian territories, on the assumption that separation from their homelands would lead to a faster assimilation into Soviet society.[24] In their places, other nationalities (often Russians) were brought in.

In the period of 1935 to 1938 at least nine Soviet nationalities suffered ethnic cleansing, and from 1941 to 1948 the total of exiled or resettled people reached an estimated 3.3 million people.[25] Before, during, and after the Second World War Poles, Romanians, Volga Germans, Estonians, Latvians, Lithuanians, Finns, Crimean Tatars, Crimean Greeks, and other nationalities experienced mass deportations to labor camps. Although motives for cleansing varied (for example, Crimean Tatars allegedly posed a fifth column risk and Chechens were suspected to have separatist aspirations), after such deportations Russian immigration into the newly cleansed territories followed.[26] The allegedly deliberate famine in Ukraine of 1933–33, which has been called "the classic example of Soviet genocide," took around 5 million Ukrainian lives.[27] In 1944 more than

190,000 Crimean Tatars were deported from Crimea to Uzbekistan and lost their national autonomy.[28] Only 40 percent of the prewar population of Crimean Tatars remained in the peninsula by 1945.[29] During the resettlement and industrialization campaign in the Baltic States, Russian workers, military personnel, and (in the 1980s) convicts arrived from other parts of the Soviet Union.[30] As a result, the number of Russians in Latvia increased from 10.5 percent in 1935 to 35 percent in 1989 and in Estonia grew from 8 percent in 1934 to 30 percent in 1989.[31] Only in Lithuania was the increase much lower, from 3 percent in 1939 to 9 percent in 1989.[32] Thus, the Baltic States, Ukraine, Crimea, Central Asian countries, and others were left with mixed ethnic populations and large numbers of Russian minorities. At the same time, the Soviet Union pursued the contradictory national policy of preserving national boundaries of the Soviet republics and trying to create a monolithic Soviet (but Russified) identity. This further contributed to the large populations of Russian-speaking peoples of various ethnicities residing across the territory of the Soviet Union.

Stalin's rule lasted nearly thirty years, and during those brutal decades he did achieve much that he set out to accomplish. By 1991 when the Soviet Union fell, the former Soviet republics that gained independence were ethnically mixed. Large numbers of ethnic Russians and Russian speakers were concentrated in certain territories in every independent state of the former USSR, and this situation remains largely unchanged until the present day. The Russian Federation that emerged in 1991 inherited this problem and an ideological dilemma. Should the concept of the Russian nation in the new Russian state include the Soviet diaspora? Should the Russian nation be based on civic, ethnic, or imperial concepts? These were the questions that Presidents Boris Yeltsin and Vladimir Putin and their advisers would in time have to answer.

THE RUSSIAN NATION AND COMPATRIOTS

The present-day concept of the Russian compatriot both stems from and relates to a broader understanding of the Russian nation. Professor of Russian studies Vera Tolz in her book *Russia* identifies five distinct conceptions of the Russian nation in the post-Soviet period derived from intellectual debate and political statements.[33] The first conception emphasizes the Union (or imperial) identity. It sees the Russians as destined to create and maintain a multinational state. This viewpoint is supported by nationally minded Communists, rhetorical ultranationalists, and Eurasianists. The political project of these people, in its maximal form, is the restoration of the Russian Empire or of the USSR. According to this conceptualization of Russian nationhood, Russian compatriots would include all former citizens of the USSR and their descendants. A second way to conceptualize the Russian nation is to include the entire community of Eastern Slavs: the Russians, Ukrainians, and Belarusians who speak closely related languages and traditionally share the Orthodox Christian faith. This vision of Russian identity could present a narrower notion of Russian compatriots based on religious and cultural affinities. The third conception of the Russian nation inclines instead to a broader vision, including all who use Russian as their first or habitual language, regardless of their ethnicity. This view would lead to a redrawing of Russian borders to include Russian-speaking parts of Ukraine, Moldova, Kazakhstan, Latvia, and Estonia, and most if not all of Belarus. The fourth conception offered by Tolz is racial, including only those who are Russian by blood. This is aimed above all at excluding Jews and peoples from the Caucasus and Central Asia. As these approaches suggest, the range of ways of conceiving the Russian nation includes visions that emphasize ancient historical and religiously rooted prejudices, while other visions emphasize more secular ways of thinking.

The fifth conception of the Russian nation is civic, embracing the citizens of the Russian Federation. Tolz points out that Yeltsin, Putin, and some of their ministers, while in theory committed to this civic definition of the Russian nation, have in practice on many occasions implicitly extended it to ethnic Russians and "Russian-speaking populations" residing in the former Soviet republics, only a few of whom are citizens of the Russian Federation. As scholar of Russia Charles Ziegler notes, the term "compatriot" generally refers to culturally Russified peoples and to ethnic Russians living in the fourteen independent states of the former Soviet Union.[34]

In his New Year's address to the Russian nation in January of 1994, Yeltsin specifically appealed to Russian speakers in the near abroad (rather than solely to Russian citizens), saying: "Dear compatriots! You are inseparable from us and we are inseparable from you. We were and we will be together. On the basis of law and solidarity, we defend and will defend your and our common interests. In the New Year, 1994, we will do this with greater energy and greater resoluteness."[35] Yeltsin repeated a similar statement later that year in his annual address to the Federal Assembly. Though in general Yeltsin failed to consistently back up his rhetoric with action, this demonstrated both how a new concept of compatriots had emerged and the fact that the notion of a civic state was still very novel in Russia in the 1990s. Instead, the definition of Russianness emphasized language and culture.[36] Certainly, the official dissolution of the Soviet Union in 1991 left many ethnic Russians and Russian speakers outside the border of the Russian Federation—a population still often looking to Moscow rather than the capitals of their respective post-Soviet states for guidance. However, Moscow's response to this dilemma and potential opportunity would take nearly two decades to fully formulate and would be articulated in some twenty documents released from 1994 to 2014 (see Tables 1 and 2 for a list of the main compatriot policies under Yeltsin and Putin).

THE YELTSIN ERA: EARLY COMPATRIOT POLICIES

In the early 1990s, Russian foreign policy was still in its infancy and thus it took some time for Moscow to start formally conceptualizing compatriots and formulating official compatriot policies.[37] Under Yeltsin's presidency six important policies would eventually emerge that related to Russian compatriots (see Table 1). The delay from 1991 to 1994 in addressing the burning problem of millions of Russian compatriots left outside the borders of Russia was due in part to Russia's domestic political difficulties of the early 1990s.[38] In addition, poor economic conditions prevented implementation of policies to assist the compatriots and reinforced the belief that potential migration of Russians to the motherland would only be an economic burden that all hoped to avoid.[39] While Yeltsin's seeming desire for ethnic Russians and Russian speakers to integrate in their "host" countries could be seen as a sign that Russia was ready to support the sovereignty of the newly independent republics, the facts on the ground soon demonstrated that compatriots could be a means of influence.

Despite the fact that neither the term "compatriot" nor "compatriot policy" was yet articulated, as early as in 1992 there were indications that compatriots were being used for Moscow's foreign policy and particularly its military agenda. A good example could be the negotiation process to withdraw some 120,000 Soviet troops from the Baltic States (completed in Lithuania in 1993 and in Latvia and Estonia in 1994). During its negotiations with the Baltic capitals, the Russian side grounded its military presence in the Baltic States as a means of safeguarding the rights of compatriots in the region.[40] The withdrawal of the Russian troops was halted because in Yeltsin's words in 1992, he was "profoundly concerned over numerous infringements of the rights of Russian speakers."[41] Later the same year Yeltsin also stressed that development of Russian-Baltic relations would "largely depend on the situation of the Russian-speaking population."[42] As will be shown in Chapter 5, the basis of Yeltsin's concern was probably first of all the fact that two Baltic countries, Estonia and Latvia, decided not to grant automatic citizenship to individuals (including many Russians) who had immigrated there during the Soviet era, but also Moscow's lack of preparations to house the returning military and their families. Refusing to withdraw troops by citing excuses regarding compatriots was among the first signs of efforts to utilize the diaspora for Moscow's aims and influence abroad. Similar statements linking Russia's foreign policy toward a target country with the conditions of its Russian and Russian-speaking population were repeated over the next decades by Yeltsin's successors in relation to a number of former Soviet republics.

In the context of rising tensions over Russian compatriots, Sergei Stankevich, historian and presidential counselor from 1992 to 1993, emerged as one of Russia's early policymakers in this area. Together with the political opposition, Stankevich argued that Russians in the near abroad should be seen as an integral part of the Russian nation.[43] He was among the first to suggest that the Russian diaspora was not a potential problem, but on the contrary, a source of power in the former Soviet space.[44] Looking back, Stankevich seems a surprising figure to have become instrumental in conceptualizing the compatriot policies that would become a tool for Russia's reimperialization efforts. A former perestroika and glasnost activist, the baby-faced former history teacher was still in his thirties when he became Yeltsin's adviser. His fall from grace was as rapid as his rise—in 1996 he was charged with graft related to a $6 million blowout of public funds for a Red Square gala concert and retreated to live abroad.[45] But before his ousting, in 1993 Stankevich au-

Table 1

Compatriot Policy Documents under Boris Yeltsin, 1993–1999

DATE	DOCUMENT	SUMMARY OF CONTENTS
January 1993	Report on Urgent Measures for Socio-cultural Cooperation between Citizens of the Russian Federation with their Compatriots Abroad	The first official document addressing the compatriot issue and containing possibly the earliest formulation and usage of the term.
11 August 1994	Presidential Decree No. 1681, Guidelines on State Policy regarding Compatriots Living Abroad[a]	First document in the field of policies toward compatriots abroad, regardless of the failure to give a clear definition of the term "compatriot." Document also supported the idea of dual citizenship.
31 August 1994	Resolution of the Russian Government No. 1064, List of Primary Measures to Support Compatriots Abroad[b]	Supplemented Presidential Decree No. 1681 (above).
8 December 1995	Declaration on Support of the Russian Diaspora and Protection of Russian Compatriots[c]	First official definition of compatriots: "all the natives of the USSR and Russia and all their descendants regardless of their nationality and ethnicity, language, religion, gender, occupation and place of residence and other circumstances."[d]
17 May 1996	Resolution of the Government No. 590, Action Program for Protecting Compatriots Abroad[e]	Declared a need to create "a legal definition of the concept 'compatriot' and its further use in the legislation."[f] Stated that Russia was ready "to assist governments of newly independent states"[g] in ensuring that Russians enjoyed the full range of their rights.

(continued)

Table 1 (continued)

Compatriot Policy Documents under Boris Yeltsin, 1993–1999

DATE	DOCUMENT	SUMMARY OF CONTENTS
24 May 1999	Federal Law on the State Policy of the Russian Federation Concerning Compatriots Abroad No. 99-FZ[h]	This document regulated relations with compatriots. The term "compatriot" was automatically applied to all persons who in the past lived in the former USSR, or their descendants (but excluding the descendants of members of titular nations of the foreign states).

Source: Compiled by the author.

Notes

a. Ukaz Prezidenta Rossiyskoy Federatsii "Ob osnovnykh napravleniyakh gosudarstvennoy politiki Rossiyskoy Federatsii v otnoshenii sootechestvennikov, prozhivayushikh za rubezhom" ot 11 avgusta 1994 g., № 1681, http://base.consultant.ru/cons/cgi/online.cgi?req=doc;base=EXP;n=218892.

b. Postanovleniye Pravitelstva Rossiyskoy Federatsii "O merakh po podderzhke sootechestvennikov za rubezhom" ot 31 avgusta 1994 g. N 1064, http://www.consultant.ru/document/cons_doc_LAW_106359/.

c. Deklaratsiya Gosudarstvennoy Dumy Federalnogo Sobraniya Rossiyskoy Federatsii "O podderzhke rossiyskoy diaspory i o pokrovitelstve rossiyskim sootechestvennikam," http://igrunov.ru/gdrf/sng/sng-archive/declar_sng.html.

d. Ibid.

e. Postanovleniye Pravitelstva Rossiyskoy Federatsii ot 17.05.1996 № 590 "O programme mer po podderzhke sootechestvennikov za rubezhom," http://www.lawmix.ru/pprf/108396/.

f. Ibid.

g. Ibid.

h. Followed by a number of amendments, the most significant in July 2010 (see below, Table 2). Federalnyi zakon ot 24.05.1999 № 99-FZ "O gosudarstvennoy politike Rossiyskoy Federatsii v otnoshenii sootechestvennikov," http://base.consultant.ru/cons/cgi/online.cgi?req=doc;base=LAW;n=150465.

thored and presented to Yeltsin a report on the Russian diaspora entitled "On Urgent Measures for Socio-cultural Cooperation between Citizens of the Russian Federation with Their Compatriots Abroad." It was the first official document addressing the compatriot issue and contains possibly the earliest formulation and usage of the term as it would come to be employed in the coming decades. The Stankevich report called for official measures to establish links between compatriots and the Russian state as well as public organizations to implement this task.[46]

Despite some initial delay, Stankevich's policy document did not go unnoticed. In February 1994, Yeltsin officially declared to the Federal Assembly the necessity of formulating a policy toward compatriots abroad. He also determined the future conceptualization and discourse regarding Russia's compatriots: Russia should help its compatriots not with coming back to the "historically native land," but with settling down in foreign states. In his speech, Yeltsin issued a call that "everywhere, where our compatriots live, they should feel themselves full and equal citizens," and defined a range of tasks of foreign policy aimed to support the "interests of Russians in the CIS countries and the Baltic states."[47] Although at the time these measures were probably mostly intended to assist Russians in settling into their countries of residence, the seeds of Russian compatriot policy as a means of influence in the former Soviet republics were planted for future use by Putin's regime. Since then, Russian politicians have maintained the notion of a certain duty to defend the rights of Russians and Russian speakers against the ethnic elites of the former Soviet republics as they pursued in Moscow's eyes a "decolonizing" process.[48]

The mechanisms to support Russian compatriots, however, were lacking, until in August 1994 the government passed a resolution approving two documents: "Guidelines on State Policy regarding Compatriots Living Abroad" and "List of Primary Measures to Support Compatriots Abroad." The government also established a Governmental Commission on Affairs of Compatriots Abroad composed of government, presidential office, and social organization officials and representatives of other groups.[49] Regardless of the failure to clearly define "compatriots," the documents maintained that state policy would be implemented toward two categories of people: emigrants from Russia and the USSR (including their descendants) and the Russian-speaking population of the former Soviet Union republics.[50] Two different policies were proposed regarding these two categories of compatriots. Emigrants to the West were to be encouraged to regain Russian citizenship and return to the "historically native land" of Russia. Probably few emigrants to the United States and Europe were actually expected to return to Russia. In contrast, for Russian speakers in the near abroad, the policy focused on "prevention of mass migration" from the former Union Republics to Russia. Sociologist Hilary Pilkington aptly noted that at the time the Russian government was in favor of preventing "compatriots" becoming "repatriates."[51] This policy of limiting repatriation was named as one of the main factors in changing the migration dynamics of the Russian population from Central Asia, which had rapidly decreased but at a slower rate after the limits were imposed in 1994. In that year 234,000 Russians migrated from Kazakhstan to Russia, but in 1995 this number fell to 144,000; 93,500 Russians left Uzbekistan in 1994, but in 1995 only 64,200; 42,900 left Kyrgyzstan in 1994, and 13,400 in 1995.[52] Still, most Russians who wanted to repatriate had already done so in the early 1990s.

Certainly, it appears ironic that Moscow seemed to want to claim this population, but not necessarily bring it back to the motherland. While it is impossible to ascribe this policy to a single motive, several reasons are possible. First, as Russia's own domestic population was experiencing severe economic hardships following the fall of the USSR, Moscow could not have provided for another 25 million returnees. Russia's housing, pension, education, and health care systems were already under strain. Secondly, unemployment and underemployment were rampant in Russia in the 1990s so there were simply not enough jobs for repatriates. Thirdly, it is likely that the Kremlin already saw the strategic potential of its compatriots as long as they remained in the near abroad. As will be discussed later, some of the Kremlin's advisers like Sergey Karaganov were highlighting the role that compatriots could play in foreign policy. During the Soviet era, the Russian minorities had served administrative, bureaucratic, intelligence, and military roles in the Soviet republics and later they often gained prominence in the economic and to a lesser extent political systems of the independent post-Soviet states, thus serving as a useful interest group for Moscow.[53] Many factors probably influenced Russia's decision to promote the integration of the diaspora into the newly independent post-Soviet states while at the same time seeking to protect it.

First, however, Moscow had to define the term "compatriot." The first official definition appeared in the end of 1995 when the State Duma adopted the "Declaration on Support of the Russian Diaspora and Protection of Russian Compatriots."[54] The document defined Russian compatriots as "all the natives of the USSR and Russia and all their descendants regardless of their nationality and ethnicity, language, religion, gender, occupation and place of residence and other circumstances, who are not citizens of the Russian Federation but explicitly declare their spiritual, cultural, and ethnic ties with the Russian Federation or with any districts of Russian Federation and confirm this relationship."[55] However, the declaration did not specify or prescribe how this spiritual, cultural, and ethnic affiliation should be demonstrated.[56] Clearly, this definition was exceedingly broad. As a result, at the end of 1995, almost anyone who was not a Russian citizen but had any connection with Russia or the USSR could have been deemed a Russian compatriot. Also, any former citizen of Russia or the USSR and his or her direct descendants could be classified as a "compatriot" if they expressed this preference. While the declaration and its definition had little practical effect on the Russian compatriots, it signaled that Russia sought to define them in a broader rather than a narrower sense of the word.

As it was immediately evident that the breadth of this definition would make it difficult to enact policies, the Russian government's "Action Program for Protecting Compatriots Abroad" of May 1996 called for "a legal definition of the concept 'compatriot' and its further use in the legislation."[57] The new policy document maintained the position of 1994 limiting repatriation and argued that Russian compatriots "had to live and determine their own destiny in complex political, economic, social, cultural, [and] psychological conditions and they need assistance and support both from the states where they reside and from Russia."[58] The Russian state once again opted for the integration of compatriots into their countries of residence rather than repatriate. The role of the Russian government was reasonably envisioned as rather limited: "Russia as the successor of the USSR has a moral responsibility to compatriots" and should assist other states in safeguarding their rights.[59] The document of 1996 also pointed out that "the issue of compatriots is a significant factor in the formation of relations between Russia and the members of the CIS and the Baltic States."[60] Already in June 1995, while visiting Kaliningrad Yeltsin stated that "guaranteeing the basic rights and freedoms of our compatriots [in the Baltics] is a priority for me" and that "abuse of Russians' civil rights in Latvia and Estonia was hindering attempts by Moscow to improve ties with the Baltic states."[61] Russian minorities in Estonia and Latvia did arguably face some legitimate discomfort over the need to undergo the naturalization process as well as uncertainty over their future legal residential status, but the exaggerated rhetoric of "basic rights and freedoms," in light of the fact that the Russian government did not welcome the repatriation of compatriots and had not legally defined them, brings into question the sincerity of Yeltsin's concern.

Russia's domestic political conditions also had an impact on the adoption of these documents. Parliamentary and presidential elections held in December 1995 and June 1996 prompted broader debates about compatriots and the country's obligations to Russian citizens.[62] A likely reason that Moscow still had failed to formulate legal definitions and policies toward its diaspora, despite the millions of ethnic Russians outside the borders of the Russian Federation, was that from 1993 to the end of the decade it simultaneously pursued a strategy toward its compatriots that contradicted its policy documents—one of turning them into Russian citizens. In the early 1990s, Moscow did not systematically pursue the passportization policy of handing out Russian citizenship to Russians and Russian speakers who are residents or citizens of foreign countries. Instead, the focus was on promoting the concept of dual citizenship in the former Soviet republics. Both methods of providing Russian citizenship would eventually come to serve Moscow's policies of expansion in Ukraine's Crimea, Moldova's Transnistria, and Georgia's South Ossetia and Abkhazia. Initially, though, the dual citizenship strategy was favored by another young reformer in Yeltsin's team—Foreign Minister Andrey Kozyrev (1991–96). Appointed foreign minister a year shy of his fortieth birthday, Kozyrev was a sophisticated, experienced diplomat with a Ph.D. in history. Like others in Yeltsin's circle, he believed in Western liberal democratic ideals and at the same time insisted that Russia be treated as a great power in international relations. Kozyrev held that promoting dual citizenship policies could serve as a "vital instrument" of Russia's foreign policy toward the near abroad, and he aimed to issue Russian passports to all ethnic Russians living in former Soviet republics, as well as to people from other ethnic groups who had historical ties to Russia.[63]

As foreign minister, Kozyrev personally sought to sign agreements with the former Soviet republics regarding dual citizenship, but the newly independent states were hardly enthusiastic. With the exception of Estonia and Latvia, all post-Soviet republics awarded their own citizenship to their entire populations, including Soviet-era immigrants. In November

1993, the Kazakh President Nursultan Nazarbayev made it clear that Kazakhstan's Russian minority does not need Moscow's passports or protection. The man who had once turned down Mikhail Gorbachev's offer to run as vice president of the Soviet Union was once again turning down Moscow's overtures. He presciently warned, "whenever one starts talking about the protection of Russians in Kazakhstan, not Russia, I recall Hitler who began to 'support' the Sudeten Germans at one time. I start feeling deep anxiety for Russians who live outside Russia. Really, they did not ask to be defended, did they? They are citizens of Kazakhstan."[64] The only states that signed up for dual citizenship agreements were Turkmenistan in 1993, when Yeltsin was also ceremonially offered a Turkmenistan passport, and Tajikistan in 1995. However, our discussion of Central Asia will show, Turkmenistan went to great lengths to prevent its citizens from gaining Russian passports and withdrew from the agreement in 2003.[65] Spreading Russian citizenship was no success but it did not mean that Moscow abandoned this project altogether.

Yeltsin's Legacy: Defining a Legal Framework for Compatriots
By 1999, the decade of the ailing Yeltsin's leadership was winding down. Despite having issued four documents related to compatriots since 1994, the Russian government still lacked a coherent legal framework to address the approximately 25 million Russians living in the former Soviet states in addition to Russian speakers and other people of Russian descent living across the globe. Passportizing the compatriots also had not shown much progress. Overall, Yeltsin's call to support and defend Russian compatriots was largely rhetorical, diplomatic, and tactical (as in the case of the Baltic States). Despite the rhetoric, Yeltsin generally pursued a policy of respect for international borders, as seen in his resistance to politicizing the Russian speakers of Crimea, who were already demonstrating for autonomy and separation from Ukraine in the early 1990s, his negotiation of the Friendship Treaty with Ukraine in 1997 recognizing its borders, and his eventual withdrawal of Russian troops from neighboring states without successfully extracting any guarantees for the local Russian-speaking populations. As the policies of the Yeltsin era demonstrated, compatriots were never a top priority for the Russian government.

In May 1999, with less than a year before Yeltsin's resignation, the government released the "Federal Law on the State Policy of the Russian

Federation Concerning Compatriots Abroad." This law finally set the basic legal framework for and definition of compatriots. It defined them as those "who were born in one [Soviet Union or Russian] state, are living or lived in it" and who "share common language, history, heritage, traditions and customs," as well as their direct descendants "residing outside the territory of the Russian Federation and related to peoples historically living on the territory of the Russian Federation," except for "descendants of persons who belong to titular nations of foreign states."[66] For instance, it meant that an ethnic Russian woman and her descendants living in Ukraine would forever be compatriots, whereas an ethnic Ukrainian woman born during the Soviet era would be a compatriot while her Ukrainian children born after the fall of the USSR would no longer be compatriots. Likewise it implied that an Ossetian and his descendants living in Georgia or Uzbekistan would forever remain Russian compatriots. This contradiction is partly born from Stalin's Soviet nationalities policies and his propagation of concepts of *natsionalnost'* (ethnic rather than civic nationality, such as is customarily entered in passports) that are to this day preserved in Russia's compatriot policies.

Furthermore, neither the aforementioned ethnic Russian nor the Ukrainian woman nor anyone else could request to be a Russian compatriot. The new law changed the right, set out in 1995, of the Soviet Union's nationals to claim the status of compatriot. Instead, that status was automatically granted both to nationals of the former USSR and to Russia's emigrants' descendants if they self-identified as such. Self-identification, like the concept of compatriot itself, was a muddled affair. It was defined as identification with Russia or Russianness or declaration of loyalty to the Russian Federation, the process for which was never formalized in practice.[67] The law also provided for compatriot ID cards but the project never achieved momentum and no such cards were ever issued.[68] As a result, by 1999 there were two distinct elements in Russia's compatriot policies: the imposition of the category on foreign states and peoples and room for self-identification as a compatriot. It is unlikely that with this definition Moscow would have tried to claim the entire 150-million population of the fourteen former Soviet republics as compatriots since most of them would not have self-identified as such, but it is feasible that the some 30 million Russian speakers would have been likely targets.

This broad concept of compatriots held some additional contradictions. First, there was a hierarchy in which a Russian "citizen" outranked a Russian "compatriot." A compatriot was never equal to a Russian passport holder residing outside Russian borders (an expatriate), though an expatriate could also be called a compatriot. Second, the concept included Russian émigrés from the tsarist and Soviet eras and their descendants. Thus, an American-Russian woman or French-Russian woman with Russian ancestors who had fled the Soviet regime following the Revolution would also be included. In practice, however, there was a geographical distinction between regions where Moscow sought to protect and support compatriots. Generally, Russia was more interested in doing so in the post-Soviet republics, which it perceived as being part of its special sphere of influence. Despite state-funded Russian language schools and special status for the Russian language in most post-Soviet states— privileges not available to Russian speakers in the West—Russia increasingly took a combative line with the post-Soviet republics on compatriots' rights. Compatriots in other parts of the world like North America or Western Europe, where Moscow held less sway, generally received less attention.[69] Despite its contradictions and vagueness, however, the 1999 law remained in place for a decade with the most significant revisions coming into force in July 2010.[70]

THE PUTIN ERA: COMPATRIOTS AS TOOLS OF FOREIGN POLICY

Compatriot Policies in the Early 2000s
When Vladimir Putin was sworn in as president in May 2000, standing next to the increasingly unwell Yeltsin, he looked the picture of youth, vigor, and strength—a new hope for Russia. Only in his late forties, Putin had already made a meteoric rise from the circle of Yeltsin's loyalists and had served as prime minister, head of the FSB (KGB's successor), and first deputy chief of the presidential staff, among other posts. Nonetheless, in May 2000, few could have thought that this little-known man, who had only arrived on Moscow's political scene in 1996, would come to rule Russia for decades as both president and prime minister. In fact, if Putin wins reelection in 2018 for his fourth presidential term, he will

have effectively been in power from December 1999 to May 2024—a total of nearly twenty-five years, which approaches Stalin's twenty-nine-year tenure.

During his rule, Putin has built on Stalin's ethnic policies and Yeltsin's diaspora laws to shape Russia's compatriot policies as a powerful tool of foreign policy and a means to reimperialize territories of the former Soviet republics. Putin's policy direction was likely highly influenced by another Yeltsin-era ideologue of Russian compatriot policy, influential political scientist and head of the Russian Council for Foreign and Defense Policy Sergey Karaganov, who served as a presidential adviser from 2001 to 2013, and was named one of the world's top-hundred public intellectuals by *Foreign Policy* magazine in 2005.[71] In 1992 he published an article proclaiming what was later named the "Karaganov Doctrine" that suggested that Russia should play an active postimperial role and protect Russian speakers.[72] Although Karaganov did not use the term "compatriots," he fully captured the importance of not only ethnic Russians but also Russian speakers in foreign policy. According to Karaganov in 1992, "everything must be done to keep Russian speakers in those regions where they live right now. Not only because we cannot afford to welcome large crowds of refugees, but also because we must leave there strings of influence with a further perspective."[73] It seems that Putin borrowed Karaganov's ideas, which gained full momentum only in the 2000s.[74] Over the course of Putin's rule some fifteen documents and policies would be adopted (see Table 2), and numerous other initiatives taken in relation to Russian compatriots.

In January 2000 when Vladimir Putin assumed office as acting president he adopted the "National Security Concept of the Russian Federation," which had already been formulated and approved under the outgoing Yeltsin in December 1999. While the main emphasis of this document was not on compatriots, it did strategically reference Russian citizens abroad. The document stated that the foreign policy of the Russian Federation should spearhead the protection of "the legitimate rights and interests of Russian citizens abroad, including by taking political, economic, and other measures."[75] Certainly the protection of one's citizens by political, economic, and other means is nothing out of the ordinary for most states. The policy, though, takes on new dimensions in light of the fact that since the 1990s the Russian Foreign Ministry sought to establish dual citizenship in the former Soviet republics, thus turning the Russian diaspora into citizens who could then be protected. This two-fold thrust of Russian foreign policy to (1) provide Russian citizenship to the Russian compatriots in the near abroad and (2) protect the "legitimate rights and interests" of Russian citizens abroad, is set to remain for the foreseeable future. Indeed, in May 2009, less than a year after the Russo-Georgian war fought over protecting Russian citizens and compatriots, an updated document, "Russia's National Security Strategy to 2020," reiterated and reinforced the effective defense of the rights and interests of Russian citizens abroad.

Meanwhile, before the compatriots could be turned into Russian citizens by the methods used in Georgia's South Ossetia and Abkhazia, Moldova's Transnistria, and Ukraine's Crimea, the question of how to define and assist them still remained. In June 2000 Putin approved a new document, "The Foreign Policy Concept of the Russian Federation"—the first foreign policy document where compatriots were explicitly mentioned. It stated that "the Russian Federation will seek to obtain adequate guarantees for the rights and freedoms of compatriots in states where they permanently reside and to maintain and develop comprehensive ties with them and their organizations."[76] Two months later a clearer definition of compatriots was finally offered. In August 2001, the "Concept of Support to Compatriots Abroad by the Russian Federation in the Current Period" was released. For the first time ever, the definition of compatriots did not evoke the Soviet Union, and thus former Soviet citizens or their descendants were no longer conceptualized as compatriots. Furthermore, compatriots did not need to be former citizens of Russia or their descendants. Instead, the focus was solely on having some connection to Russia, as compatriots were defined as "constantly living abroad, but having historical, ethnic, cultural, linguistic, and spiritual ties with Russia, trying to preserve their Russian authenticity and having a need to maintain contacts and cooperation with Russia."[77] Again, the definition was broad and malleable thanks to the deployment of fluid and abstract concepts such as cultural or spiritual connections to Russia. Though the new definition was somewhat narrower due to the exclusion of citizens of the Soviet Union, it included a much broader group of people than solely ethnic Russians or Russian speakers abroad and seemingly evoked the peoples of the historic Russian empire.

Table 2

Compatriot Policy Documents under Vladimir Putin and Dmitry Medvedev, 2000–2014

DATE (PRESIDENCY)	DOCUMENT	SUMMARY OF CONTENTS
10 January 2000 (Putin)	Presidential Decree No. 24, The National Security Concept of the Russian Federation[a]	One of Russia's foreign policy goals is defined as protecting the legitimate rights and interests of Russian citizens abroad, including by taking political, economic, and other measures.
28 June 2000 (Putin)	The Foreign Policy Concept of the Russian Federation[b]	Compatriots are included for the first time in a foreign policy document.
30 August 2001 (Putin)	Concept of Support to Compatriots Abroad by the Russian Federation in the Current Period[c]	Compatriots are defined as "constantly living abroad, but having historical, ethnic, cultural, linguistic, and spiritual ties with Russia, trying to preserve their Russian authenticity and having a need to maintain contacts and cooperation with Russia."[d]
31 May 2002 (Putin)	Federal Law No. 62-FZ On Russian Federation Citizenship[e]	Simplifies the procedure of acquiring Russian citizenship and grants Russian passports to stateless people from the former Soviet Union.
28 November 2002 (Putin)	Basic Guidelines for Support of Compatriots Abroad by the Russian Federation for 2002–2005[f]	Signifies change in official discourse toward compatriots. Previously seen as a problem, compatriots become a resource.

Date (Leader)	Document	Description
18 June 2005 (Putin)	Government document No. MF-P12-2990, Program of Measures of Organizational, Legal, Administrative, and Socio-economic Character for the Purpose of the Long-term Stimulation of Voluntary Resettlement of Compatriots From Abroad to Russia[g]	Document focused on improving long-term migration policy legislation and economic stimulation measures to attract voluntary settlers.
8 July 2005 (Putin)	Government document No. MF-P2-3405, The System of Measures to Support Russian Compatriots Abroad and Facilitate Their Voluntary Resettlement to the Russian Federation[h]	Sets out measures for compatriots abroad and for voluntary resettlement including financial and transportation assistance.
29 December 2005 (Putin)	Government decree No. 833, The Russian Language Federal Target Program[i] (2006–2010)[j]	Supports Russian language teaching as the basis for the development of integration processes in the CIS. Also aims to meet linguistic and cultural needs of compatriots living abroad.
22 June[k] 2006 (Putin)	Presidential Decree No. 637, National Program of Support to Voluntary Migration of Compatriots Living Abroad to the Russian Federation[l]	Provides a resettlement plan to distribute new arrivals to Russia.[m] Aims to address the Russian demographic crisis.
2 October 2006 (Putin)	Government decree No. 1370-r, Program for Working with Compatriots Abroad,[n] 2006–2008[o]	Priorities include consolidation of the Russian diaspora, support for the print and internet resources of compatriot organizations, efforts to preserve national and cultural traditions.

(continued)

Table 2 (continued)

DATE (PRESIDENCY)	DOCUMENT	SUMMARY OF CONTENTS
27 March 2007 (Putin)	Ministry of Foreign Affairs, Russian Federation, Foreign Policy Review[p]	Distinguishes a separate foreign policy dimension called the "humanitarian trend," which includes protection of compatriots abroad.
12 May 2009 (Medvedev)	Presidential Decree No. 537, Russia's National Security Strategy to 2020[q]	Sets goal of "more effective defense of the rights and lawful interests of Russian citizens abroad."[r]
23 July 2010 (Medvedev)	Amendment No. 179-FZ to Federal Law On the State Policies of the Russian Federation with Regard to Compatriots Abroad[s]	Status of compatriot in addition to principle of self-identification has to be supported by the person's activity in preserving the Russian language and culture, and community participation.
7 May 2012 (Putin)	Presidential Decree No. 605, On Measures for Implementation of the Foreign Policy of the Russian Federation[t]	Calls for budget increase for projects implemented through the Government Commission for the Affairs of Compatriots Abroad.[u]
12 February 2013 (Putin)	Concept of the Foreign Policy of the Russian Federation[v]	Aims to ensure "comprehensive protection of rights and legitimate interests of Russian citizens and compatriots residing abroad, to expand and strengthen the space of the Russian language and culture, support consolidation of organizations of compatriots."[w]
4 April 2014 (Putin)	Resolution of the State Duma No. 4077-6 GD, Amendments to Article 14 of the Federal Law on Citizenship in the Russian Federation[x]	Eases procedures for obtaining Russian citizenship by foreign citizens and stateless persons recognized as native Russian speakers.[y]

Source: Compiled by the author.

Notes

a. Ukaz Presidenta Rossiyskoy Federatsii ot 10 janvarya 2000 g. N 24 "O Konceptsii natsionalnoy bezopasnosti Rossiyskoy Federatsii," https://fas.org/nuke/guide /russia/doctrine/gazeta012400.htm.

b. *The Foreign Policy Concept of the Russian Federation,* 28 June 2000, http://www.fas.org/nuke/guide/russia/doctrine/econcept.htm.

c. "Konceptsiya podderzhki RossiyskoyFederatsii sootechestvennikov za rubezhom na sovremennom etape," http://www.whiteworld.ru/rubriki/000022/000 /0110302.htm.

d. Ibid.

e. Federal Law No. 62-FZ On Russian Federation Citezenship, 31 May 2002, http://www.legislationline.org/documents/action/popup/id/4189.

f. Rasporyazheniye Pravitelstva Rossiyskoy Federatsii ot 28.11.2002 № 1663-r. "Osnovnye napravleniya podderzhki Rossiyskiyey sootechestvennikov za rubezhom na 2002–2005 gody," http://docs.procspb.ru/content/part/63062.

g. "Programma mer organizatsionnogo, pravovogo, administrativnogo, socialno-ekonomicheskogo kharaktera, napravlennykh na dolgosrochnoye stimulirovaniye dobrovol'nogo pereseleniya v Rossiiu sootechestvennikov iz-za rubezha," utverzhdennaya Pravitelstvom Rossiyskoy Federatsii 18 yunya 2005 g. (№ MF-P12-2990).

h. "Kompleks mer po podderzhke rossiyskikh sootechestvennikov za rubezhom i sodeistviyu ikh dobrovolnomu pereseleniyu v Rossiyskuyu Federatsiyu," utverzhdennyi Pravitelstvom Rossiyskoy Federatsii 8 yulya 2005 g, http://www.materick.ru/index.php?section=analitics&bulid=115&bulsectionid=1284

i. The program was later updated. See Government decree No. 492. *The Russian Language Federal Target Program (2011–2015),* 20 June 2011 (Postanovleniye Pravitel-stva Rossiyskoy Federatsii ot 20.06.2011 № 492. "O federalnoy tselevoy programme 'Russkiy yazik' na 2011–2015 gody"), http://www.consultant.ru/document /cons_doc_LAW_161668/.

j. Postanovleniye Pravitelstva Rossiyskoy Federatsii ot 29.12.2005 № 833. "O federalnoy tselevoy programme 'Russkiy yazik (2006–2010 gody)," http://www .consultant.ru/document/cons_doc_LAW_10301/.

k. Signed on the symbolic date 22 June—the beginning of the Great Patriotic War of 1941–45. A new version of the program came into effect in July 2010. See Alexander Zhuravsky and Olga Vykhovanets, "Compatriots: Back to the Homeland," Russian International Affairs Council, 31 May 2013, http://russiancouncil.ru/en/inner/?id_4=1908#top.

l. In other sources also called the *State Program for Assisting Compatriots in Foreign Residence in Their Voluntary Resettlement to the Russian Federation.* (Ukaz Presidenta Rossiyskoy Federatsii ot 22.06.2006 № 637. "O merakh po okazaniyu sodeistviya dobrovolnomu pereseleniyu v Rossiyskuyu Federatsiyu sootechest-vennikov, prozhivayushikh za rubezhom"), http://base.garant.ru/189653/.

m. Country Profile of Russian Federation, *Focus Migration,* no. 20 (July 2010), http://focus-migration.hwwi.de/Russian-Federation.6337.0.html?&L=1.

(*continued*)

Table 2 (continued)

n. The Program was later updated three times. See Government decree No. 1646-r, *Program for Working with Compatriots Abroad, 2009–2011*, 10 November 2008 (Rasporyazheniye Pravitel'stva Rossiyskoy Federatsii ot 10.11.2008 № 1646-r. Ob utverzhdenii Programmy raboty s sootechestvennikami za rubezhom na 2009–2011 gody), http://www.consultant.ru/document/cons_doc_LAW_81532/; also Government decree No. 1799-r, *Program for Working with Compatriots Abroad, 2012–2014*, 13 October 2011 (Rasporyazheniye Pravitel'stva Rossiyskoy Federatsii ot 13.10.2011 № 1799-r. Programma po rabote s sootechestvennikami za rubezhom na 2012–2014 gody), http://government.consultant.ru/page.aspx?1576773 and Government decree No. 2321-r, *Program for Working with Compatriots Abroad, 2015–2017*, 19 November 2014 (Rasporyazheniye Pravitel'stva Rossiyskoy Federatsii ot 19.11.2014 № 2321-r. Programma raboty s sootechestvennikami, prozhivauschimi za rubezom, na 2015–2017 gody), http://government.ru/media/files/ZXiQGZwhcwc.pdf.

o. Rasporyazheniye Pravitel'stva Rossiyskoy Federatsii ot 02.10.2006 № 1370-r, Programma raboty s sootechestvennikami za rubezhom na 2006–2008 gody, http://russia.bestpravo.ru/fed2006/data01/tex10044.htm.

p. Ministerstvo inostrannykh del Rossiyskoy Federatsii, Obzor vneshney politiki Rossiyskoy Federatsii, http://www.mid.ru/brp_4.nsf/sps/3647DA97748A106BC325 72ABoo2AC4DD#%Do%92%Do%92%Do%95%Do%94%Do%95%Do%9D%Do%98%Do%95.

q. Ukaz Presidenta Rossiyskoy Federatsii ot 12.05.2009 № 537, "O Strategii natsional'noy bezopasnosti Rossiyskoy Federatsii do 2020 goda," http://www.rg.ru/2009/05/19/strategia-dok.html.

r. *Russia's National Security Strategy to 2020*, 12 May 2009, http://rustrans.wikidot.com/russia-s-national-security-strategy-to-2020.

s. Federalnyi zakon ot 23.07.2010 № 179-FZ, O vnesenii izmeneniy v Federalnyi zakon "O gosudarstvennoy politike Rossiyskoy Federatsii v otnoshenii sootechestvennikov za rubezhom," http://www.rg.ru/2010/07/27/sootech-dok.html.

t. Ukaz Presidenta Rossiyskoy Federatsii ot 07.05.2012 № 605, "O merakh po realizatsii vneshnepoliticheskogo kursa Rossiyskoy Federatsii," http://kremlin.ru/acts/15256.

u. See more in Grigory B. Karasin, "Russian World Is Becoming a Reality," *Rossiyskaya Gazeta*, 24 October 2012, http://www.mid.ru/bdomp/brp_4.nsf/f68cd37b84 7116c326f6foo541094/35bdddgo489408994425?aaeoo4c4b4!OpenDocument.

v. *Concept of the Foreign Policy of the Russian Federation*, 12 February 2012, http://www.mid.ru/brp_4.nsf/0/76389FEC16818gED44257B2Eoo39B16D.

w. Ibid.

x. Gosudarstvennoy Dumy Federalnogo Sobranija Rossiyskoy Federatsii ot 04.04.2014 № 4077–6 GD, "O Federal'nom zakone 'O vnesenii izmeneniy v stat'i 14 i 27 Federal'nogo zakona "O grazhdanstve Rossiyskoy Federatsii"' (proyekt N 417698–6)," http://www.rg.ru/2014/04/23/grazhdanstvo-dok.html.

y. "On Submission to the State Duma of a Draft Law Simplifying Procedures for Receiving Russian Citizenship for Some Categories of Foreigners," The Russian Government, 4 March 2014, http://government.ru/en/news/10896.

Once again, while claiming the Russian compatriots for itself, Moscow had little intention of letting them return to the homeland, even stipulating a "restriction of uncontrolled migration in Russia."[78] In 2001 this decision was somewhat surprising. On the one hand Russia was still recovering from the financial crisis of 1998, and probably could not have borne the costs of an influx of millions of immigrants. On the other hand, global oil prices were beginning to rise rapidly and Russia's wealth was increasing, resulting in a rising need for additional labor especially in the face of Russia's demographic crisis.[79] Furthermore, Putin clearly stated in October 2001, "Russia is interested in having Russians return from abroad"[80] and admitted that previous work with Russian compatriots had not been effective. Nonetheless, the early 2000s also marked a time of rigid Russian immigration policies.[81] Accordingly, the 2001 Concept largely preserved Russia's older policies vis-à-vis Russians abroad, focusing on assisting their "adjustment and integration into the life of countries of residence while voluntarily preserving their ethnic and cultural identity."[82]

The year 2002 was a turning point for conceptualizing the Russian compatriots. At the end of May Putin signed "Federal Law No. 62-FZ On Russian Federation Citizenship." The new law toughened the general naturalization rules in comparison to the law of 1991, but on the other hand, enabled the stateless former Soviet Union citizens to get Russian passports more easily.[83] Right after this law came into force, mass Russian passportization started in Georgia, where application centers were established even in the most remote areas of Abkhazia and South Ossetia. According to official Russian sources, in four years after the beginning of this policy in 2002 the proportion of Russian citizens in Abkhazia increased from 30 percent to 80 percent and in South Ossetia from 40 percent to 90 percent by 2006.[84]

In May, Putin also ordered the Foreign Ministry to develop policy guidelines toward compatriots abroad.[85] These "Basic Guidelines for Support of Compatriots Abroad by the Russian Federation for 2002–2005," approved by the government in November 2002, changed Russia's discourse regarding the Russian diaspora. As political scientist Maria Nozhenko argues, if for the previous eight years the political establishment viewed the diaspora as a problem that Russia should tackle, now Russian speakers of the post-Soviet space were considered Russia's external political resource to be employed vis-à-vis other states.[86] As Putin stated a few months after the adoption of the document, "such 'humanitarian' activities [compatriot policies] mean for the interests of the country no less than the activities of Russian business abroad."[87] The Basic Guidelines called for the "initiation of their [compatriots'] role in expanding cooperation of the Russian Federation with other states and further development of democratic transformations in the Russian Federation."[88] Though the prescriptions were still in the realm of soft power, this was the first time that compatriots were officially articulated in government policies as having a role to play in Russian foreign policy.

The decade of the 2000s saw a rising momentum of utilizing compatriots in Russia's soft power and influence efforts. As outlined in the previous chapter, the increasingly proclaimed notion of the diaspora as a "Russian World," the spread of the Russkiy Dom network, and the establishment of the Russkiy Mir Foundation and Rossotrudnichestvo reflected Russia's growing wealth and nationalism and the strengthening of Putin's regime. The summer of 2008 was marked by both the Russo-Georgian war and the record peak in oil prices of US $145 per barrel. A few years earlier, in April 2005, Putin uttered his much-quoted phrase that "the collapse of the Soviet Union was a major geopolitical disaster of the century." However, many have forgotten that in that instance the primary disaster he referenced was that of the Russian compatriots—"Tens of millions of our co-citizens and compatriots found themselves outside Russian territory."[89] Something had to be done and Moscow could finally put its money where its mouth was regarding the compatriots.

In the middle of this decade of resurrection of Russia's power and wealth, on the occasion of the sixty-fifth anniversary of the beginning of the Great Patriotic War (the Second World War as it involved the Soviet Union) in June 2006, a presidential decree launched the "National Program of Support to Voluntary Migration of Compatriots Living Abroad to the Russian Federation." Russia—the fair-weather friend to its compatriots—was finally going to invite them back home. However, the compatriots were not being invited solely out of good will. The program was intended to solve Russia's evident labor shortage and related economic imbalances.[90] Between 1992 and 2004 the country's demographic situation deteriorated significantly—the excess of deaths over births reached 10.4 million and contributed to a decline in skilled human resources.[91] Therefore, according to the program, compatriots would have to be settled in government-specified regions that had experienced a population decrease or labor shortages. The glitz and glamour of Moscow and St. Petersburg were not intended for Russian compatriots; instead, they would have to settle for the Far East and Siberia.[92] This program of compatriot resettlement demonstrated that Russia was cynically using both the term and the people—compatriots—solely for its own immediate national interests rather than to benefit the interests of compatriots.

It was no surprise that very few Russian compatriots would take up the offer to move to the Far East or Siberia where Stalin had sent his deportees to the Gulag. In contrast to the initial plans to welcome 50,000–100,000 compatriots per year, in the peak year of 2011 only 32,500 compatriots arrived (a figure greater than in all the previous years combined).[93] For instance, from Estonia in the period 2007–9, the count was only 20 to 37 repatriated persons, despite Moscow's consistent allegations that Estonia's Russian minority suffers various discriminations.[94] The poor performance of this program can also be attributed to its much delayed launch (some fifteen years after the fall of the Soviet Union) and to the onset of the world financial crisis of 2008, affecting global labor markets.[95] It is also likely that by this time most compatriots who had wanted to emigrate to Russia had already done so. Looking back, it is reasonable to question to what extent Moscow was ever sincere in its resettlement efforts, and to what extent this was merely a show for the anniversary of the Great Patriotic War. If Moscow really intended to return some Russians to the motherland, this was only a small part of a multivector strategy toward its compatriots. Just two years later in the summer of 2008, Russian tanks would be moving into Georgian territories of South Ossetia and Abkhazia, to protect local populations to whom Moscow had been dutifully offering passports in the preceding years.

Later in 2006, several programs targeting compatriots were launched, becoming long-term strategies focused on both supporting compatriots abroad and positioning them as a potential future resource. The programs also laid the groundwork for propaganda tools later used on Russian compatriots and for information warfare against Georgia, Ukraine, and beyond. The "Program for Working with Compatriots Abroad, 2006–2008" focused among other things on the provision of information support such as the creation and maintenance of websites, press publications, and TV and radio programs, collaboration with Russian-language mass media abroad.[96] Putin himself underlined the importance of the program at the World Congress of Russian Compatriots in 2006, boasting that financial resources devoted to compatriot issues that year were almost seven times greater than in 2000.[97]

The "Program for Working with Compatriots Abroad" has been updated three times, but it has maintained the same strategic direction. The initial 2006–8 version emphasized the improvement of compatriot legislation in Russia, while the 2009–11 version concentrated more on assistance in organizing cultural events and on the promotion of Russian media. In comparison to previous versions, the program for 2012–14, released in 2011, featured new "assistance in consolidation of compatriots on [a] professional basis" and "assistance in [the] moral encouragement of compatriots including awarding ceremonies."[98] This program also prioritized the increased role of the World Coordination Council of Russian Compatriots (established in 2006) and its country coordinating councils, as well as support for the print and internet resources of compatriot organizations.[99] The latest version of the program, for 2015–17, focuses more on the younger generation of compatriots and includes a new priority of "assistance in consolidation of youth compatriot organizations" such as summer schools, international sporting events, and competitions.[100] Over the past decade Russia has already engaged the Russian compatriot youth including organizing annual paramilitary camps.

Overall, unlike the efforts for repatriating the diaspora, the programs for compatriot information support have been seemingly successful. As the case studies will demonstrate, in 2014, nearly twenty-five years after the dissolution of the Soviet Union, the diaspora tends to consume Russian TV, newspapers, online news portals, and social media quite heavily across the entire post-Soviet space. However, it is difficult to determine to what extent this appeal is due to the diaspora's self-identification with Russia rather than with the significant advantages of scale and financing enjoyed by the Russian media versus the more limited media offerings of the smaller former Soviet republics.

Nonetheless, to create and maintain influence via information spread to the Russian compatriots, their Russian-language skills and those of other citizens of the former Soviet republics need to be maintained. Putin argued that "preserving a Russian-speaking territory" was "one of the priority issues" to be achieved via the compatriots.[101] Accordingly, after its approval in December 2015, in 2006 the "Russian Language Federal Target Program 2006–2010" was launched. In 2011 it was updated to cover 2011–15. The purpose of the language program is twofold: first, it supports "the Russian language as the basis for the development of integration processes in the Commonwealth of Independent States"; second, it addresses "the language and cultural needs of compatriots living abroad."[102] The means to achieve these targets include organizing research and teaching, educational and cultural events, and provision of educational materials on Russian language, literature and culture, as well as remote Russian language teaching. On the other hand, the actual funds dedicated to these programs were minimal. In 2011–15, Russia devoted some $28 million (1.5 billion rubles) to the program of which 46 percent was invested to meet the "Satisfaction of Linguistic and Cultural Demands of Compatriots Abroad."[103] In contrast, the German Goethe-Institut has an approximate annual budget of $320 million, of which 40 percent goes to language education.[104] This suggests that despite the rhetoric, Russia is not prepared to spend for purely cultural and linguistic support of the compatriots.

In March 2007, the softer and more humanitarian aspects of Russian foreign policy were conceptualized further in the "Russian Federation's Foreign Policy Review." It had been nearly a decade since compatriots were introduced into Russian foreign policy with the Foreign Policy Concept of 2000. The new review officially introduced the concept of the "humanitarian trend" of Russian foreign policy. Besides the defense of human rights, this included the protection of compatriots living abroad. The review was notable for several reasons. First, compatriots were conceptualized as important contributors to the formation of Russia's "objective image" abroad.[105] Second, to implement the "humanitarian trend" the review relied closely on "soft power" tools, which it noted were effective in producing favorable outcomes for the world's great powers.[106] However, Russia soon used compatriots for its military and territorial aims in the war with Georgia.

Just months before the start of war, Dmitry Medvedev was sworn in as president of Russia, a post he would hold until 2012, under the watchful eye and domineering hand of Prime Minister Putin. At just forty-two years of age, the former lecturer in civil and Roman law appeared to be a more youthful, liberal, and modern alternative to Putin. Yet, he lacked Putin's strongman persona and eventually came to be regarded as little more than the prime minister's shadow. Meanwhile, the summer of 2008 was a victorious one for the Medvedev-Putin duo. The so-called Five-Day War, the Russian invasion of Georgia, came and went. The world worried; the world grumbled; but the world also quickly forgot. Nonetheless, Russia clearly won this war, not only on the battlefield but in its permanent separation of South Ossetia and Abkhazia from Georgia. It was also a victory for Russia's long-term strategy vis-à-vis its compatriots. As will be seen in Chapter 4, the Russian speakers and Russian citizens of South Ossetia and Abkhazia had become willing beneficiaries of Russia's passports and thus its protection. Before Russian troops entered Georgia, Medvedev stated that "under the constitution and federal law . . . I must protect the life and dignity of Russian citizens wherever they are."[107] Later Medvedev repeated the same pretext vis-à-vis the South Ossetians, stating that "protecting the lives and dignity of our citizens, wherever they may be, is an unquestionable priority for our country"[108] and "this is one of our foreign policy priorities."[109] Certainly Georgia's first military move against the separatist territories made Russia's call for protection of its citizens and compatriots seemingly more legitimate.

Subsequently, flushed with success in Georgia, in September 2008 Medvedev founded the Federal Agency for the Commonwealth of Independent States, Compatriots Living Abroad, and International Humanitarian Cooperation. This autonomous agency under the Russian Ministry of Foreign Affairs, headed by member of the Federation Council of the Russian Federal Assembly Konstantin Kosachyov, is responsible for supporting and developing relations between Russia and the CIS as well as other countries, including guiding compatriot issues.[110]

In May 2009 "Russia's National Security Strategy to 2020" was launched by presidential decree of Medvedev to supplement the "National Security Concept of the Russian Federation of 2000." The new document reiterated and further reinforced as a long-term goal the "more effective defense of the rights and lawful interests of Russian citizens abroad."[111] Considering that Russia had just fought a war to defend the interests of its compatriots and citizens abroad, the rather ambiguous wording would seem to imply more than just diplomatic initiatives of compatriot support. And though the strategy did not reference compatriots directly, thanks to Moscow's passportization efforts compatriots were often just one step shy of being citizens.[112] The document also noted the importance of using "Russia's cultural potential" to strengthen its national security: television and radio programs, internet sources, and cinematographic works. Such media initiatives would later become important tools of not only Russia's soft power but also information warfare campaigns.

Contemporary Compatriot Policies and Laws

In July 2010 the fourth attempt was made to define Russian compatriots with an amendment to the 1999 "Federal Law on the State Policies of the Russian Federation with Regard to Compatriots Abroad." The newest and final definition was equally if not more ambiguous. The amendment included the older 1999 definition of compatriots as those who were born in the same state (Russia and its predecessor the Soviet Union) and who share Russian cultural attributes. This was in direct contrast to the definition introduced in the 2001 Concept of Support to Compatriots that did not evoke the Soviet Union. For the first time, Russian citizens permanently living abroad were also included as compatriots. However, the new definition added another category of "individuals who live outside the Russian Federation and belong to the nations historically residing on the territory of Russian Federation and who also have made a free choice in favor of maintaining spiritual, cultural, and legal ties with Russian Federation."[113] Based on this definition, neither Russian ethnicity nor Russian language is necessary to be a Russian compatriot, nor is former Russian or Soviet citizenship. Any person who feels a spiritual or cultural connection with Russia and is descended from any of 185 current nationalities inhabiting the Russian Federation and of the many more nationalities that used to inhabit the Russian imperial territories could be called a compatriot.

Most crucially, the 2010 amendment both eliminated the necessity of legal self-identification by compatriots and at the same time required that a compatriot express his or her self-identification by actively participating in Russia's cultural and political project. The earlier (never enacted) provision on compatriot identification cards was struck, thus eliminating compatriots as a legal category.[114] Instead, the compatriot now had to engage and demonstrate: "civic or professional activity in preserving the Russian language and the native languages of the peoples of the

Russian Federation, developing Russian culture abroad, strengthening friendly relations between the state in which the compatriot resides and the Russian Federation, supporting compatriot community associations, protecting the rights of compatriots, and maintaining spiritual and cultural connections with the Russian Federation in any other freely chosen way."[115] Therefore, by 2010 the definition of compatriots had shifted from something solely defined by one's identity to something that must be also certifiable by membership in relevant organizations or by the person's activities. Being a compatriot became a seemingly political or activist undertaking.

This shift has several consequences. On one hand, it marks an effort to conceptualize compatriots as active rather than passive members of the Russian World. On the other hand, the conditionality of activism likely narrows the ranks of compatriots. As political scientist Oxana Shevel outlines, the 2010 amendment once again enables Moscow to define all former Soviet citizens as compatriots, but does not legally require Moscow to do so.[116] Furthermore, the concept of self-identification reduced the scope of the paradoxical situation created in 1999 where some 150 million former Soviet citizens could be considered compatriots under the law, including (in the wording of the amendment) "residents of Finland and Poland because these countries at some point were within the territory of the Russian state, and Mikheil Saakashvili and elites of the Baltic States because they are from the former USSR."[117] Certainly, Georgia's President Mikheil Saakashvili who had just fought a war against Russia could not be counted among Russian compatriots though he had previously held Soviet citizenship. On the other hand, Georgia's South Ossetians and Abkhazians could still be included presumably because they had historically resided in the Russian Empire and because many had acquired Russian citizenship.[118]

At the same time, various initiatives to support compatriots continued. In the spring of 2011, Medvedev established a Foundation for Supporting and Protecting the Rights of Compatriots Living Abroad, which aims "to provide Russians abroad with the necessary support to protect their lawful rights and interests in their countries of residence."[119] Also that year the Ministry of Foreign Affairs launched a website, ruvek. ru—a self-described portal for Russian compatriots—to assist their voluntary resettlement to Russia.[120]

A momentous shift in Russian foreign policy vis-à-vis compatriots occurred after Putin returned to the presidency. In May 2012, he signed a decree "On Measures for Implementation of the Foreign Policy of the Russian Federation." This document had one strategic difference from "Russia's National Security Strategy to 2020" of 2009 and the earlier "Russian Foreign Policy Concept" and the "National Security Concept," both of 2000 that presaged changes in compatriot policy: for the first time, it explicitly set out to protect Russian compatriots in addition to Russian citizens. It instructed the Ministry of Foreign Affairs of Russia and other executive agencies "to ensure the full protection of the rights, freedoms and legitimate interests of Russian citizens and compatriots living abroad."[121] Thus the document called for an increase in budget financing for relevant projects, to be implemented through the Foundation for Supporting and Protecting the Rights of Compatriots Living Abroad and the older Government Commission for the Affairs of Compatriots Living Abroad established in 1994.[122] This commission, chaired by Russian Minister of Foreign Affairs Sergey Lavrov, aimed to coordinate the work of Russian federal and regional executive bodies in pursuing and implementing state policy toward "Russians residing abroad"—terminology that again seems to equate Russian compatriots and Russians in general.[123] In the same year, during the Fourth World Congress of Compatriots, Putin stated that documents regarding Russian compatriot policy were no longer vague, as "support for the Russian diaspora is one of the most important policies of our state."[124]

In February 2013 the Russian Ministry of Foreign Affairs published a new "Concept of the Foreign Policy of the Russian Federation," which further reiterated the notion of protecting both Russian citizens and compatriots. Among its goals, the concept aimed to ensure "comprehensive protection of rights and legitimate interests of Russian citizens and compatriots residing abroad" through the mechanisms of international law and treaties. It also supported "consolidation of organizations of compatriots to enable them to effectively uphold their rights in the countries of residence while preserving the cultural and ethnic identity of the Russian diaspora and its ties with the historical homeland."[125] As the next chapter will show, this concept of equating compatriots and citizens was demonstrated in 2014 in Crimea and eastern Ukraine, although Moscow's policies of protection there did not employ international laws and treaties but rather opted for annexation and military means.

Shortly after the annexation of Crimea in March 2014 and at the start of conflict in eastern Ukraine in the beginning of April 2014, the Duma approved a bill to simplify the procedure for Russian-speaking foreigners to obtain Russian citizenship. The need to develop simplified procedures for granting citizenship was already clearly expressed at the end of 2012 by Putin when he stated in a public address that "Russia needs new blood,"[126] and that the process of obtaining citizenship was too complicated. Amendments to Article 14 of the "Federal Law on Citizenship in the Russian Federation" specified that the new procedure for obtaining Russian citizenship could be used by foreign citizens and stateless persons recognized as native Russian speakers, for example, speaking fluent Russian and regularly using it at home, in social, cultural, and other spheres, and whose lineal ancestors permanently lived on territories of the Russian Empire or the USSR, on the condition that they renounce their present foreign citizenship. Also, according to the amendment, a native Russian speaker would be determined via an interview with a special commission.[127] The condition that new Russian citizens renounce their foreign passports marks a departure from Russia's previous policy of seeking to spread dual citizenship across the post-Soviet states. It can be interpreted as a means to demarcate more clearly the allegiances of compatriots. Leaving no ambiguity about their citizenship would be more favorable to Russia's efforts at protecting them and possibly seeking to acquire territories where they reside.

In many ways the development of Russian compatriot policies follows the arc of Russia's power, ambition, and struggle for national identity. In the two decades between 1994 and 2015, the Russian government promulgated more than twenty policies, programs, and laws to both conceptualize and assist compatriots. These were an ever-present dilemma and opportunity for Moscow; however, the manner in which Moscow chose to engage or at times ignore the 30 million Russians and Russian speakers varied over these two decades. In the early 1990s, as Russia grappled with severe economic decline and new statehood, the compatriot issue remained vague and ill defined. Early on Moscow decided that the diaspora would not be invited to return to Russia and stipulations were made to block mass repatriation. Only fifteen years later, some half-hearted attempts at resettlement followed. Nonetheless, even in the Yeltsin era there were efforts to link issues of foreign policy and compatriots as in the cases of the Baltic States and the failed efforts to introduce dual citizenship across the post-Soviet states.

Since the 2000s under Putin's leadership, as the Russian economy and stature on the world stage grew along with rising oil prices, the compatriot issue increasingly came into focus. Russia redefined itself as a great power on the world stage and a leader of a Slavic, Russian-speaking, Orthodox Christian civilization—in other words, of the Russian World. Russians, Russian speakers, and other minorities in the near abroad were the crucial part of this world and were politicized and conceptualized as compatriots. Many early compatriot policies appeared like confused and heavy-handed attempts to use soft power. Under Putin, the compatriots were increasingly conceptualized as a resource for Russian foreign policy and geopolitical ambition in the near abroad. After the Georgian war of 2008 over compatriots, Russian policies became more clear and focused on protecting citizens and compatriots abroad.

This chapter has also demonstrated that Russian compatriot policies cannot be viewed in isolation. Compatriots are not only part of Russian humanitarian outreach programs, but rather are enshrined in Russia's national laws and linguistic, cultural, and information programs. Furthermore, compatriots are part of the basic foundations of the Russian state: in national security strategies, foreign policy concepts, and definitions of citizenship. Finally, compatriot policies should not be viewed as a reflection of certain times or leaderships. Just as Yeltsin inherited the compatriot issue from the debris of the Soviet Union's dissolution and Stalin's ethnic policies, so too will the compatriot issue persist long after Putin retires from power. Russian compatriots will remain relevant to Europe and Eurasia in the decades to come, regardless of the leadership in the Kremlin. As I argued in the previous chapter, Russian compatriots serve a key role in the reimperialization trajectory, which aims to maintain neo-imperial influence over and regain territory in the former Soviet republics. The following four case study chapters will demonstrate how and to what extent these compatriot policies and the reimperialization trajectory have been enacted in Ukraine, Georgia, Moldova, the Baltic States, and Central Asia, as well as Belarus and Armenia.

CHAPTER FOUR

Separatism and Annexation

MOLDOVA, GEORGIA, AND UKRAINE

The most obvious risk was that the Russian-speaking population was threatened and that the threats were absolutely specific and tangible. This is what made Crimean residents, the people who live there, think about their future and ask Russia for help.

—*Vladimir Putin, 17 April 2014*

AT FIRST GLANCE, the three former Soviet republics of Moldova, Ukraine, and Georgia appear to have little in common. Moldova is a small country of just four million people, sandwiched between Ukraine and Romania. Despite its historical, cultural, and linguistic ties to EU and NATO member Romania, Moldova has been a forgotten corner of Europe since the Soviet Union's disintegration. Neighboring Ukraine is a juggernaut in comparison. Ukraine's landmass makes it the largest country entirely within Europe, and its population of approximately 43 million is also substantial.[1] Often called the breadbasket of Europe, the country has been a prize that neighboring powers such as Poland, Lithuania, the Crimean Khanate, the Ottomans, and Russia have jostled over for hundreds of years. As fellow Slavs, Russians consistently perceive the Ukrainians as a "brother-nation," inherently related to themselves. Across the Black Sea from Ukraine, nestled in the Caucasus Mountains, is the country of Georgia. The Georgians, or Kartvelians, number just 5 million people today, and, as part of their distinct position at the crossroads of Eastern Europe and Western Asia, possess a unique alphabet, language, and identity.

Yet these distinct countries possess some striking similarities. All three have had a long and difficult history with imperial and Soviet Russia, facing aggressive Russification and deportation policies. A sizable proportion of the population of all three states belongs to the Eastern Orthodox Church, a feature in common with Russia. All have struggled with corrupt regimes and remain among the poorest countries in Europe with an annual GDP per capita of less than $4,000. Partly as a result, all three have experienced "colored" revolutions, civil movements seeking change in the government and a turn to the West: Georgia's Rose Revolution in 2003, Ukraine's Orange Revolution in 2004, and Moldova's Grape or Twitter Revolution in 2009. And they were the three top performers within the EU's Eastern Partnership Initiative since it was launched in 2009.[2]

Perhaps the most significant commonality shared by Moldova, Georgia, and Ukraine is the clarity with which their recent histories reveal the trajectory of Russian reimperialization. Equally striking is the similarity with which Russian policies (particularly passportization, information warfare, and calls for protection) have been enacted in these three states at different time periods. Indeed, while the 2014 annexation of Crimea came as a shock to most, many of the same processes of compatriot passportization and calls for their protection had been ongoing since the early 1990s in all three states. On Moldova's eastern border, Transnistria has been an internationally unrecognized breakaway territory bolstered by Russia since the 1990s. Moscow has been stoking separatism in Georgia's Abkhazia and South Ossetia since the 1980s and has turned these territories into puppet states since the Russo-Georgian war in 2008. The groundwork of Crimea's annexation and separatism in eastern Ukraine's two newly minted "people's republics"—the People's Republic of Luhansk and the People's Republic of Donetsk—has been laid over the last decades. In 2015, both of these "people's republics" increasingly look likely to turn into frozen-conflict zones like Transnistria, Abkhazia, and South Ossetia. As Georgia's president from 2004 to 2013, Mikheil Saakashvili, wrote in the *Washington Post* as the crisis in Ukraine was unfolding in March 2014, "there are striking similarities between the early stages of Russian aggression against Georgia and what is happening in Ukraine."[3] The current Georgian President Giorgi Margvelashvili reiterated this, stating that "What happened in 2008 unfortunately also echoed in 2014 in Crimea, Donetsk, Luhansk and Mariupol."[4] Indeed, Russia's reimperialization trajectory has been almost identical in Ukraine, Georgia, and Moldova.

RUSSIA

LATVIA
Riga

LITHUANIA
Vilnius

BELARUS
Minsk

UKRAINE
Kiev

KHARKIV
LUHANSK
DONETSK   3
DNIPROPETROVSK   2

MOLDOVA   1
Chişinău   ODESSA
GAGAUZIA   MYKOLAIV
                 KHERSON
                 ZAPORIZHIA

ROMANIA

Black
Sea   ☆ 4

▲ Self-declared republic	*ODESSA* Administrative unit	1. TRANSNISTRIA
Significant Russian speaking populations	**Kiev** ■ Capital	2. 'DONETSK PEOPLE'S REPUBLIC'
☆ Annexed region		3. 'LUHANSK PEOPLE'S REPUBLIC'
☒ Conflict regions		4. CRIMEA

MAP 2. Distribution of Russian speakers and disputed territories across Belarus, Ukraine, and Moldova. Map drawn by Giedrė Tamašauskaitė

MAP 3: Distribution of Russian speakers and disputed territories across the Caucasus. Map drawn by Giedrė Tamašauskaitė

There are also important distinctions in the way Russian reimperialization efforts have been pursued in Ukraine, Georgia, and Moldova. Since the Transnistrian conflict of 1991 until the annexation of Crimea in 2014, there have been notable changes in Russia, its leadership, and its policies, as well as in the geopolitical context of Europe—all of which have colored the developments in the countries concerned. Russia's participation in the Transnistrian conflict was partly a reflex response of the old Soviet empire (and Soviet troops on the ground) to a (from their point of view) advantageous course of events. The Russo-Georgian war of 2008 was a successful trial experiment in reimperialization by Putin's regime, in no small part because it garnered little response from the West. Crimea's annexation and the war in eastern Ukraine appear as a culmination of these measures that have been methodically and systematically pursued by the Kremlin since the 2000s. In all three countries—in Moldova's Transnistria, in Georgia's South Ossetia and Abkhazia, and in Ukraine's Crimea and eastern territories—Moscow has consistently evoked the protection of Russian compatriots as reasons for its involvement and military operations. Before outlining Russia's policy in the three states, however, it is helpful to place them geographically (see Maps 2 and 3) and start with a brief overview of their Russian compatriot populations, their historical ties to Russia, and the background to conflict.

BACKGROUND TO CONFLICT

Georgia

The populations of Russian speakers and so-called Russian compatriots of Georgia, Moldova, and Ukraine could not be more different, particularly because of differences in their ethnicities. Indeed in the case of Georgia and Moldova it is surprising that Moscow would conceptualize those populations as compatriots. Georgia's South Ossetians, numbering only fifty thousand, have little to do with Russia ethnically, culturally, or linguistically. Ossetians are descendants of the Alans, warrior tribes speaking a language akin to Persian, who have lived here since the early medieval period.[5] For hundreds of years, South Ossetians and Georgians lived in harmony, and most Ossetians spoke Georgian in addition to Ossetian. Their recent affinity with Russia can be explained by their geographical proximity to North Ossetia (also inhabited by Ossetians), which is part of the Russian Federation. The Georgians, Abkhazians, and Ossetians also share a common Orthodox Christian faith with Russia. Like the Ossetians, Georgia's Abkhazians are also a distinct ethnic group, now numbering just a few hundred thousand. In the eighth century, they formed a Christian kingdom with close ties to either united Georgia or the Georgian Principality until they came under Ottoman rule and then that of the tsarist Empire. During the nineteenth century, the tsarist regime carried out an ethnic cleansing policy along the northeast shore of the Black Sea and the North Caucasus, which resulted in the annihilation of around 1.5 million locals and the expulsion from the region of a similar number of indigenous Abkhazians, Circassians, and Muslim tribes.[6] Subsequently, Russians, Armenians, Greeks, and Georgians colonized the region.[7] The Georgian-born Stalin pursued aggressive Georgianization policies in Abkhazia, which was the turning point that forever spoiled Abkhaz-Georgian relations. Instead, Abkhazians increasingly looked to Moscow for support.[8]

Moldova
In Moldova, Moscow's perception of local minorities and even ethnic Moldovans as "compatriots" is likewise puzzling. Sharing the same language and culture with neighboring Romania, the Moldova principality came under the influence of Moscow at the beginning of the nineteenth century with its incorporation into the Russian Empire. For the next two hundred years, Moldova would face Russification policies while the native Romanian was eliminated from official use.[9] The Stalin era saw executions and deportations of locals to Siberia or Central Asia while new, Russian-speaking workers were brought in.[10] In addition the "Moldovan" language was introduced, which was essentially the same as Romanian but written in the Cyrillic alphabet.[11] The conflict in Transnistria emerged following Moldovan independence from the USSR, when Chisinau reinstated Romanian as the state language and in 1990 Transnistria declared its independence from Moldova, seeking instead to continue to be part of the Soviet Union.[12] Initially the Kremlin was skeptical toward Transnistria's independence and ability to control the region, and the Russian media described the independence movement as "rebellion against perestroika."[13] Transnistria's activists also toyed with the idea of integrating with Ukraine but increasingly the idea of autonomy and identity tied to Moldova's Soviet history gained ground.[14] Today, the people of Transnistria whom Moscow has long sought to protect as Russian compatriots in fact are almost equally divided between Moldovans, Ukrainians, and Russians, with Moldovans being the most numerous. There are two more regions in Moldova with separatist proclivities and Russian support: the Taraclia district, where some 65 percent of the residents are

Russian-speaking ethnic Bulgarians; and the autonomous region of Gagauzia, where some 80 percent of the population are Gagauz—an Eastern Orthodox nation of Turkish and Bulgarian descent. Though the Gagauz have their own Turkic language, the majority today are Russian speakers, in great part due to Soviet Russification policies.[15]

Ukraine

Unlike Georgia and Moldova, Ukraine is a Slavic nation, making it easier for Russia to impose a Kremlin-driven narrative of its culture and history, with the aim of appropriating Ukraine for its imperial project. Moscow likes to promote the concept that Kievan Rus' formed the ninth-century cradle of Slavic (Russian, according to Moscow) civilization in the territory of Ukraine. This is argued as evidence that Ukrainians and Russians are essentially one and the same people.[16] Ukrainians lay claim to their own distinct history and identity, and argue that "Rus'" historically referred to the lands and peoples of Ukraine and Belarus. Until 1547 Russia was never referred to as such but rather by the name of its capital city: Moscovia—officially known as the Grand Duchy of Moscow. The relatively modern concept of Russia only developed during the reign of Ivan the Terrible, who inherited the title of Grand Prince of Moscow from his father, Vasili III, and in 1547 assumed the title of Grand Prince and Tsar of All the Russias.[17] At most, Ukrainians acknowledge their common roots with Russians until the tenth century, but some even question whether Russia is truly a Slavic nation.[18] Ukraine's history with its so-called brother-nation has been difficult since the end of the eighteenth century when Kiev lost the remains of its autonomy to the Russian Empire.[19] In the nineteenth century the Ukrainian nation faced aggressive Russification policies from Moscow, including closure of its main institution of higher learning, the Kiev-Mohyla Academy, suppression of its culture, prohibition from publishing books and teaching in Ukrainian, and even banning of building churches in the Ukrainian Baroque style.[20] The Stalinist era was the cruelest to Ukraine. In the early 1930s, most Ukrainian intellectuals and officials were repressed and killed, while the repression of Ukrainian peasants took the shape of the politically motivated famine, the *Holodomor* (extermination by hunger), in which around 5 million Ukrainians perished.[21] Throughout the Soviet era, Russification policies and an influx of Russian immigrants persisted.

In eastern Ukraine the developments were similar but Russification was more pronounced. Before the 1850s, Ukraine's eastern regions of Donetsk and Luhansk were inhabited predominantly by rural Ukrainians, but one could also meet peasants of various ethnic origins—Russians, Greeks, Germans, Tatars, and others. Industrialization brought labor migrants from central Russia and elsewhere.[22] During Soviet times, many prisoners were deported from all over the Soviet Union to the Donbas to work in coal mines and factories, resulting in a more diverse ethnic composition in the Donetsk and Luhansk regions than elsewhere in Ukraine.[23] However, while the Russian language was popular, ethnic Ukrainians remained the majority.[24]

Crimea's history is distinct from Ukraine's. The peninsula was ruled by the Golden Horde and then formed part of the Crimean Khanate from the fifteenth to the eighteenth century. The Russian Empire annexed Crimea in 1783, which resulted in the emigration and deportation of the local populations of Crimean Tatars and Greeks, while the peninsula was colonized mainly by Russians.[25] In 1944, on the night of 18 May Stalin deported the remaining Crimean Tatars to Uzbekistan, other Central Asian republics, and Siberia.[26] Herded to railway stations and packed into cattle cars, many of the Tatars died during the journey, while starvation and disease also took their toll in the resettlement camps.[27] As noted by Lilia Muslimova, aide to the Crimean Tatar leader Mustafa Jemilev, "this tragic event resulted in the deaths of 46% of the Crimean Tatar population and achieved what many historians consider to be the Russian desired final solution—a Crimea without Crimean Tatars."[28] The most recent transparent population census, that of 2001, in Crimea showed that 58.5 percent called themselves Russians, 24.4 percent identified as Ukrainians, and 12.1 percent called themselves Crimean Tatars, with other ethnic groups making up the remainder.[29] Muslimova adds that "in the twenty-first century Crimean Tatars are once again struggling for their dignity and homeland because of the Crimea's brutal and illegal occupation by the Russian Federation."[30]

PORTRAITS OF RUSSIAN SPEAKERS

To illustrate the complexity of views and sentiments of contemporary Russian speakers and "compatriots" of Ukraine, Georgia, and Moldova, this section will draw on interviews with Russian speakers to offer readers the voices and portraits of people that facts and figures cannot provide. There is an important distinction between Russian speakers residing in separatist territories like Transnistria and those in Moldova and Georgia proper. Russian speakers in Transnistria, South Ossetia, and Abkhazia have been more thoroughly Russified and have increasingly grown loyal to Moscow over the past two decades. Russian speakers in Moldova, Georgia, and Ukraine proper are more integrated into their states and are more likely to perceive themselves as Moldovan, Georgian, and Ukrainian. These observations were indirectly confirmed in an internet survey conducted in September 2014 by Russian opposition leader Alexei Navalny and his Anti-Corruption Foundation, in which they tried to learn the attitude of two traditionally pro-Russian regions in Ukraine, Odessa and Kharkov, toward separatism and Russian involvement in Ukraine. While this survey demonstrated people's skeptical position toward the Kiev government (with 26 percent describing their attitude as "negative," 25 percent as "neutral," and only 11 percent as "positive"), it also revealed other sociological trends such as 34 percent support for the statement that "the Ukrainian future should be with Europe" (compared with 17 percent for Russia), a 50 percent "negative" attitude toward Putin (with only 12 percent "positive"), and most importantly, 87 percent of support for the statement "I'd like to see my region as part of Ukraine," as against only 3 percent expressing a preference for becoming "part of Russia," and 2 percent in favor of "a part of Novorossiya").[31] As I noted in the introduction, the following interviews should not be construed as a scientific survey, as it was not possible to gather a representative sample of every age and social group, especially considering the ongoing war in Ukraine and the frozen conflicts in Transnistria, Abkhazia, and South Ossetia. Instead, these interviews offer a glimpse into the views of mostly young Russian speakers in late 2014. The focus on the younger generation, born after the fall of the Soviet Union, is due to the fact that they represent the future of Russian compatriots in their countries. This generation may play a significant role in how their countries respond to the reimperialization policy.

In Ukraine, the interviewed youths were from Ukraine's third largest city, Odessa. In 2014, Putin emphasized that Odessa was part of the region of Russia's historic empire known as Novorossiya (New Russia), implying that that region should be part of the Russian Federation.[32]

Today, the port city of Odessa boasts a vibrant multiethnic population that includes more than ten nationalities. While ethnic Ukrainians make up more than 60 percent of the population, the city is mostly Russian-speaking with most ethnic Ukrainians using Russian as their native language. The subject I will call Margarita is a Russian speaker and a student of marine logistics at Odessa University.[33] She dreams of working in the merchant marines. With Russian roots on her paternal side, she considers herself half Russian, but certainly not a Russian compatriot or Russian patriot. As she explains, "Russia and Ukraine are two separate countries" and "I have never lived in and will never live in Russia." She would prefer Russian to be the second national language of Ukraine, so that Russian speakers could choose to conduct their education and bureaucratic procedures in their mother tongue. However, she does not think that Ukrainian Russian speakers need Russia's protection and that "all problems can be solved within the border of our own country."

Another Russian-speaking Odessan, whom I will call Viktoriya, is a young marketing professional.[34] She enjoys speaking English and hopes to travel to America someday. Like Margarita, she does not feel she is a Russian compatriot and has no grievances as a Russian speaker in Ukraine. As she says, "in a democratic society everyone has the freedom and right to speak the language of their choice. We don't have fascism or totalitarianism. Nobody dictates the language we speak here and certainly not in my region." She thinks Russian protection or support is unnecessary and that in fact "Russia should turn its attention to its own domestic problems and not to the domestic problems of a neighboring country."

Yelena, a recent university graduate from Odessa, moved to Kiev not long ago to seek employment.[35] Born and raised in Odessa in a Ukrainian family, she grew up speaking Russian. But, as she explains, "here everyone speaks in Russian, but we are not Russian. We are Russian-speaking Ukrainians and patriots of our country." Based on her personal experience, she refutes myths that Russian speakers are discriminated against, pressured, or intimidated anywhere in Ukraine, including western Ukrainian-speaking territories. She adamantly rejects the prospect of Moscow's protection—"I wonder from whom Russia is going to protect us? From ourselves? What is happening in our country should be decided from within and we do not need outside help."

In Moldova's predominantly Russian-speaking territory of Gagauzia the sentiments are similar. Deniz is a young journalist and a native Russian speaker.[36] As he explains, "my mother is Moldavian and my father is Gagauz, but in the family they spoke Russian, so they could understand one another. This is why from my childhood I spoke in Russian." He explains that in the cities most Gagauz are Russian speakers, but in the provinces they speak Gagauz though they all know Russian as well. He rejects the notion of being identified as a Russian compatriot, declaring: "I am a citizen of Moldova. My homeland is Moldova! I was born here and I am a patriot of my own country!" He has never encountered any discrimination in Moldova other than the occasional request in the capital of Chisinau to speak Romanian. He believes that "no one here would ever want Russian protection."

In Moldova's breakaway territory, Transnistria, opinions are more divided. Yevgeny is in his thirties and a member of the leading political party.[37] He represents the vanguard of pro-Russian compatriots in Moldova. He considers himself to be a Russian compatriot and a Russian because "I was born and raised in a Russian environment and I have only one homeland—Russia." A staunch Russian patriot, Yevgeny actively supports the notion of Russia absorbing Transnistria and the latter becoming part of Novorossiya and the Eurasian Economic Union. When asked about potential grievances, he stated, "only the Western-leaning Moldovan government causes problems for Russian speakers." He also believes that "Russian protection is necessary and that a few military bases would cool down the pro-Western officials in Chisinau." Finally, when asked about Russia's 2014 policies in Ukraine, he mentioned that "Crimea always belonged to Russia" and that "a great historical mistake has been fixed."

Konstantin is a sales manager in his fifties and a former participant in the Transnistrian War.[38] Like Yevgeny, he is highly pro-Russian. Even though he holds Transnistrian, Moldovan, and Russian passports, he regards himself as a Russian because he was born there and he only moved to Transnistria in the late 1990s. Konstantin, too, is a firm Russian patriot and explains that "I grew up in the USSR, my family always spoke Russian, and we always supported the fight against the West." Although Konstantin is a hardline supporter of the Crimean annexation, he is more ambivalent about Russia's involvement in eastern Ukraine or

Novorossiya as he calls it—"simply because at the present this region is not of great importance."

Yana, a high-school teacher in her late twenties, represents the least pro-Russian segment of Russian speakers in Transnistria.[39] Although she speaks Russian today, she considers herself to be Ukrainian, because "in the family we always spoke Ukrainian" and she does not consider herself a Russian compatriot or part of the Russian World. When asked about Russia's protection of Russian speakers in Transnistria, she replied "Russia made a lot of promises to Transnistria and its people, but in reality little has changed. Unfortunately, military support is probably the only support that Russia can provide us with." She added that her "Russian friends mention being dissatisfied by the policies of both Moldova and Russia." Yana is very critical of the Russian involvement in Ukraine. She explains that "I have many friends who live in Crimea and eastern Ukraine and therefore, I have negative feelings toward Russian aggression. People die there in vain."

In the case of Georgia, it was exceedingly difficult to get responses from residents of the breakaway territories of Abkhazia and South Ossetia, as they feared discussing their national identity and sentiments toward Russia. Nonetheless, a few agreed to offer their views under strict conditions of anonymity. Boris, a university-educated man in his forties, lives with his family in Abkhazia while running a business in Russia.[40] His feelings toward Russia are somewhat ambiguous. While Abkhazian is his native language, today he primarily relies on Russian. However, this has not affected his identity: "No, I don't consider myself Russian, because I'm Abkhazian. I am not a Russian compatriot because I was not born in and have never lived in Russia. . . . My homeland is Abkhazia." However, he feels that Russia's protection of Abkhazia's Russian speakers is necessary "because Abkhazia is a small country and it cannot by itself take care of its own problems." Likewise, he is supportive of Moscow's policies in eastern Ukraine and Crimea.

Soslan is a native South Ossetian in his fifties with a notable streak of skepticism.[41] He lives in South Ossetia, but often travels to Russia and admits he could partly identify as a compatriot because he was born in the Soviet Union and holds Russian citizenship. On the other hand, he has a very strong Ossetian identity. "I speak Russian fluently, but I am not Russian, I am Ossetian and I treat the Russian passport only as a means to travel," he says. "Don't get me wrong, we don't have anything against the Russians, in fact, we appreciate their support fighting the Georgians in August 2008. Nonetheless, it would be silly to be a patriot of Russia, a country that is so incredibly rich and is treating its people so poorly. How could you ever even admire a country that is so unjust?" he asks. Surprisingly, Soslan is not supportive of the Crimean annexation— unlike many, he is rather skeptical of the Russian media's narrative.

As these interviews suggest, many Russians and Russophones in Ukraine and the separatist regions of Georgia and Moldova feel ambivalent toward Russia. Some may seek Russian protection or support for their nation or territory, but they do not all consider themselves Russian compatriots. Indeed Moscow's eagerness to claim various ethnic minorities of Georgia, Moldova, and Ukraine as compatriots appears driven by Russia's national interests rather than the interests of the so-called compatriots.

RUSSIA'S MOTIVES AND INTERESTS

Moscow has a number of ideological, military, political, and economic motives in maintaining Moldova, Georgia, and Ukraine in its sphere of influence and potentially reincorporating portions of their territories into the Russian Federation. All three are perceived as belonging to Russia's inherent sphere of influence and interests. Moldova and Ukraine are members of the CIS, while Georgia is a former member. Among Russia's foremost interests has been for the CIS states not to seek integration into Western structures, like the EU and especially NATO, nor to host any new U.S. military bases.[42]

Moldova

It may seem puzzling that Russia would seek control or influence in the small, poor, and landlocked country of Moldova. Historically, however, both the Russian Empire and the Soviet Union aspired to control the territories in the Black Sea basin (to which Moldova belongs) and the Danube river delta, which served as a trade corridor to the Balkans and could advance Russia's influence, interests, and security in the region.[43] Transnistria lies on the border of Ukraine, close to Ukrainian territories that Russia has deemed "Novorossiya." The unresolved status of Transnistria is of special interest to Moscow as it dims Moldova's chances of EU membership or closer ties to NATO. In fact, the unresolved borders of Moldova, Georgia, and Ukraine all benefit Russia by slowing NATO expansion in this region and remain a useful instrument for potential divide-and-rule tactics regarding the internal affairs of these countries.

Georgia

Georgia's position on the Black Sea and in the Caucasus, straddling Eastern Europe and Western Asia, is of clear strategic interest for Russia. As early as the 1990s, the Kremlin noted that Russia's strategic weight in the Black Sea depends on the presence of its troops on the Caucasus's western coast. Thus the territory of Abkhazia, with its long stretch of Black Sea coastline, holds military significance for Russia as well as boasting offshore oil resources (now controlled by Russian state monopoly Rosneft). As for South Ossetia, though it is a poor and sparsely populated mountain region it could offer Moscow leverage over its own Ossetian minorities and diffuse its internal problems. Just over the Russian border and the Great Caucasus mountain range is North Ossetia, an autonomous republic within the Russian Federation inhabited by ethnic Ossetians and connected to South Ossetia by the Roki Tunnel. For Moscow, dangling the carrot of union with South Ossetia could preempt any radicalization and separatist movements among the North Ossetians.[44] As my interviews revealed, many Ossetian nationalists in fact hope that one day the two territories will be united. Moscow's fears of radicalization of its ethnic minorities are considerable, especially as Russia's North Caucasus region is already roiled by separatist and Islamic movements, and even by ISIS-aligned groups in neighboring regions like Ingushetia and nearby Chechnya and Dagestan.[45] Furthermore, the frozen conflict and resulting lawlessness in South Ossetia and Abkhazia facilitate money laundering and organized crime that often has ties to Russia.[46]

Apart from its Black Sea access and location in the strategic and volatile Caucasus, Georgia itself offers few riches or natural resources that could beckon Russia's reimperialization. However, Georgia stands to be a player in the energy diplomacy of the Caucasus, particularly as Europe would like to diversify its energy mix with Caspian rather than Russian energy resources. As an energy superpower, Russia seeks control of oil and gas pipelines from the Caspian Sea that would pass through Georgian territory, including the Baku-Tbilisi-Ceyhan oil pipeline, the

Baku-Tbilisi-Erzurum gas pipeline, and the proposed Azerbaijan-Georgia-Romania gas interconnector pipeline.[47] Lastly, Georgian territory cuts off Moscow's direct access to its regional ally Armenia where it keeps a military base.

Ukraine

Ukraine's size, population, Black Sea ports, and geographical position, which make it both buffer and launching pad against the West, along with its role as both a supplier of foodstuffs and a market for Russian goods, have made it a strategic prize for the Russian imperial project for centuries. Ukraine shares a long border with Russia, a sizable Russian-speaking population, and a common Christian Orthodox faith. The ideological motives behind Moscow's imperial claims on Ukraine are significant. As Zbigniew Brzezinski noted, "It cannot be stressed strongly enough that without Ukraine, Russia ceases to be an empire, but with Ukraine suborned and then subordinated, Russia automatically becomes an empire."[48] Ukraine would be the most prized addition to the Moscow-led Eurasian Economic Union, of which Belarus and Kazakhstan are also members. At the same time Russia strongly opposes Ukraine's association agreement with the EU. Part of the imperial ideology vis-à-vis Ukraine rests on the aforementioned concept of Russia and Ukraine as "brotherly Slavic nations." Days ahead of the annexation of Crimea, on 18 March 2014, President Vladimir Putin stated that Ukraine and Russia are inextricably interlinked, saying "we are one people . . . and we cannot live without each other."[49] In August 2014, Putin reiterated, "I think that the Russian and Ukrainian peoples are practically one single people, no matter what others might say. . . . People living in what is Ukraine today all called themselves 'Russian.'"[50] The Ukrainians, on the other hand, are more ambivalent about this concept of "Slavic brotherhood" accompanied by threats.[51] Ukraine also figures centrally in Russia's perception of empire. The influential far-right, anti-Western Russian author Alexander Prokhanov has argued that Russia is now entering the stage of its Fifth Empire: "The first Russian empire was Kievan Rus', the second was the Moscow Kingdom, the third was the St. Petersburg Empire of the Romanovs, [the fourth] the Red Empire of the Soviet Union," and the fifth is now emerging under the leadership of President Putin.[52] Finally, Moscow is also concerned about the domestic repercussions in Russia, when neighboring Ukrainians are looking to the EU, seeking reforms and a democratic society.[53] Moscow likely worries that a version of Ukraine's Orange Revolution of 2004 and the Maidan movement of 2013–14 might spark in Russia, and thus attempts to delegitimize if not demonize the civic unrest by labeling it a radical, fascist, staged revolution, and alleging Western interference.

Besides these ideological motives, Russia has a number of strategic economic interests in Ukraine. The country is a significant market for Russian natural gas, oil, and nuclear fuel.[54] In 2013, according to Gazprom's data, the company sold nearly $11 billion worth of gas to Ukraine, representing some 16 percent of Gazprom's total gas exports, and earned 16 percent of its total revenue.[55] Following the conflict and a change in the Ukrainian government, in 2014 Ukraine cut its gas consumption by half to less than $4 billion.[56] Most significantly, however, Russian energy exports depend on Ukrainian territory. Through Ukraine runs Russia's key Urengoy-Pomary-Uzhhorod gas pipeline and the Druzhba (Friendship) oil pipeline, transporting Russian energy resources to European markets. Russia's economy is hugely dependent on revenues from oil and gas exports, and Russia depends on the European markets for some 80 percent of its piped gas exports. Half of that supply is piped through the territory of Ukraine. Thirteen European countries—Croatia, France, Greece, Germany, Poland, Italy, the Czech Republic, Hungary, Slovakia, Slovenia, Austria, Bulgaria, and Romania—get their gas via Ukraine.[57] Thus for Russia it is critical to maintain control and influence over a territory through which flows its most important export route and on which its main source of income depends. Leaked Russian government policy papers from February 2014 stated that in light of the changing political situation in Ukraine, Russia could not risk "losing not only the Ukrainian market for energy sales but more importantly indirect control over the gas transportation system of Ukraine. This will put at risk Gazprom's positions in Central and Southern Europe, causing great damage to the national economy."[58]

Ukraine also has its own significant natural resources. Ukraine's gas reserves are 1.2 trillion cubic meters, and if production were to be ramped up the country could fully supply its domestic needs and in the long term could even become a key European natural gas exporter.[59] In eastern Ukraine shale gas exploration was launched in 2013, and Donetsk and

Luhansk, which have become hotbeds of Russian-sponsored separatism, are highly industrialized and have notable coal and iron ore deposits. According to the Statistics Service of Ukraine, the regional GDP of Donetsk totaled nearly 12 percent of Ukraine's GDP, and Luhansk's, 4 percent.[60] Meanwhile, 70 percent of coal in Ukraine is mined in Donetsk and Luhansk regions.[61] Since the 2014 conflict erupted, Ukrainian coal from Luhansk has been transported out of the country to Russia.[62] In the face of increasing Western and Chinese interest, Russian private and state-owned companies have also sought to privatize Ukrainian state-owned companies and enterprises, including gas and oil pipelines, energy companies, engineering industry, and agricultural land.[63]

According to Ukrainian political scientist Dmytro Kondratenko, Russia's primary interests in Ukraine are military. Ukraine's domestic military industry includes manufacture of helicopters and cruise missile engines, and Russia likewise relies on Ukraine for the maintenance of its SS-18 nuclear rockets as well as its aircraft—facilities for all of which activities are located in eastern Ukraine.[64] Most importantly, for Russia, Ukraine serves as a passage to central Europe, the Balkan countries, and Moldova's Transnistria.[65] Only on 23 May 2015 did Ukraine annul a series of agreements with Russia on military cooperation and mutual security, and most importantly, it officially terminated permission for Russian troops to use Ukraine as a corridor to Transnistria.[66] The Ukrainian port of Sevastopol, which has now been annexed by Russia, had been romanticized as "Russian Glory"[67] and compared to "the Temple Mount in Jerusalem" by Putin despite there being no historical basis for this argument.[68] Sevastopol's importance has been primarily military—it has hosted the Russian Navy, affording Russia quick access to the eastern Mediterranean, the Balkans, and the Middle East.[69] Moscow has consistently argued that even the theoretical possibility of Ukraine's joining NATO would have significant implications for Russia's security. As Putin stated on 18 March 2014 regarding Ukraine's theoretical closer ties to NATO: "What would this have meant for Crimea and Sevastopol in the future? It would have meant that NATO's navy would be right there in this city of Russia's military glory, and this would create not an illusory but a perfectly real threat to the whole of southern Russia."[70] With its annexation of Crimea, Russia immediately seized various equipment—rockets, ships, aircraft, tanks, infantry fighting vehicles—from Ukrainian military bases.[71]

SOFT POWER

Russia's soft power in Moldova, Ukraine, and Georgia (as well as their separatist territories) has predominantly been based on the prevalence of the Russian language, the Orthodox Church, the Russian media, and strong business ties. The legacies of common Soviet culture and the appeal of Russian contemporary popular culture have also played a role, especially in Ukraine, Moldova, and Georgia's separatist territories. All this has been most effective in the separatist regions, but this is partly because the tiny, internationally unrecognized regions are now completely dependent on Russian patronage. As noted in Chapter 2, Russian soft power often goes beyond these means of influence, comes to resemble coercion and blackmail, and can include economic sanctions.

Ukraine

As a means of economic influence, Russia has conducted numerous trade wars against Ukraine, especially since the Orange Revolution of 2004. Much of the economic pressure was aimed at forcing Ukraine's hand to join the Russian-led Customs Union and later the Eurasian Economic Union.[72] Cutoffs of natural gas flow to Ukraine due to tensions over debts, pricing, and politics (including the notorious cuts of 2006 and 2009 that affected the EU's supply) have been the most prominent and consistent instrument of Russia's political and economic coercion of and influence over Kiev.[73] Other Russian embargos targeted Ukrainian agricultural, metal, and manufactured products.[74] Russia also offered carrots as well as brandishing sticks in its economic policies toward Ukraine. For instance, in the aircraft industry, Russia at times promised cooperation in exchange for political concessions.[75]

Since the 2000s, Russian soft power in Ukraine has centered on the Russian cultural centers, including in the western Ukrainian city of Lviv and the Crimean Peninsula. The sizable and well-funded Crimean center, besides cultural events and distribution of Russian textbooks and flags, has consistently sought to influence the identity of the Crimean inhabitants and propagate separatism, including supporting the Crimean Cossacks militant pro-Russia group.[76] It has continually organized such initiatives as the Day of Russia, the Day of Moscow, and the Day of the Reunion of Crimea with Russia.[77] Every week the center's TV Studio telecast the *Kuranty* (Chimes) program targeting the Crimeans and offering information on Russian government activities, the Moscow-Crimea Foundation, and the like. Through the 2010s, Ukraine imported three times more books from Russia than it published on its own, while Ukrainian cinemas and TV channels spent more than a hundred million dollars annually on films produced in Russia.[78] However, it is evident that throughout the 2000s, rather than cultural appeals, intense ideological pressure on the Ukrainian people marked Russia's soft power.[79]

Often intertwined with cultural and political means of influence, Russia's economic influence has been overwhelming over the past twenty years. Russian citizens own 10 percent of Ukraine's two hundred largest strategic companies.[80] Russian companies and businessmen donate funds to different pro-Russian organizations, often blurring the lines between Russia's economic, cultural, and political soft power. For example, Russian-born oligarch and billionaire Vadim Novinskiy is a well-known sponsor of the Ukrainian Orthodox Church of the Moscow Patriarchate.[81] He helped elect a relatively pro-Russian candidate as the new metropolitan of the church, which answers directly to the Kremlin ally Patriarch Kirill of Moscow and competes with the two independent Ukrainian Orthodox Churches, the Kievan Patriarchate and the Autocephalous Orthodox Church, which are not subordinate to Moscow.[82]

Moldova

As in Ukraine, in Moldova the soft power of the Russian Orthodox Church is also important. The Metropolitan Church of Moldova is canonically subordinate to the Russian Patriarchate, and administers about 70 percent of all Orthodox parishes in the country and benefits from the status of the country's most trusted institution.[83] The church has generally lent its support to pro-Russian political parties at election times. In return, the Communist Party of Moldova, while in power from 2002 to 2008, renovated a series of churches, often using public funds.[84] Another cultural source of Russian soft power in Moldova is Soviet nostalgia, which was progressively revived after the Communist Party became the largest political party in the parliament in 1998. The 9 May celebrations, commemorating Soviet victory in the Second World War, have been the main rallying point, with Soviet-era wartime songs performed by prominent Moldovan and Russian singers invited to Chisinau. Since around 2012, the Russian Embassy has introduced a new tradition of sporting a

Russian nationalist and military symbol, the St. George Ribbon, which has been enthusiastically adopted by the Moldovan Communist Party.

In Moldova and Transnistria, Russia has leveraged its position as a dominant investor, energy provider, and consumer of Moldovan wine. Russia contributes to some 40 percent of all investment in the Moldovan economy (including Transnistria) as a player in some 350 enterprises.[85] While Moldova accounted for some 10 percent of the wine consumed in Russia in 2013, Russia has enacted several bans against it including in 2006 and in 2013 when Moldova signed an association agreement with the EU.[86] At the same time, Russia started favoring wines from Moldova's Gagauz region, thus lending informal support to its separatist tendencies.[87] Transnistria has also received some carrots from Moscow in the form of "free" gas from Gazprom, running up an outstanding bill of $5 billion.[88] Moldovan authorities are not financially able to pay the debt, but separating the debt from Moldova and demanding that Transnistrian authorities pay it themselves would be a step toward recognizing the independence of the region—something Chisinau is not prepared to do.[89]

Georgia

As in Transnistria, in Georgia's Abkhazia and South Ossetia Gazprom has consistently provided subsidized gas as a tool of economic soft power. By contrast, Moscow has consistently pressured Georgia, which used to be 100 percent dependent on Gazprom gas, to pay its massive energy debt.[90] Amid political tensions, in the winter of 2006, the coldest in some twenty years, unknown saboteurs bombed the gas pipeline supplying Georgia and Armenia.[91] Tbilisi called this Moscow's foul and in the subsequent years diversified its gas supply away from Russia and toward Azerbaijan.[92] The same year Russia also applied economic sanctions against Georgia, blocking imports of Georgian wine and mineral water.

Trade with Russia has been another soft power tool used in South Ossetia. In the 1990s, the South Ossetian administration received significant revenue from controlling illegal trade in Russian gasoline and wheat, which was conducted on the side of the road to Vladikavkaz and the Roki mountain tunnel connecting the region with Russia. The South Ossetian government would resell these goods to Georgia and apply "transit taxes" though the region was still officially part of Georgia. Likewise, throughout the 1990s, Russia paid the salaries of Russian soldiers and peacekeepers stationed in the region in rubles rather than the Georgian lari, to further tie the territories economically to Russia.[93] To this day, much of Russia's soft economic power in the separatist territories is tied to illegal commercial practices that steer resources to a few people in these poor and underdeveloped regions. The economic vulnerability of these regions makes them attractive targets for the next stage of humanitarian policies of Russia's reimperialization trajectory.

In addition to Russia's policies toward the separatist territories, since the 2010s as Tbilisi increasingly turned Westward and NATO-ward, Russia's soft power activities intensified vis-à-vis Georgia's domestic politics. There were increased signs and allegations of Russian intelligence activity, including infiltration of government bureaucracies, officials, and even the military.[94] In 2012, the rapid rise of the former Georgian Prime Minister Bidzina Ivanishvili was described as "the sudden transformation of a shady Russian billionaire into a populist Georgian politician" and was perceived by some "as a Kremlin-organized plot."[95] Regardless of the truth or falsehood of these allegations, they contributed to an immense polarization of Georgian domestic politics, growing mistrust, and distraction from national priorities.

The Georgian Orthodox Church (GOC), as one of the most ancient (from the fourth century) of the family of Orthodox churches, benefits from a unique position. Out of all Eastern Orthodox Churches in the post-Soviet states, only the autocephalous GOC is independent from Moscow and has not become a clear mechanism of Russia's soft power.[96] South Ossetia and Abkhazia officially still belong to the GOC's canonical territory, and the GOC has responded harshly to the Russian Orthodox Church's plans to build churches in Russian military bases in Abkhazia.[97] However, it is possible to discern that traditional Georgian society has been targeted by Russia's narrative of "a common [Orthodox] front against Western influence on society."[98] In the 2010s there has also been a notable challenge to Georgia's Euroatlanticist agenda from within the country as various local pro-Russian NGOs and organizations like Eurasian Choice, the Eurasian Institute, and Earth Is Our Home that have been supporting Georgia's integration into the Eurasian Economic Union instead.[99] Also, NGOs and interest groups that openly receive funding from Russian sources, such as the Russian-Georgian Public Center, the Foundation of Russian and Georgian People, and the Gorchakov Fund, which is directly affiliated with the Russian Ministry of Foreign Affairs, regularly hold events in Tbilisi, including conferences, roundtable discussions, and seminars. Pro-Russian rallies and political leaders who oppose integration to NATO have become increasingly common, demonstrating that Russia's soft power is not just a singular phase leading to conflict but rather a long-term consistent effort that persists even after the war is officially over.[100]

HUMANITARIAN POLICIES

Russia's humanitarian policies have varied from softer means of assistance to harder methods of troop introduction under the pretext of peacekeeping in Moldova and Georgia. In Moldova's Transnistria, Russia has consistently provided a large amount of financial support to the Tiraspol administration, in the form of humanitarian aid, bonuses, additions to pensions, and other means of support. To illustrate the scope of this, in the period 2007–11, Russia spent some $75 million to pay out pensions in Transnistria.[101] In Georgia on the other hand, Russian humanitarian policies in the 1990s were directly tied to its military activities. The first presence of Russian troops in the region can be traced directly to Russia's "humanitarian operations" or, specifically, peacekeeping in the early 1990s in South Ossetia and Abkhazia following the wars of these two territories for independence from Georgia.[102] For Russia peacekeeping has arguably been not about keeping peace but at a minimum gaining influence and at a maximum carrying out acts of aggression, in accordance with General Gerasimov's argument that peacekeeping is an important component of new methods of war.[103] The first Russian peacekeepers arrived in South Ossetia in 1992 as part of a multinational force and essentially never left. In the Russo-Georgian war of 2008, the safety of Russian peacekeepers (and the newly minted South Ossetia's Russian citizens) was used as the reason for military intervention in Georgia.[104] Other humanitarian efforts in South Ossetia included an OSCE mission set up in 1991 to reach a peaceful political settlement, but the mission was perceived to be highly influenced by the Russian state.[105] Similarly, in May 1994, following a cease-fire in the Abkhaz-Georgian conflict, peacekeeping was to be conducted by CIS countries yet only Russia sent its troops, who remained in Abkhaz territory until the outbreak of war in 2008.

During the 2000s, Russia's humanitarian efforts in Ukraine have centered not on "peacekeeping" troops (as no prior conflict existed) but instead on the narrative of supporting the rights of Ukraine's Russian minority. However, it is worth mentioning that in fact Russia had considered yet ultimately refrained from using "peacekeeping" troops in 2014 in eastern Ukraine both before and after the request from militants in Donetsk.[106] Moscow's interest in Ukraine's Russian minority policies intensified following Ukraine's attempts to turn West with the Orange Revolution of 2004. The paradox of these policies stemmed from the fact that no international human rights organizations had ever received any complaints from ethnic Russians or Russian speakers living in Ukraine.[107] Instead, the Russian government tried to appeal to the OSCE High Commissioner for National Minorities on a number of occasions.[108] In October 2008, the Russian ambassador to Ukraine, Viktor Chernomyrdin, called on the OSCE to monitor the rights of Russians there, claiming that Ukraine is using "restrictive measures without taking into account the interests of the Russian-speaking citizens of Ukraine, who appeal to the Russian embassy."[109] Russia has also appealed to the Council of Europe regarding these alleged violations.[110] Most surprisingly, Russian policy deemed that Ukraine's recognition of its historical Ukrainian Insurgent Army, which fought against the invasion of the Nazis and Soviets, is a violation of international law and a violation of the rights of Soviet army veterans.[111] These incoherent attempts at raising the issue of human rights violations in Ukraine were backed by Russia's simultaneous compatriot policies. Once again, soft power and humanitarian policies lay the groundwork for the most significant policy thread in the reimperialization trajectory—that of reclaiming Russian compatriots.

COMPATRIOT POLICIES

Georgia

In Georgia and Moldova, Moscow's efforts to claim the South Ossetian, Abkhazian, and Transnistrian populations as Russia's compatriots started in the early 1990s with economic and cultural support and peacekeeping operations long before Russia had fully formulated its official policies toward compatriots. In the 1990s Russia promoted Russian-language education in Abkhazia and South Ossetia, which had just 9 percent and 1 percent ethnic Russians respectively. As a result Russian became the language of instruction in all schools and higher education institutions while the educational content was redesigned to promote a new national identity.[112] In April 2008, before the Russo-Georgian war that summer, Putin called for a package of economic and legal assistance to Russian compatriots, resulting in a formal program, Main Directions of the Development of Relations with Abkhazia and South Ossetia. This program established consular, economic, social, educational, and cultural cooperation and assistance. The Russian media described it as a step to protect "the legitimate interests" of Russian citizens "residing in so far unrecognized republics."[113] The real aim and result of these policies was to start treating the separatist regions as independent states and sidelining the Georgian government in its territories. Outside of the separatist regions, Russia's compatriot policies toward the Russian diaspora in Georgia proper have been much more limited and have garnered little success, primarily due to the small numbers of ethnic Russians and Russian speakers and their generally successful integration into Georgian society.[114]

Moldova

Moldova and Transnistria have both been targets of Russia's official compatriot efforts. While most of these efforts started long after the de facto independence of Transnistria, here, Russian compatriot support can be barely distinguished from Soviet-era Russification policies. In Transnistria, though Russian, Ukrainian, and Moldovan are the official languages, the Russian language is the de facto language of communication. According to Transnistria's 2014 official report, ethnic Moldovans number 32 percent of the population, Russians 30 percent, and Ukrainians 29 percent, but 96.5 percent of school and university students study in the Russian language.[115] In 2009, out of Transnistria's 182 schools, only thirty-three taught in the "Moldovan" language and only two in Ukrainian, with the rest teaching in Russian. Moreover, the majority of the region's government leaders come from Russia, so that most government proceedings are in Russian.[116]

In Moldova, there is a plethora of nongovernmental organizations spearheading Moscow's support for the so-called Russian compatriots. The Russian Community (comprising 26 territorial branches) and the

Congress of the Russian Community (comprising 11 organizations, plus 20 local branches) are both part of the Coordinating Council of Russian Communities (comprising an additional 22 associations and 9 territorial branches). Besides their many branches, these entities host joint events in Gagauzia. Many of their activities are cultural (such as the "Days of Russian Culture" festival) or educational (such as the "Time to Study in Russia" project), but they also promote joining the Eurasian Economic Union and "reunification with Russia."[117] Delegates of the Congress of the Russian Community in Moldova participate in the World Congress of Russian Compatriots.[118] A smaller organization, Friends of Russia, advocates closer relations with Russia and boasts many prominent Moldovan public figures, including ex–Prime Minister Vasile Tarlev, governor of Gagauzia Mikhail Formuzal (2006 to present), and former Deputy Prime Minister Nicolae Andronic as members.[119] The extensive efforts to support Russian compatriots are somewhat surprising considering that Chisinau has long emphasized that "Moldova is a multiethnic state,"[120] and is perceived to have enacted some of the best policies in the region as regards ethnic and linguistic minorities.[121]

Ukraine

Under Putin's regime, Ukraine has also faced escalating Russian compatriot policies despite the fact that Russians and Ukrainians have lived together peacefully for decades: intermarrying, speaking predominantly Russian in some regions, and often sharing the same faith. Nevertheless, starting in about the year 2000 the Russian government began creating various compatriot organizations and culture centers and supplying them with legal, financial, informational, logistics, and organizational support, but these activities intensified after the mid-2000s.[122] After the 2004 Orange Revolution, Russian citizens started creating illegal and semilegal organizations in Ukraine and providing members with paramilitary training, resulting in Kiev banning some Russian politicians from entering the country.[123] For instance, Donetsk's pro-Russian separatist organization "Donetskaya Respublika" was registered in 2006 and started receiving military training no later than 2009, according to media reports and information from social networks.[124] Other Russian organizations in Ukraine also became more active at this time. In 2007 a former member of the Ukrainian parliament, Vadim Kolesnichenko, became the head of the newly founded Coordinating Council of Russian Compatriot Organizations in Ukraine—a post he maintained until he absconded to Russian-occupied Crimea in 2014.[125] Yet the most significant policy related to Russian compatriots in Ukraine, Georgia, and Moldova was Moscow's passportization effort.

PASSPORTIZATION

Georgia

The Georgian and Ukrainian cases are the best examples in the post-Soviet states of Moscow's highly concerted effort to provide Russian citizenship to inhabitants of specific regions. Handing out Russian citizenship and passports was often conducted simultaneously with efforts to politically and ideologically reconstruct these foreign citizens as Russian compatriots. In Georgia, Russia started its early efforts of passportization in the 1990s, and they gained further momentum under Putin's presidency in the 2000s. Tbilisi granted automatic Georgian citizenship to all former citizens of the Georgian Soviet Socialist Republic immediately following independence—including South Ossetians and Abkhazians.[126] Yet many people from these regions did not acquire Georgian passports due to both separatism, tensions with Tbilisi, and the fact that many people living in remote villages saw no need to apply. In 2000, Moscow made a strategic move and withdrew from Georgian citizens the right to visa-free travel to Russia but allowed it for Abkhazians and South Ossetians. This had significant consequences economically for some 600,000 to 900,000 Georgian labor migrants in Russia and in particular for the breakaway regions that bordered Russia.[127] For these poor regions trade with neighboring Russia had become an important source of livelihood. As a result, many South Ossetians and Abkhazians, including those interviewed and profiled here, obtained Russian passports, driven by the economic necessity to travel visa-free to Russia. Russian citizenship provided additional benefits such as pensions and allowances, winning the loyalty of the population.[128]

In 2002, Moscow started large-scale distribution of Russian citizenship and passports, shortly after Russia's new citizenship law, which simplified the naturalization procedure.[129] The new law stipulated that stateless peoples of the former Soviet Union could hand in their Soviet passports and in exchange receive Russian passports. Despite the fact that Abkhazians and South Ossetians were officially Georgian citizens, a pass-portization blitz followed across these territories. For instance, within a month of the new law, Russian application centers were set up in six out of seven regions in Abkhazia, in which special field brigades distributed documents within days across remote and inaccessible mountain villages. The proportion of Russian citizens in Abkhazia and South Ossetia rose consistently: from 30 percent in Abkhazia and 40 percent in South Os-setia in 2002, to 80 percent and 90 percent respectively in 2006. Dur-ing the war of August 2008, passportization was allegedly assisted by Russian troops. For instance, some two thousand Russian passports were found in the vehicle of a Russian officer in South Ossetia's capital of Tskhinvali. Pressure and compulsion to accept Russian citizenship were reported even in ethnically Georgian territories, though some of the interviewed ethnic Georgians from nearby regions such as Gori had also acquired Russian passports for economic motives. By 2009, nearly 90 percent of Abkhazia's and South Ossetia's population were Russian citizens.[130]

Ukraine

In Ukraine, Russia started handing out citizenship and passports to members of the Russian minority in Crimea during the 1990s, and am-plified its policies in the 2000s. In addition, discharged officers of the Black Sea fleet would obtain Ukrainian citizenship and remain in the country. In 2008, the Vice Admiral of Ukraine, Volodymyr Bezkorovainiy, as well as the Sevastopol prosecutor's office, announced that some 1,595 navy personnel from the fleet stationed at the port had illegally acquired Ukrainian citizenship, all of them while maintaining their Russian citi-zenship.[131] The Ukrainian media in 2008 started covering stories such as that a librarian in a Sevastopol library was systemically handing out Russian passports.[132] While estimates suggested that the number of Crimeans with Russian citizenship ranged from eight to forty thousand or 0.4 to 2.1 percent of the total population, Russian officials continued to deny the distribution of passports there.[133] Generally, many Crimeans, especially ethnic Russians, were ambivalent both toward Ukrainian citizenship, and often accepting of the opportunity to have a Russian passport.[134] The rapid passportization of the Crimeans was a reflection of Russia's successful implementation of previous stages of the reimperialization trajectory, namely soft power and compatriot policies.

The Russian passportization activities were not unknown to the Ukrainian officials, though Kiev made no consistent policy response. In the early 2000s the representatives of Crimean Tatars presented evidence that Russian consulates in Simferopol and Sevastopol were massively handing out Russian citizenship.[135] In 2008, The minister of foreign affairs, Volodymyr Ohryzko, confirmed in an interview that the Russian consulate general in Simferopol was providing Russian passports to Ukrainian citizens in unknown numbers.[136] In September 2008, Ukrainian members of parliament from then Prime Minister Yulia Tymoshenko's bloc drafted legislation to strengthen penalties for offenses against the Ukrainian Law on Citizenship, which forbids dual citizenship, but the law was never passed. In February 2015, the Ministry of Foreign Affairs stated it would start introducing "sanctions" against holders of dual citizenship.[137] Indeed what is evident from the cases of Georgia and Ukraine is that the weakness and incoherence of these countries' policies toward their own citizens and minorities and their lack of response to Russian soft power and compatriot policies enabled Russian passportization and paved the way for more aggressive reimperialization activities.

Moldova

The process of passportization was somewhat different in the case of Moldova's Transnistria than in Georgia or Ukraine. Passportization followed rather than preceded the region's separatism and served to solidify rather than establish proseparatist and pro-Russian leanings. Much of this is due to the fact that Transnistria's separatism emerged long before Russia's compatriot and accompanying citizenship policies were developed. Since Transnistria declared independence in 1990 almost immediately following Moldova's independence but before the Soviet Union collapsed, most Transnistrians remained Soviet citizens. While Transnistria has issued its own passports (which are internationally unrecognized) many people have opted for Russian and Ukrainian citizenship. Estimates from the late 2000s suggest that there were some 150,000 Russian citizens in Transnistria out of the total population of half a million.[138] However, in comparison to South Ossetia, Abkhazia, and Crimea,

Moscow's effort at passportizing the population has been less concerted. In the 2000s Moscow opened a consular office in Transnistria's capital Tiraspol, despite Chisinau's objections. Yet reports indicate that Transnistrians have difficulty acquiring Russian citizenship and to do so generally pay significant fees and bribes to middlemen.[139] Passportizing the Transnistrians has become a profitable business for some. In the end, the inhabitants of South Ossetia, Abkhazia, and Transnistria all succumb to the same necessity: people living in internationally unrecognized territories without internationally recognized passports have no choice but to resort to obtaining Russian passports if they want to legally travel to Russia or anywhere else. Yet with a Russian passport these individuals wittingly or not become targets of Moscow's claims to protect.

INFORMATION WARFARE

Possibly the most active and sophisticated Russian information warfare campaign in the whole of the post-Soviet space was enacted against Ukraine in the year leading up to Crimea's annexation and the separatist war. As in Abkhazia, South Ossetia, and Transnistria, Russian information warfare leveraged the widespread Russian language and the dominance of Russian media that had been established over earlier years through soft power efforts, cultural appeals, compatriot policies.

Ukraine

In Ukraine, the main targets of Russian information warfare have been Russians and Russian speakers, who mainly reside in the southeastern parts of the country, while Ukrainian speakers have been targeted to a much lesser degree.[140] The main vehicles of this information campaign have been Russian and Russian-language TV, online media, and social networks. In the autumn of 2013, Russian TV channels like Perviy Kanal, Rossiya 24, Life News, Euronews (Russian edition), Russia Today, and others pursued a number of strategies. The first was to discredit Ukraine's European integration efforts and the Maidan protests.[141] Simultaneously, the Russian media turned to their favorite tactic of smearing its opponents as "fascists," and tried to convince eastern and southern Ukrainians of the narrative that "fascism is returning to life" in Kiev and western Ukraine.[142] Russian TV channels urged Russian speakers to resist and even to take aggressive actions against the authorities and their Ukrainian neighbors.[143] The Russian mass media also tried to promote the idea of "federalization of Ukraine"—introducing greater autonomy for various regions through referendums.[144] Russian foreign minister Sergey Lavrov likewise demanded that "Ukraine should abandon the unitary position and Ukrainization."[145] As time progressed, but before the annexation of Crimea and ahead of the military clashes in Donetsk and Luhansk, Russian authorities started to produce fake reports about mass refugee flows from Ukraine to Russia.[146] Much of this propaganda was also targeted at domestic TV viewers to gain support for Moscow's stance toward Ukraine.

As with passportization, Kiev was ill-equipped, outmatched as it was by Moscow's resources and political will, to respond to Russia's information campaign. Generally, Ukrainian television is considered to be quite pluralistic, without explicit pro- or anti-Russian content, with the possible exception of the Inter channel which in 2015 was accused by the government of broadcasting "Russian propaganda" but continues in operation.[147] Inter is the second most popular national channel in Ukraine, owned by Dmitry Firtash and Sergey Levochkin, oligarchs aligned with ousted President Victor Yanukovich who allegedly have strong connections with Russian business.[148] Ukraine stopped transmitting several Russian TV channels on its territory, though one Kiev-based pro-Russia newspaper (and corresponding internet site), *Vesti*, continues to operate as of 2015, allegedly financed in cash by Russia.[149] On the other hand, Russian troops and pro-Russian militias immediately switched off Ukrainian TV channels and switched on Russian ones after taking control of a city or town in the conflict since 2014.[150] Less than a year after Crimea's annexation, internet users in the peninsula faced Russian censorship and could not access more than eleven thousand banned websites including Ukrainian ones.[151]

In addition to a vigorous information warfare offensive, since 2014 pro-Russian hackers have been carrying out a cyber warfare campaign not only against the Ukrainian government but also against NATO. Shortly after Yanukovych fled Ukraine on 28 February 2014, by sabotaging fiber optic cables and raiding the facilities of the Ukrainian telecommunications company Ukrtelecom, Russian troops rendered the entire Crimean peninsula virtually inaccessible from the mainland.[152] Subsequently, the main Ukrainian government website was shut down for over seventy-two hours and pro-Russian hackers also managed to compromise the mobile phones of Ukrainian parliamentarians.[153] This tactic, which essentially followed the Russian hybrid warfare scenario, severely hampered communications between the Ukrainian military and decision makers during the crucial hours of the Crimean annexation. Furthermore, it has been observed by security analysts that dozens of computers in Ukraine have been hit by Snake—a sophisticated computer virus probably originating from Russia, which can gain access to, remotely control, and steal large amounts of data.[154] Ultimately, following the Russian offensive in Ukraine and the Western sanctions in 2014, a surge of cyber attacks has been documented against NATO, Western government departments, and telecoms—all probably linked with cyber groups based in Russia.[155]

Moldova

In both Moldova and Transnistria, Russian media are almost equally pervasive. According to Moldova's 2014 Barometer of Public Opinion, the media are the third most trusted institution after the church and the army. Television is the most important source of information for 83 percent of Moldovans.[156] The most watched Moldovan TV channel, Prime TV, mostly retransmits the Russian channel, Perviy Kanal. About half the newspapers are in Russian and also mostly published in Russia, while some, like the business newspaper *Kommersant Plus,* are financed by Transnistria's regime.[157] The propaganda of Moldova's and Transnistria's pro-Russian media focuses on negatively portraying the European Union and the West, and positively portraying Russia and the Eurasian Economic Union. In the case of Transnistria, there has been a tendency to build anti-Moldova public sentiment, which in times of tension between Chisinau and Moscow has been described as reaching a level of "psychosis."[158]

Georgia

In Georgia's South Ossetia and Abkhazia, however, the Russian policies went beyond propaganda tactics: as in the Ukrainian case, the propaganda served as a tool to justify an eventual invasion, which was facilitated by a concerted information warfare campaign. As the 1990s progressed, Georgia lost the information space and the allegiance of South Ossetia and Abkhazia to Russia. In 2006, the two separatist regions blocked the broadcasting of Georgian channels, giving Russian media the monopoly.[159] Ahead of the war in 2008, there was a notable increase in Russian coverage of the hardships and discrimination allegedly faced by the South Ossetians and the Abkhazians at the hands of the Georgians and the Georgian government.[160] Following these allegations, in the spring of 2008 Moscow sent reinforcements to its peacekeeping operations in Abkhazia, declaring that force would be used to protect Abkhazia's Russian citizens if the alleged hostilities resumed. In June 2008 Russian Lieutenant General Alexander Burutin warned in reference to the allegations of abuses, "In the future we cannot guarantee that our servicemen will act in this patient way. Their patience is not limitless. The consequences will be grave and there could be bloodshed. It is beyond doubt that the Georgian side will have to assume the responsibility for these provocations and their consequences."[161]

In the lead-up to the war in the summer of 2008, Russia's information warfare became increasingly aggressive, reporting on completely unsubstantiated claims of "genocide" and "ethnic cleansing" being carried out by the Georgians.[162] During his visit to Russia's North Ossetia in August 2008, Prime Minister Putin stated, "we are seeing elements of a kind of genocide against the Ossetian people" and "They are mostly women, children, and the elderly. Of course, they faced a dramatic tragedy. What they told me is beyond any war rules. I believe there were elements of genocide."[163] Yet these dramatic accounts were no more than a disinformation ploy. The Independent International Fact-Finding Mission on the Conflict in Georgia concluded in 2009 that there was no evidence of genocide committed by the Georgian side during the war or its aftermath. Rather, the report concluded that ethnic cleansing had been practiced against ethnic Georgians in South Ossetia both during and after the war.[164]

As war approached, Russia's information campaign turned to cyber warfare and included cyber attacks on Georgian government and media websites.[165] It was the first known case (which would later be repeated in Ukraine) where cyber warfare and a military campaign were coordinated, with pro-Kremlin hackers reportedly working alongside Russian military forces.[166] Weeks before the invasion, Russian hackers began attacks against Georgian internet infrastructure with coordinated barrages of millions of requests—known as distributed denial of service, or DDoS, attacks—that overloaded and effectively shut down Georgian servers.[167] The DDoS attacks also targeted the websites of the president, the parliament, the foreign ministry, news agencies, and banks.[168] Ultimately, while Russian tanks and troops were crossing the Georgian border and bombers were flying, the hackers began simultaneously attacking key Georgian military, communications, finance, and government websites (fifty-four of them were targeted), thus rendering some of them inaccessible during the crisis and spreading chaos and panic.[169]

PROTECTION

Moscow's call for protection of Russian compatriots was carried out under quite different circumstances in Moldova, Georgia, and Ukraine. However, in all three cases there were already Russian troops on the ground who served as the means for this "protection" process. In the early 1990s in Moldova it was Soviet troops; in the 2000s in Georgia it was Russian peacekeepers; and in 2014 Ukraine it was Russia's military presence on the Sevastopol naval base. The calls for protection and subsequent military operations in the case of Georgia and Ukraine were preceded by much earlier groundwork of wooing and co-opting Russian compatriots and even providing them with paramilitary training.

Ukraine

In Ukraine, Moscow's calls for Russian compatriot protection were already voiced sporadically following the country's Orange Revolution in 2004 and were often launched in response to Ukraine's domestic political developments, such as elections or a change in leadership.[170] Increasingly, however, some Russian intellectuals and political scientists associated with the Kremlin tended to speak about splitting Ukraine and absorbing some of its regions. In an interview in May 2009, a prominent Russian philosopher who argues for a restoration of the Russian Empire, Alexander Dugin, called for the integration of the southeastern regions of Ukraine with Russia. He even outlined the process, arguing that the residents of these regions should initiate a referendum on integration with Russia, and protest if such a referendum were prohibited.[171] Another Odessa-born Russian political commentator, Anatoliy Vasserman, proposed that each local commune of Ukraine should hold a referendum about whether its residents wanted to join Russia.[172] According to a 2015 report begun by Boris Nemtsov and finished by his colleagues after his death, long before Crimea's annexation Ukrainian officers and politicians were being recruited by the Russian security services to switch sides and support the separatists at key moments, and being paid for their efforts by Moscow and by Crimean businesses that received loans from Russian banks.[173] Indeed the subsequent events in Crimea, Luhansk, and Donetsk unfolded as if according to the Kremlin's playbook.

By early 2014, following the Maidan protests and Yanukovich's departure from government and Ukraine on 21 February, Moscow's protection changed from rhetoric to a hybrid warfare campaign. On the night of 27 February 2014, Russian special forces took over the local legislature of Ukraine's Autonomous Republic of Crimea.[174] During the day, several legislature members gathered and illegally named a new prime minister of the Crimea (without proper procedure, quorum, or the Ukrainian president's permission).[175] At the same time, Russian troops, previously stationed in Crimea and the city of Sevastopol under the Black Sea Fleet Treaty of 1997, started besieging and attacking Ukrainian troops, government buildings, and infrastructure in direct violation of the 1994 Budapest Memorandum which guaranteed the territorial integrity of Ukraine.[176] On 16 March, Russian authorities and pro-Russian separatists conducted an illegal "referendum" for Crimea and Sevastopol to join Russia with the reported but unlikely outcome of 96.7 percent supporting annexation. At the same time, the president of Russia's Council on Civil Society and Human Rights unexpectedly published in a blog (which was quickly removed a short time later) that "50–60 percent voted for unification with Russia, with a turnout of 30--50 percent."[177] Putin himself later acknowledged that around twenty thousand Russian troops were present in Crimea during the "referendum," which has been perceived as influencing the outcome.[178] In Sevastopol the Russian authorities created new leadership by appointing a so-called people's mayor without any procedure. On 18 March, two days after the "referendum," the Russian Federation signed the treaty of accession for Crimea and the city of Sevastopol, and thus enacted what the world considers an unlawful annexation of Ukrainian territories.

In eastern Ukraine, violence by small militant groups broke out on 1 March. The real fighting began after 11 April, when a special Russian

military detachment, commanded by Colonel Igor Girkin (who had earlier taken part in capturing Crimea) crossed the Russian-Ukrainian
border and captured the city of Sloviansk in the region of Donetsk.[179]
Pro-Russian militias continued capturing and advancing on other towns
and cities in eastern Ukraine. Despite the Ukrainian army's efforts to
liberate Donetsk and Luhansk regions, subsequent offensives in 2014
and 2015 enabled the militants that were supported, armed, and largely
manned by Russia to maintain control over some territories. On 11 May
2014 Russian militants in Donetsk and Luhansk conducted internationally unrecognized referendums and pseudo-elections on 2 November
2014. The future consequences of these actions as yet remain unclear,
since the militants declared "state sovereignty" but not independence
for the so-called Donetsk and Luhansk people's republics.[180]

On 17 July 2014 the conflict acquired an international dimension
when Malaysia Airlines Flight MH17 was shot down over Donetsk by pro-
Russian separatists with an SA-11 Buk missile likely given them by Russia, killing 298 people, seemingly because the separatists confused the
plane with a Ukrainian military aircraft.[181] From the beginning, investigation of this tragedy was compromised by efforts of Russian propaganda
to assign responsibility for the tragedy to Kiev, presenting fake pictures
of Ukrainian fighter aircraft next to the airliner and coming up with non-
existent witnesses who claimed to see Ukrainian involvement.[182] However, all evidence suggested the opposite. On 17 July 2014, approximately
at the same time the contact with MH17 was lost, Colonel Girkin posted
on the Russian social network Vkontakte about shooting down a Ukrainian An-26 plane in eastern Ukraine, but deleted the post as soon as the
news about the MH17 crash started to emerge.[183]

Meanwhile, in August and September 2014, pro-Russia militias
seized the city of Novoazovsk in Donetsk region and tried to capture the
city of Mariupol.[184] In September 2014, a first cease-fire agreement
(Minsk-1) was signed between Kiev and the separatists, but it was broken
several days later when fighting started for control of the Donetsk air-
port.[185] In February 2015 a second cease-fire agreement (Minsk-2) was
signed but constant shelling by pro-Russian forces persisted.[186] The war's
toll from 2014 to mid-2015 was more than six thousand dead, tens of thousands wounded, and nearly 1.3 million displaced persons.[187]

Throughout the war, the Russian government and media emphasized the narrative of "protecting" Russian compatriots as if to justify forceful intervention and pseudo-referendums. In early March and again at the beginning of April 2014 there were reports in the Russian media that Russians were calling for protection in Crimea, Donetsk, and Luhansk regions, and the city of Odessa.[188] In April 2014, Putin argued that protection of Russian speakers was Russia's primary motive in the annexation of Crimea:

> The most obvious risk was that the Russian speaking population was threatened and that the threats were absolutely specific and tangible. This is what made Crimean residents, the people who live there, think about their future and ask Russia for help. This is what guided our decision. I said in my recent speech in the Kremlin that Russia had never intended to annex any territories, or planned any military operations there, never. . . . But we also thought, and have always hoped, that all native Russians, the Russian-speaking people living in Ukraine, would live in a comfortable political environment, that they would not be threatened or oppressed.[189]

Just a month earlier, however, Putin had been far less studiedly pacifistic when he argued cynically that Russia is not worried about war with Ukraine: "If we make that decision [to go to war with Ukraine], it will only be to protect Ukrainian citizens. And let's see those [Ukrainian] troops try to shoot their own people, with us behind them—not in front, but behind. Let them just try to shoot at women and children! I would like to see those who would give that order in Ukraine."[190] Indeed Russia's "protection" of its "compatriots" is nothing more than an undeclared hybrid war against Ukraine. The goal appears to be to destroy Ukraine in its present form as a unitary state and to gain control over Ukrainian territories.

Georgia

In Georgia as in Ukraine, propaganda about mistreatment of "compatriots," in this case the South Ossetians and Abkhazians, also set the stage for "protection." In hindsight it appears that Georgia served as a rehearsal for the line that Moscow would later take in Ukraine. However, unlike in

Moldova and Ukraine, in 2008 there had been a heated debate over whether Georgia was completely blameless in the outbreak of the Russo-Georgian war. Some have argued that it was Georgia's use of military force against South Ossetia and Abkhazia and the killing of two Russian peacekeepers that resulted in the escalation of the conflict.[191] Others point to the fact that Russian troops had been in South Ossetia and Abkhazia under the guise of peacekeepers since the 1990s and that Moscow stepped up its aggressive polices in Georgia after the country indicated its desire to join NATO at the Bucharest summit in 2008. In the end, the Russo-Georgian conflict became an all-out direct war without Russia hiding behind proxies and paramilitary groups as in the case of Ukraine or Moldova. Under the leadership of pro-Western Georgian President Mikheil Saakashvili, the conflict also took on the character of a personal conflict between him and Putin. The Columbia University–educated lawyer Saakashvili gained his wild popularity and made his ascent to the presidency by his bold charisma, his call to curb the country's corruption, and his penchant for riding the run-down Tbilisi metro. In the summer of 2008, Ossetians began shelling Georgian villages while Russian troops and military equipment were moving toward Georgia. Arguably in response or arguably to recapture the breakaway territory, Saakashvili launched a military operation on the night of 7–8 August. On 8 August Russia officially moved its army and air force into South Ossetia in addition to the large "peacekeeping" contingents there and started air strikes against Georgia proper.

The Russian side called the operation "peacekeeping enforcement."[192] On 9 August 2008, Russian Foreign Minister Sergey Lavrov argued that the Russian constitution and Russian laws made it "unavoidable for us to exercise responsibility to protect," which was little more than a manipulation of the R2P (Responsibility to Protect) concept coined by Western analysts.[193] On another occasion, he reiterated, "Russia will not allow the death of its compatriots to go unpunished . . . the life and dignity of our citizens, wherever they are, will be protected."[194] The military intervention was justified by allegations of genocide of the Ossetian population by the Georgian forces, and as a move to protect South Ossetia's Russian citizens and Russian peacekeeping forces on the territory.[195] Certainly, the fact that South Ossetians and Abkhazians were now Russia's citizens gave Moscow greater grounding in its efforts to "protect" them. On 10 August 2008, at an emergency meeting of the Security Council in New York, Russian Permanent Representative Vitaly Churkin was highly emotional, accusing the Georgians of carrying out "ethnic cleansing" and "genocide" in South Ossetia, but it would be a vast understatement to call his claims exaggerations. He claimed Georgia's attack on South Ossetia's capital in one day resulted in 2,000 casualties of mostly Ossetian Russian citizens.[196] "Can it be described as genocide when 2,000 out of 120,000 people died the first day of the war? What should be the [numbers of the] victims to describe the situation as genocide?"[197] However, the Independent International Fact-Finding Mission on the Conflict in Georgia concluded that the overall South Ossetian civilian losses in the August 2008 war were 162 in total rather than the 2,000 in a day cited by Russian officials.[198]

Moldova

In the case of Moldova, there have been two scenarios of attempted Russian compatriot protection. The first was in 1991–92 when the some twenty to thirty thousand Soviet troops who were still on the ground in Moldova fought together with and on behalf of the separatists of Transnistria, thus establishing the de facto independence of the territory. The Soviet military involvement was largely justified on the pretext of protecting Moldova's Russians and Russian speakers. While today the Russian military remains on the ground as a "peacekeeping force," it has also been observed that Russia has been providing Transnistrian soldiers and officers with service passports and rotating them through elite Russian officer training courses.[199] In 2014, furthermore, there was an arguably orchestrated effort similar to that in Donetsk and Luhansk to destabilize Moldova's region of Gagauzia. Like Transnistria, Gagauzia had declared itself independent in 1991, but Chisinau had assuaged tensions in 1994 by giving the region autonomy. In early February 2014, however, Gagauzia held an illegal referendum on whether Moldova should join the Russia-led Eurasian Economic Union, or the EU, which resulted in more than 98 percent voting in favor of the Eurasian option. Likewise, the voters voted 99 percent in favor of Gagauzia seeking independence from Moldova if the latter lost its sovereignty or were to try to join Romania.[200] In early 2014, the security services of Moldova successfully arrested a number of Gagauz who had participated in military training camps in

Russia, and others fled to Russia fearing arrest.[201] Allegedly young Gagauz men had been recruited by Gagauz officials close to the Gagauz *bashkan* (governor), Mihail Formuzal, and were supposed to complete training in a Russian camp on how to defend themselves against police special forces as well as to attack, make Molotov cocktails, and launch grenades.[202] In late November 2014, other pro-Russian organizations also came to the attention of the Moldovan police, including AntiFa, Social Shield, Restruct [*sic*] Moldova, the Russian Legion, the New Legion, and the Cossack movement, after the police found large amounts of ammunitions, rifles, grenade launchers, and currency in fifteen locations where members of AntiFa were active.[203] Many in Moldova have concluded that the upsurge of these organizations was related to parliamentary elections in November 2014. The former acting director of Moldova's Department of Homeland Security, Valentin Dediu, stated: "Immediately after the elections these forces will try to destabilize the situation to the maximum, and the Russian Federation aims at creating the new Russian Empire."[204] Essentially Dediu argued that electoral losses by pro-Russian candidates could result in violent protests carried out by the specially trained militant groups. In May 2015, calls for protection were again heard when sixty-six Transnistrian NGOs requested Putin to protect the territory and guarantee peace there in light of the fact that Ukraine had terminated its agreement with Russia on military transit to Moldova.[205]

ANNEXATION

Among the three countries analyzed in this chapter, only Ukraine in the case of Crimea experienced an official annexation of its territories by Russia. In fact Crimea stands alone as a case of Russia's annexation of territory following the fall of the USSR. Even though the vast majority of the international community has rejected the validity of Crimea's referendum and subsequent annexation, it does appear a lost cause for decades to come. The future of Ukraine's territories of Luhansk and Donetsk looks more uncertain. Annexation does not seem to be the most likely scenario in the near to medium term. For one, Western sanctions since 2014 and falling oil prices have taken a toll on the Russian economy and the Kremlin is unlikely to pursue such an openly confrontational path. Kondratenko and another Ukrainian analyst, Inna Vedernikova, argue that the aim of Russia is to keep these territories in medium-intensity war mode and under the Ukrainian flag but with near complete Russian control.[206] This lower-cost strategy could help Russia interfere in Ukrainian domestic affairs, torpedo Kiev's reforms, and hinder any plans to join the EU and NATO through the resulting instability and unresolved territorial boundaries. It is likely that other parts of Ukraine could become targets of conflict. Russia's interfering hand could reach Ukraine's Kharkiv, Zaporizhia, or Dnipropetrovsk region and even further, but at greater cost. Going forward the reality on the ground for Luhansk, Donetsk, and Crimea will likely resemble the no-man's-lands of Transnistria, South Ossetia, and Abkhazia, with limited rule of law and no international recognition.

In the case of Transnistria, the isolated territory's "independence" has never been recognized by Russia. In fact, Soviet President Mikhail Gorbachev annulled Transnistria's declaration of independence by a presidential decree in December 1990.[207] As the territory has remained isolated for a quarter of a century with Moscow as its sole supporter and protector, Russia holds all the cards of Transnistria's future in its hands. In March 2014, following the annexation of Crimea, the leadership of Transnistria submitted their application to join the Russian Federation, but have not received a response to date.[208] Transnistria's geographical position and lack of a border with Russia make it unlikely to become formally incorporated into the Russian Federation. However, this possibility cannot be excluded as Russia's Kaliningrad Oblast is also not connected territorially to the rest of the country. Nonetheless, formal annexation is not necessary for Russia's reimperialization aspirations, and de facto control suffices for Russia to dominate Transnistria and indirectly influence Moldova's foreign and domestic politics. The status quo in Transnistria as well as eastern Ukraine will continue to benefit organized crime and even terrorist organizations, as has been the case in South Ossetia and Abkhazia. According to the former Moldovan ambassador to the United States, Ceslav Ciobanu, Transnistria is rife with criminal activities such as "money laundering; contraband; and illicit trafficking of drugs, alcohol, tobacco, and weapons" which have made their way to other conflict zones, "falling into the hands of criminal and terrorist groups."[209]

South Ossetia and Abkhazia's "independence" has not received recognition in the international arena outside of Moscow's closest allies.[210] It is likely that in the years to come these breakaway territories will follow the Crimean example and be absorbed by Russia. Some signs are already present. On 24 November 2014 Russia and Abkhazia signed the Moscow-proposed Alliance and Integration Treaty, which aims to create joint defense and law enforcement structures as well as to integrate the region into Russia's economic, social protection, and health care systems.[211] In March 2015, South Ossetia signed a similar agreement and effectively handed over control of its border, military, and economy to Russia, while also creating a joint defense and security zone and integrating customs agencies.[212] It is possible that South Ossetia will merge with the Russian Federation's territory of North Ossetia, but the Abkhazians appear to be interested in maintaining at least some degree of independence. In October 2014, Aslan Basaria, a representative of the prominent Abkhazian media club Ainar, which focuses on ensuring cooperation between Abkhazia and Russia, offered a perspective that seems to reflect the position of Abkhazia's leadership, "I am deeply convinced that Abkhazia would be much more useful for Russia as an independent state. We need to simply develop the concept for the country having in mind the processes of integration to the Eurasian Economic Union."[213] Meanwhile, the Georgian government and Abkhazia's government in exile have been pursuing "Involvement without Recognition," a policy of public diplomacy toward the region without recognizing its independence. The policy aims for support and cooperation in health care and education. According to the chairman of the Supreme Council of Autonomous Republic of Abkhazia (in exile in Georgia), Elguja (Gia) Gvazava, "Today, strengthening public diplomacy is essential and it should be taken on the political level. We do not have any other chances. . . . If relations with the occupied territories will not be built, of course, frozen conflict will persist and we will have to wait for what the future will bring. . . . It must be acknowledged not only inside Georgia, but also on the international arena that if we forgo our nonrecognition policy, even by insignificant steps, we must realize that these territories will be lost forever."[214]

In sum, it seems possible that in the years to come Russia will consolidate the gains of its reimperialization trajectory by absorbing the breakaway territories of Ukraine, Georgia, and Moldova. However, it is more likely that Moscow will pursue an opportunistic, low-cost, high-return

strategy of maintaining these frozen conflicts and continue to use compatriots as a vehicle to achieve its foreign policy goals and thus make life
difficult for Kiev, Tbilisi, Chisinau, as well as for NATO and the EU. Specifically, the lack of territorial integrity of these states will hinder any
ambitions they may have for membership in those organizations. In the
end, annexation may not be the very end goal of Moscow despite the domestic appeal of rebuilding the Russian Empire. With annexation come
costs—isolation in the international community, the threat of sanctions
from the West, and a lack of legitimacy in international law. With frozen
conflicts, on the other hand, Moscow is still able to boast gains while the
torn-apart countries of Ukraine, Georgia, and Moldova shoulder many
costs.

CHAPTER FIVE

NATO's Achilles' Heel

THE BALTIC STATES

We continually raise questions about our compatriot situation in some European Union countries, specifically in the Baltic States, where the completely uncivilized perception of a person as "non-citizen without the rights and freedoms" still exists.

—*Vladimir Putin, 19 December 2013*

NOWHERE ARE THE RUSSIAN REIMPERIALIZATION TRAJECTORY and compatriot policies of greater concern for the current European post–Cold War order as in the Baltic States. The three Baltic countries of Estonia, Latvia, and Lithuania are unique among the former Soviet republics because they have carved out their own geopolitical destiny, joining the EU and NATO in 2004. In comparison with other new EU and NATO members such as Poland, Hungary, and the Czech Republic, however, the Baltic States are vulnerable to Russia's policies of "compatriot protection" because of their sizable populations of ethnic Russians and Russian speakers. Since the 1990s, all three Baltic States have been consistently targeted by Moscow's soft power, humanitarian and compatriot policies, information warfare, and, to some degree, its passportization efforts. Following Russia's annexation of Crimea in March 2014, its compatriot and information warfare policies gained further momentum in the Baltic States. Russia's shadow war in Ukraine also prompted discussions in the Baltic States and their allies of whether Russia would carry out a similar intervention in these NATO member states and thus challenge the alliance and its collective security guarantees provided by Article 5 of the NATO Treaty. Certainly, any success Moscow achieves in destabilizing Estonia's, Latvia's, or Lithuania's territorial integrity or fueling separatism either will elicit an effective response from NATO or will result in discrediting the authority of the alliance and in turn the entire international system built on its security guarantees. Indeed, some have argued that this is precisely Moscow's aim as it has notched up pressure on the Baltic States since Crimea's annexation.

While the three countries are often grouped together under the somewhat arbitrary "Baltic States" label due to their geographical position and history of Soviet occupation, they are in fact quite distinct. The northernmost, Estonia, located on the Gulf of Finland and the Baltic Sea, is a small country of little more than a million people, and shares more cultural and linguistic ties with Finland than Latvia and Lithuania. Its fairytale medieval capital of Tallinn was once a thriving city of the Hanseatic League. Today it is just a two-hour ferry ride from Helsinki, testimony to the country's geographical and cultural proximity to the Nordic countries. In fact, Estonia has spent much of the 2000s trying to position itself as a Nordic rather than a Baltic or certainly a post-Soviet country. Nonetheless, fifty years of Soviet rule has also left a mark on Estonia, with both Tallinn and an eastern part of the country now inhabited by many Russians and Russian speakers. Latvia, neighboring to the south, is slightly larger than Estonia with nearly two million inhabitants. It is sandwiched between two bodies of water: the Baltic Sea and the Gulf of Riga. Latvia's history was closely tied to that of Estonia when both states were part of German Livonia and their capitals part of the Hanseatic League. The dynamic capital, Riga, has a fine collection of Art Nouveau buildings and is reminiscent of other Scandinavian capitals. Today, though, Russian is heard as often as Latvian on the streets of Riga due to the presence of a sizable Russian minority. Linguistically and ethnically, Latvians have more in common with their southern neighbor, Lithuania, as both nations and their languages stem from ancient Baltic tribes. The southernmost Baltic country, Lithuania, boasts a long history of statehood that goes back to the Middle Ages. Most Lithuanians will proudly recount that in the fourteenth century the Lithuanian Grand Duchy was the largest state in Europe and included parts of present-day Latvia, Poland, Belarus, Ukraine, and Russia. In defense of their statehood following the Second World War, many Lithuanians resisted the Soviet occupation through partisan guerrilla warfare as late as 1953. This broad hostility toward the Soviet regime, coupled with fewer industrial jobs, have likely been the main reasons for Lithuania's smaller numbers of Soviet-era Russian immigrants than Latvia and Estonia.[1] The Baroque-style pastel-colored capital, Vilnius, is reminiscent of Italian cities; historically it has been a lively multicultural capital where Jews, Poles, Russians, Belarusians, and Ukrainians lived in harmony for centuries and today also has a sizable population of minorities.

All three Baltic States are affected by a factor that facilitates Russia's "compatriot protection": large, concentrated populations of ethnic Russians and Russian speakers residing on the borders with Russia. Estonia and Latvia have particularly large ethnic Russian minorities, totaling about 24 percent and 27 percent of the general population respectively, while Lithuania's Russian population falls just under 6 percent. Percentages of Russian speakers, rather than ethnic Russians, are even higher since Soviet-era Russification policies caused other Baltic minorities such as Poles, Ukrainians, Belarusians, and people of mixed ethnic origin often to adopt Russian as their native language. Latvia's Russian speakers make up nearly 34 percent of the population, Estonia's approximately 30 percent, and Lithuania's almost 8 percent.[2] While Baltic Russian speakers may not identify themselves as Russians, they matter greatly in the reimperialization trajectory. First, because Russian "compatriot" policies target not only Russian citizens or Russians but a much broader group that has any cultural or linguistic affinity toward Russia. Second, because Russian speakers often rely on Russian media and are thus more receptive to the Kremlin's viewpoints and policies.

Over the past decades Russia has maintained political, economic, and social ties with the Baltic Russians and Russophones, and in particular, its humanitarian and compatriot policies have evolved beyond softer means of influence toward passportization and more muscular information warfare. Despite their NATO and EU membership, the Baltic States possibly represent the second set of post-Soviet states that have experienced the most aggressive efforts of Russian reimperialization. Unlike the more authoritarian Central Asian states, the open and democratic Baltic governments have had less capacity to counter many Russian policies. Likewise, the Baltic States have faced much more aggressive rhetoric and actions from Moscow than Russia's traditional ally states of Belarus and Armenia. Initially, the main source of tension between Moscow and the Balts has been Estonia's and Latvia's nonautomatic citizenship poli-

Significant Russian speaking populations

IDA-VIRU Administrative unit

Tallinn
■ Capital

Narva
● City with Russian speakers

MAP 4. Distribution of Russian speakers across the Baltic States. In Estonia and
Latvia the shaded regions represent high-density Russian-speaking populations:
80 percent in Ida-Viru county, 36 percent in Harju county, 40 percent in Riga district,
and 55 percent in Latgale region. In comparison, the shaded regions in Lithuania
indicate relatively lower-density Russian-speaking population of around 20 percent
in Vilnius municipality, nearly 18 percent in Šalčininkai municipality, 17 percent in
Švenčionys municipality, 28 percent in Klaipėda municipality, and around 22 percent
in Zarasai municipality. Map drawn by Giedrė Tamašauskaitė

cies following independence—policies on which Moscow has been able to capitalize. Hence, citizenship policies continue to matter not only for the relatively small but persistent proportion of Baltic Russians and Russophones without citizenship, but also as a condition that creates a space for Russian influence and amplifies the effectiveness of Moscow's passportization policies. This chapter will assess the success and failures of Russia's policies by drawing on past examples such as the 2007 Bronze Soldier riots in Tallinn and calls for separatism since 2014, and compare them to the cases of Ukraine, Georgia, Moldova, and other post-Soviet states. To understand the complexity of the dynamics faced by populations of the Baltic States, it is helpful to start with a snapshot of Baltic Russians and Russian speakers and their views.

PORTRAITS OF RUSSIAN SPEAKERS

Neither Baltic Russian speakers nor ethnic Russians are uniform groups, but vary from country to country, from generation to generation, and in their socio-economic environments. Here I will focus on individuals born following the fall of the Soviet Union and after Baltic independence who are symptomatic of the young generation of Baltic Russian "compatriots." Certainly they are more integrated into Baltic societies and much more likely to perceive themselves as Estonian, Latvian, and Lithuanian than their parents or grandparents who immigrated during the Soviet era. They offer nuanced perspectives on their relationship to Russia. On one hand, they shun the idea of Moscow's protection of Russian compatriots along the model of Crimea and eastern Ukraine. On the other hand, some are open to Russian cultural support or even to citizenship and passports. Having spent their entire lives in the Baltic States, they do not necessarily identify with the Russian state. However, particularly in Latvia and Estonia, they do feel the shortcomings of societal integration and insufficient political representation based on their ethnic identity. The profiles here offer a glimpse into the viewpoints and identities of Baltic Russian compatriots, rather than providing a full scientific survey.

Meet Darya from Riga, where the Baltics' largest Russian-speaking population resides.[3] This articulate master's student in Middle Eastern studies is of Russian and Polish descent. Born and raised in Latvia, she considers herself a Russian speaker. However, she shies away from the label of "Russian compatriot" because "I have never been to Russia and

I don't know much about Russian culture in particular." While Darya is skeptical of the support Moscow could garner among Latvia's Russian speakers, in her opinion the philosophical basis of Latvia's nation-state is problematic for other ethnicities: "The biggest problem in my opinion is Latvia's view of Russian-speaking people as 'others.' It makes Russian-speaking people feel alienated and not wanted in the society. Another problem is that Latvia might give citizenship to Russian-speaking people, but they can never be called 'Latvians' because Latvia strictly differentiates between citizenship and nationality. My citizenship is Latvian, but my nationality can be only Russian or Polish. It shows that the Latvian country was formed from and for one nation—Latvians—making other ethnic groups 'citizens' and not Latvians." While classification by "nationality" among Baltic citizens is a leftover from the Soviet era, it creates tensions in contemporary societies. Darya also argues that Baltic Russian speakers do not need Russia's protection and that the integration issue could be solved domestically. Nonetheless, she is supportive of Latvia's noncitizens acquiring Russian citizenship based on their ethnic ties to the latter country.

In addition to the question of language and identity, political leanings also play a role in determining Russian speakers' views on the compatriot issue. Artyom, a doctoral student from Riga, considers himself a Russian speaker but bristles at the notion of being called Russia's compatriot: "No, why should I? I'm a Latvian citizen and I do not think of myself somehow involved in Russia's political project. Besides, I think that Russia is rolling into the darkness these days, and I cannot accept on any level their contemporary aggressive national rhetoric."[4] On the question of Putin's protection of Latvia's Russian speakers in general, Artyom is also adamant. "Protection from what?—Gays and freedom from censorship? All enemies of Baltic Russian speakers are imaginary. Russian national rhetoric uses these images to produce divergence in multiethnic societies." Like the majority of the Baltic Russian people interviewed, Artyom also believes that separatism is impossible in the Baltic States because it would lack the support of the majority of Baltic Russians and because of the states' NATO membership. However, Artyom warns: "But it doesn't mean Russia doesn't want to increase its political influence in the inner politics of Baltic States through the so-called 'Russian parties,' which mask pro-Putin beliefs behind the 'language question.'"

Nadia is an accountant from Riga in her forties and represents the middle-aged generation of Latvia's Russian minority.[5] Born in a Russian family during the Soviet era, she only learned the basics of the Latvian language as an adult, in contrast to most younger Baltic Russians who are fluent in Latvian or Estonian. Although Nadia identifies herself as Russian, she does not consider herself as a compatriot, making a sharp distinction between Russian culture and politics, saying that "I do not sympathize with politics, I treat politics critically. As a native Russian speaker, I love Russian culture and feel my belonging to it." When she was asked whether Russian speakers have legitimate grievances, she stated that "generally speaking no, but it was not nice not to grant citizenship for people who were born in Latvia." (However, it is worth mentioning that the 1998 Citizenship Law amendments have provided the opportunity for descendants of noncitizens to obtain Latvian citizenship. If such a descendant is a child under fifteen, then the parents have to submit an application form; descendants between fifteen and eighteen years old can simply submit an application on their own initiative and after passing the Latvian language test obtain citizenship.)[6] Darya was also skeptical of Russia's protection, saying that "the law, which is based on common human values, should protect the people and not political interests."

Anton is a Russian-speaking university student from Tallinn and considers Estonia to be his home.[7] He shuns the notion of being defined as a "Russian compatriot" and argues that "I do not consider myself as a compatriot, because apart from Russian language, nothing ties me to Russia," and adds that he has "sworn allegiance to Estonia." When asked if he thinks that Russian speakers in Estonia have legitimate grievances, he was quick to respond: "What a provocative question.... I'm fine." However, he wittily added: "The ones who do all the complaining do not do anything. At school they needed to learn [the Estonian language], but not drink in the alleys." For those Russian speakers who say they need Russia's protection, he provided a short but firm answer: "If they think they need Russia's protection, so please . . . luggage, station, Russia."

Yelena, a schoolgirl from Estonia, is also a fine example of the intricate Russian-Estonian dynamics.[8] She emphasizes that while her mother tongue is Russian, this does not make her a Russian compatriot. "I was born in Estonia," she explains. "It is my homeland." She is skeptical that

Russian speakers in Estonia have genuine grievances, and suggests that "people imagine some kind of problems."

In Lithuania, sentiments are similar. Alisa is a young professional born and raised in Lithuania in a Russian family.[9] Having undergone primary schooling in the Russian language and later Lithuanian university-level education, she now works for an American multinational company. Her Lithuanian speech is a bit halting and she admits that she feels more at ease with English than with Lithuanian. She considers carefully the notion of "compatriot" and concludes that according to the strict definition of the term, she is indeed a "Russian compatriot." However, subjectively and emotionally she has trouble identifying with the label: "Russians who were born and grew up in Lithuania differ a lot from Russia's Russians. Mostly they are culturally and mentally closer to Lithuanians, even though they perceive themselves as Russians." When considering the potential grievances of Russian speakers in Lithuania, Alisa notes: "If we omit the fact that there is one obviously predominant anti-Russian line in the public sphere that makes you feel uncomfortable if you are Russian, there are no grievances. Some examples of discrimination can be met with in Lithuanian society (e.g. while searching for a job), however they are not numerous. As there are no grievances, no [Russian] protection is needed. However some support [from Russia], especially in cultural and educational spheres, would be very useful."

Many of those who are often simplistically grouped among Lithuania's Russian speakers in fact harbor complex identities. Yaroslav, an electrician in his early twenties, lives with his Polish-Russian family in his native village in southeast Lithuania.[10] He grew up speaking Russian but because he received his education in Lithuanian he is also fluent in that language. Because only his father is Russian-born and his mother is Polish, he considers himself partly a Russian "compatriot" but mainly a true Russian "patriot" because he admires Russian culture and history. Yaroslav does not think that today Lithuania's Russians or Russophones need Moscow's protection, but he believes that in general "Russia should protect Russians, because every nation must protect 'its people' and it does not matter in which country they are based. Even military protection is needed sometimes, it depends on that situation . . . for instance, in the case of Crimea, I think it was necessary." Ultimately, Yaroslav supports Russia's recent policies in eastern Ukraine and Crimea since "many Russian speakers and ethnic Russians live there" as well as the Russian leadership: "I support Vladimir Putin, because he rules a huge and strong country, therefore he must be categorical and strong."

Nataliya is an art teacher in her fifties and represents the older generation of Lithuania's Russian speakers.[11] Born and raised in the country in a predominantly Lithuanian environment, she identifies herself as a Russian-speaking Ukrainian and does not consider herself a Russian compatriot. She does not see any legitimate complaints of Russian speakers in Lithuania and explains: "I used to hear complaints and whining from my Russian-speaking friends and acquaintances. However, the only people who have grievances are the ones who are not doing anything and those who do not try to understand the nation with which they live." Still, when asked about the recent events in Ukraine, she sides unequivocally with Moscow: "Crimea historically is Russian," and "I am myself Ukrainian but I feel shame for the Ukrainians who staged a massacre in Ukraine."

The older Baltic Russian and Russophone generation, while not outright calling for Russia's military protection, tends to have less straightforwardly skeptical views of Russia. For instance, Alyona, a sixty-four-year-old pensioner who lives in Tartu, Estonia, and identifies herself as Russian and a Russian speaker, would welcome some support from Moscow and nonmilitary protection: "I would like to see protection from Russia's side. Maybe Russia should conduct negotiations and defend Russian citizens in Estonia because discrimination still is clearly visible."[12] She is also dissatisfied with the Estonian government and believes that a Crimean scenario is feasible in the border city of Narva: ". . . people are not satisfied. Many people leave Narva because of unemployment and the Estonian government is not able to provide work places for people."

Lidiya, a seventy-year-old retired biology teacher of Russian origin who now lives in the Estonian city of Kohtla-Järve in Ida-Viru county, has had difficulty integrating into Estonian society because of the language barrier and is critical of the fact that state-funded education is increasingly moving toward instruction in the Estonian language: "We aren't allowed to teach our children in their mother tongue, which makes the educational process more difficult. A teacher who was teaching in Russian his entire life now should teach children who hardly speak Estonian in the national language."[13] Also, when asked whether Russia should help its compatriots solve these problems, she noted that "it should be solved from the inside, but Russia could push them more to do this."

At first glance, the picture of the younger Baltic Russian speaker is not one that lends itself very easily to Moscow's manipulation. None of those interviewed, even among the older generation, called for Russian military protection in their home country. Nor do any support separatism outright, as in Ukraine or Georgia. However, based on Moscow's definition of compatriots, most Baltic Russians and Russian speakers would qualify for Russia's protection based on its laws and compatriot policies, even if they do not identify themselves as compatriots. The interviews with the younger generation also paint a more optimistic picture than that of the sentiments of the Russian minorities as a whole. According to Estonian political scientist Raivo Vetik, who studies Estonia's social integration issues, many Russians and Russian speakers, especially of the older generation, still feel a number of grievances.[14] Laurynas Kasčiūnas, of Lithuania's Eastern European Study Centre, also argues that while local Russians or Russian speakers tend generally to be ambivalent about Russia's policies, during times of tension and crisis they tend to rally behind Moscow.[15] This is not surprising, given the receptiveness of most Baltic Russians and Russophones to Moscow's points of view and propaganda. Meanwhile, manufacturing propaganda to support Russia's foreign policy interests is an important and frequently practiced aspect of the reimperialization trajectory.

RUSSIA'S MOTIVES AND INTERESTS

When the Baltic States gained NATO and EU membership ten years ago, the dual accession was believed to have resolved their security dilemma vis-à-vis the regional hegemon, Russia. Would Moscow risk a showdown with the West by stoking tensions or destabilizing EU and NATO member states? Certainly, NATO membership and its Article 5 accord the Baltic States a much stronger geopolitical position than that of Ukraine, Georgia, and Moldova. In fact, before Russia's war in Ukraine, a territorial assault on the Baltic States seemed implausible even though Moscow's efforts to maintain influence in the Baltic region were undoubted. What are Moscow's motives in seeking, if not reimperialization, then dominance in the Baltic States? Certainly the compatriots are only a means to a broader end.

In addition to the perennial ideological drive to unite Russians and Russian speakers of the near abroad under the Russian flag, Moscow has a number of historical, security, political, and economic motives to reincorporate the Baltic States into its "empire" or at least its sphere of influence.[16] Russia pursued imperialization and Russification of the Baltic territories since the eighteenth century. Its power grab began in 1721 under Peter the Great, when it established control over some territories of modern-day Estonia and Latvia.[17] During the reign of Catherine the Great, Lithuania was incorporated into the Russian Empire as a result of the partitions of the Polish-Lithuanian Commonwealth in 1772, 1793, and 1795.[18] In all three Baltic States, Russian imperialization resulted in a clampdown on national identity, with the printing of books banned except in the Cyrillic (rather than the native Latin) alphabet. Colonization by Russian officials and immigrants followed.[19] The Soviet era saw a similar effort for Russification as well as dramatic population loss and an influx of Russian and Russian-speaking immigrants. The deportations, evacuations, flight, and executions amid German and Soviet expansionism resulted in the loss of about 20 percent of the population in Estonia, 30 percent in Latvia, and 15 percent in Lithuania between 1941 and 1945.[20] In fact, during the Soviet occupation 10 percent of the entire adult Baltic population was either deported to other Soviet or Russian territories or sent to prison camps.[21] In their place arrived the Soviet military and their families as well as Russians and other nationalities to work in industrial jobs.

In the post–Cold War era, Estonia, Latvia, and Lithuania remain of strategic importance to Russia. The Baltic territories serve as a buffer zone for Moscow, between its territories and those of Western Europe. Before 2004 they used to serve as a buffer zone against NATO; thus, the Baltic accession to the alliance was one that Russia contested vigorously.[22] Historically, the Baltic States also served a buffering role: Estonia and Latvia protected against Scandinavian and Germanic invasions while Lithuania's territory separated Russia from the Napoleonic armies. Today, the territory of Belarus and Lithuania separates the highly militarized Russian enclave of Kaliningrad from the rest of Russia by some 225 miles. The tiny enclave is of paramount strategic importance for Moscow, because it houses the fifty-six-warship-strong Baltic Fleet at the port of Baltiysk, which is the country's only ice-free European port and the home of the Iskander-M nuclear-capable missile complexes.[23] The early 1990s saw diplomatic tensions between Vilnius and Moscow as Russia unsuccessfully tried to negotiate a corridor through Lithuania to supply its forces in Kaliningrad, and bilateral transit agreements were signed only in 1993 and 1994.[24] Needing to finalize its border demarcation with Russia for EU accession, Lithuania had to give, and in early 2003 it agreed to concessions that made passage through Lithuania significantly easier for Russian military traffic, which nonetheless remains highly regulated.[25]

Russia's economic interests in the Baltic States are equally important. Like Crimea, which serves as the base of Russia's Black Sea Fleet and a pathway to the Mediterranean, the Baltic States contain ice-free ports and constitute a window to the West, which has made them targets of Russia's expansionism since the time of Peter the Great.[26] Despite increasing Baltic trade and ties with the EU, the Baltic and Russian economies still have many legacy links. The ports of the Baltic States have historically served to transport Russian oil and oil products to European markets. For instance, throughout the 1990s until the opening of an oil terminal in the Russian port of Primorsk in 2001, Latvia's Ventspils Nafta operated as the second largest exporting terminal for Russian oil, and the largest exporter outside Russian territory.[27] Since the 2000s, Russia has directed its energy flows away from the Baltic States by building up its own ports, terminals, and new pipeline systems on the northern Baltic and North Sea.[28] Nonetheless, Baltic territories and ports still continue to serve as transit routes for Western goods that Russia imports.

While generally the Baltic States are energy-poor countries, Estonia's Ida-Viru county is energy-rich. It is located in the eastern part of the country near the border with Russia, nestled between the Gulf of Finland and Lake Peipus, and is predominantly inhabited by Russians and Russian speakers. The region's large deposits of shale oil are used for heating and electricity production, meeting 80 percent of Estonia's electricity needs. For a country with few natural resources that is still 100 percent dependent on Russian gas, Ida-Viru shale oil is of highest strategic importance, but like eastern Ukraine's coal mines it could be a tempting target for separatist forces or Moscow.

Finally, Russia's ideologically and strategically driven view of the Baltic States as part of its sphere of influence, despite their membership in NATO and the EU, is another potential motive for Moscow's softer

reimperialization efforts. For instance, in 2008 President Dmitry Medvedev asserted Russia's right to "privileged interests" in its neighboring
states and "[c]ertainly the regions bordering [Russia]."[29] This Russian viewpoint is problematic. On one hand, Moscow often treats the Baltic States
as part of the post-Soviet space, the "near abroad," and as new states first
established in 1991.[30] Thus in certain cases (as in its compatriot policies), Russia seems to pursue similar policies toward the Baltic States as
in regard to the CIS states, their different status notwithstanding.[31] Nonetheless, EU and NATO membership precludes Russia from openly dom-
inating the Baltic States or carrying out military aggression as it would
in the current and former CIS countries. This explains why Russia mostly
applies soft power and softer coercive measures to the Baltic States.

SOFT POWER

Since the early 1990s much of Russia's soft power effort in the Baltic
States has been tied to its insistence upon its presumptive right to maintain a guiding influence in the region. Much of Russia's existing influence in the Baltics is inherent, the result of tsarist and Soviet legacies as
much as current policies. Russia's soft power is greatly amplified by the
fact that the Russian diaspora and Russian and Soviet culture have been
part of the social matrix for more than half a century.[32] In recent years,
Russia's use of soft power has been best exemplified by the extensive use
of Kremlin-friendly networks of influence in the Baltic cultural, economic, and political sectors, often involving loyal interest groups and decision makers in order to advance its agenda.[33] Though Russia's soft power
instruments overlap and include various issue areas, the principal vehicles in the Baltic States have been the Russian language, the Orthodox
Church, culture, and sports, as well as business and political ties.

The Russian language remains an important tool of Russian influence as most of the Baltic population educated before the collapse of the
Soviet Union speak Russian as their first foreign language. In Latvia and
Estonia, where Russians and Russophones are numerous, the Russian
language is even more prevalent. However, since the 1990s there has
been a decline in the popularity of the Russian language among the non-
Russian Balts. In a seeming response to this decline and to support the
Russian and Russian-speaking minorities, in 2008 the Russian state–
sponsored Russkiy Mir Foundation opened a Russian-language center

in Estonia, two in Latvia, and by 2009 one in Lithuania. Russkiy Mir's activities seemingly go beyond the simple promotion of language and culture in the Baltic States. The Estonian security police has indicated that members of the "former Soviet intelligence cadre are active within the Estonian Chapter" of the Russkiy Mir Foundation, suggesting that the foundation also works to advance Moscow's interests in the Baltics.[34] Since the mid-2000s Moscow has also actively sought to promote exchanges and education opportunities in Russia for Russian compatriots.[35] For instance, the Russian Ministry of Education, Culture, and Science reserves more than ninety scholarships for graduates of Estonian schools to study in Russian universities.[36] However, in the Baltic States the success of such policies has been rather insubstantial as the vast majority of the Baltic youth, both Russians and the titular nations, choose to study either at home or in EU institutions and opt to study English rather than Russian.

The Russian Orthodox Church has served as an instrument of Russia's soft power to varying degrees across the Baltic States. In nominally Protestant Estonia, where religion plays a small part in most people's lives, the Orthodox Church has emerged as the biggest religious group and mostly includes the Russian minority. In Latvia the Orthodox Church is the third largest denomination, following Lutheranism and Catholicism.[37] The Estonian, the Latvian, and the smaller Lithuanian Orthodox Church all answer directly to the Moscow Patriarchate. The local priests and their preaching are perceived to be politicized and heavily influenced by Moscow, suggesting another manner that Kremlin's policies can be promoted on the ground in the Baltic States.[38] Sometimes they focus on social issues. In Estonia, for example, the Orthodox Church lobbied against the country's gender-neutral draft law on cohabitation.[39] The traditional views espoused by the Russian Orthodox Church and the Russian government have to a degree also found appeal among segments of the Baltic titular nationalities. In Lithuania, some people disenchanted with liberal values promoted in the West and the EU have found appealing Putin's portrayal of Russia as the bastion of traditional Christian culture.[40] There is also a growing tendency by Moscow to leverage the natural societal tensions in the Baltic States (and Europe more generally), to drive further divisions between supporters of liberal values and those of traditional values whom Russia has courted.[41] This is particularly noticeable among some ethnic Lithuanians with competing opinions regarding the notion of nationality. As Kasčiūnas explains, "some people hold that the Lithuanian nationality should be pro-Western, others argue that it should be pro-Russian, and the third group argues that it should be neither pro-Western nor pro-Russian," and within these divisions there has emerged a "significant number of Lithuanians who embrace a Russian mentality."[42]

Both Russian high and popular culture remain salient for various generations of the broad Baltic population but particularly for Russians and Russian speakers. Russian cultural events are primarily apolitical, though they often receive funding and support from both the Russian government and local businesses interests. In Latvia, which is perhaps the greatest recipient and consumer of Russian culture among the Baltic States, since 2004 the cultural center House of Moscow has been a key player in promoting Russian culture and is funded by the Moscow city government. Other important mechanisms are the government-supported cultural festivals "Days of Russian Culture in Latvia" and "Days of Latvian Culture in Russia," both launched in 2007 following a détente in Latvian-Russian relations. Following the success of the 2007 and 2008 festivals, Russia expanded its cultural presence in Latvia with additional cultural festivals.[43] Russian high culture events are often organized and sponsored by local businesses that are owned by ethnic Russians or work with Russian markets. For example, Vladimir Romanov, a Lithuanian businessman of Russian origin and the former owner of the now defunct Ūkio Bank of Lithuania used to organize an annual high-profile Russian cultural charity event and also owned the legendary Lithuanian basketball team Kauno Žalgiris.[44]

Sport is another means to reinforce Russia's soft power in the Baltics. Since 2008 Russia's Continental Hockey League has united teams from the former USSR, and the Latvian team Dinamo Riga, which is sponsored by the Russian gas distributor Itera, is an active participant in the league.[45] Elite basketball teams from the Baltics also participate in the Russian-organized VTB United Basketball League, sponsored by the Russian state–owned VTB bank. The president of the league is Sergey Ivanov—an FSB official, former deputy prime minister of Russia, and a close aide to Putin.[46] However, since 2014 Lithuanian basketball teams ceased to participate in this league in response to Russia's aggression in

Ukraine, though Latvian and Estonian teams continued to play.[47] In the past, some Baltic athletes have chosen to play for Russian teams or to train in Russia where they sometimes receive better funding.

Russian economic and business ties also exert soft power on the Baltic States. Since their independence, the Baltic States have been significantly reliant on Russian sources of energy: most notably, they were 100 percent dependent on Russian gas. As a result, through various nontransparent payment schemes and direct threats the Kremlin has been able to build up significant economic and energy influence, coercion, and lobby structures in the Baltics.[48] Gazprom and other Russian energy companies have used various lobbying channels to convince favorable politicians, NGOs, and local communities to hinder diversification projects away from Russian energy.[49] Following decades of energy vulnerability, Lithuania launched a new liquefied natural gas (LNG) terminal in Klaipėda in 2014 that will for the first time ever give the country access to non-Russian sources of gas via sea routes rather than via Gazprom-owned pipelines. Nonetheless, due to geographic proximity and commercial considerations, in the near term the Baltic States will likely remain highly dependent on Russian oil and gas.[50]

Ultimately, looking back since the 1990s, ebbs and flows in Russia's soft power influence over the Baltic countries in general and the Russian and Russian-speaking diaspora in particular can be discerned. It fluctuated with global developments, the economic performance of Russia versus the West, and Baltic domestic conditions. For example, during the global financial crisis of 2008–9 that highly impacted the Baltic States, Russia and its leadership were more positively regarded by a broader segment of the population than during the boom years of the early and mid-2000s, which were fueled by optimism over economic growth and EU and NATO accession. In 2014, Russia's annexation of Crimea and war in eastern Ukraine has raised skepticism and concern among the Baltic publics. Russia's influence over the Baltic Russians and Russophones, which the Kremlin sought to co-opt and support through various humanitarian and compatriot policies, has also not been static.

HUMANITARIAN POLICIES

Russia's so-called humanitarian policies emerged vis-à-vis the Baltic States shortly after the dissolution of the USSR. The newfound independence

of the three states resulted in sizable numbers mostly of Soviet-era immigrants from Russia and other Soviet republics losing their Soviet citizenships and needing new passports and in many regards new identities.
The 1991 decision by Riga and the 1992 decision by Tallinn not to grant
automatic citizenship to Soviet-era immigrants in Estonia and Latvia
has been one of the most divisive issues with Moscow and the source of
arguably legitimate criticism of Baltic minority policies. While the law
did not single out ethnic Russians or Russian speakers, many of these
groups had immigrated during the Soviet era and in practice were directly impacted. Estonia and Latvia's noncitizens were issued so-called
alien passports, which significantly restricted their civic rights compared to full citizens.[51] The motives for such a decision were strongly
tied to Estonia's and Latvia's "doctrine of continuation" of their statehood
and their citizenship status. Essentially it meant that all Estonia or Latvia's inhabitants and their descendants who were citizens before the
Soviet occupation (irrespective of their nationality) were automatically
granted citizenship, while those who had immigrated during the Soviet
era (irrespective of their nationality) had to apply for citizenship.[52] It is
highly likely that the Estonian and Latvian governments opted for this
distinction in an effort to prevent the titular majorities from being outvoted
by the Russian minorities on issues involving the strategic direction
of the state such as independence, EU rather than CIS integration, and
NATO membership. Russians and Russian speakers were also feared as a
potential fifth column.[53] Meanwhile, Lithuania, having a much smaller
Russian minority, granted automatic citizenship to all its residents.

The citizenship laws and Russian minority rights immediately became a source of contention during the negotiations between the Baltics
and Moscow over the withdrawal of some 120,000 Soviet troops in the
first years of independence. Similarly to the case of Moldova, the Russian side repeatedly linked the withdrawal of Soviet military to the well-
being of Russians and Russian speakers and demanded legislation
safeguarding their rights.[54] In October 1992, President Boris Yeltsin announced a halt to the troop withdrawal due to the treatment of the Russian minorities in the Baltic States, though the real reason for the halt
was reportedly the shortage of housing in Russia for the returning military families.[55] Likewise, as we saw, in the 1990s Moscow had little
interest in resettling the Russian diaspora (including the families of

servicemen) back to the motherland. Yet Yeltsin said he was "profoundly concerned over numerous infringements of the rights of Russian speakers," and demanded treaties regulating the troop withdrawal and guaranteeing "measures of social protection" for the servicemen and their families.[56] Yeltsin also emphasized that Russian-Baltic relations would "largely depend on the situation of the Russian-speaking population."[57] In the year 1994, referring to the citizenship laws in Latvia, Yeltsin argued that "Instead of taking the path of aligning its policy with the high world and European human-rights standards, Latvia chose to divide its residents into first-rate and second-rate people.... It legalized the discrimination of people on the basis of their ethnicity."[58] Yeltsin's rhetoric aside, there was little evidence that the Russian minorities were discriminated against in the Baltic States, and apart from the controversial Estonian and Latvian citizenship laws there were no systemic policies that could be perceived as targeting Russians or Russian speakers.[59]

Moscow's policies toward the passportless populations drove its "humanitarian" efforts in the region. For much of the 1990s Russia tried to enlist international organizations such as the Council of Europe, the Organization for Security and Cooperation in Europe, and the United Nations to support the rights of the Baltic Russian minorities. Following the grossly overstated Russian accusations of human rights abuses in Latvia and Estonia, international human rights observers and several fact-finding missions, visiting at the invitation of the Estonian and Latvian governments—notably those led by Ibrahima Fall, the director of the United Nations Center of Human Rights, in 1992, and by Max von der Stoel, High Commissioner for Ethnic Minorities of the Commission on Security and Cooperation in Europe in 1993—have found no systematic human rights violations in Estonia or Latvia.[60] On the eve of Estonia's admission to the Council of Europe in 1993, Russia even objected to this on grounds of Estonian human rights violations, but this proved to be an embarrassing failure.[61] In reality, many of these Russian "humanitarian" policies were used tactically to discredit the Baltic States in the eyes of their European partners and to hinder their efforts to join the EU rather than assist the Russian minorities.[62] Despite changes in Estonian and Latvian citizenship laws in the late 1990s and the reduced scope of the problem, the citizenship issue still persists in both countries. Though the numbers of noncitizens are relatively small and in decline, they persist mainly among the older generation which cannot or choose not to meet the citizenship requirement of passing a Latvian or Estonian language exam. In Estonia some 7 percent of the entire population, mostly Russians and Russophones, do not have Estonian citizenship and in Latvia around 13 percent—a total of more than 300,000 across both states.[63] Besides tensions with Moscow, Estonia's and Latvia's citizenship policies have had notable negative long-term consequences, including creating divisions in society and blocking effective integration of ethnic Russians and Russian speakers.[64] They have also arguably hindered creating states on the basis of civic nationalism in place of ethnic nationalism.[65] Citizenship issues have also spawned security concerns by creating a space for Russian influence and facilitating Moscow's policy of handing out Russian citizenship.

COMPATRIOT AND PASSPORTIZATION POLICIES

Over the past decades Russia has expended great efforts to maintain political, economic, and social ties with its "compatriots" in the Baltic States. Numerous cultural, academic, veteran, and other organizations, associations, communities, unions, funds, and centers in the Baltic States are oriented to local ethnic Russians and Russian speakers (61 in Estonia, 81 in Latvia, 97 in Lithuania), many of which are funded by Russkiy Mir.[66] In Estonia, the majority of compatriot organizations are managed by the Coordinating Union of Russian Compatriots in Estonia, and a large share of their activities focuses on the initiation and media coverage of events linked to the Great Patriotic War and the role of the Soviet army in Estonia during the war, such as the anniversary of Tallinn's liberation and Russian Navy Day. Special attention is also paid to detailed coverage of the situation of those of the Russian and Russian-speaking population who cannot obtain Estonian citizenship because of inability to comply with the language requirements.[67] The head of the Coordinating Union of Russian Compatriots in Latvia, Viktor Gushchin, lists among his chief concerns the protection and promotion of the Russian language's status as a "native language" of Latvia and the promotion of political and civil rights of the Russian-speaking population, while also expressing hopes that the Russian Federation would eventually state its firm position toward these issues.[68] In Lithuania, the 2011 Congress of Russian Compatriots defined the aim of Russian compatriot organizations as, first and foremost, maintaining Russian cultural identity (especially among the young Russian generation) and widening access to the Russian information space.[69] As Vytis Jurkonis, a lecturer in international relations at Vilnius University, notes, "these organizations and their activities are constantly questioning the success of the post-communist transition, seeding mistrust in the public institutions and playing with nostalgia for the Soviet past."[70] Ainārs Lerhis, chairman of the board of the Centre for East European Policy Studies in Riga, explained that "Russia's institutions are making no effort to conceal their attempts to promote an opposite integration of the Russian speaking section of the Latvian population in the direction of Moscow in the broader context of reintegration of the entire Post-Soviet territory under Russian dominance."[71] The Russian-Ukrainian conflict has made some of the more radical Baltic compatriot organizations increasingly vocal and aggressive. Andrei Zarenkov, head of the "antifascist" committee in Estonia, says that "now they pay attention to us. They started to speak more carefully while trying to avoid hurting our feelings. They are afraid we will follow the Donbas scenario. Northeastern Estonia is the same as southeastern Ukraine."[72] Another member of an Estonian "antifascist" organization, Nochnoy Dozor (Night Watch), Maksim Reva, supports this statement by claiming that Putin's position on Russkiy Mir and Moscow's readiness to protect Russian compatriots has been a great inspiration among Russian communities in the Baltic States. Sergei Dmitriev, head of the Union of Russians in Lithuania, says that the Crimean annexation has been interpreted as the people's will to self-determination and that Kiev's behavior in eastern Ukraine has deeply troubled Russians in Lithuania.[73]

Russian compatriot support has not been all cultural and linguistic. Moscow encourages Baltic Russian and Russian-speaking youths to participate in paramilitary camps where they receive military and informational warfare training as well as psychological preparation. For instance, in the 2010s high-school students from Russian-language schools in Estonia, Latvia, and Lithuania were traveling to the paramilitary camp Soyuz (Union—as in Soviet Union).[74] One former participant, Lithuanian high-school student Maksim Smechov, subsequently joined Russia's Ryazan Airborne Senior Command Academy.[75] Another Russian compatriot policy, that of diaspora resettlement, launched in 2006 has had limited success in the Baltic States despite Moscow's allegations of abuses and discrimination against the region's Russian minorities. Resettlement was most popular in Latvia where some 770 persons moved to Russia between 2007 and 2014.[76] In Lithuania in the same period, only 190 Russians repatriated through the program.[77] In Estonia in 2007–9, only some 20–37 persons chose to repatriate.[78] To get a better idea of Russian compatriot and passportization policies and the Baltic Russian and Russian-speaking populations that they target, however, it is necessary to look at Estonia, Latvia, and Lithuania one by one.

Estonia

Estonia's sizable ethnic Russian minority is concentrated in the capital, Tallinn, and Ida-Viru county, and comprises 24 percent of the country's population, or around 315,000 people. Tallinn's ethnic Russians number more than 150,000 and make up about 37 percent of its population.[79] Tallinn's Russian speakers are an even larger group, comprising 46 percent of the population, or about 200,000 people.[80] As a result, left-leaning political parties favored by the Russian and Russophone minority have long dominated Tallinn's local politics. Since independence, three mayors of Tallinn have belonged to the Centre Party, which counts 75 percent of ethnic non-Estonians as its supporters. In 2004 the party signed an undisclosed cooperation agreement with Russia's pro-Kremlin United Russia party.[81] The current mayor, Edgar Savisaar, is also the "face" of the Centre Party. The burly ethnic Estonian, who has served as mayor from 2001 to 2004 and from 2007 to the present, has become a somewhat controversial fixture on Tallinn's political scene. In 2011 he was investigated by the Estonian authorities for being an "agent of influence" for Moscow and named a "security threat" by Estonia's security police.[82] He allegedly received €1.5 million in party funding from a Russian NGO run by Vladimir Yakunin, the head of Russian Railways and a former KGB officer. While Savisaar's defense was that the monies were to be used for building a Russian Orthodox church in Tallinn, the timing of the donation (ahead of the parliamentary election of 2011) raised doubts. Though in the end no legal action was taken against Savisaar, who has retained his post of mayor, the public and the media remain critical. Overall, however, since the 1990s outright pro-Russian political parties and movements have gained little success in Estonian politics.[83] The only time a party representing ethnic Russian interests got into the national parliament was in 1995 when the Russian Party in Estonia received nearly 6 percent of the votes.[84] By 2015, most of the ethnic Russian or Russian-speaking politicians had either quit their careers or joined larger political parties without any specific ethnic delineations.

Ida-Viru county, where Russian passportization policies have been most successful, possibly has even greater implications for the Russian-Estonian relations. Here ethnic Russians number nearly 73 percent of the population while the ethnic Russians together with Russian speakers number around 80 percent.[85] The region's largest city, Narva, which is also Estonia's third largest city, is 82 percent ethnic Russian, and together with the Russian speakers they amount to 97 percent of the less than 60,000 population.[86] With a declining, but still relatively high unemployment rate of 10 percent in 2013 and probably the highest HIV rate in the EU, namely 3 percent of the adult population, Narva seems anything but a desirable place to live.[87] Still, some local enthusiasts believe Narva is an up-and-coming city with potential to attract investments and new inhabitants. A book by Katri Raik, head of Narva College of Tartu University, *Minu Narva* (My Narva), describes the city as an exotic place and tackles ethnic tensions through humor.[88] However, the statistic that bears perhaps the most significance, and one that can truly be a vehicle for Russia's "compatriot protection" efforts, is the number of Russian citizens. In 2013, 36 percent (or about 23,000 people) of Narva's population held Russian citizenship.[89] With Moscow's encouragement through the easing of Russian citizenship requirements in 2006 and again in 2014, a number of residents who had not acquired Estonian citizenship opted for Russian citizenship instead.[90] The Russian passports qualify them for Russian pensions, universities, and visa-free travel to Russia.[91] As in other post-Soviet republics like Georgia, Moldova, and Armenia, the appeal of visa-free travel cannot be underestimated, as many residents visit their families in Russia or travel for work and business reasons. Indeed, Tallinn and St. Petersburg are nearly equidistant from Narva. In addition, Estonian residence permits enable these Russian citizens to travel freely in the EU's Schengen area, thus providing the best of both worlds.

Narva's sizable population of Russian citizens is a security concern for Estonia since Moscow's policy for protecting its citizens is even more explicit than that for protecting ethnic Russians and Russian speakers in general, as seen in Crimea, Abkhazia, and South Ossetia. Estonian academics, politicians, and NGO workers, however, generally hold the view that Estonia's Russian and Russian-speaking minority is not very receptive to Kremlin's manipulative foreign and compatriot policies, and that therefore, there is no imminent danger looming over Estonia. Narva's current mayor, Eduard East, argued in 2014 that Russia is not as alluring for the city's inhabitants as might appear, since in recent years, "it's hard to find anyone that wants to be part of Russia."[92] Ultimately, as Ivan Lavrentjev, coordinator of Russian-speaking NGOs at the umbrella organization called the Network of Estonian Nonprofit Organizations, notes: "In Estonia people view themselves as European, even though they can like Putin. They also prefer to live in a stable society, with greater economic stability."[93] Still the numbers of Russian citizens in Estonia suggest that Moscow's compatriot and passportization policies have been somewhat successful.

Latvia

Latvia's Russian minority population is the largest of the Baltic States, namely 27 percent, or roughly 537,000 people, and is concentrated in Riga and the region of Latgale. In Riga, ethnic Russians make up 40 percent of the population (around 257,000 people) while the entire ethnic Russian and Russian-speaking minority totals nearly 50 percent (approximately 321,000 people).[94] In fact Riga is a nearly bilingual city and Russian is widely heard on the streets, spoken both by locals and by frequent Russian tourists. The center-left Russian minority party Harmony Centre, which reportedly has close ties to Putin's United Russia party, has dominated Riga's local politics since 2009.[95] That year Nils Ušakovs of Harmony Centre became the first Russian-speaking mayor of the Latvian capital. His reelection to the mayor's office in 2013 demonstrated the solid political position of the Russian minority and of Harmony Centre. In the 2011 and 2014 parliamentary elections Harmony won the greatest number of votes of any political party but was not included in the resulting government coalition led by the center-right parties. Riga has not experienced substantial ethnic tensions since the 2000s, though the Russian minority has been active politically, often with the encouragement of various compatriot organizations. In 2014 a small group of Russian speakers protested against educational reforms dictating that 60 percent of courses should be taught in the Latvian language in the country's state-funded Russian schools. However, the issue has clearly lost salience since 2004, when it had galvanized thousands of Russian protestors.[96]

Latvia's eastern region of Latgale borders Russia, Belarus, and Lithuania, and historically has had a large Russian and Russian-speaking population. It remains among the poorest regions of the European Union, but like Estonia's Ida-Viru county, Latgale is also of some strategic importance. Through its territory runs an oil pipeline that used to transport oil for export from Russia to Latvia's Ventspils seaport until it was shut down by Moscow following a political and commercial dispute with Riga in 2003.[97] In Latgale, ethnic Russians number more than 100,000 and make up nearly 39 percent of the population.[98] Latgale's Russian speakers also include people of Belarusian and Polish ancestry, tallying 55 percent of the population.[99] Many ethnic Russians arrived during the Soviet era, joining those who came around the time of the First World War and others who came centuries earlier. The earliest Russian émigrés belonged to the Old Believers community that split from the Russian Orthodox Church in the seventeenth century. In the region's largest city, Daugavpils, ethnic Russians total nearly 54 percent of the population, while Russian speakers make up 79 percent of the city inhabitants.[100] Yet, unlike in Narva, in both Latgale and Daugavpils the number of Russian citizens is notably small—totaling 2 and 4 percent respectively.[101] Reports indicate that 685 Latgalians in 2011 and 621 in 2012 applied for Russian passports, a trend that picked up during the Latvian economic crisis of 2009.[102] Their motivation has been primarily economic—a lower retirement age in Russia and ability to receive Russian pensions.[103] The small number of Russian citizens somewhat reduces worries about Russia's interference in the region, though since 2012 there has been concern that separatism is being stoked by pro-Russian groups who proclaim the region's distinct identity embodied in the Latgalian dialect of the Latvian language.[104] Likewise, Latgale's Russians and Russian speakers have consistently demonstrated their preference for raising the status of the Russian language. In the 2012 referendum on making Russian the second official language only 15 percent of Daugavpils residents opposed the initiative.[105] In contrast, about 75 percent of Latvian citizens voted against the proposal.[106]

Overall, the sentiments of Latvian Russians and Russophones whom Moscow has sought to co-opt as compatriots have been mixed. According to a 2013 study organized by Immanuel Kant Russian State University, only 24 percent of ethnic Russians in Latvia can be described as "highly receptive" to Russian policy. Meanwhile 42 percent of those polled from middle-income families have adapted to Latvian society and 34 percent are indifferent to their political or social status.[107] On the other hand, Latvia's Russians and Russophones have been more likely than not to support Russia's actions in Crimea and Ukraine of 2014. Polls conducted in Latvia in April 2014 showed that 36 percent of Russian speakers believe that Russia's interference in the internal affairs of Ukraine is not justifiable while 44 percent supported Russia's actions.[108] Another poll in 2015 demonstrated that 66 percent of Latvia's Russians support the annexation of Crimea.[109] In the view of Andis Kudors, executive director of the Centre for East European Policy Studies in Latvia, the biggest problem is the fact that Russian compatriot policies encourage compatriots to make political demands for changes in language and citizenship policies in Latvia and Estonia, and to disseminate historical interpretations that split Latvian and Estonian (and Ukrainian, and other) societies among ethnic lines.[110] For instance many Russkiy Mir Foundation grants to Russian-Latvian NGOs are dedicated to projects promoting the Kremlin's viewpoint on history rather than supporting the Russian language or culture. They include books and films praising the greatness of the Russian nation, while often whitewashing the more sinister aspects of the USSR such as Stalinist crimes or the invasion and occupation of the Baltic States.[111]

Lithuania

Because of its relatively low numbers of ethnic Russians and Russian speakers, Lithuania has often been regarded as the Baltic state least vulnerable to Russian compatriot measures. In some ways Lithuanian policymakers have been complacent in this respect, in the erroneous belief that by granting automatic and universal citizenship, Vilnius solved its minority problem in the 1990s.[112] Nonetheless, as in Latvia and Estonia, the integration of Russians and Russophones into Lithuanian society is far from complete. Lithuania's smaller Russian minority—totaling 6 percent of the population, or some 175,000 people—is divided between three regions. Like Tallinn and Riga, Lithuania's capital, Vilnius, also has a significantly higher proportion of Russian speakers than the rest of the country. Its population is 12 percent Russian (around 62,000 people) while nearly 27 percent are Russian speakers (around 140,000 people), including many ethnic Poles.[113] Due to Soviet Russification policies, 23 percent of Lithuania's ethnic Poles (totaling under 7 percent of the population, or around 200,000 people) report that their mother tongue is Russian.[114] The port city of Klaipėda, located on the Baltic Sea close to the Russian territory of Kaliningrad, also has a more concentrated Russian minority than Lithuania overall. Here ethnic Russians make up nearly 20 percent of the population (around 31,000), while Russian speakers total 28 percent (around 44,000).[115] Klaipėda is also a strategically important port, where much of Lithuania's trade is conducted and which is the site of the country's new "floating" LNG terminal. Lithuania's third concentration of Russian speakers is found in the small eastern city of Visaginas. Like Estonia's Ida-Viru county and Latvia's Latgale, the Visaginas region has also been one of strategic importance. Lithuania's Ignalina nuclear power plant operated in this region until 2009 and the same city is designated as the site of Lithuania's proposed new nuclear project. It is the only Lithuanian city with more than 50 percent ethnic Russian population, while Russian speakers number 77 percent of the total population of approximately 20,000.[116] A significant number of Visaginas's inhabitants are former employees of the original nuclear power plant, which was built by Russian and Russian-speaking specialists brought in during the Soviet era. In 2014 Lithuanian media interviews and reportage concluded that the Visaginas population was not receptive to the Crimean model, and no reports of separatism or calls for autonomy have been noted since.[117]

Politically, the situation in Vilnius, and in Lithuania as a whole, is more complex than the relatively small numbers of Russians and Russian speakers imply. Since the mid-2000s the Russian minority has come to be overshadowed by the Polish minority, particularly by the upsurge of Lithuania's Polish party, Electoral Action of Poles in Lithuania. In 2008, the Polish party "absorbed" the main Russian minority political party, the Russian Alliance, and since then both parties jointly participate in Lithuanian parliamentary, municipal, and European parliamentary elections. However, many experts believe that the footprints of Russian influence can be traced in this endeavor: by combining the Polish and Russian minorities, the Kremlin has succeeded in building enough critical mass to advance its own agenda. As Kasčiūnas notes, "the newly established political party has no links with deeply rooted Polish political or cultural traditions and can be viewed as merely an attempt for Russia to get involved in Lithuanian politics."[118] The Polish minority, with its leader Valdemar Tomaševski, have been raising issues of discrimination to explain the economic underdevelopment of the regions the party represents as well as courting ethnic Russians and Russian speakers, and positioning themselves as the "voice" of all minorities in Lithuania. Tomaševski also recently embarked on pro-Russian policies like supporting Russia in the Crimea question and wearing a Russian imperial military and patriotic symbol, the St. George's Ribbon. Moscow's clout is not new in Lithuanian politics. Lithuanian member of the European Parliament Viktor Uspaskich, former President Rolandas Paksas (who was impeached due to suspicious links with Russian organized crime), and former Minister of Agriculture Kazimira Prunskienė all are known for their close and controversial relationships with Russia.[119]

INFORMATION WARFARE

Russia's information warfare vis-à-vis the Baltic States has centered on its own interpretation of Soviet history, smearing Baltic governments and societies as fascists and Nazis, and creating propaganda about alleged abuse of the Russian minorities. The prominence given to these matters has ebbed and flowed. However, since Crimea's annexation in 2014, the narrative of discrimination against the Russian minorities has intensified. The propaganda has served to reinforce Russia's soft power efforts to create a network of co-opted communities of compatriots in the Baltic States as well as sow societal ethnic divisions. The goal has been to encourage Russians and Russian speakers (but not only these) to develop loyalty to modern-day Russia, including its interpretation of history and current events.[120]

In the historical sphere, the main source of tension since the 1990s has been the interpretation of the Soviet occupation of the Baltic States. In the early years of Yeltsin's presidency the high point of Baltic-Russian historical accord was the agreement signed on 29 July 1991 between Lithuania and the Russian Soviet Republic. It recognized that Lithuania had been "annexed" by the Soviets (though Moscow avoided the word "occupation").[121] By the mid-1990s, however, the Russian government started to move away from acknowledging Soviet annexation.[122] Possibly the last time Russian officials acknowledged the Soviet occupation of the Baltics was in 1993 when the foreign minister of the Russian Federation, Andrey Kozyrev, confirmed that the Soviet Union had indeed occupied the Baltic States in 1940.[123]

With the start of Putin's presidency in 1999, tensions over the historical record increased as the new regime began to consciously rehabilitate Soviet-era leaders and symbols and the Soviet version of history, and to deny occupation of the Baltic States.[124] For instance, during the massive 2005 commemoration of the sixtieth anniversary of Soviet victory in the Second World War, Putin stated: "The world has never known such heroism. . . . Our people not only defended their homeland, they liberated 11 European countries."[125] Thereafter, Russian leaders interpreted the Baltic occupation as either liberation from fascism or a voluntary act of joining the Soviet Union on the part of the Baltic States.[126] In 2005, the chief of European affairs at the Kremlin, Sergey Yastrzhembsky, seconded Putin, declaring that "There was no occupation. There were agreements at the time with the legitimately elected authorities in the Baltic countries."[127] Overall, Putin's regime has consistently sought to demonstrate that the period of independence and sovereignty of the Baltic States was an "abnormality," as against the "normality" of the period when the region was under Russian or Soviet rule.[128]

Much of Moscow's propaganda has been carried out by its extensive state-controlled media apparatus, which has allowed it to manipulate the perceptions of Baltic populations. Russian media have carved out a sizable role in the Baltic information environment and convey world and regional news to large segments of Baltic society.[129] For instance, in 2013, the four main Russian TV channels, namely NTV Mir, First Baltic Channel PBK, RTR Planeta, and Ren Lietuva, attracted some 15 percent of Lithuania's viewers—more than the combined total percentage of Lithuania's Russian and Polish minorities.[130] In contrast, the national Lithuanian broadcaster LRT attracts only 8 percent of the total Lithuanian television audience. Russian television channels, Russian and local Russian-language newspapers and internet news portals, and radio stations that target the Baltic States have consistently disseminated information with a Kremlin bias.

The Russian media have not only gained a foothold among Baltic viewers, but since the late 2000s Russian investors have sought a larger stake in the Baltic, and especially the Lithuanian media. For instance, from 2009 to 2011 the Russian-owned Lithuanian bank Snoras owned 34 percent of the largest Lithuanian media group, Lietuvos Rytas, which consists of the main national daily, a television station, a news portal, and other publications.[131] Political scientist Nerijus Maliukevičius of the Institute of International Relations and Political Science of Vilnius University considers Russian media expansion as information geopolitics. He argues that since the 2000s Russian media entered the European market in order to gain control over this "media territory" and to leverage the easygoing and flexible European media regulation for Moscow's information warfare campaigns.[132]

There are numerous examples of Kremlin-biased reporting that targets Baltic domestic politics and societies, but the most notorious example of Russian information warfare was a campaign that contributed to the 2007 riots by Russians and Russian speakers in Tallinn. Tensions started with the Estonian government's decision to relocate a Soviet war memorial to a military cemetery away from the city center. The timing of the move—just weeks ahead of the 9 May Russian Soviet Victory Day celebrations—was particularly sensitive. According to Estonian perceptions, Moscow was instrumental in inciting unrest and discontent by spreading false accounts in the Russian-language press that the monument, and presumably the nearby tombs of unknown soldiers, had been destroyed. The Russian embassy allegedly also took part in organizing the riots, while Russian activists, including members of the Nashi pro-Kremlin youth movement, traveled from Russia to take part in the violence.[133] Teenage Estonians of Russian origin, despite the fact that they had never lived under the Soviet Union, also rioted and held up signs saying "The Soviet Union Forever."[134] Lavrentjev, who was still a high-school student at the time, reflected on the 2007 propaganda campaign: "When you are told something every day on the news and in the media, you start to believe it even if you do not want to believe. Then it does not matter if there were soldiers buried there or not, since the outcome [of the riots] would have been the same."[135] The violence was also accompanied by cyber attacks against Estonian websites. While Russia vehemently denied its involvement, Estonian government officials accused Moscow of taking down the websites of the Estonian presidency and parliament, numerous political parties, three of the country's six big news

NATO'S ACHILLES' HEEL 165

organizations, two of the biggest banks, and firms specializing in communications.[136] The attack prompted the establishment of the NATO Cooperative Cyber Defense Centre of Excellence in Tallinn in 2008.[137]

In Latvia, examples of Russian media influence include the 2010 parliamentary elections when the First Baltic Channel lobbied for the Russian minority party, the Concord Centre.[138] Likewise, during the 2012 campaign for the referendum on making the Russian language official, Russian media published false and inflammatory reports that Russians who intended to participate in the vote were threatened by their employers with layoffs.[139] Similarly, following language policy reform in Estonia in 1999 that obliged public officials to speak Estonian while at work, the Russian media outlet Russia Today presented this to the wider public in a rather demonizing manner as a "language inquisition" that threatened to silence the Russian minority.[140] Hence, to counter the Kremlin's propaganda, in 2015 Estonian Public Broadcasting and Latvian Public Service Television concluded a cooperative agreement to develop Russian-language TV channels in both countries that could provide the Russian-speaking populations with quality journalism that is based on a variety of sources.[141]

As in the cases of Ukraine and Georgia, Russia's information warfare has been most potent during times of political tensions and in the lead-up to military conflict. Not surprisingly, by 2014, following the annexation of Crimea, Russia's information warfare in the Baltic States intensified. Russian media included the "Baltic threat" to Russia in its general anti-Ukrainian narrative. First, the influential Russian journalist Dmitry Kiselev consistently argued fantastic theories that Sweden, Poland, and Lithuania were behind Kiev's Maidan events, allegedly to take revenge on Russia for its victory over Sweden in the long-ago battle of Poltava in 1709.[142] Second, the Russian NTV television station (notorious for its smear campaign against the U.S. ambassador to Russia in 2011–14, Michael McFaul) ran a pseudodocumentary, which among many historical falsehoods invented the myth of Baltic snipers shooting at crowds during the episode of Soviet aggression in 1991 in Vilnius and the 2014 protests in Kiev.[143] As a result, in 2014 the Lithuanian Radio and Television Commission restricted the broadcasts of the three most popular Russian TV channels in the country.[144]

The threat of Russia's information campaign was increasingly recognized and publicly acknowledged by the Lithuanian government. In

2014 the Lithuanian internal security service announced that Russian media sources were pursuing a consistent anti-Lithuanian propaganda campaign by attempting to "humiliate Lithuanian domestic and foreign policies" and that "[e]ven if the audience susceptible to this information is not very large, however, it still may incite hostile moods and encourage discontent with the government."[145] Also, the 2014 Lithuanian internal security service activities summary noted that both Russia's foreign intelligence and its military intelligence agencies had significantly ramped up their efforts to obtain information about NATO defense plans and EU policies related to Ukraine.[146] In late 2014 President Dalia Grybauskaitė stated: "Every day we are witnessing new information warfare attacks and the target is our people. They are being told not to trust their government, their history, military, membership in the EU and NATO."[147] Thus, it hardly came as a surprise when in March 2015, the Lithuanian internal security department conducted large-scale raids on the apartments of more than nine suspects, in the framework of an investigation into operations of anticonstitutional groups that had threatened the Lithuanian president, called for attacks on the Lithuanian state, and challenged NATO membership.[148]

The escalating information campaign against the Baltic States has been among the most visible aspects of the reimperialization trajectory in the Baltic. This stage is particularly worrying due to the fact that Russia has often coupled reports of "compatriots'" grievances with calls to protect them. Certainly "grievances" can be easily fabricated and politicized in the age of media, particularly those that are fully controlled by the Russian state. The separatist unrest and hybrid warfare in eastern Ukraine were bolstered by Moscow's information warfare machine and these developments have caused alarm bells to ring in the Baltic States. However, it is also important to consider that the states' small size makes dissemination of falsehoods more difficult over the long term than in Ukraine. As Lavrentjev notes, Estonia's total population is significantly smaller than that of just the Donetsk region in Ukraine, and while the Baltic population may be swayed and even incited in the short term, over time Baltic residents are less likely to believe false reporting because they are more likely to know the goings-on in their cities and regions.[149]

SEPARATISM, ANNEXATION, PROVOCATION

Despite Russia's escalating information warfare against the Baltic States, to date these three NATO members have not faced Russian efforts to militarily protect compatriots. Nonetheless, as recently as December 2013 Putin publicly stated: "We continually raise questions about our compatriot situation in some European Union countries, specifically in the Baltic States, where the completely uncivilized perception of a person as 'noncitizen without the rights and freedoms' still exists."[150] In the 1990s and since 2014 there have been some minor provocative calls for separation in various Baltic regions. Shortly after Crimea's annexation, in March 2014 a petition was launched on an activist website, avaaz.org, for Lithuania's port city Klaipėda to join Russia's Kaliningrad. Putin himself insinuated support for this move in 2005, as did Gorbachev at the time of Lithuania's independence movement.[151] However, the 2014 petition barely gathered one hundred signatures and was abandoned as it clearly did not reflect the sentiments of the vast majority of Lithuania's Russian population. Likewise, the Visaginas population has not been receptive to the Crimean model.[152]

In April 2014, a sparsely attended rally took place in front of the Latvian embassy in Moscow calling for Latgale to become part of Russia, and in early 2015 a Latvian activist was arrested by the authorities because he was collecting signatures for a petition sponsored by the website avaaz.org for Latvia to be annexed by Russia.[153] However, separatist sentiments are generally the exception rather than the norm among the Russian minority, both in Latgale and in Latvia as a whole.[154] Likewise, in Estonia in 2014 there were no calls for separation in Ida-Viru county or the city of Narva. It is important, though, not to forget that in 1991 and 1993 several attempts were made to proclaim an autonomous or even an independent Narva, with referendums held and local councils voting for this initiative. The last referendum of July 1993 in the cities of Narva and Sillamäe reported 98 percent support for independence with a turnout exceeding 50 percent. The Estonian State Court ruled the results illegal.[155]

While Russia has had very limited success in targeting specific Baltic territories for separatism or annexation, its other recent policies have violated the usual international norms of neighborly conduct in peacetime. A provocation on Estonian territory in 2014 is a particular example. On 5 September that year, an officer of the Estonian Internal Security

Service was kidnapped by the Russian Federal Security Services and
taken to Russia where he has been charged with espionage. According to
Estonia's Internal Security Service, in the course of illegally detaining
the Estonian officer at gunpoint the abductors jammed radio communications and threw a smoke grenade.[156] The incident allegedly occurred
on Estonian territory and marks a significant departure from Russia's respect for Estonian statehood and territorial boundaries.

In 2014 the Russian government also issued what could be perceived
as a challenge to Lithuania's statehood in an effort to enforce Soviet laws
on Lithuanian citizens. In September that year Russian legal authorities
reopened twenty-five-year-old criminal cases against Lithuanians who
had refused to serve in the Soviet army in the 1990–91 period. This affects approximately fifteen hundred Lithuanian men who, following Vilnius's declaration of independence in March 1990, avoided or hid from
the Soviet draft, often being arrested and tried by Soviet authorities.[157]
Moscow's decision is puzzling, because it involves enforcement of legislation of a country that vanished from the world map almost twenty-five
years ago. The Lithuanian government has issued a warning to these
men, now in their early forties, against traveling to Russia or outside
NATO countries, lest they be arrested or prosecuted. The Lithuanian defense minister, Juozas Olekas, argued in 2014 that this is clearly a "provocation from the Russian Federation," and Artūras Paulauskas, chairman
of the parliament's National Security and Defense Committee, called it a
provocation "not so much against these men as against Lithuanian society."[158] Moscow's reopening of these cases not only demonstrates that
Russia perceives itself as a continuation of the Soviet Union but could also
be interpreted as nonrecognition of Lithuania's declaration of independence. Ultimately, as a direct response to rising tensions with Russia and
the Ukrainian crisis, in early 2015 the Lithuanian government temporar-
ily reinstated compulsory military service.[159] According to the government's proposal, the military will call up annually around three thousand
men aged nineteen to twenty-six, while permitting all males up to the age
of thirty-eight to volunteer for military service.[160] Estonia, for its part, also
became more conscious of the dangers that Russia poses. In 2014, enroll-
ment in organizations such as the Estonian Defense League spiked, and
in total around fifteen thousand volunteers joined citizen militias, which
are headed by officers from the Estonian military.[161]

In 2014 the Baltic States also experienced a severe increase in Russian military provocations, coming especially from Kaliningrad. NATO jet fighters patrolling the Baltic airspace were scrambled 68 times along Lithuania's border, by far the highest count in more than ten years. Latvia registered 150 "close incidents" where Russian aircraft purposely engaged in provocative and risky behavior, and Estonia registered 5 airspace violations all in the year 2014.[162] In March 2014, the Russian Baltic Fleet conducted unexpected tactical exercises with some thirty-five hundred personnel along the Baltic coast.[163] At the same time Poland invoked Article 4 of the North Atlantic Treaty, which grants any NATO member the right to consultation whenever its territorial integrity, political independence, or security is threatened.[164] As a result, in April 2014 NATO increased its air presence in the region by deploying six warplanes to the Baltic States and sending six hundred troops to the Baltic States and Poland, to reassure them (rather symbolically) that the alliance is taking its security commitments seriously.[165] In June 2014, NATO stepped up its support when ten member countries (the United States, Canada, Denmark, Estonia, Finland, Latvia, Lithuania, Poland, Norway, and the UK) kicked off military exercises in the Baltic States with some forty-seven hundred troops and eight hundred military vehicles. Russia viewed NATO's buildup as a sign of aggression and deployed twenty-four warships and bombers to Kaliningrad.[166] In November 2014, NATO also launched a two-week-long multinational military drill in Lithuania, which gathered twenty-five hundred servicemen from the alliance.[167] Moreover, taking into account Russia's muscular foreign policy, NATO has been strengthening its long-term military presence in the Baltic States. In late 2014, NATO decided to establish a five-thousand-strong rapid reaction force that, if necessary, will deter Russian aggression and will be controlled from six NATO command centers, of which three will be located in the Baltics.[168]

The incidents and developments of 2014 and 2015—provocations regarding separatism, attacks on Estonian officials, imposition of Soviet laws, airspace violations, and military exercises—all demonstrate that Moscow is increasingly challenging not only the boundaries but also the very notion of statehood of the Baltic States, even if it has not called for military protection of its compatriots there. Indeed, Moscow's actions have moved beyond its previous claims to privileged interests in the Baltic

States. Since 2014, its actions are more reminiscent of policies it would be expected to pursue toward its protectorates. Nonetheless, NATO membership, the recent military support demonstrated by the allies, as well as the United States' $1 billion European Reassurance Initiative appear to have assuaged immediate fears in the Baltic States.

Possibly the greatest and most evident concern today in the Baltic States stems from the sizable numbers of Russian citizens in Estonia's Narva, on the border with Russia. Overall, the largest and most concentrated numbers of Baltic Russians and Russian speakers is found in Latvia's Latgale that also borders Russia. Finally, contrary to popular misconception, Lithuania is likewise not immune to Russia's meddling in its minority populations. Moscow's ability to conduct a hybrid war in Ukraine, the increasing Russian military activity in the Baltic Sea region, and Putin's insistence on protecting Russian compatriots abroad are all legitimate red flags for the Balts and their allies. On one hand, as NATO members, the Baltic States have the security of Article 5 not afforded to Ukraine. On the other hand, as the conflict in eastern Ukraine has demonstrated, Russia no longer relies on traditional military fighting power but rather on shadow war using proxy military groups. The resulting military conflict can thus be made to resemble civil war or separatist efforts by local Russian populations. Furthermore the Kremlin's tactics do not require enlisting local majorities among such populations but often just minorities to support its neo-imperialist aims.[169] Small, loyal, organized minorities supported by special forces could be sufficient for destabilizing Baltic cities with Russian and Russian-speaking populations even if no outright efforts were to be made to seize Baltic territories. The case of the Soviet Bronze Soldier monument in Estonia in 2007 has already shown how easily riots and instability can be stoked.

In fact, the Baltic States have already been targets of Russian reimperialization efforts with compatriots being instrumentalized for territorial expansion. Yet one should not focus solely on the policies of the Russian government. The Baltic States need also to assess their policies toward their Russian (and in the case of Lithuania also its Polish) minorities. The recent successful political mobilization of Latvia's Russian minority parties is not an issue of concern. On the contrary, the active and especially the transparent participation of Baltic Russians in Baltic political life will make Baltic societies more cohesive and less vulnerable to opaque influence from Moscow. The political participation of the Russian minorities would be even more welcome if it was not mobilized along ethnic lines that point up the ongoing divisions in society. If, however, the Baltic States are unable to fully integrate their Russian and other minorities, or if they lose the soft power war with Russia for their loyalty, then it is possible that their territories could become more vulnerable targets of Russia's expansionism.

CHAPTER SIX

State Building and Shifting Loyalties

Whenever one starts talking about the protection of Russians in Kazakhstan, not Russia, I recall Hitler, who began to "support" the Sudeten Germans at one time. I start feeling deep anxiety for Russians who live outside Russia. Really, they did not ask to be defended, did they? They are citizens of Kazakhstan.

—Kazakhstan's President Nursultan Nazarbayev, November 1993

THE FIVE CENTRAL ASIAN STATES of Kazakhstan, Kyrgyzstan, Taji-kistan, Uzbekistan, and Turkmenistan have all carved out new identities for themselves since the fall of the Soviet Union—turning inward, away from Moscow, to carry out their nation-state-building projects and attempting to develop independent foreign policies. Yet they maintain a close relationship with Russia and balance it with relations with other prominent states active in the region such as the United States and China. At the same time, the resurgence of nationalist moods in some Central Asian states coupled with strong local leaders and their personalities have to some extent driven their relations with Russia. The fact that some of these countries remain largely closed and authoritarian also affects the extent to which the Russian reimperialization policy trajectory has been successful in Central Asia, because strongman regimes have limited Moscow's influence. The limited flow of information, especially from Uzbekistan and Turkmenistan, also presents challenges in interpreting their policies in regard to Russian compatriot initiatives. In addition, each of these five states is affected by unique circumstances and has a distinct form of relationship with Russia.

In Russo–Central Asian relations, the question of reimperialization is not immediately evident. The Central Asian states were among the few former Soviet republics that never declared their independence from Russia, but rather found themselves independent after the Soviet Union was formally dissolved by Moscow. Their leaders were not even invited to the inaugural meeting of Russia, Ukraine, and Belarus that set up the Commonwealth of Independent States on 8 December 1991.[1] These facts could certainly bring into question to what extent post-Soviet Russia sought to keep the Central Asian states in its "empire" or subject them to its subsequent reimperialization project. In fact, however, since 1990, Russian policy toward the Central Asian states has evolved through three stages. In the early 1990s Moscow had relatively little interest in the region. During the mid-1990s, Russian Minister of Foreign Affairs Yevgeny Primakov promoted increasing involvement and assertion of Moscow's interests in the region. Starting in the 2000s under the leadership of Vladimir Putin, Russia's presence in Central Asia became still stronger despite the fact that many of the region's countries had long drawn a red line against Russia's invasive activities targeting its diaspora such as passportization, protection of compatriots, and stoking of separatism.[2]

THE CENTRAL ASIAN BACKGROUND

Kazakhstan

Kazakhstan is without a doubt the regional leader—by far the largest and wealthiest state among the five. It is the second largest former Soviet republic after Russia, but its vast steppes are sparsely populated with some 17 million inhabitants; neighboring Uzbekistan, on the other hand, is the most populous, with 30 million people. Both countries dwarf their neighbors Tajikistan (8 million), Turkmenistan (5 million), and Kyrgyzstan (almost 6 million). Kazakhstan's GDP per capita of $13,610 is almost ten times that of Uzbekistan ($1,878), Tajikistan ($1,037), and Kyrgyzstan $(1,263), and twice that of Turkmenistan ($7,987).[3] Its abundant natural resources, large territory, and relatively small population have allowed Kazakhstan to acquire a much higher standard of living than its neighbors, putting it nearly on equal footing with Russia and former communist states in Eastern Europe, despite significant regional inequalities and a rural-urban divide. Kazakhstan is often praised for its interethnic stability and its peaceful coexistence between its Russian minority and the titular nationality. In comparison to more autocratic Uzbekistan and Turkmenistan, Kazakhstan's political model can be described as "softer" authoritarianism that relies on occasional coercion but mostly on the consent of the population.[4] It is one of the two Central Asian states, the other being Uzbekistan, that have not witnessed a change in the leadership since independence in 1991.

Kazakhstan's President Nursultan Nazarbayev (1991–present) is usually described as a very experienced and crafty politician who managed to acquire political power in the turbulent 1990s and hold on to it ever since. His position toward Russia is complicated: on the one hand, he has repeatedly assured Moscow of Astana's loyalty; on the other hand, he has also been known for his critical remarks about the northern neighbor. In 2012 he described Kazakh-Russian relations as follows: "we were first a colony of the Russian Empire and then of the Soviet Union. Over these 150 years Kazakhs nearly lost their national traditions, customs, religion, language."[5] His approach toward Russia can perhaps best be explained by his view that "neighbors can't be chosen."[6] As a result, for the last twenty years or more Nazarbayev has pragmatically pursued a policy of cooperation with Russia within the framework of his "multivector" foreign policy and drawn red lines where Kazakhstan's security or interests are challenged. Nonetheless, Nazarbayev has remained Russia's closest ally in the region and remains so despite the events in Ukraine since 2014.

Uzbekistan

Uzbekistan has aspired to rival Kazakhstan's leadership in the region, and the country's President Islam Karimov (1990–present) is another example of a Soviet-bred politician who has managed to hold on to political power for more than two decades.[7] From the beginning, Karimov's state building has been based on nationalism and Uzbek dominance, with the country's independence being interpreted as an opportunity for a revival of the nation's historic glory.[8] The Uzbek leadership's ideology is centered on pride in the country's historical legacy (often mythologized), notably the conquests of Timur the Great, who in the fourteenth century founded the ruling Timurid dynasty in Central Asia. Karimov's regime emphasizes the historic link between those times and contemporary Uzbeki-

STATE BUILDING AND SHIFTING LOYALTIES   175

stan. The country's symbol is the capital of Tashkent, which was founded
between the fifth and third centuries B.C., and somewhat less enthusiastically, the ancient cities of Bukhara and Samarkand, which are especially rich in historical monuments and sites but are often regarded as
culturally more Persian than Uzbek. Unlike Nazarbayev, Karimov never
even tried to appear democratic, and has made 180-degree turns in his
foreign policy, breaking his commitments to multilateral organizations of the post-Soviet space whenever they did not suit his personal
agenda. He has varied from helping launch the Moscow-led Collective
Security Treaty Organization (CSTO) of 1992 in Tashkent, to appealing
to Russia when the Taliban were threatening Uzbekistan's borders, to
suspending his country's membership in the CSTO and the Eurasian
Economic Community, and even briefly joining the counter-Russian
GUAM (Georgia, Ukraine, Azerbaijan, Moldova) Organization for Democracy and Economic Development from 1999 to 2005. Karimov has
also developed partnerships with both the United States and Russia
without playing favorites, and overall, like the leaders of Kazakhstan and
Turkmenistan, he has pursued a flexible foreign policy.[9] Following U.S.
plans to withdraw from Afghanistan, in 2012 the United States started to
supply Uzbekistan with weapons intended to strengthen the country
against radical Islamic threats. Yet Karimov has also turned once again
to Russia since he recognizes that he cannot face the threat alone in the
region.[10] While he has not officially recognized Crimea's annexation, his
rhetoric has supported Russia's actions in Ukraine.[11]

Kyrgyzstan

Neighboring Kyrgyzstan has been much more dependent on Russian
support and financial aid, in part due to its weak economy and unstable
political situation following two mass revolts. Among the Central Asian
countries, its political development has been unique. Kyrgyzstan has often been cited as the most democratic state of the region due to the initial reforms of its first president, Askar Akayev (1990–2005), and the
mass uprisings against the ruling regimes in the Tulip Revolution of
2005 and the Second Revolution of 2010. The subsequent two presidents,
Kurmanbek Bakiyev (2005–10) and particularly Almazbek Atambayev
(2011–present), have viewed Russia as a "strategic partner."[12] Nonetheless, Bakiyev had notoriously failed to deliver on his end of the bargain

with Moscow by not terminating the U.S. lease of the local Manas air base. Overall, Kyrgyzstan remains consistently the vulnerable junior partner in its relationship with Russia.[13]

Turkmenistan

In strong contrast to Kyrgyzstan, Turkmenistan is the most authoritarian and closed country of the region mostly known for its leadership's cult of personality. The symbol of Turkmenistan is Turkmenbashi Palace (Oguzkhan Presidential Palace) built in 1997 in the capital of Ashgabat by the order of the first president, Saparmurat Niyazov (1990–2006). The palace's ostentatious luxury reflects both the president's near absolute power and the country's vast natural gas resources that mostly benefit the national elite.[14] Turkmenistan's foreign policy is based on the doctrine of "positive neutrality," which implies self-imposed isolation and avoidance of all alliances. However, in practice the country has been known to cooperate with external actors and organizations. For example, Ashgabat was a transportation hub for U.S. and NATO forces during their operation in Afghanistan.[15] Despite some hopes for change and reforms, the second president, Gurbanguly Berdymukhamedov (2006–present), has pursued a similar authoritarian style of governance, keeping the country closed to external influences. The country's closest economic partner is increasingly China, but Berdymukhamedov has named both Russia and China as "strategic partners" and carried on a flirtation with the United States.[16]

Tajikistan

Tajikistan has possibly been the least endowed among the Central Asian states due to its difficult topography that consists of mountains and isolated regions, and its lack of natural resources. The Persian origins of the Tajik people distinguish them from the neighboring Kazakhs, Kyrgyz, Uzbeks, and Turkmens, who all count as Turkic. The Tajiks believe themselves to be the most ancient ethnic group in Central Asia.[17] Unfortunately, Tajikistan could be considered an all but failed state on account of its corrupt regime, weak underdeveloped economy, dependence on external financial aid, lack of control over some of its territories, and drug trafficking from neighboring Afghanistan. Some of Tajikistan's problems are the legacy of a violent civil war (1992 to 1997) and the subsequent fail-

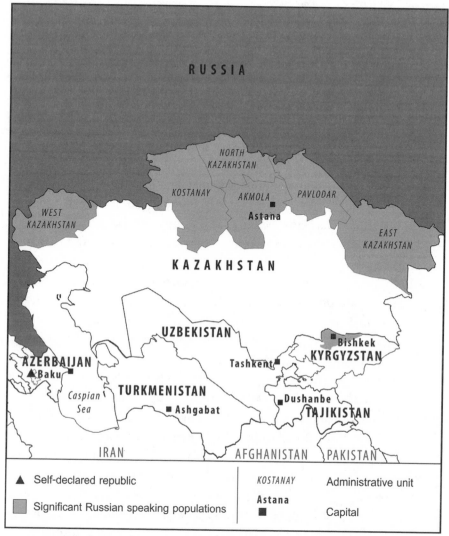

MAP 5: Distribution of Russian minorities across Central Asia. Map drawn by Giedrė Tamašauskaitė

ure of the government to achieve national consolidation and power centralization, as seen in clashes between the forces of President Emomali Rahmon (1994–present) and local insurgents in central and eastern Tajikistan in 2010 and 2012.[18] The weak Rahmon government has been unable and, perhaps more importantly, unwilling to address the country's problems including its corruption. Russian support for Rahmon's ascent to power as well as significant Russian financial and military aid have made his regime and the country in general highly dependent on Moscow, with the official position outlined as: "Russia is our main strategic partner and natural ally."[19]

PORTRAITS OF RUSSIAN SPEAKERS

After the collapse of the Soviet Union and the subsequent massive departure of ethnic Russians and Russian speakers from Central Asia, those remaining had to adjust to the new reality of sovereign nation-states where Russians were no longer in the position of a ruling elite but rather just another ethnic minority. In the period from 1989 to 1999, approximately 1.5 million Russians departed from Kazakhstan to Russia, 300,000 from Kyrgyzstan, more than 500,000 from Uzbekistan, 200,000 from Turkmenistan, and 300,000 from Tajikistan.[20] In the 1990s ethnic Russians and Russian speakers often faced discrimination, being expelled from government and other leadership positions as titular nationalities entered political life. Some forms of discrimination still persist. However, these nationalist policies were never targeted against Russians specifically but against all minorities—Tatars, Germans, and Uzbeks living in Kazakhstan and Kyrgyzstan, or Kyrgyz living in Tajikistan.[21] Nonetheless, due to the Russification policies of the Soviet era the Russian language had become and remains the predominant language of communication not only among ethnic Russians but also among a large part of the titular nationalities. In the 2010s Russian has remained popular among the urban populations of Kazakhstan, Kyrgyzstan, and Tajikistan, where many have graduated from Russian-speaking schools and universities. For instance, 75 percent of ethnic Kazakhs speak Russian either as a second language or as their primary language.[22] In Uzbekistan and Turkmenistan, the focus on reviving the national languages has somewhat reduced the role of Russian, especially among the younger generation, but it remains popular among the urban population and also among those in search of economic opportunities in Russia.[23] Here I will focus on younger ethnic Russians and Russian speakers because they represent the next generation of a population that Moscow would like to co-opt as "Russian compatriots." Attitudes to this policy both across the region and within each state are diverse. As with the other post-Soviet countries, the profiled individuals serve to give a glimpse into the different views and opinions of the region's Russian minority but should not be taken as a scientific survey of this group.

Anya is a Kazakh college student.[24] Being half Russian, she feels great affinity for Russian literature, culture, and movies but states, "I don't consider myself 100 percent Russian, because I've never lived in Russia, and sometimes I feel a bit foreign when I go there." She thinks that the Russian minority in Kazakhstan may have some grievances: "Discrimination always exists when you are a minority. Fortunately, neither my family nor I have suffered much from it, but I've witnessed it." Nonetheless, she does not consider herself a Russian compatriot and is against Russian interference in Kazakhstan's internal affairs, especially Moscow's efforts to "protect" those it identifies as compatriots: "It's none of Russia's business. We are citizens of Kazakhstan and if need be protection should come from our own country." She is aware of very different perspectives of the Russian and Western media on the Ukrainian crisis, but she is firmly against Moscow's annexation of Crimea: "I do not support it. I don't know why Moscow did what it did."

Stanislav is a recent college graduate with a degree in linguistics who now works as a Kazakh government immigration officer.[25] Despite his Russian ethnicity he does not identify much with Russian nationality and instead considers himself more of a cosmopolitan person. He further declares: "I do not consider myself a Russian compatriot. The main reason is that a Russian compatriot with his civil duties has to support Putin's inadequate policy, though I would like to support the opposition to Putin." Like Anya he is also critical of Russia's foreign policy toward Ukraine, which he regards as illegitimate: "I do not support Moscow's policy in Crimea and eastern Ukraine. The Russian interference in the resolution of Ukrainian conflicts was not legal."

Viktoriya is an ethnic Russian in her late thirties and holds a degree in international law.[26] Like Stanislav, she too is dubious about the need for Russian protection. Being an employee of an international NGO, she rejects Russian policies in Ukraine as a "violation of international norms and the sovereignty of Ukraine." She feels that her connection with Russia is mostly linguistic as Russian is her native language. She does not speak Kazakh because it is not needed in her day-to-day life. However, in all other matters she strongly identifies herself as a Kazakhstani citizen: "I was born and have been living in Kazakhstan for all my life and there is only one Motherland for me: Kazakhstan." Though she admits that there is some discrimination against Russians, in her view, this is more a matter of a "general unfair system" affecting all citizens, and of individual cases, rather than of policies targeted against particular ethnicities. She is firmly against the idea of Russian assistance to the Russian minority in Kazakhstan, as she believes "we need sovereign independence from Russia."

Oleg, in his twenties, is an instructor in English and Spanish language and exemplifies the complex views of Russians in Kazakhstan.[27] Coming from a Russian family, Oleg states: "I consider myself Russian because my relatives are originally from Russia, Russian is my mother language, but in all other aspects I'm a Kazakhstani citizen." He elaborates his strong ties to Kazakhstan: "I'm a patriot of the country that I was born in and where I'm living now." Oleg is skeptical that Russian speakers in Kazakhstan have legitimate grievances and echoes an argument often times repeated in the Baltic States: "In most cases it's their own fault. Lack of interest in studying culture, traditions, customs, and of course local language results in their being on the sidelines in the country they live in without fully integrating into the nation." However, Oleg is not against the idea of Russian protection of the Russian minority, insisting only that this protection "should occur in strict accordance with international norms and practices." Although Oleg is against Russian interference, he is among the few young people interviewed in Kazakhstan who supports Russia's reclaiming of Crimea, saying that it has "reunited with its historic Motherland," and that "I believe that Russian policies in this conflict are largely defensive."

In Turkmenistan, the closed nature of the regime made holding interviews problematic; nonetheless, a few young Russian speakers shared their different views. In many ways, Yolbars exemplifies those urban ethnic Turkmens who are Russian speakers.[28] Yolbars is currently studying abroad and identifies himself as a Turkmen with some Tatar roots. He would never consider himself a Russian compatriot since in his words: "Russia for me is a foreign state." He emphasizes that Russians from Central Asia have a unique identity: ". . . not only many Russians, but also many Russian speakers feel themselves a part of the local culture, so-called 'Central Asian Russians.' Many of them even returned after their emigration to Russia in the early 1990s because they had adaptation problems there." He thinks Russian speakers in Central Asia may face some discomfort in employment or higher education because they do not speak local languages, but does not think Russia's involvement is necessary: "Instead of Russia's protection, they need more support from local governments, tolerance and acceptance by titular nations, and state integration incentives like free language courses." Yolbars finds Russia's takeover of Crimea "unacceptable" and explains, "It would be like my neighbor who would come and occupy part of my garden claiming that the roots of his tree are there. Every state has to respect the sovereignty of other states and solve problems using the instruments of international diplomacy."

Berdi is a Turkmen engineering student whose stance toward Russian compatriot policies is more ambivalent than that of Yolbars.[29] Berdi's grandmother is Russian and speaking the language at home makes him feel somewhat though not completely Russian. He notes that among his family and friends the feeling of Russianness is less prevalent among the younger generation born and raised after the collapse of the Soviet Union than among the Soviet generation. He thinks he could potentially identify himself as a Russian compatriot because of cultural and political similarities between the former Soviet republics and Russia: "The USSR left a strong impact on the government and political development of its allies." He notes: "In Turkmenistan there was a time when it was hard for Russian compatriots, especially those who were working for the government [because of a Turkmen language requirement]. But now it is not that bad." He thinks that Turkmenistan's Russians need Russia's protection: "Of course not militarily but at least with some regulations, or helping them move to Russia, or by influence over the government."

Many Kyrgyzstanis perceive Russia as a partner and protector of Kyrgyzstan and this is reflected in the views of those interviewed. Artur is twenty-one years old and works in advertising in northern Kyrgyzstan.[30] Ethnically, he is Russian-Armenian and was born in Uzbekistan. Despite his mixed background, Russian is his native language and he considers himself a Russian compatriot. When asked about the grievances of the Russian minority in Kyrgyzstan he notes that "things in the north are very good, but there are often nationalistic problems in the south [faced by all minorities]. If a person is Russian, then there is no opportunity for career development and starting a business. It is different in the north. People do not care about your nationality and appearance." He adamantly

182 STATE BUILDING AND SHIFTING LOYALTIES

supports Russian protection of compatriots in Kyrgyzstan: "I consider Russian military protection necessary. Everyone has long known that Russia helps us under any circumstances. We are very much dependent on Russia." Although Moscow ignored calls from pro-Russian factions of Kyrgyzstan to intervene in ethnic clashes in the south of the country in spite of having fought a war in 2008 against Georgia on behalf of South Ossetia and Abkhazia, Artur believes that it would provide military assistance to compatriots in Kyrgyzstan even without being asked. Overall he is convinced of the benevolence of Moscow and its altruistic willingness to protect Russian compatriots everywhere, and would like to see "all former Soviet republics united in a strong union" once more.

In neighboring Tajikistan, which is also highly dependent on Russia and is among Russia's closest allies, sentiments are similar. Yusuf is a twenty-seven-year-old native Russian speaker and office worker.[31] Although born in Uzbekistan with both Jewish and Ossetian blood, inherited from his paternal and his maternal side respectively, he considers himself a Russian compatriot. He is skeptical that compatriots face grievances in Tajikistan: "I almost never hear anyone saying something vile or discriminatory against me or my Russian-speaking friends." However, Yusuf believes that Russian protection might be necessary. He argues that "currently we are safe . . . but who knows what might happen tomorrow? If there is a political change or any other situation that would endanger Russian speakers in Tajikistan, there should be someone who could protect them." Yusuf also wholly supports Moscow's policy in Ukraine, arguing that "the fascist actions of Ukraine (with the support of the West and European countries) against its people are not allowed."

Katerina, a twenty-year-old Russian-speaking manager from Tajikistan, also considers herself a Russian compatriot because in her words "our life is directly dependent on Russia!"[32] Even though she grew up in Tajikistan and does not have any relatives in Russia, Katerina also considers herself a true Russian patriot. She does not think that there are any significant grievances for Russian speakers in Tajikistan: "Even if there are isolated cases of harassment, I have not witnessed any cases of discrimination or any violations of their rights." Nonetheless, she firmly believes that Moscow's protection is necessary: "of course we need protection, because we are directly dependent on Russia." Finally, Katerina also completely supports Russia's policy vis-à-vis Crimea, because "In the past Crimea belonged to Russia, therefore it should always belong to Russia."

Anatoly is a twenty-four-year-old ethnic Russian working in an IT company in Tajikistan.[33] Born in Uzbekistan but now a citizen of Tajikistan, Anatoly does not like the "compatriot" label and explains: "I am a patriot of the world, not Russia. I am not going to die for Tsar or Homeland." With a sarcastic sense of humor he explains that signs of his Russian identity are his partiality to "the balalaika, Russian *matryoshka* dolls, and bears on a chain." Anatoly is very skeptical of any grievances of Russian compatriots in Tajikistan. He explains, "I've never seen any violations of human rights or discrimination based on ethnicity." When asked if he thinks that Russia's protection of its compatriots is necessary, he explains that "On the one hand, Russia must take all necessary actions to ensure the peace and stability in our country. On the other hand, at the moment there are no internal or external threats to Russian compatriots. Therefore no protection is currently needed." Anatoly also has mixed views regarding Russia's policies in eastern Ukraine and Crimea: "although I do believe that it is good that Crimea joined Russia, I cannot say the same about Moscow's involvement in eastern Ukraine simply because a military conflict is bad. Russia ought to focus its resources on ending the conflict and not prolonging it."

Gash, a Russian-speaking bureaucrat from Uzbekistan, is much more pro-Moscow than Anatoly.[34] Now in his late twenties, Gash was born and raised in an Ossetian household and he does not fully regard himself as a Russian patriot or compatriot. Nonetheless he supports the Russian Federation because he feels it has been defending Ossetians from Georgia before and after the 2008 Russo-Georgian war. While he does not think that Russian speakers are generally discriminated against in Uzbekistan, he nonetheless concedes that there are some day-to-day problems. Thus he supports the idea of Moscow's protection, arguing that "there always has to be a strong guardian and that both sides would benefit from this relationship." Moreover, echoing the Russian media, he believes that Russia's policy vis-à-vis Crimea and eastern Ukraine was ultimately a good thing because "Moscow's policy was a carefully measured response to the American intention of establishing new military bases in the region." In the end, notwithstanding his seemingly pro-Russian stance, Gash regards himself as an Ossetian nationalist who lives in Uzbekistan. He believes that "one day North Ossetia and South Ossetia will become a single independent state, not under the Russian Federation or even less under Georgia."

Karina, a thirty-one-year-old Uzbek public-sector worker, believes in Uzbekistan's closer integration with Russia.[35] Although born and raised in Uzbekistan, in a mixed Russian and Tatar household, she does not speak the Uzbek language and understands only a little. She is a native Russian speaker and regards herself as a Russian compatriot. Karina adds: "in the foreseeable future I intend to acquire a Russian passport." While she does not think that the Russian minority in Uzbekistan has any serious grievances, she nonetheless believes that Russian support and Russo-Uzbek cooperation are somewhat of a necessity because "Uzbekistan is surrounded only by pro-Russian countries." Unsurprisingly, she is also a staunch supporter of the Eurasian Economic Union (EEU) project. Lastly, when asked about Moscow's recent policies in Crimea and eastern Ukraine, Karina answers that she definitely supports this trend of Russian foreign policy: "Russia has the right to protect its compatriots."

Overall, interviews in Central Asia demonstrated that while the ethnic Russian and Russian-speaking youth of the region identify somewhat less with Russia than does their parent or grandparent generation, they nonetheless harbor a spectrum of views toward Russia that includes staunch support of Moscow's policies. While many of the interviewees in Kazakhstan and elsewhere argued against Russia's protection of compatriots in their countries, this finding does not account for the likelihood that their opinions may change in the face of, say, perceptions of rising discrimination against Russian minorities—a perception that can result from Russian information warfare or a change in local policies. Despite the current mixed views on Russian compatriot and foreign policies represented in this sample of young voices from the Central Asian countries, Moscow has strong motivations for pursuing policies of influence and reimperialization in the region.

RUSSIAN MOTIVES AND INTERESTS
Russian interests in Central Asia are above all geopolitical—to maintain the region as a special zone of influence in the face of rising engagement from powers like China and especially the United States.[36] As with other CIS states, during the second half of the 2000s Moscow's attention has

been increasingly dedicated to preventing projection of American or NATO military power in the region, in contrast to the early 2000s when Moscow cooperated with the United States during Operation Enduring Freedom in Afghanistan and agreed to U.S. military bases in Kyrgyzstan and Uzbekistan as well as to adhesion to NATO's Partnership for Peace program of all five Central Asian countries.[37] Likewise, the Central Asian states serve as Russia's buffers against the volatile states of Afghanistan, Iran, and Pakistan as well as against Islamic extremism and the drug trade, with the latter nonetheless being an important source of income for players in Kyrgyzstan, Tajikistan, and Russia itself.[38] Kazakhstan is the most important buffer state, shielding Russia from the other Central Asian nations and sharing with it a border of more than four thousand miles. Moscow's economic and security interests in the region are based on energy transit, labor migration, defense of common boundaries, and in particular countermeasures against the emergence of Islamic extremist and to some extent nationalistic movements.[39]

Among the five states, Kazakhstan is typically viewed by Moscow as the most reliable regional partner, though the smaller, weaker Kyrgyzstan is a close second.[40] Following the 2014 crisis in Ukraine, Putin named Kazakhstan Russia's "closest strategic ally and partner," but the Kazakh-Russian relationship remains highly complex.[41] The Central Asian states, similarly to Ukraine and Belarus, host a variety of Russian military and strategic sites. In Kazakhstan these include the world's first and largest space launch facility, the Baikonur Cosmodrome, the Russian Ministry of Defense's 929th State Flight Test Center, the 4th State Central Polygon (a weapons testing range), the Dnepr and Balkhash space surveillance and early warning radar stations, the Sary-Shagan anti–ballistic missile testing range, and an air transport base at Kostanay.[42] Likewise, Kazakhstan, like Ukraine, is a former nuclear state and remains an important player in this sphere due to its uranium production. In the 2000s Kazakhstan emerged as the world's leading uranium producer, in 2013 producing 38 percent of the global total.[43] Russia's nuclear industry is one of the largest buyers of Kazakh uranium, and Kazakhstan's uranium industrial giant Kazatomprom works closely with its Russian counterpart Rosatomprom. This close relationship has not escaped controversy. The ex-head of Kazatomprom, Mukhtar Dzhakishev, who was arrested in 2009 on corruption charges and later sentenced to a decade in prison, has claimed that his persecution was caused by Russian struggles for control over Kazakhstan's uranium assets and in particular his opposition to Rosatomprom's acquisition (completed in January 2013) of one of the world's largest uranium mining companies, Uranium One, which has sizable operations in Kazakhstan.[44] Nonetheless, the Kazakh-Russian collaboration seems intact. In May 2014, Russia and Kazakhstan signed an agreement for construction of a nuclear power plant in Kazakhstan, and a Comprehensive Development Program for Russia-Kazakhstan Cooperation in the Peaceful Uses of Atomic Energy.[45]

Since the 2000s, Russia has consistently expanded its military presence in Kyrgyzstan and Tajikistan where it keeps troops permanently stationed. In 2003 Russia reopened the 999th Air Base in the Kyrgyz town of Kant, just twelve miles from the nation's capital of Bishkek.[46] Its main function is monitoring the Central Asian airspace and if necessary launching counterterrorist strikes.[47] Russia's 201st Motorized Rifle Division, previously involved in the Tajik civil war, has been based in Tajikistan since 1945. Only Uzbekistan and Turkmenistan do not have any Russian military sites on their territory. However, between 2006 and 2012 when Uzbekistan was a member of the Moscow-led Collective Security Treaty Organization, Russian forces reportedly used the Uzbek Karshi-Khanabad air base.[48]

Three of the Central Asian states are members of various Russian-led regional integration projects such as the EEU (Kazakhstan, Kyrgyzstan), as well as the CSTO (Kazakhstan, Kyrgyzstan, and Tajikistan).[49] However, this picture is not quite so simple. While Kazakhstan's president has long had reservations regarding further integration with Moscow-led organizations, he has seemingly been more vocal about this following Crimea's annexation in 2014.[50] In September 2014, Nazarbayev emphasized that Kazakhstan's participation in the EEU is purely economic and that the country will never be a "part of organizations that represent a threat to its independence."[51] The government of Uzbekistan, in spite of having participated in various Moscow-led regional organizations in the past, has also preferred to maintain bilateral diplomacy whenever possible.[52] In January 2015 Karimov stated that Uzbekistan has no intention of ever joining post-Soviet organizations.[53] In the case of Kyrgyzstan, though Atambayev's government joined the EEU in 2015, there are nationalistic groups among the Kyrgyz elite that do not support

Moscow-led Eurasian integration.[54] Finally, following tensions with the West and a rapprochement with China, Russia has cautiously started a new approach to cooperation in the region by signing in May 2015 a joint statement on integration between EEU and the China-led Silk Road economic development framework.

Moscow's efforts at Eurasian integration are in no small part motivated by the region's energy wealth. Turkmenistan, Kazakhstan, and Uzbekistan boast significant energy reserves. The natural gas reserves of these three states are estimated to be 400 to 700 trillion cubic feet—among the largest in the world.[55] Most of this gas lies in Turkmenistan (an estimated 265 to 618 trillion cubic feet) and the country also has notable reserves of oil.[56] Kazakhstan has about 2 percent of the world's proven oil reserves, 1 percent of gas reserves, and almost 4 percent of coal reserves. Uzbekistan's natural gas reserves are almost as large as Kazakhstan's and the country also has some oil reserves.[57]

Kazakhstan greatly depends on Russian-controlled pipelines for its exports of oil and gas.[58] More than three-quarters of Kazakh crude oil exports are transported through Russian territory via the Caspian Pipeline Consortium and Atyrau-Samara pipeline linked to the Russian Transneft pipeline distribution system.[59] Because Kazakhstan has been unable to agree with Russia on increasing its pumping capacity via the CPC pipeline and negotiate acceptable transit fees, since 2008 it has used tankers to deliver oil across the Caspian Sea to Russia's competitor, the Azerbaijani Baku-Tbilisi-Ceyhan pipeline. In 2009 Kazakhstan opened another, larger non–Russian-controlled export route—the Atasu-Alashankou oil pipeline to the Xinjiang region of China.[60]

Turkmenistan has been most successful in reorienting its export routes away from Russia toward China, which in 2011 gave Ashgabat a $4.1 billion loan in exchange for future gas supplies.[61] By 2013, 70 percent of Turkmen gas was being exported to China via the Central Asia China pipeline, which opened in 2009.[62] Iran has been the second largest buyer of Turkmen gas via the Korpezhe-Kurt Kuri pipeline since 1997 and Dauletabad-Khangiran pipeline since 2010, though these volumes may fall as Iran boosts its own domestic production.[63] Earlier Turkmenistan's main export routes depended on Russian territory and the Central Asia Center pipeline, which was opened in 2004.[64] Moscow and Ashgabat had initially agreed that CAC would export almost all of Turkmen gas production by 2009, but the ambitious plans came to nothing because of CAC's lack of capacity for larger volumes, disagreement between Moscow and Ashgabat over the price, and a 2009 explosion that caused a nine-month halt in operations.[65] By 2011 Russia was buying only a third of previously planned Turkmen gas.[66]

In contrast to Kazakhstan, Uzbekistan, and Turkmenistan, the resource-poor countries of Kyrgyzstan and Tajikistan are dependent on Russia for energy, and much of their population depends on Russian remittances for their livelihood. Tajikistan is the most remittance-dependent country in the world and Kyrgyzstan usually falls within the top five. A large share of the adult Tajikistani population (totaling between 1–2 million) works in Russia and in 2012 remittances from Russia made up 52 percent of the national GDP.[67] Meanwhile, there are from half a million to a million Kyrgyzstani labor migrants working in Russia.[68]

As with Ukraine and Belarus, there is also an ideological element in Russia's perception of Central Asia. Whereas Moscow considers Ukraine and Belarus as essentially the same nation as Russia, Moscow has often viewed the Central Asian republics as artificial states that the Soviets created in the 1920s.[69] Aleksandr Solzhenitsyn once stated that Kazakhstan's territory in essence consists of the Russian lands such as "southern Siberia, territory bordering the Urals, and central desert spaces," with the Kazakhs occupying only the southern regions.[70] The borders of the five central Asian states were indeed drawn rather artificially favoring economic considerations, often regardless of ethnic boundaries. National identity was weak during the Soviet era, though the Soviets rather encouraged national divisions while at the same time persecuting Islam and introducing the Cyrillic alphabet to break cultural links with Turkey and Iran. Putin's statement in August 2014 that the "Kazakhs never had possessed a state before Nazarbayev built it" reflected Moscow's disdainful sentiment toward Central Asia though it aimed to compliment Nazarbayev's regime.[71] The Kazakh president had earlier made similar statements himself, but in light of Russia's challenge to the statehood of Ukraine, he did not welcome Putin's comments. In October 2014 Nazarbayev announced that throughout 2015 the country would be celebrating 550 years of statehood, looking back to the fifteenth-century rise of the Kazakh Khanate despite its somewhat arbitrary connection to modern Kazakhstan.[72]

SOFT POWER

As with the Baltic States and Ukraine, Russia's soft power in Central Asia stems primarily from the presence of ethnic Russians and Russian speakers, from economic ties, and from a dose of Soviet nostalgia especially among the older generation—all factors that are in fact legacies of the Soviet era. In Kazakhstan, Russia's soft power has been influential because of the sizable Russian population and the generally cooperative orientation toward Moscow of the country's leadership. Kyrgyzstan's general vulnerability predisposes it toward Russian influence, which is furthermore welcomed by Bishkek. These factors are to a certain degree counterbalanced by a strong nationalist element among some of the newly emerged Kazakh and Kyrgyz elites. Tajikistan's favorable stance toward Moscow and general state weakness likewise predispose it toward Russian influence, yet there is little public information on Russian policies and programs in the country. Uzbekistan and Turkmenistan, due to the closed nature of their regimes and societies, are least susceptible to Russian soft power and influence over their domestic politics but are not completely immune to it.

In Kazakhstan and Kyrgyzstan the Russian language has a special status enshrined in the constitution as an "officially used language,"[73] while the Tajik constitution designates Russian as the "language of interethnic communication."[74] In Kazakhstan, there are more than 3.5 million ethnic Russians, and three-quarters of them do not speak any Kazakh. In addition, as seen in the interviews, Russian is the native language of people of mixed ethnic background and even of many urban members of the titular nation. In Kazakhstan in 2000 about 1.6 million school students (51 percent of the total) were studying in the Kazakh language, and 1.5 million (45 percent) in Russian. The government started to promote the national language in the 2000s, but this did not harm Russian speakers—there are around two thousand Russian schools in the country. Kyrgyzstan made Russian an "official language" in 2000, although a 2004 law stipulated that all state officials must know the Kyrgyz language.[75] In Tajikistan, due to the Russian military presence and strong economic dependence on Russian financial aid, the state has not introduced any nationalist policies to weaken the role of the Russian language, as it did with the language of the Uzbek minority,[76] though in 2009 legislation stipulated that all government documents were to be published in Tajik only. Nevertheless, due to the civil war some 200,000 of the 388,500 Russians had fled the country by 1993 and the remainder now constitute less than 1 percent of the population, leading to a significant decline of the Russian language. In contrast to the other three Central Asian states, in Uzbekistan and Turkmenistan the Russian language lost its privileged position in the early 1990s as governments distanced themselves from their Soviet past and focused on nation building and promoting a cultural renaissance of the titular nations. In Uzbekistan the Russian language does not have any official status since 1995, though it remains in use in Tashkent. In Turkmenistan, all state officials have been required to speak Turkmen since 1992.[77]

Despite this being a predominantly Muslim (albeit not highly practicing) region, the local Russian Orthodox Church also plays an influential role, in part due to its ties with Russia and the presence of Russian minorities,[78] the only possible exception being Turkmenistan. Across the region, the church is considered to be most influential in Kazakhstan. In 2009, Orthodoxy was the second most widely practiced religion there and about 26 percent of Kazakhstani citizens identified themselves as Orthodox.[79] As several scholars note, the church's relative success can be largely explained by the considerable support of President Nazarbayev and other state officials.[80] For instance, in 2010 Nazarbayev was awarded a high church honor by Russian Patriarch Kirill for his approval of and political assistance for the construction of the Uspensky Cathedral in Astana.[81] Nazarbayev stated in 2013 that "Islam and Orthodoxy are foundations of national spirituality" in Kazakhstan.[82] Astana's support for the Russian Orthodox Church is surprising in light of the fact that overall since 2011 there has been a trend of less tolerance for and more state control of religion, following a law that obliged official reregistration of all religious communities. This perhaps can be explained by the fact that the Russian Orthodox Church has desisted from challenging political regimes in Central Asia, unlike some regional Islamic movements. The trend has been similar in Kyrgyzstan and Tajikistan where since 2009 checks on religious communities have increased, including on Orthodox Christians. In Uzbekistan and Turkmenistan, the Russian Orthodox Church has the least influence, since these most autocratic states of the region have considerably limited its role.[83]

The influence of Russian big business has been most notable in Kazakhstan, though Kyrgyzstan and Tajikistan are overall dependent on Russian economic aid. In Kazakhstan, the most notable Russian business interests are energy companies.[84] The Russian oil company Lukoil owns 15 percent of Kazakhstan's Karachaganak Petroleum Operating Company, which develops the Karachaganak oil and gas field, and 5 percent (through its subsidiary Lukarco) of Tengizchevroil, which operates the Tengiz oil field. Russian pipeline operator Transneft owns 31 percent of the Caspian Pipeline Consortium, which transports Kazakh oil to Russia.[85] Nazarbayev emphasized the importance of continued future cooperation between Russia and Kazakhstan in the oil and gas sphere at the Eleventh Russia-Kazakhstan Interregional Cooperation Forum in September 2014.[86] However, in the other Central Asian states, Russian companies and business interests have faced some pushback. The failure of Russian oligarch Oleg Deripaska's company RusAl (Russian Aluminum) to gain a foothold in Tajikistan is one example of this. In 2004 RusAl sought to make a deal with the Tajik government to construct a hydroelectric plant in exchange for letting RusAl privatize an aluminum plant.[87] In 2007, however, the Tajik government claimed that RusAl had not lived up to the agreement by failing to provide adequate financing and terminated the deal, saying it would build its own hydroelectric plant and preserve ownership of the aluminum plant.[88]

As in other post-Soviet regions, the element of nostalgia for some Soviet features, such as a strong state, social security, education, and industrialization, is still widely persistent among various sections of society and serves as another form of Russia's soft power in Central Asia. In Kazakhstan this nostalgia stems from the fact that the government's moderate "Kazakhization" of the country since the 2000s, coupled with the transition to market economies, has resulted in growing economic inequality and social discontent, so that a number of Kazakhs and various minorities feel a longing for the simpler Soviet times.[89] A 2005 survey of some fifteen hundred Kazakhs regarding their assessment of current and Soviet government showed that 50 percent "strongly agreed" that Soviet government "responded to citizens' needs" and only 10 percent "strongly disagreed," while 48 percent "strongly disagreed" that Kazakhstani government responds to citizens' needs and only 9 percent "strongly agreed."[90] In some respects, Kazakhstan's participation in political and economic unions with Russia and Belarus, like the revival of many Soviet practices in the CIS, can be viewed as a form of "neo-Sovietism."[91] In fact, a 2013 a survey of Kazakhstani citizens also demonstrated that one of the reasons for the high popular approval of the EEU (68 percent) was "nostalgia for Soviet Union."[92] However, since the 2014 events in Ukraine the EEU is being increasingly criticized by the national opposition and the Kazakhstani population.[93] Overall, among the Central Asian states, Russia's soft power has been successful in Kazakhstan, Kyrgyzstan, and Tajikistan without significant efforts on the part of Moscow thanks to the prevalence of the Russian language, the presence of the Russian Orthodox Church, Russian economic influence, and nostalgia for the Soviet era.

HUMANITARIAN POLICIES

While Moscow has not actively pursued humanitarian policies to protect Central Asia's Russian-speaking minorities as it tried to do in the Baltic States, it has engaged in humanitarian aid and peacekeeping operations, particularly in Kyrgyzstan and Tajikistan. According to the Russian Ministry of Foreign Affairs the total humanitarian aid to the region during 2010 to 2014 was estimated at $4.5 billion, with the largest share of assistance going to those two countries. For instance, in 2013, Russia was the largest donor to Tajikistan, providing financial and economic aid such as debt restructuring, nontariff energy supplies, and humanitarian aid including food products.[94] The most significant Russian peacekeeping operations in Central Asia took place during the Tajik civil war of 1992–97. However, Russia's peacekeeping role was not without controversy. In 1992, the Garmis and Pamiris, underrepresented clans or regional groups that included both liberal democratic reformists and Islamists, formed an opposition and rose up against the government of the Leninbadi and Kulyabi regional groups that had been in power since the Soviet era.[95] Russia and Uzbekistan got involved in the conflict on the side of the government militias while the opposition turned to the Tajik diaspora in Afghanistan for refuge and allegedly to Iran for financial support.[96] In 1993 Russia, Kazakhstan, Kyrgyzstan, Tajikistan, and Uzbekistan created the CIS Collective Peacekeeping Force, but as in the case of Russia's peacekeeping in Georgia's South Ossetia and Abkhazia, most of the troops were Russian. In Tajikistan the troops were drawn from the Russian 201st Motorized Rifle Division, which had been present in the country since 1945.[97] On the one hand, Moscow's efforts contributed to the achievement of a peace accord in 1997 and the pacification of the country; on the other hand, there was some international and domestic criticism that Moscow had used its twenty-five-thousand-strong peacekeeping forces to establish a zone of influence in Tajikistan.[98] At that time, Yeltsin announced that "withdrawing Russian troops from Tajikistan would mean leaving a whole nation to perish, something that Russia would not accept."[99] In 2004 despite Tashkent's resistance, Russia created a permanent military base in Tajikistan for this peacekeeping force with the stated goal of preserving stability in the country.[100] The base remained Russia's second largest military presence abroad (after its Black Sea Fleet in Sevastopol) with a military contingent of seven thousand people (some 20 percent of whom are now permanent residents of Tajikistan) focused on monitoring Tajikistan's border with Afghanistan and on illegal militarized groups.[101]

In contrast to Tajikistan, Russia evaded peacekeeping operations in the 2010 ethnic clashes in southern Kyrgyzstan between Uzbek and Kyrgyz populations despite a public request from Kyrgyzstan's interim government. At the time, President Dmitry Medvedev quickly rejected the idea of sending in troops, explaining that Russia did not want to intervene into Kyrgyzstan's "internal affair."[102] In reality, Moscow's ambivalence toward the conflict stemmed from the fact that Russian interests were not at stake, from the persistent international criticism of Russia's recent actions in the Georgian war, and probably from a desire not to antagonize the lukewarm ally Uzbekistan. Naturally this raised many eyebrows and much criticism in view of Russia's "humanitarian" intervention in Georgia just two years earlier and its assistance to Tajikistan in 1992–97.[103]

COMPATRIOT POLICIES

Russia has pursued compatriot policies to different extents and with varying success in the five Central Asian states, owing to their different responses to Russian policies and their different overall relationships with Moscow. Kazakhstan, Kyrgyzstan, and Tajikistan have the most cooperative relations with Moscow and thus they have accepted (if not quite welcomed) Russian compatriot policies. However, as the interviews and profiles of young Central Asians show, the region's ethnic Russians and Russian speakers do not have uniform views on Russia and do not necessarily perceive themselves as compatriots. Kazakhstan's large Russian minority of some nearly 3.7 million people (21 percent of the total population) is concentrated in two regions bordering Russia: North Kazakhstan, where they are just over 50 percent of the regional population, and Kostanay, where they number nearly 43 percent.[104] As the cases of Ukraine, Georgia, Moldova, Estonia, and Latvia have shown, Russia has been best able to exploit compatriots for purposes of reimperialization when they are concentrated in territories on Russian borders. However, compatriot policies have had little notable success in Kazakhstan apart from resettlement of Russians back to the motherland.

In Kazakhstan, the Russian minority sought a foothold in domestic politics in the early 1990s. In 1994 Lad, a political party representing the interests of that group, won 80 percent of the seats in regional elections in cities with large Russian populations such as Temirtau, Aksu, Stepnoy, Rudny, and Ust-Kamenogorsk. This political success, along with the mere presence of a large Russian minority on the border with Russia, raised some concern for Nazarbayev's government. In seeming response, in 1995 a presidential decree created an Assembly of the People to represent nontitular ethnic groups.[105] However, it is largely considered to be an ineffective bureaucratic organization that does not genuinely represent minorities. In any case, Lad has since lost its political prominence in the face of government pressure and the division of the party into two branches in 2004.[106] However, the number of organizations representing ethnic Russians and Russian speakers has consistently increased from the 1990s to 2014, when there were thirty-eight organizations working to preserve Slavic culture, "interethnic stability," and Cossack traditions,[107] among them the Association of Russian, Slavic, and Cossack Organizations and the Russkaya Obshchina (Russian Community). Arguably due to Astana's pressure, however, they tend to take a moderate approach in their efforts to promote Russian identity, despite their possible hidden political objectives, collaborating with the Kazakhstani Ministry of Culture and promoting the Kazakh language in addition to Russian. Organizations like the Eastern Kazakhstan Regional Society of Slavic Culture and the Russian Cultural Center promote Russian culture.[108] In 2014, the Russian government's Russkiy Mir Foundation had ten branches in Central Asia—three in Kazakhstan, three in Kyrgyzstan, and four in Tajikistan. Kazakhstan's Russkiy Mir offices—located in Astana and the cities of Aktobe and Ust-Kamenogorsk—were founded in 2008 in close cooperation with the Presidential Center of Culture of Kazakhstan.[109]

The Russian minorities in Tajikistan (34,000, or 1 percent of the population) and Kyrgyzstan (420,000, or 8 percent) are much smaller than in Kazakhstan, but compatriot organizations are likewise active.[110] In Tajikistan, the Coordinating Council of Russian Compatriots (formerly Russkaya Obshchina) works with various Russian cultural organizations including those of Crimea's Tatars and Georgia's Ossetians who are also counted as "compatriots." According to the council, there are eleven Russian organizations in Dushanbe, two in Khatlon region, and one in Sogd region.[111] Kyrgyzstan, being both the most politically liberal Central Asian state and one that has close relations with Russia, has a much higher number of associations that promote Russian language and culture. The most prominent is the Slavic Fund, but there are more than twenty-five registered organizations representing the Russian minority such as Russkiy Soyuz (Russian Union) and the Compatriot Guild Association.[112] The Cossack community is an East Slavic semimilitary group living across Ukraine, Russia, and parts of Central Asia that preserves close ties to Cossacks in Siberia. In Kazakhstan it includes the Semirechiye Cossacks in the south and center, whose leader was arrested in the 1990s for organizing marches and rallies favoring separatism; the Ural Union of Cossacks in the west; and the Union of Cossacks of the Gorky Line in the north and east.[113] The Cossacks are quite numerous in Kyrgyzstan, and have their cultural center Vozrozhdeniye (Rebirth), which also publishes *Slavyanskiye Vesti* (Slav News), in Bishkek.[114]

In 2014, a highly controversial event for international compatriot youth took place in Kyrgyzstan: a patriotic and military camp targeting Russian youths from former Soviet republics, "Soyuz 2014—Victory's Heirs," that included representatives from all Central Asian states except for Turkmenistan.[115] Most of the participating Russian or Russian-speaking high-school students belonged to military sports teams: Kazakhstan's Albatros Youth Military-Patriotic Club from Kostanay, three teams from Kyrgyzstan (the Rodina Sport-Military Club, Veterans of the Kyrgyzstan Air Force, the Edelveis Military-Patriotic Club), and Uzbekistan's national freestyle wrestling team, as well as individuals from

Tajikistan.[116] This was the eighth annual Soyuz gathering held in the post-Soviet space.[117] The camp offers military training to the participants, including in information warfare, as well as teaching a Moscow-approved version of history.[118] The camps are funded by private companies but officially supported and organized by the Ministry of Defense of the Russian Federation, the Russian State Duma, the CIS intergovernmental military alliance CSTO, a patriotic organization aimed at consolidating Russian speakers abroad called Doblest Otechestva (Prowess of the Fatherland), and sports organization the Russian All-Round Fighting National League.[119] The event reflects Russia's growing efforts to militarize its compatriot populations. While one of organizers of the Soyuz camp, Oleg Bakanach, explains its purpose in innocent-sounding terms—"after the dissolution of the USSR, with the achievement of independence, the republics started to regress and grow distant from each other. This led us to the idea of organizing military-patriotic gatherings that would unite youth under the idea of internationalism."[120] In reality, however, the camp has a record of recruiting youths from post-Soviet states to Russian higher military academies.[121]

Unlike Kazakhstan, Kyrgyzstan, and Tajikistan, both Turkmenistan and Uzbekistan have resisted Russian compatriot policies and organizations. In Turkmenistan the Russian population is small, totaling under 150,000 (less than 3 percent of the population) in 2007. As seen in the interviews, some ethnic Turkmens are Russian speakers though the numbers are declining. In 1999, Turkmenistan's President Niyazov stated that he would not recognize any Russian-based associations, and in 2001 he even banned all Russian cultural events, declaring them "contrary to the spirit of Turkmen people."[122] Leaders of Russkaya Obshchina in Turkmenistan have been persecuted and the government refused to officially register the organization.[123] Since President Berdymukhamedov came to power at the end of 2006, the hard line against Russian compatriot activities has eased somewhat though there is very little information about these activities.[124] Uzbekistan's Russian population is likewise small, numbering only 800,000 in 2007 (3 percent of the population).[125] However, the Russian embassy in Tashkent in 2009 counted 1 million Russian compatriots in Uzbekistan including 200,000–300,000 Bashkirs and Tatars. Half of the Russian minority lives in Tashkent (around 400,000), and most of the rest lives in the city of Samarkand, Navoy and

Bukhar regions, and the Fergana valley. The Uzbek government is generally cautious about Moscow-driven Russian compatriot activities, and instead, since 1994 it has directly supported the largest nongovernmental organization of its kind in the country, the Russian Cultural Center of Tashkent, which organizes cultural festivals and has twenty-four offices across the country.[126]

Russia's compatriot resettlement program has had some success in Central Asia. Unlike with other Russian compatriot policies, Uzbekistan and Tajikistan were not directly opposed to this Russian initiative, perhaps because Uzbekistan's leadership focused on nation-state building based on the titular nationality and Tajikistan had a very small Russian population to begin with. Kazakhstan, with the largest Russian minority, has had the largest number of people participating. According to the Russian Federal Migration Service, in the period 2006 to December 2013, the resettlement program has been most popular in Kazakhstan and Uzbekistan with 41,308 and 29,194 individuals resettled to Russia respectively, while Tajikistan (13,571) and Kyrgyzstan (8,557) have had smaller numbers.[127] In 2011 the program gained momentum in Kazakhstan and the number of participants doubled.[128] The most active Kazakhstani cities in the program include Karaganda and Temirtau (Karaganda region), Petropavlovsk (North Kazakhstan region), Ust-Kamenogorsk (East Kazakhstan region), and Semei (East Kazakhstan region), with participants citing limited opportunities to use the Russian language as the main motive for resettlement. In contrast, in Tajikistan and the rest of the Central Asian states, and as with the resettlement of ethnic Armenians from that country (see Chapter 7), half of the people who want to take part in the resettlement program are ethnic Tajiks who want to acquire Russian citizenship and move to Russia primarily for economic reasons and because of marginalization of the Russian language and lack of Russian schools.[129] As noted earlier, many Tajiks in Russia are migrant workers and legalizing their status via the compatriot program is appealing. Nonetheless, considering that the Central Asian states, unlike Armenia, have not objected to Russian resettlement programs, the numbers of Central Asian returnees to Russia since the 2000s have been relatively small in comparison to their total population. Overall, outside of resettlement programs, Russian compatriot policies have not been welcomed in Turkmenistan and Uzbekistan and have thus had limited success.

Moscow's compatriot efforts have been more successful with Kazakhstan's large Russian minority as well as in Kyrgyzstan and Tajikistan
despite these countries' small Russian population.

PASSPORTIZATION

While Kazakhstan, Kyrgyzstan, and Tajikistan have been somewhat open
to Russian compatriot policies, all Central Asian countries have eventually rejected Russian passportization and dual citizenship efforts with the
sole exception of Tajikistan. The Central Asian states along with Belarus
have seemingly been more successful than Estonia, Ukraine, and Georgia, which have also tried to resist Russian passportization efforts, due
to the more authoritarian nature of their regimes. Only Tajikistan has
an agreement with Russia on dual citizenship, with some seventy-five
thousand Tajiks having acquired Russian citizenship.[130] This exceptional
position of Dushanbe can be explained by the country's dependence on
remittances, negligible Russian minority, and particularly Russia's leverage over the country: peacekeeping in the Tajik civil war 1992–97, humanitarian aid, and a sizable military base on its territory.[131]

Turkmenistan
In contrast, while Turkmenistan also signed an agreement on dual
citizenship with Yeltsin in 1993, the good will did not last and Ashgabat
generally discouraged Russia's passportization of Turkmens.[132] In 2003,
Putin and Niyazov officially terminated the agreement, a concession by
Putin, who argued that all ethnic Russians who wanted to emigrate from
Turkmenistan to Russia had already done so.[133] However, in reality Russia
was looking to placate Ashgabat and get access to Turkmen gas. The turn-
about was driven by the gas deal struck between Moscow and Ashgabat by
which Russia was to receive almost all Turkmen gas exports. In return for
its gas, Turkmenistan was allowed to terminate dual citizenship on its territory. Subsequently Niyazov gave an ultimatum to Turkmens with dual
citizenship (some thirty to fifty thousand) to choose one of the two nationalities within two months.[134] As a result emigration of Russians from
Turkmenistan sharply increased.[135] Following an intervention by the Russian Ministry of Foreign Affairs, Turkmenistan agreed that only new ap-
plicants would not have the right to dual citizenship, thus exempting
existing Russian citizenship holders.[136] However, in September 2008,

possibly in response to the Russo-Georgian war in August, new President Berdymukhamedov introduced a new constitution that again stated that "citizens of Turkmenistan cannot have citizenship of another state," and gave a five-year grace period to choose between citizenships.[137]

Moscow's 2003 gas deal with Ashgabat demonstrated the cynicism of its policies toward its diaspora. Russia has sought to "protect" and passportize Russian minorities in Georgia, Moldova, Ukraine, and the Baltic States when it suited its foreign policy goals but abandoned these policies when this was less convenient. In fact, if Russia had really wanted to protect or passportize its compatriots it should have been above all in Turkmenistan, where conditions for Russians were most difficult. Starting from 1992 Russians have been gradually removed from the public sector. By 2001–2, most Russian schools were closed (with the exception of one Russian high school opened in Ashgabat in 2002 during a visit by Putin), and all educational institutions were obliged to use Turkmen as their language of instruction. Head of Russia's Central Asia program of the Human Rights Center "Memorial" Vitaliy Ponomarev said in 2013 that the Moscow-Ashgabat gas deal was interpreted as an act of betrayal of Turkmenistan's Russians, with anti-Moscow sentiments running high and "even portraits of Putin were burned in front of the Russian embassy."[138]

Kazakhstan

Kazakhstan, Uzbekistan, and Kyrgyzstan have firmly resisted Russian passportization policies from the start and in fact have made dual citizenship illegal. In Kazakhstan, when Moscow raised the issue in 1993–94, Nazarbayev decisively rejected dual citizenship.[139] In May 1994 a Russian delegation headed by the chairman of the Committee on Citizenship of the Russian Federation, Abdullah Mikitayev, visited Kazakhstan to discuss dual citizenship but Almaty rejected even such discussion. It seems that if Moscow was pushing the dual citizenship agenda in order to gain leverage over Kazakhstan, Almaty rejected the idea for the very same reason. Nazarbayev's government minced no words and explained that dual citizenship was a threat to nation-state building and an opportunity for Moscow to interfere in the country's internal affairs.[140] In 1994, using a remark by Kazakh poet Olzhas Suleimenov, Nazarbayev compared dual citizenship with giving parachutes only to half the passengers in an airplane, instead of checking it to ensuring its proper functioning: that would be the effect of focusing on the Russian minority rather than building the Kazakh state.[141]

In 1995, Moscow and Almaty signed two treaties that addressed issues of citizens of each country living in the other, and the acquisition by Russian citizens of Kazakh citizenship.[142] To some extent these treaties addressed the interests of Russians in Kazakhstan and introduced a variety of favorable conditions and concessions for Russian citizens there. To put an end to the question of dual citizenship, in 1995 Article 10 was added to the constitution of Kazakhstan stating: "Foreign citizenship of a citizen of the Republic shall not be recognized."[143] In 2014 Kazakhstani Deputy Minister of Foreign Affairs Samat Ordabayev emphasized that the grand integration project of the EEU of Russia, Belarus, and Kazakhstan would not have any legal consequences for citizens of Kazakhstan such as the introduction of common citizenship.[144] Nonetheless, it is likely that some degree of dual citizenship exists among the Russian minority. There are occasional mentions in the Kazakhstani press that illegal acquisition of Russian passports is popular in the North Kazakhstan region, but no official statistics are given.[145]

In Uzbekistan, the 1992 Law on Citizenship established nonrecognition of any other citizenships of Uzbek citizens and this has remained unchanged.[146] Kyrgyzstan's position has become more ambiguous, with the introduction in 2007 of a citizenship law that theoretically recognizes possession of another citizenship, but only if international agreements exist with the country concerned.[147] It is likely that Russia's efforts at passportization and information warfare have been more cautious in autocratic Kazakhstan, Turkmenistan, and Uzbekistan so as not to jeopardize ties with the strongmen leaders.

INFORMATION WARFARE

As in much of the post-Soviet space, Russian media have a strong presence in Kazakhstan, Kyrgyzstan, and Tajikistan, but the Uzbekistan and particularly the Turkmenistan governments try to severely limit them. As in Ukraine, the Baltic States, and elsewhere, in Central Asia the local media have trouble competing with Russian media not only among ethnic Russians or Russian speakers but also among the broader population due to their more limited resources, less exciting programming, and shorter track record, and the persistent popularity of Russian pop culture.[148] Following the announcement of the launch of the new Russian international media project Sputnik with offices in all ex-communist states except Turkmenistan,[149] Sputnik Kyrgyzstan started its work in December 2014 with its head, Yelena Cheremenina, stating that Russia is Kyrgyzstan's strategic partner and given Kyrgyzstan's accession to the EEU there was a need to tell people what is "happening in the country."[150] This was somewhat surprising considering that some members of the Kyrgyz and other Central Asian elites had already expressed concern over the dominance of the Russian media. The chief of staff of the former interim government, Edil Baisalov, wrote an op-ed in 2014 about the pervasiveness of Russian propaganda in Kyrgyzstan which, he declared, inspired ill-considered and irrational lawmaking and encouraged homophobia. In Kyrgyzstan the Russian-state run Channel One is already the second most watched TV channel, after the country's national broadcaster OTRK.[151]

Likewise, in 2013 Kazakhstan's former Secretary of State Marat Tazhin urged modernization of local mass media and an increase in its appeal to people.[152] In 2014, according to polls, 50 percent of the Kazakhstani population regularly watched Russian TV channels, with 38 percent of them choosing Russian state-owned channel RTR-Planeta, which broadcasts programs of the Rossiya channel to the post-Soviet space.[153] Polls also indicate that the most watched TV channel in Kazakhstan is Pervyi Kanal "Euraziya" (Channel One Eurasia), which rebroadcasts TV programs and news of Russia's Channel One.[154] This widespread reliance on Russian TV, print, and online media colors the views of the Kazakhstani population especially on foreign policy. In 2014, a survey conducted by the Center for Social and Political Research Strategy demonstrated that 61 percent of those surveyed supported Russian policy in Ukraine, only 5 percent supported Ukraine, and the rest were undecided.[155] Moreover, of the 31 percent of respondents who named Russian mass media as their primary source of information, 84 percent supported Russia and only 4 percent did not do so. Interestingly, in response to a question about whether respondents believed in the possibility that Russia could use military force against Kazakhstan, 57 percent said "no," 28 percent answered "more no than yes," 8 percent could not give an answer, and only 7 percent indicated "yes" and "more yes than no."[156]

In Tajikistan, Turkmenistan, and Uzbekistan Russian cable TV channels also remain popular, even in the most remote villages where people have installed satellites (despite official but not very efficient resistance from the Turkmen and Uzbek governments).[157] Uzbekistan's official policy restricts broadcasting in the Russian language and the state tries to ban some Russian channels deemed to show improper content.[158] Uzbekistan has consistently shut down mainstream Russian TV channels such as the business news channel RBK and entertainment channels such as REN TV, TNT, and Domashniy.[159] However, even the most rural Uzbekistani population still has wide access to Russian television channels through satellites, as President Karimov has himself confirmed.[160] Though the authoritarian regimes and the lesser regard for freedom of expression and diverse opinions has given Uzbekistan and Turkmenistan more room for countering the influence of Russian media, their efforts have not been entirely successful.

Unlike Georgia, Moldova, Ukraine, the Baltics, and Armenia, the Central Asian countries have not faced a concerted information warfare campaign by the Russian mainstream media regarding the conditions of the region's Russian minorities. There has even been little coverage of the actual tough minority policies that Turkmenistan has pursued. From the 1990s to the 2010s there has only been sporadic, low-profile coverage of compatriot issues. For instance, in 1995 the Kazakh authorities detained for three months Nikolai Gunkin, leader of the Semirechye Cossacks who were calling for North Kazakhstan's secession, on account of unauthorized rallies in Almaty. Russian television broadcast Gunkin's outlandish allegations that Kazakhstan was a "fascist state" that engaged in "genocide of Russians."[161] The publicity around Gunkin's case garnered some attention to Cossack nationalist claims but the story quickly subsided. Apart from traditional media outlets, Russian actors also take advantage of Central Asia's internet space. Websites such as those of the Russian Center for Terrorist Threat Analysis, headed by former deputies of the Russian Duma, which in 2013 registered an office in Kazakhstan, and Kyrgyzstan's "Eurasians—the New Wave" organization intensively propagate anti-American conspiracy theories and encourage integration of Kyrgyzstan and Kazakhstan into the EEU.[162]

Since Russia's annexation of Crimea in 2014, the situation has remained largely unchanged, though comparisons have been drawn on both sides between Crimea and North Kazakhstan. In October 2014, the independent Russian website Meduza published a reportage on the poor conditions of Russian speakers in Kazakhstan. The story also contained interviews with representatives of Russian and Kazakhstani organizations such as Russkiy Mir, Lad, and Russkaya Obshchina who were convinced that East Kazakhstan's history was similar to that of Crimea. "As Putin said, we were given away [by Russia] like a sack of potatoes," said Oleg Navozov of Lad. He was backed up by Oleg Maslennikov from Kazakhstan's branch of Russkaya Obshchina: "I have no idea why Lenin came up with the idea of giving away Rudny Altai [a territory in eastern Kazakhstan]," referring to Lenin's demarcation of Kazakhstan's borders. The reportage was immediately blocked on the territory of Kazakhstan.[163] Apart from such sporadic incidents, perhaps to avoid upsetting relations with the Central Asian states and their leaders, Moscow has largely refrained from information warfare campaigns on the treatment of Russian minorities.

Russia did, however, launch a campaign against one regional leader, Kyrgyz President Bakiyev, that contributed to his ousting from power in 2010 and serves as an example of the possible outcomes of Russia's targeted propaganda in Central Asia. The 2010 protests against Bakiyev were primarily driven by domestic factors, namely the public's dissatisfaction with nationwide corruption and deteriorating standards of living, but in that general context, Russian media had a powerful effect that was highly destabilizing to the Bakiyev regime.[164] Bakiyev's relations with Moscow deteriorated in 2009 when the Kyrgyz leader, against Russia's wishes, decided not only to prolong the U.S. lease on the Manas air base but also to approve building along with the Americans a new military training center in southern Kyrgyzstan.[165] In response, in March 2010 Russia increased tariffs on energy exports to Kyrgyzstan, while the Russian mass media started an anti-Bakiyev campaign that significantly added to the negative sentiments toward the government among Kyrgyzstanis who received much of their information from Russian cable TV channels.[166] The criticism of Bakiyev resounded both in strongly pro–Russian government media such as the newspaper *Izvestiya* and the NTV channel, and in relatively independent outlets such as online Gazeta.ru and radio station Moscow Echo. The reports told of the corruption and clientelism of Bakiyev's regime (especially involving Bakiyev's son Maxim Bakiyev) and its close and allegedly unseemly relationship with the United States, and raised accusations of Bakiyev's alleged involvement in the notorious murder of Kyrgyz journalist and regime critic Gennadiy Pavluk in 2009.[167] Bakiyev was also compared to Turkmenistan's deceased dictator, President Niyazov.[168] Although there has not been direct evidence that Russia participated in a deliberate campaign to force Bakiyev out or that the Russian media campaign was decisive in his ousting, there have been reports of meetings of Russian representatives with the Kyrgyz opposition. After the revolution, Russia was the first country to offer financial aid and to recognize the interim Kyrgyz government that came to power after Bakiyev fled the country.[169] Overall, Russia's information warfare campaign in Kyrgyzstan has been the exception rather than the rule in Central Asia and Moscow's calls for compatriot protection have also been more muted in this region than elsewhere.

PROTECTION OF COMPATRIOTS

While there has been a discernible increase in Russian media reports on the Russian diaspora in Central Asia and support for Russian compatriot and cultural organizations across the region since the 2010s, there have been no official calls from the Russian government to "protect" these people. In fact, the only calls for "protection" occurred in the early 1990s under Yeltsin's administration and were met with such a firm rebuff that the Putin administration has chosen its words more carefully.

In general, in the early 1990s Moscow was not overly concerned with Russian compatriots in Central Asia and lacked any consistent strategy (see Chapter 3). Only a couple of notable episodes of Moscow's expressed concern took place in the 1993 to 1995 period. In 1993, Moscow's efforts to create a new currency zone that excluded Central Asian states was at best ill received in Kazakhstan and interpreted as a betrayal at worst, thereby contributing to anti-Russian sentiments and rumors of violence.[170] In 1993, Russian Deputy Prime Minister Shokhin commented on the alleged anti-Russian violence in Kazakhstan: "Russia has sufficient means of responding to bullying methods of 'people's diplomacy' to make the 'architects' of this policy regret it. . . . Russia can and will defend its current interests."[171] Nazarbayev made his famous response, comparing Moscow's protection of Russians in Kazakhstan to Hitler's support of Sudeten Germans.[172] Subsequently, Russian Foreign Minister Andrey

Kozyrev and Deputy Defense Minister Boris Gromov visited Almaty in November 1993 but Nazarbayev refused to meet them personally, delegating the foreign minister and the prime minister instead. Kozyrev presented a memorandum on the situation of Russians in Kazakhstan commenting on the Russian language policy, the Cossacks, Russian education and culture, and the status of Russian military personnel, and made a public statement of Moscow's support for dual citizenship. Kazakhstani Prime Minister Sergey Tereshchenko responded that "all citizens of Kazakhstan enjoyed equal rights and protection of the law." To make the situation more awkward, eccentric Russian politician Vladimir Zhirinovsky promised in 1993 and during his 1996 presidential election campaign to grant Russian citizenship to all Russians in former Soviet republics. Nazarbayev responded by saying that this type of statement "under the pretext of protecting Russian-speaking population, sow discord between our countries. . . . Our task is to protect Russians as well as other ethnic groups who live in Kazakhstan."[173] Nazarbayev's political party also issued a statement calling upon "democratic forces [in Russia] to rebuff such defenders of the Russian people's interests."[174] Additionally, government authorities organized leaders of industrial plants in the city of Semipalatinsk (where there is a large population of ethnic Russians) to send a telegram to Yeltsin condemning Zhirinovsky.[175]

While Putin's regime fought two wars in Georgia and Ukraine over the "protection" of Russian compatriots, in Central Asia, at least in official discourse, Putin has shown more pragmatism and diplomacy over the compatriot question. For instance, early in his tenure, when Putin met with leaders of compatriot organizations in Astana in October 2000, he emphasized that existing Russian agreements with Kazakhstan ensured satisfactory conditions for the Russian diaspora population and called only for promoting Russian culture and language.[176] Although the head of Kazakhstan's branch of Russkaya Obshchina, Yuri Bunakov, called for the return of Russians from Kazakhstan to Russia, Putin steered the conversation to positive opportunities and assured that Kazakhstani authorities were not interested in Russians leaving the country.[177] Putin's official discourse on the issue of protecting Russian compatriots has been muted for the same reason that Moscow has been hesitant to aggressively push compatriot or passportization policies in the region. Openly antagonizing strongman leaders in Kazakhstan, Uzbekistan, and Turkmenistan is unlikely to yield results in these closed societies and authoritarian states. In contrast, in Kyrgyzstan and Tajikistan Moscow can wield a freer hand, but these countries are in any case loyal to Russia so that the pretext of compatriot protection is unnecessary to exert influence.

SEPARATISM AND SECESSION MOVEMENTS

Among the Central Asian states only Kazakhstan has the large, concentrated population of ethnic Russians and Russian speakers along the border with Russia that could favor separatist or secessionist movements. While Kyrgyzstan and Tajikistan have become Russia's de facto protectorates, only Kazakhstan faces imminent risks implied by the re-imperialization trajectory. The risk of separatism in Kazakhstan has persisted from the 1990s and Nazarbayev has consistently tried to counter it. For instance, in 1994, a survey showed that 42 percent of the population in East Kazakhstan and 37 percent in North Kazakhstan believed that these border regions should be part of Russia.[178] In general, during the 1990s Russians in Kazakhstan remained oriented toward Russia: a United States Information Agency survey in 1997 showed that 66 percent of Kazakhstan's Russians favored the idea of a closer union with Russia compared to only 35 percent of Kazakhs.[179] In response to these pro-Russian sentiments among the Russian minority, the Kazakhstani government introduced an "administrative rationalization" program in 1997 that redrew the boundaries of regions, merging northern Russian-populated regions with neighboring ones to diffuse the Russian population.[180] Nazarbayev's most drastic move to secure the northern regions was in 1998 when he transferred the nation's capital from southern Almaty to northern Astana.[181] Manifestations of separatism have been dealt swift blows by the government. In one prominent episode in 1999, in the city of Ust-Kamenogorsk with about 67 percent Russian population, twenty-two people were accused of pro-Russian separatism and arrested.[182] Twelve of them were Russian citizens led by Viktor Kazimirchuk of the Rus' patriotic movement who tried to organize a referendum for East Kazakhstan to become an autonomous region of Russia. They were convicted of organizing "terroristic acts."[183]

In the lead-up to Russia's annexation of Crimea and the declaration of a Cossack separatist "people's republic" in eastern Ukraine in 2014,

the Kazakhstani government took a stricter approach as separatist rhetoric increased. In February 2014, the Kazakhstani media reported that
Cossacks from the eastern part of the country wanted to fight on the side
of the Crimean separatists. These pro-Russian sentiments were attributed to the work of the Russian Eurasian Youth Union, formed by the
chief Russian promoter of Eurasianism, Alexander Dugin, when one of
its members, Pavel Zarifullin, said in an interview that Kazakhstani
members of the union "actively support idea of Russian empire and that
the outcome of the Crimean incident will be decisive in the development of whole Eurasian world."[184] In April 2014, such sentiments were
indirectly echoed in an interview with Viktor Sharonov, one of the leaders of the Kazakhstan Cossacks: "In terms of the immutability of state
borders . . . talking about some actions as being fixed for eternity is
simply incorrect. . . . Then what right would the Scots have to hold a
referendum on separating from Great Britain?"[185] Earlier that month,
Kazakhstan introduced criminal penalties for separatism in a revised
version of the country's criminal code.[186]

At the same time, Russia-Kazakhstani relations became more complicated when Russia's nationalist groups started calling for a revival of
the Russian Empire. In February 2014, Russia's popular extreme left political activist Eduard Limonov called for outright annexation of northern Kazakhstan.[187] Four days later, Russian Ambassador to Kazakhstan
Mikhail Bocharnikov tried to defuse the situation, describing Limonov
as "a marginal social network figure," and said there was no need to
comment on his statements.[188] Likewise, in April 2014 the Chairman of
the Supreme Council of the Republic of Khakassia (part of the Russian
Federation and close to northern Kazakhstan), Vladimir Shtygashev, said
that "the East Kazakhstan region or Rudny Altai was always a part of
Russia . . . and that in total we ceded five regions to Kazakhstan."[189]
The Kazakh Ministry of Foreign Affairs immediately issued a statement
expressing concern about "alleged Russian historical rights to eastern
parts of Kazakhstan."[190] Russia responded that "irresponsible comments
from Russian regional governments" did not reflect the official Russian
position on Kazakhstan's territory.[191] In August 2014, Zhirinovsky reiterated that Russia should annex Kazakhstan after Ukraine.[192] In light of
Crimea's recent annexation and the effort to create a "New Russia" in eastern Ukraine, it would be surprising if Moscow's assurances, combined

with simultaneous unofficial pronouncements of Russia's claims on Kazakhstan, were implicitly believed in Astana.

In sum, given the active Russian compatriot measures in Kazakhstan and
across Central Asia, all five Central Asian countries face the reimperialization trajectory. To date, though, Moscow's policies have largely failed
in Kazakhstan, Turkmenistan, and Uzbekistan. All Central Asian states
have encountered Russia's soft power, including compatriot activities that
ranged from benign cultural support to more aggressive programs of military training for youths, propaganda campaigns, efforts at passportization, and possibly stoking of separatist movements in northern
Kazakhstan. The five Central Asian states have each drawn different red
lines when it came to reimperialization efforts via the Russian minority.
While the regime of Kazakhstani President Nazarbayev has generally
taken a pragmatic and diplomatic approach with Russia and allowed Russian cultural organizations, it has rejected passportization, calls for protection, and separatist movements. Nazarbayev's pragmatism and the
authoritarian nature of his regime have enabled him to both assuage
Kazakh nationalism and find support among the ethnic minorities who
perceive him as a guarantor of interethnic peace.[193] As the most powerful state in Central Asia, Kazakhstan has been able to cultivate its partnership with Russia without making itself vulnerable.

Tajikistan's and Kyrgyzstan's positions have been much different.
Both of these poor, weak states depend on Russia for economic aid and
security assistance and host Russian military bases. They have been left
vulnerable to much greater Russian influence despite their lack of shared
borders with Russia and large Russian minority populations. Tajikistan
is also the only Central Asian state to have accepted Russia's policy of dual
citizenship. Here Moscow has largely succeeded in its neo-imperial aims,
and Tajikistan and Kyrgyzstan that have become Russia's dependents like
Belarus and Armenia. Admittedly Moscow's success has been only in
small part if at all due to the presence of ethnic Russians and Russian
speakers. Instead, as in Georgia, Moldova, and Armenia, Moscow has leveraged the vulnerability of these states, resulting from their civil wars,
ethnic conflicts, and economic weakness, in order to exert influence over
them. In the future, Kyrgyzstan and Tajikistan could likely see even
greater economic, political, and security dependence on Russia.

Much of the success of those Central Asian states that have thwarted Russia's efforts is tied to the specifics of their regimes. In contrast to Kyrgyzstan and Tajikistan, both Uzbekistan and Turkmenistan, as the richer, more closed and authoritarian regimes of Central Asia, have been the least cooperative with Russia's compatriot policies, rejecting Russian passportization efforts and even restricting Russian cultural initiatives. Uzbekistan and particularly Turkmenistan have been the least permeated by Russian reimperialization efforts because of the fact that they remain relatively closed to outside influence and because their autocratic regimes facilitate greater control over society. Nonetheless, the populations of both states are highly dependent on Russian media, while the appeal of the Russian World is evident from the participation even of Uzbek youths in the Soyuz military camp.

Among the Central Asian states, Kazakhstan finds itself most at risk of a challenge to its territorial integrity. This challenge is unlikely to emerge as long as Kazakhstan's foreign policy remains in line with Moscow's. Yet, if Kazakhstan were ever to shift its foreign policy, say, toward the West or to seek NATO membership, it could face increasing pressure from Moscow as have Ukraine, Georgia, and others. The most likely conduit for this pressure would be the Russian compatriots residing in northern Kazakhstan. A change in leadership in Kazakhstan or in any of the Central Asian states could result in a change in these states' foreign policies and their relationships with Moscow. With Kazakhstan's Nazarbayev and Uzbekistan's Karimov both well into their seventies and Tajikistan's equally long-ruling Rahmon in his sixties, changes of leadership are certainly on the horizon for these states. During periods of transition, opportunities may emerge for Russian influence and interference. Some scholars have emphasized the importance of clan politics and local kinship identities in Central Asia.[194] This could suggest that ethnic or clan infighting may emerge as a risk in leadership transition periods. However, while Moscow will probably try to exploit ethnic, regional, and family interest groups, this risk and the importance of clan politics are probably overstated, except as they affect Tajikistan. While discourses of local identity have been given a boost in the postindependence period, the national identities that have emerged from the Soviet period and modern Central Asian authoritarian political systems are complex and do not fall within narrow definitions of traditional clan-based societies.[195] The broader Kazakh and Uzbek elites have consistently taken a nationalistic line in the last twenty years and Moscow will not have an easy time gaining significant political influence over these large, strong, energy-rich states as it has been able to do so in Tajikistan and Kyrgyzstan. Nonetheless, in the future, as the more closed autocratic Central Asian regimes perhaps change and open up, they could become more vulnerable targets of the reimperialization trajectory, and thwarting Russia's soft power, compatriot, information, and separatist efforts will be more difficult in more liberal societies.

CHAPTER SEVEN

Allies or Targets?

BELARUS AND ARMENIA

Belarusians and Russians are one people.

—*Russian Defense Minister Sergey Ivanov, February 2006*

Armenia can only live with Russia or not live at all.

—*Former Russian Ambassador to Armenia Vyacheslav Kovalenko, July 2013*

BELARUS AND ARMENIA have been among Russia's closest military, political, and economic allies since the end of the Cold War. Belarus, Russia's neighbor and so-called Slavic brother nation, in the late 1990s even considered forming a union with Russia, in which the Belarusian President Alexander Lukashenko saw himself as a possible leader and successor to Boris Yeltsin.[1] Russia's closest friend in the Caucasus, Armenia, has looked to Moscow for support in light of its troubled relationship with neighboring Turkey, which goes back to the Ottoman-led Armenian genocide of 1915–23 and the bloody ethnic war with neighboring Azerbaijan in and around Nagorno-Karabakh since the early 1990s. It may seem counterintuitive to seek to identify a Russian reimperialization trajectory toward its closest allies. The paradox lies in the contrast between the cooperative relationship of these two states with Moscow and the fact that the trajectory implies coercive means of influence that may end in aggression and even annexation. However, this analysis of Belarus and Armenia offers a unique perspective on the relevance of Moscow's compatriot and reimperialization policies toward cooperative post-Soviet states where there is no sizable ethnic Russian minority. There is indeed something to be learned about how the reimperialization trajectory is pursued with countries that are allies versus countries such as the Baltic States and Georgia that have had more adversarial and troubled relations with Russia. While the declared Russian policies toward Belarus and Armenia have been ones of fraternity, their close relationship with and dependence upon Russia have been sources of weakness for both states and have limited their independence.[2]

DIVERGENT BACKGROUNDS

While Belarus and Armenia share a similar cooperative relationship with Russia, the sources of Russian influence over these two countries are different. In Belarus, it stems from a strong cultural and political affinity as well as from economic dependence. For Armenia, the perceived external security threats from Turkey and Azerbaijan are the main motive for closer relations with Moscow. However, Russia's influence over Armenia finds some resistance due to the country's strong and distinct cultural identity. Still, Moscow has already arguably achieved significant military, political, and economic integration of both Belarus and (albeit to a lesser degree) Armenia. "Reimperialization" may not be the best word to describe Belarusian-Russian and Armenian-Russian relations, since Minsk and Yerevan have never been lost to Moscow's orbit of influence. Russia's activities regarding Belarus and Armenia may best be understood as an effort to maintain the countries in its "empire." However as the case of Ukraine has demonstrated, even a Slavic brother nation and a historic ally of Russia can become a target of reimperialization and annexation efforts. Likewise, the case of Belarus points, if not to Russian annexation, more likely to a gradual and slow merger—a process that in many ways began not only before Putin's reign, but even before the Soviet era.[3]

Belarus

The dependence of Belarus and Armenia on Russia is a product of centuries of history. Indeed the so-called alliance between Belarus and Russia has long been one of vassal and master. Belarus has been under Moscow's domination since 1772 when the Russian Empire took over territories of eastern Belarus from the Polish-Lithuanian Commonwealth. From that time, Belarus faced severe Russification policies including conversion of locals from the Greek Catholic Church to the Russian Orthodox Church of the Moscow Patriarchate.[4] As in Ukraine, the Baltic States, and many other countries in the tsarist empire, printing books in the local language using the Latin alphabet was outlawed and the Russian Cyrillic alphabet was imposed. During the Soviet era the pressure continued. The Belarusian population faced massive purges while the Belarusian language was Russified and stigmatized.[5] The force of Sovietization and the pressure to eradicate national identity were so successful that the Belarusians were considered models of *Homo Sovieticus* (Soviet Man).[6]

President Lukashenko's ascent to power in 1994 marked a new page in Belarusian history—but one that had an uncanny resemblance to its past. His victory in 1994 elections was unexpected and was met with mixed feelings ranging from surprise ("a president by accident") to embarrassment at having a Soviet *kolkhoznik* (collective farmer) running the country. However, by gradually monopolizing the reins of power, marginalizing the opposition, and atomizing the nascent civic society, Lukashenko has secured his presidential throne for more than two decades.[7] Eventually Belarus became a self-isolated terra incognita, best known for having "Europe's last dictator." In Lukashenko's era, Belarusian authorities simultaneously pursued Sovietization and Russification, as the leader tried to revert to a Soviet Politburo style of government. In 1995, following a referendum, Russian was introduced as the second official language, once again increasingly marginalizing Belarusian. As in the Soviet time, the Russian language was used for teaching all subjects in the education system. As a result of centuries of such policies, the Belarusian nation has been robbed of its national identity—of its "self," according to contemporary Belarusian philosopher Valiantsin Akudovich's book *Nesaties Kodas*.[8] Today, the majority of Belarusians speak Russian day-to-day and due to Minsk's policies have become an inseparable part of Moscow's ideological project—the Russian World. Still, the current Belarusian identity is complex. As Lukashenko stated in 2014, "there is no other country in the world [outside of Russia and Belarus] that would care so much for the great Russian language and the great Russian culture," but also emphasized that "we are not Russians, we are Belarusians."[9] The younger generation, less trapped in a Soviet identity, has been engaged in various initiatives of alternative culture. Speaking Belarusian, before considered provincial, now has become hip for some urban youth. This process has been boosted by the popular campaign *Budzma Belarusami* (Let's Be Belarusians), which expresses national pride through urban music and is backed by international funding.[10] The Belarusian diaspora (some 3 million worldwide) also supports various language, history, literature, and cultural initiatives.[11]

Armenia

The sense of national identity is an area where the similarities between Armenia and Belarus end. Armenia's geographical position in the Caucasus between Western Asia and Eastern Europe has dictated its history and its identity. This ancient civilization, the first state in the world to adopt Christianity, boasts its own unique alphabet and has always had a strong sense of self. This national identity has been threatened on numerous occasions by the Romans, the Parthians, the Persians, the Ottomans, the Turks, and the Soviets. Being the closest of powerful "European" nations and one with whom Armenia shares a common Orthodox Christian faith, Russia has emerged as an unlikely friend, security guarantor, and protector.[12] The institutionalization of Russian-Armenian relations can be traced back to the early eighteenth century, when Armenian diplomat Israel Ori sought an alliance with Russia in the hopes of freeing Armenia from the Ottoman and Persian yokes when other allies in Europe could not be found.[13] There has followed a long and difficult history, with Russia sometimes acting as more of a foe than an ally, and with Armenia being forcibly incorporated into the Soviet Union with deportations and Russification programs similar to those that took place across the Soviet republics. In the late 1980s and early 1990s, ethnic clashes between Armenians and Azeris broke out in the long-contested region of Nagorno-Karabakh, which was formally part of neighboring Soviet Azerbaijan but was historically inhabited by Armenians (see Map 3, p. 97).[14] During this time the Soviet government sought to uphold the status quo and keep Nagorno-Karabakh within Soviet Azerbaijan. By 1990–91 Armenian militias engaged in direct combat with the Soviet Army and security forces in both Armenia and Nagorno-Karabakh as Soviet forces sought to deport Armenians from the contested territory.[15] By 1992, an all-out war broke out between newly independent Azerbaijan and Armenia with the self-proclaimed Nagorno-Karabakh Republic.[16] Echoing its history, Armenia once again would turn to Russia for assistance and protection and thereby lay the ground for an enduring alliance in the decades to come. But this turn to Russia was not immediate and not without hesitation. Initially, Armenian activists sought to win the support of the West as well as Russian democrats to stop Moscow's involvement on the side of Azerbaijan.[17] After the fall of the Soviet Union, Yeltsin's ascent, and the West's refusal to get involved, in 1993 Turkey also emerged as a threat, launching an economic embargo and massing its troops on the border with the Turkish leadership threatening invasion.[18] That was when the Armenian government turned to Russia and requested that a Russian division remain in Armenia as a deterrent against Turkey.[19] As editor of *The Armenian Reporter* Emil Sanamyan explained, "While both Armenia and Azerbaijan sought Russia's assistance throughout the Nagorno-Karabakh conflict and since, it was the potential Turkish factor that cemented the Russian-Armenian alliance."[20] Subsequently, Moscow's role in the Nagorno-Karabakh conflict and its relationship with Armenia have remained complex.[21] Through a combination of corruption and political decisions Russia armed and supported both Armenia and Azerbaijan in their conflict.[22]

PORTRAITS OF RUSSIAN SPEAKERS

Compared with most of the other countries' cases analyzed here, such as the Baltic States, Ukraine, and Georgia, the situations of Russian compatriots in Belarus and Armenia are exceptional. In Belarus, ethnic Russians are just 8 percent of the population, or nearly 800,000 people.[23] Furthermore, they are relatively evenly dispersed across the country rather than concentrated in specific regions. The largest concentration of Russians is 10 percent, in the Vitebsk region bordering Russia. However, most Belarusians are Russian speakers, with just 23 percent knowing Belarusian and less than 5 percent using their native language in daily communication.[24] Given their shared language, faith, and arguably culture with Russia, and their membership in the Russian World, most of the 9.6 million Belarusians could potentially be regarded as Russian compatriots according to Moscow's loose definition of the term.

In Armenia the situation is quite different. With their distinct language and culture, the Armenians do not fit the compatriot definition so easily, and the country's ethnic Russians amount to just some eleven thousand people. Native Russian speakers total fifteen thousand, mostly in the capital, Yerevan, and in the second largest city, Gyumri, in the Shirak region, where a Russian military base with four thousand troops is located (Map 3, p. 97).[25] Most Armenians speak Russian as a second language with various degrees of fluency, though the use of Russian has been in decline since the 1980s. In fact, of all the former Soviet republics, Armenia shows the least use of Russian and has the fewest state-funded Russian-language schools. However, the language still persists among the younger generation of Armenians, some of whom study in Russian-language institutions of higher learning such as the Russian-Armenian (Slavonic) University.

The Armenian and Belarusian Russian speakers in general differ notably from each other and from those interviewed in other countries, first by virtue of the fact that the majority of Belarusians are Russian speakers, while in Armenia they are a small minority. In Armenia, younger Russian speakers in particular are often ethnically Armenian and urban, and tend to have higher education. Many have lived or studied in Russia and have a close affinity with Russian culture. Nonetheless, their views of Russian foreign policy and their self-identification as compatriots may differ vastly. While there has been considerable Soviet nostalgia in Armenia and approval of Putin among the older generation (both Russian-speaking and Armenian-speaking), the younger generation has been more critical. Most Belarusians are Russian-speaking, yet they are a diverse group—some identify with Russia while others have a strong national identity. Because of the closed and authoritarian nature of the Belarusian regime, those who agreed to be interviewed there generally have had greater exposure to and ties with Europe and the West than is the case in Belarusian society in general. This factor and their being part of the younger generation undoubtedly has colored their views toward Russia and their unwillingness to self-identify as Russian compatriots. The following profiles of younger Russian-speaking Armenians and Belarusians will show their wide range of identities and their self-identification (or lack thereof) as Russian compatriots.

Artyom, a graduate student at the Russian-Armenian (Slavonic) University in Yerevan and a correspondent for a foreign newspaper, demonstrates the complex identities of Armenian Russian speakers who feel strong ties to their homeland and identify themselves as Russian compatriots.[26] Born in Yerevan to an Armenian family, Artyom was raised in Russia, where he moved with his family in the 1990s as did many Armenians seeking economic opportunities. Today he considers Russian to be his native language but insists that he feels Armenian "almost at a genetic level." He also considers himself a Russian compatriot, since "For many years I lived in Russia, side by side with Russians, and managed to acquire certain habits and even ways of thinking." He feels that in Armenia the Russian-speaking population has great possibilities to thrive, and declares that Russian "protection, in whatever form it may take, is not necessary, but support such as new Russian literature for Armenian libraries would be welcomed." He is highly critical of Russian actions in Crimea and especially in eastern Ukraine, because "I always thought Russia should attract other countries and pull them toward itself—but not by force under any circumstances. Russia, even while acting as the guarantor of the territorial integrity of Ukraine, brazenly took land from a sister country. In my deep conviction, Russia has now lost Ukraine for decades."

Araxya is another Yerevan native raised in a Russian-speaking ethnic Armenian family who considers herself a Russian compatriot.[27] She completed her graduate studies in Moscow where she lived for nearly a decade and now teaches at a university in Yerevan. Araxya calls herself not Russian but "a bearer of Russian culture with a strong Armenian ethnic identity," and a Russian compatriot "since most of my life activity has been linked to Russia (education, family, friends)." She does not think Russian protection is necessary for Russian speakers in Armenia, but "it would be enough to finance educational and cultural projects" because "in Armenia Russian culture is insufficiently promoted, there are few Russian schools and universities and few Russian-speaking young people."

Valentina is another Armenian who was raised in Russia.[28] She is a recent Ph.D. graduate teaching Russian literature at the Slavonic University and has equal affinity with both Russian and Armenian culture and literature. She considers herself only to a certain extent a Russian compatriot, since she was a child during the Soviet era and has never held Russian citizenship. However, she does feel a "kinship of the spirit rather than blood" with Russia, and concludes that "common language and cultural heritage, certain traditions and customs, strong ties with Russia, long-term residence in the territory of the Russian Federation . . . make me in a sense a compatriot." She thinks Armenia's Russian speakers require no protection from the outside and is on the fence about Russia's policies in Ukraine and Crimea, which she compares to the frozen conflict in Nagorno-Karabakh.

Kristina's case demonstrates the divergence between language and national identity that is common among Russian speakers who do not consider themselves Russian compatriots.[29] A thoughtful and articulate student in her last year of undergraduate studies in international relations, she hopes one day to work in the Armenian government. While her hometown is in Russia where she was born and raised in an Armenian family, she says that she does not consider herself a Russian compatriot because Russia is not her homeland: "My homeland is Armenia. Here I feel completely at home." In response to the question whether Russian speakers in Armenia have grievances she is adamant: "Absolutely not! In Armenia, two leading newspapers are printed in Russian, *Golos Armenii* [Voice of Armenia] and *Novoye Vremya* [Modern Times], TV programs and films are in Russian, cafe and restaurant menus are in Russian, Armenian, and English, as well as many street signs in Russian, and so on." She follows Russian domestic and foreign policy, especially the situation in Ukraine, concluding: "I do not like the current policy of Russia. I do not support it; I think it is imperialist. Maybe my assessment is related to my identity as a representative of a small nation— Armenia. . . . I do not think that Russians or Russian speakers in Russian tanks are needed in Ukraine." As a young student of international relations she believes that "Firstly, the era of empires in this world has long sunk into oblivion; secondly, the great powers must seek alliances and soft power rather than tanks and artillery. On the other hand, as the classic writers have said, Russia can only exist as an empire or it will disappear."

Ivan, an ethnic Belarusian, also does not identify himself as a Russian compatriot despite being a Russian speaker.[30] In fact, he is very certain about his ethnic identity: "I am Belarusian—period. But the so-called compatriots do exist, some of them are affected by the doctrine of *Zapadnaya Rus'* [Western Russia],[31] which says that though Belarusians differ from Russians, they belong to Russia and the Russian World." Now in his early thirties, Ivan hails from a small city close to the border of Lithuania, where growing up he also learned Belarusian. Following his university studies in Poland, he returned to Belarus to work in the NGO sector and is therefore able to travel frequently. Ivan has many friends in Ukraine and is terrified of Moscow's actions and its manipulative allegations of Kiev's fascism and discrimination against Russian minorities. "No, Russians are not discriminated against in Belarus. In fact, they feel right at home here"—Ivan sighs—"but that isn't comforting either."

Nastya is twenty-eight years old and was raised in Brest region, which borders Poland, in a quite religious Orthodox family, but now considers herself an atheist.[32] A historian by education, she speaks Belarusian, Russian, Ukrainian, and Polish, but admits that "technically speaking the absolute majority of Belarusians are native Russian speakers. All of us are fluent in Russian, except for the few elderly living in distant villages." Nastya is currently a housewife in Minsk, but used to be a youth activist supportive of the revival of the Belarusian identity. She certainly does not consider herself a Russian compatriot, but "unfortunately, the pro-Russian mood, though latent, is rather strong in Belarusian society." As she is at home, she is following closely the developments in Ukraine. When asked about her opinion on the annexation of Crimea she replied with a grin, "Ask the *vatniki* [the patriotic "rednecks"] instead."[33] Nonetheless, thanks to the aggressive Russian propaganda, a broad spectrum of Belarusian society, including the intelligentsia and the middle class, support the idea of a "Great and Strong Russia" and Putin's leadership.[34]

Tatsiana's case illustrates the fact that Belarusians who may not consider themselves Russian compatriots can still feel an affinity for their neighbor.[35] A talkative Belarusian lawyer in her fifties with two advanced degrees, she gladly speaks Belarusian when the rare opportunity presents itself, but most of the time she speaks Russian. She emphasizes the difference between national identity and language use: "I wonder why people link us with the Russians just because we speak Russian on a daily basis. This is essentially wrong. I am Belarusian, my parents and my grandparents were Belarusians. . . . I don't consider myself a Russian compatriot as I have a country of my own. Russia is just a neighboring country. Nothing more." After a little pause she smiles and clarifies: "I might be cheering for Russia during the hockey match with Canada, though, but this is a different thing." In Belarus Tatsiana does not think there is any discrimination against Russian speakers—"On the contrary, those who speak Belarusian might feel discriminated against much more as the absolute majority of public institutions use the Russian language."

Olga is a young IT professional from Minsk. Like all Belarusians she speaks fluent Russian, but she actually prefers speaking Belarusian.[36] Her interest in Belarusian identity emerged relatively recently—following the national movement sparked by the fraudulent presidential elections of 2006. She admits that Russian is her native language, but she is categorical that she is neither Russian, nor has any feelings for Russia or the Soviet Union. "The majority of Belarusians do not care about the Soviet Union," she says. "Soviet Union collapsed? Soviet Union was restored? Nobody cares." She is convinced that Belarusians are indifferent to ideology and most of them are pure pragmatists. "There is no ideology of Pan-Slavism or any other of that kind," she impatiently insists. "The only motive for those preachers is pragmatism. It's either money or career opportunity. These so-called ideologists are no more than mercenaries." Olga's cynicism may not be completely unfounded. The end goal of Russian policies is not necessarily supporting its compatriots, let alone Pan-Slavism, but expanding its resources, defending its security and economic interests, and fulfilling its neo-imperial ambitions.

RUSSIAN MOTIVES AND INTERESTS

Russia's interests in Belarus and Armenia are quite different but in both cases center on the strategic, military, and economic spheres. Belarus's geopolitical position is similar to that of Ukraine—buffering Russia against Western Europe and at the same time serving as a corridor to Russia's territory of Kaliningrad on the Baltic Sea (Map 4, p. 139). Over the years Moscow has hardly treated Belarus like a separate entity. Moscow's confidence in Minsk's loyalty may have been the only reason that Belarus has not suffered a threat to its territorial integrity like Ukraine, Moldova, Georgia, and others.[37] Meanwhile, Armenia has been labeled the "Russian outpost in the South Caucasus" since 2004, when the visiting Duma Speaker Boris Gryzlov coined the expression.[38] Likewise, in 2000 when the two countries signed a Declaration on Cooperation in the Twenty-first Century, Putin said this reflects the fact that Armenia is Russia's "traditional ally."[39]

Armenia

Armenia has been a close military ally of Russia since it invited its forces to serve as a deterrent against Turkey. Following the retention of a Russian division at Gyumri, in 1997 a formal treaty transformed the force's quarters into a Russian military base and in 2010 Armenia extended the lease until 2044 in exchange for long-range missile systems.[40] The garrison includes air defense units and a fighter jet squadron as well as anti-aircraft missile troops.[41] Since January 2015, the Gyumri base and surrounding area have been rocked by tensions after a Russian serviceman brutally murdered an Armenian family of seven including a two-year-old girl and a six-month-old boy.[42] The Russian government's refusal to have the suspect tried in an Armenian court as provided by the 1997 treaty has led to protests by Armenians and clashes near the base, undermining Armenians' trust in Russian military forces and possibly even future Armenian-Russian military cooperation.[43]

Armenia has generally pursued close cooperation with the Russian armed forces and together with Belarus, Kazakhstan, Kyrgyzstan, and Tajikistan is a member of the Moscow-led Collective Security Treaty Organization (CSTO). Since 2005 Armenia has also been cooperating with NATO via the Individual Partnership Action Plan, though it does not aim at becoming a full-fledged member. It is also cooperating with the alliance to build a center in the country to assist with crisis management and counterterrorism, and has been sending troops to Iraq, Afghanistan, and peacekeeping missions in Kosovo. Russo-Armenian military cooperation is reflected in the fact that the Russian Federal Security Service work jointly with Armenian border guards to protect and patrol Armenia's borders with Turkey and Iran, while Armenian armed forces are part of the CIS's united air defense system.[44] In 2013, Moscow and Yerevan signed a defense deal regarding military technology cooperation. Still, roughly three-fourths of Armenia's military has been deployed against Azerbaijan, and Russia has no direct role in those forces. In 2013, for the first time ever, the Gyumri base commander stated that "in case Azerbaijani leadership makes a decision to re-establish its jurisdiction over Nagorno-Karabakh with forceful means, the base may engage in military conflict in accordance with the contractual obligations of the Russian Federation in the framework of the Collective Security Treaty Organization,"[45] raising Azerbaijani objections.[46] Overall, Russian policies appear aimed at protracting the Nagorno-Karabakh conflict by supporting Armenia via its military base while selling arms to Azerbaijan—all to preserve influence with both conflict parties.

Russia also has close economic cooperation with Armenia though the small country of just some 3 million people with a meager annual GDP per capita of under $6,000 in 2013 is hardly a prize for Russia in economic terms. Still, Armenia pays half of the expenditures of the Russian military base and also does not charge Russia for the lease of the land or for the base itself.[47] Armenia's economy relies on small-scale manufacturing, services, remittances from abroad (mainly Russia, France, Germany, and the United States), and agriculture, as well as on loans from the World Bank, the IMF, the Asian Development Bank, and Russia.[48] Russia has been the leading investor in the Armenian economy via business giants like ArmRosGasProm (a Gazprom subsidiary), Russian Railways, telecom operators MTS and Beeline, and leading Russian banks and insurance companies.[49] Although the EU is Armenia's largest trading partner,[50] Yerevan is dependent on Russia in strategic economic sectors such as energy and to a lesser degree communication and transportation; this is reflected in Russia's share in Armenia's imports, which, including energy, is almost twice the EU's.[51] Russia has also successfully leveraged Armenia's economic vulnerability and energy dependence. In 2002 the two countries launched the "Property-for-Debt" (or "Equity-for-Debt") deal, transferring Armenia's underemployed and largely nonoperational state-owned industrial companies to the Russian state in order to cover Yerevan's $100 million loan debt to Moscow and to spur investment.[52] Since then, Armenia has been forced to cede to Russia more state-owned properties and assets in order to pay for gas imports.[53]

Belarus
In contrast to Armenia, the Belarusian armed forces are often viewed as almost part of the Russian military. For instance, in Russian military doctrine, in the event of conflict with the West the Belarusian army would be deployed as part of the Russian army to defend Russia's western boundaries.[54] Russia and Belarus have joint regional air defense systems and regularly conduct massive military exercises under the name Zapad (West) near the borders of Poland and Lithuania. Russia's military and naval communications center and its early warning radar are located on the territory of Belarus in Vileyka and Baranovichi respectively, covering the North Atlantic and Europe.[55] The Baranovichi base also hosts jets, and there are further plans for more bases in the western city of Lida and

the eastern city of Bobruisk.[56] Russia also relies on the Belarusian military industry, including companies like Belomo, famous for its night vision devices, military enterprises like Beltechexport, and the tank manufacturing plant at Borisov.[57] The Minsk Wheel Tractor Plant, despite its pedestrian name, produces mobile transporter launchers for Russian intercontinental ballistic missiles.[58] Thus keeping Belarus in Russia's sphere of influence is of strategic and military importance for Russia.

The Belarusian economy arguably holds less appeal for Russia than its strategic position. Nonetheless, Russia has consistently sought to integrate Belarus into its economic zone and gain access to its resources and industries. Since 1995, Belarus has been embedded as an inaugural member in the Moscow-led Eurasian Economic Union. Since 2014, Belarus, along with Armenia and Kazakhstan, has been part of Moscow's latest economic project—the newly formed Eurasian Economic Union. Russia has consistently been the leading foreign investor in the Belarusian economy as well as the biggest export and import partner, doubling the volume of all other top ten trading partners combined.[59] Over the years Russia has also sought to privatize a number of strategic Belarusian enterprises, including among others the world's largest potash producer, Belaruskali, and energy sector entities like oil-refining companies Naftan and Mozyr.[60] The Belarusian national gas pipeline Beltransgaz (known as Gazprom Transgaz Belarus since 2013) was bought up in stages by Gazprom from 2007 to 2011, a procedure that the Russian gas company described as "Beltransgaz returns to Gazprom family"—a turn of phrase that somewhat reflects the philosophy that Belarus (like Ukraine) belongs to the Russian family.[61]

For the Russian energy sector, Belarus holds a similar position to that of Ukraine and (historically) the Baltic States—as a transit country for exports; in fact, half of Russian crude oil exports go via Belarus. However, as in the case of the Baltic States, Moscow has been trying to cut Belarus out of the transit business by constructing alternative gas and oil transit routes such as North Stream and Baltic Pipeline System-2.[62] Belarus itself has a sizable domestic oil field and undeveloped reserves of oil shale that are estimated at some 9 billion tonnes, but with subsidized energy pricing from Russia there has been little incentive for their development. There is also speculation that Russian companies and authorities launder money through Belarus as they do through Ossetia and Abkhazia (especially in the arms and energy trades).[63]

What sets Belarus apart from Armenia and most post-Soviet states is the unique ideological or perhaps even psychological role the country holds in Russia's imperial project as "the 'last chance saloon' in the European theater."[64] Belarus remains the only European post-Soviet country that is still squarely in Moscow's orbit. The Baltic States have joined the EU and NATO, Moldova and Ukraine have forged their "colored revolutions," and former Warsaw Pact states like Poland and Romania are long integrated with the West. Only Belarus quaintly remains a sort of European colony of Russia. In some regards, Armenia holds a similar position in the Caucasus—the last bastion of pro-Russian support, as Georgia fought a war with Russia, while Azerbaijan uses its oil and gas resources in full to claim more autonomy. Belarus also shares a post-Soviet political and economic model with Russia. As political scientist and expert on Belarus Vytis Jurkonis explained, "Belarus is like a role model for the Kremlin—it is an example of holding on to power for twenty years, atomizing society, controlling opposition by playing the divide-and-rule game, and oppressing activists (by detaining, arresting them, expelling from universities)."[65] On the other hand, Belarus expert and head of the Center for Political Analysis and Prognosis Pavel Usov argues the opposite: that Russia's autocratic tendencies, born in the Yeltsin era and expertly enacted under Putin, have made an authoritarian regime possible in the much smaller Belarus.[66] Nonetheless, while the fellow Slavic Ukrainians launched their Orange Revolution in 2004 and the Maidan movement in 2013 seeking a change in government, Lukashenko's grip on power has never wavered. As Jurkonis explained, "perhaps the Kremlin does not like Lukashenko that much, but it appreciates his loyalty and his ability to create a system of successful control."[67] In contrast, though the Armenian political system is also not quite democratic, it is pluralist with highly competitive elections. Unlike the self-isolated Belarus, Armenia is also influenced by its diaspora (especially in the United States) and Western-funded NGOs. Yet Belarus's welcome for the Soviet-inspired economic and political model and Armenia's acceptance of Russia's alliance and support have paved the way for Russia's notable success in exercising its soft power over these two states.

SOFT POWER

Belarus

Among the CIS states, Russia's soft power project has possibly been most successful in Belarus, with Armenia trailing close behind. This success has been helped in both countries by the prevalence of the Russian language and Orthodox faith, as well as by strong economic and military ties. While Belarus and Russia have been close allies over the last twenty years, Belarus has also been a target of Russia's soft power and influence via economic, financial, cultural, social, and political measures. As political scientist Laurynas Jonavičius aptly summarizes, "One should also not forget that today Russian television, Russian money and investments, Russian language, Russian armed forces, Russian oil and gas are daily routine in Belarus. Irrespective of whether Lukashenko likes it or not."[68] Yet for most of the past two decades, the Lukashenko regime has mounted no resistance to Russian soft power and has consistently favored the Russian language.

In 2014, following Crimea's annexation, some Russian media reported that Lukashenko has started showing signs of "soft Belarusization" of the country.[69] In his State of the Nation Address in April 2014, Lukashenko tried to indirectly address Moscow's efforts to politicize the Russian language in Belarus and Ukraine: "I would like to make it clear once again for those who want to 'privatize' the Russian language. The language is ours. It is neither Russia's nor Ukraine's. It is ours. It is a living asset of Belarusians, too."[70] In January 2015, the Belarusian Ministry of Education announced that history and geography would be taught in Belarusian, a move that was interpreted by the media as "de-Russification" and "revival" of Belarusian culture.[71] However, it seems unlikely that Lukashenko will seek to directly constrain Russia's soft power by drastically turning to the Belarusian language. Instead, he will likely try claiming the Russian language as Belarus's own with the Belarusian language as window dressing to improve his bargaining position with Brussels and the Kremlin.[72]

A common religion is another form of Russian soft power. The Belarusian Orthodox Church is part of the powerful Russian Orthodox Church under the Moscow Patriarchate. It is Belarus's most trusted public institution, with a 63 percent trust rating—higher than the army

(44 percent) and unions of entrepreneurs (40 percent).[73] Some 80 percent of the Belarusian population belongs to the church, though most are not practicing.[74] Meanwhile some 15 percent belong to the Catholic Church, which has more than occasionally experienced pressure from the Lukashenko regime. To leverage the faith, Russia has reportedly been working in Belarus through organizations that promote traditional Orthodox and family values.[75] Since 2014, organizations like Holy Russia, various Cossack groups, and the Orthodox Brotherhood have been promoting the idea of "Western Russia," the narrative of Belarus belonging to the larger Slavic and Orthodox world, as well as of patriotism and dedication to the motherland, Russia.[76] The Cossack organizations, in particular, target youths and organize paramilitary training camps.

A somewhat unusual and to some extent inadvertent aspect of Russia's soft power in Belarus is the enduring Soviet nostalgia in Belarusian society and official policies. While Putin's regime tried to rehabilitate Soviet-era leaders and history in the 2000s, in Belarus the glory of the Soviet regime has been extolled under Lukashenko's guidance ever since the 1990s. For instance, victory in the Second World War is not only the most important event in the Russian national psyche, but as polls show, 80 percent of Belarusians also consider the victory to be their greatest symbol of pride in the twentieth century. Meanwhile, only 36 percent think that Belarusian independence in 1991 is the country's proudest moment.[77] Belarus is also unique in the post-Soviet space in its relations vis-à-vis Russia, because as noted earlier, it has not only been a ready importer of Russia's soft power, but also arguably an exporter of its own post-Soviet ideology and regime style that has potentially served if not a model to than a mirror of Putin's Russia.

Armenia

In strong contrast to Belarus, while the Armenians are also Orthodox Christians the Armenian Apostolic Church has throughout its history always remained independent. Due to its long-standing traditions as the first Christian state church, the Armenian church has never been under the influence of the Moscow Patriarchate. In fact, there has been a contentious history between the Russian authorities and the Armenian church. In 1902, the Russian government moved to expropriate Armenian church assets, resulting in an attempted assassination of the viceroy by Armenian revolutionary groups the following year. In a further crackdown, the Russian authorities armed regional groups, resulting in a chain of violent confrontations that became known as the Armenian-Tatar War (1905–6) which set a precedent for future Armenian-Azerbaijani conflicts.[78] Since the 1990s, however, the role of the Russian Orthodox Church is more visible as go-between Armenia and Azerbaijan. Armenian Catholicos Garegin II has on numerous occasions within the past decade appealed to the Moscow patriarch, seeking mediation with Azerbaijani religious leaders in the Nagorno-Karabakh conflict.[79]

While the Russian language has become the native tongue for most Belarusians, Moscow has been pushing for some kind of official status for Russian in Armenia. The most important actors in this campaign have been Russian government institutions like Rossotrudnichestvo and state-sponsored NGOs like Russkiy Mir.[80] The head of Rossotrudnichestvo's office in Yerevan, Viktor Krivopuskov, has argued that "Russian is the language of Armenia's security."[81] He seemed to imply that if Armenia seeks its national security it should privilege the Russian language. In 2014, Kremlin spokesperson and Russia's chief propagandist, Dmitriy Kiselev, called once again for a special status for the Russian language in Armenia.[82] However, the Armenian government has consistently tried to resist this initiative.[83] Indeed, Moscow's soft power and linguistic support in Armenia have verged on coercion and even blackmail.

Armenia has also seen a rise in secondary education in the Russian language. In 1997 the Russian-Armenian (Slavonic) University was established by intergovernmental decree, offering higher education in Russian rather than Armenian to more than twenty-five hundred students—including many of the Armenians profiled above.[84] A number of branches of other Russian universities function in Armenia, and in August 2014 the Armenian government agreed to launch a branch of Moscow State University in Yerevan in 2015, pledging to cover its operational costs, and thus creating a public outcry.[85] In addition, various Russian language course centers operate in the country under the auspices of Slavonic University or funded by Russkiy Mir.[86] This form of Russian soft power has largely been welcomed by Russian speakers in Armenia, as the interviews above show.

Russia's soft (and not so soft) economic power in Armenia has been best exemplified by Moscow's pressure on Yerevan since 2012 to join the

Eurasian Economic Union rather than establish closer ties to the EU.[87] For years Armenia tried to pursue EU-led reform and at the same time maintain pragmatic relations with Moscow.[88] Moscow's "convincing" of Armenia to join the Eurasian Economic Union followed its usual tactic in the post-Soviet space, namely wielding its energy weapon. Between 2005 and 2012 Gazprom increased the gas price for Armenia four times though this was in no small part related to the rising global gas prices.[89] In 2012, Moscow made repeated official and unofficial threats to cut trade preferences with Armenia and to raise gas prices yet again.[90] Top-level Russian representatives were part of this campaign including Putin's chief economic adviser Sergey Glazyev and Russian Ambassador to Armenia (2009–13) Vyacheslav Kovalenko.[91] In December 2013, during Putin's official visit to Armenia, Gazprom extended the olive branch to Yerevan and agreed not to increase the gas price by another 30 percent, instead offering to sell it at the much lower domestic Russian price—but only after Yerevan decided to join the Eurasian Economic Union.[92] The threat of higher gas prices that would have impacted many sectors of the economy certainly influenced Armenian President Serzh Sargsyan's decision on 3 September 2013 to turn toward the Eurasian Union, although, as we will see, information warfare and security considerations played a possibly even more important role. Subsequently, Yerevan also failed to secure funding from the United States and France for a new nuclear power plant that would reduce the country's dependence on Russia. Instead it accepted a $300 million loan from Russia in May 2014 for extending the life of its existing nuclear power plant to 2026.[93]

Another aspect of Russia's soft power efforts in Armenia is their focus on trying to limit the influence of Western-funded NGOs and of organizations run by the Armenian diaspora. In May 2014, Russian Ambassador to Armenia Ivan Volynkin in an interview urged Yerevan "to neutralize those NGOs in Armenia that want to drive a wedge into Russian-Armenian relations," offering as an example the controversial Russian law that equated foreign-funded NGOs with "foreign agents."[94] Armenian civil society and the government protested, with the usually soft-spoken Armenian Foreign Ministry stating outright: "All organizations in Armenia are registered and function according to laws of the Republic of Armenia."[95] In February 2015, Russian Senator Konstantin Kosachev reiterated Moscow's demand, declaring that nearly 350 NGOs were working in Armenia against Eurasian integration and in favor of rapprochement with the EU, and noting that this was "unacceptable."[96] More broadly both the civil society and the government in Armenia have largely tried to resist such Russian efforts, including the more aggressive Russian compatriot policies.

HUMANITARIAN, COMPATRIOT, AND PASSPORTIZATION POLICIES

Russia's policies in these areas have been quite different in Belarus and Armenia, despite the similar soft power influence and close cooperation Moscow enjoys with the two states. This is partly due to Russia's different perceptions of the two countries, the differences in their domestic structures, and Armenia's Nagorno-Karabakh conflict. The different responses in Minsk and Yerevan to Moscow's overture have been another distinguishing factor.

Belarus

In Moscow's eyes, much of the Belarusian population can be deemed Russian compatriots, since together with Ukrainians they are part of the so-called tripartite Russian nation. As Russian Defense Minister Sergei Ivanov said in February 2006, reiterating a belief that is deeply ingrained in Russia, "Belarusians and Russians are one people."[97] Lukashenko echoed the same belief, saying in 2014 that "we are de facto one country."[98] In 2009 a sociological study showed that 75 percent of Belarusians do not consider Russia to be a foreign country.[99] That might partly explain why Russia has not pursued consistent humanitarian and compatriot policies in Belarus. Russkiy Mir opened its first Belarusian office only in December 2014, in the western border city of Brest.[100] Since June 2014, Brest has also been home to the Russian Centre of Science and Culture, which since late 2010 has also had an office in Minsk and is due to open another one in the second largest Belarusian city, Gomel, in 2015. Both Russkiy Mir and the Russian Centre are perceived to be tools of Russian intelligence.[101] Rossotrudnichestvo has had offices in Belarus since June 2004 and mostly targets organizations of Russian compatriots, aiming to consolidate and coordinate their activities, though it also engages in cultural and educational outreach and disseminates positive information on Russia.[102] Lukashenko has also personally enacted many policies that have placed Belarus as part of the Russian World, including making Russian a second official language in 1995, outlawing Belarus's historic coat of arms (the *Pahonia*) and its white-red-white flag, and instead mainstreaming the history of the Soviet past.[103] According to Jurkonis, because of the contemporary and historical Russification of Belarus, the country has arguably been perceived by Moscow as an inherent part of the Russian World where not many further efforts need to be made.[104] Nonetheless, the developments in Ukraine became a signal that nothing should be taken for granted and that the Russian World needs to be sustained, which explains Moscow's post-2014 upsurge of compatriot policies.

Likewise, historically Russia has not aggressively pursued passportization policies in Belarus, first of all because Belarusian law does not allow dual citizenship. This may seem surprising considering that Russia has consistently lobbied for dual citizenship in the former Soviet republics and Minsk has generally followed most Moscow's policy leads. However, as one Belarusian diplomat recalled, in the early 1990s, the Belarusian authorities did not really consider Russia a separate country: "We didn't have enough time for Russia. Some thought: we will find a way to deal with the 'ours' ["our people," namely the Russians]. Moscow was not considered as an abroad. . . . We were still living [as if] in the united Soviet Union."[105] The issue of dual passports was likely never considered by Minsk since both countries viewed themselves almost as one and the same. The lack of serious passport checks at the Belarusian-Russian border throughout the 1990s is a testament to those views.

In 2010, it was reported that there were only some 88,000 Russian citizens living in Belarus permanently—a small number considering the country's total population of more than 9 million.[106] There are also a number of Belarusian labor migrants in Russia: 67,000 Belarusians working in Russia officially in 2010. Including undocumented workers the number could be as high as 100,000 to 300,000.[107] As has been seen by the cases of Estonia's Narva region, Georgia's South Ossetia and Abkhazia, and will also be seen in the case of Armenia, Russian citizenship holds economic advantages for populations living near the border with Russia and particularly for labor migrants and people who often travel to Russia on business. However, these "economic citizens" can quickly turn into citizens whom Russia wishes to protect. Belarus's labor migrants and those living close to the border could one day be the most likely targets of Russia's passportization. However, considering Moscow's general ambivalence about passportizing Belarusians, a swift change of policy does not seem likely in the near future without a change in Belarusian leadership or foreign policy.

Armenia

In contrast to Belarus, in Armenia the main thrust of Russia's policies toward its compatriots since 1994 has been passportization. Surprisingly the targets of these policies were never solely ethnic Russians or Russian speakers (due to their small numbers), but rather (if not primarily) ethnic Armenians. As the first Russian ambassador to Armenia, Vladimir Stupishin, writes in his memoirs, Russia argued that all people living in Armenia were eligible for Russian passports on the basis of their "former USSR citizenship."[108] This was a surprising policy formulation considering that there were no stateless people in Armenia and Yerevan had granted universal citizenship to all its inhabitants. The issue of Russian citizenship became salient for many ethnic Armenians who sought emigration to Russia in the early 1990s, looking for greater economic opportunities and seeking to avoid the ongoing Nagorno-Karabakh war. Thus, compatriot status and Russian citizenship were appealing to many Armenians. Yet the Kremlin did not systemize the passportization process in Armenia until 2008 and 2009.

Passportization gained greater momentum after 2008 but was tied to Russia's new efforts for resettling compatriots from all post-Soviet countries back to Russia. In 2009, shortly after Rossotrudnichestvo was established by the Russian government in 2008, it opened an office in Armenia[109] whose main activity was implementing the 2006 compatriot immigration program for compatriots, which enables citizens of post-Soviet republics to become residents in select remote provinces of the Russian Federation.[110] The resettlement program soon became a source of contention in Armenia. By the summer of 2011, civil society activists and public figures voiced their opposition to the concerted effort to resettle Armenians to Russia, including calling for parliamentary hearings on the matter in an open letter to the prime minister and the speaker of the National Assembly.[111] Armenia's then Prime Minister Tigran Sargsyan echoed these concerns and in July 2011 stated: "We have invited the attention of our Russian partners on this matter, and said [that] in Armenia this program cannot be implemented as a [general] standard, and this issue will be discussed on inter-governmental level. . . . We shall resolve this issue on a political level."[112] The Russian consul general in Gyumri, Vasily Korchmar, tried to assuage fears in August 2011, stating that "the compatriots program does not aim at leaving Armenia without Armenians, but at strengthening the existing ties between the two nations."[113] Nonetheless, criticism of Moscow's policies continued.

By 2012 the Armenian government, media, public figures, and Western-funded NGOs intensified their opposition to the passportization and resettlement programs.[114] In October 2012, Armenian Deputy Foreign Minister Shavarsh Kocharian said that Armenia "is concerned regarding the part of the program that openly aims at transmigrating Armenian citizens to Russia and giving them citizenship. We are strongly against that."[115] Prime Minister Sargsyan stated: "Our political position is that we do not approve this state program, we did not consent to such a program in Armenia."[116] He reiterated that the Armenian position "is known to the political leadership of Russia. The 'Compatriots' program will no longer operate in Armenia in this format. The activities of such an organization in Armenia are not permissible."[117] To appreciate the significance of this strong opposition, one must bear in mind that the Armenian government has always proclaimed its fraternal relations with the Kremlin and been cautious in its criticism of Russia, since it perceives Moscow to be a guarantor of Armenia's security. But in this case, the usually cooperative and often submissive Yerevan stood its ground and in the spring of 2013, the resettlement program was terminated.[118]

Still, the program left a significant imprint. According to expert estimates, in March 2014 200,000 to 300,000 Armenian citizens had acquired Russian passports, the majority of them having dual Armenian-Russian citizenship—a considerable number in a country of just 3 million.[119] Many of these people are labor migrants who are important to Armenia's economy: remittances from abroad (including Russia) made up some 10 percent of Armenia's GDP in 2012.[120] There are also political implications. In 2014, the head of the State Migration Service, Gagik Yeganyan, argued that the Crimean scenario is unlikely in Armenia: "There the main factor was the ethnic Russians living there. . . . There is no great community of ethnic Russians in Armenia, we are a mono-ethnic state, more than 98 percent of population is Armenian."[121] However, in cases like Moldova's Transnistria and Georgia's South Ossetia and Abkhazia, even non-Russian populations have been politically conceptualized as Russia's compatriots. In Armenia's case, most Russian citizens are ethnic Armenians, many of whom returned from Russia for ethno-nationalist reasons, or to serve in the Armenian armed forces, or to join long-standing repatriate programs established by the Western diaspora such as Birthright Armenia and the Armenia Volunteers Corps. Thus, they would arguably not be easily manipulated for Russian foreign policy aims. However, as eastern Ukraine has shown, Moscow has used the mere presence of so-called compatriots as a pretext for military action regardless of the compatriots' actual preferences. The significant population of Russian citizens in Armenia can thus serve as a means for Russian influence and even result in potential security concerns in the future.

INFORMATION WARFARE

Belarus

It is questionable whether Minsk has yet faced concerted Russian information warfare; however, Russian media remain highly influential in Belarus. The Belarusian presidential race in 2010 offers some insights. The Russian media arguably initiated a propaganda campaign against Lukashenko by showing a documentary, *Krestniy Batka* (The Nation's Godfather), which portrayed the president as a tyrant and a criminal.[122] Overall the level and intensity of Russian propaganda against Belarus and its leadership has varied, and direct confrontation has been rare. Nonetheless Russian media (including Russian social networks like VKontakte and Odnoklassniki) are a powerful instrument as there are very few if any media alternatives for most Belarusians. In fact, Belarusian and Russian state-controlled media dominate the information landscape. The most popular Russian TV channels in Belarus include NTV, RTR, ONT, and since 2014, Russia Today. The only independent media consist of online platforms and foreign-funded media projects (broadcast from Poland like Belsat satellite TV and Euroradio) but they all have limited reach. In 2014, according to official data, nearly 48 percent of Belarusians stated that they regularly watch Russian television, while another 41 percent said they do so occasionally.[123] Although Belarusians' overall trust in the media has declined from 54 percent in 2010 to 32 percent in 2013, in 2014 a majority of Belarusians (52 percent) considered Russian news programs objective, while 31 percent thought them mostly or completely biased.[124] Generally, Belarusian and Russian media narratives go hand in hand. In 2014, the media of both countries as well as Belarusian official discourse were highly critical of Kiev's Maidan public protests, seeking to show that civic disobedience, public protests, and challenges to governments lead to instability, chaos, collapse of countries, and eventually war.[125] According to one of the leaders of the opposition Christian Democrat party, Vitali Rymasheuski, "The influence of the Russian-speaking media in Belarus is huge, which results in the public perception that keeping the status quo basically means distancing oneself from the war."[126] Arguably, both Lukashenko and Moscow use the threat of chaos and war to narrow the perceived options of the Belarusian public to discourage it from regime change or turning to the West. This could be construed as a form of information warfare, though it is aimed not at territorial expansion but simply at maintaining Belarus in Moscow's sphere of influence.

Armenia

In the case of Armenia, there is also insufficient evidence to suggest that Russia has been pursuing a consistent information warfare strategy meant to support its efforts at compatriot protection, prompting separatism, or acquiring territory. Instead, Russia's media efforts are aimed more at maintaining Armenia in its sphere of influence. In 2013 and 2014 there were a few episodes that suggest Moscow coupled information warfare with pressure and blackmail intended to "manufacture consent" so that Yerevan would choose integration with the Eurasian Economic Union rather than seeking closer ties to the EU.[127] In the spring of 2013, when it looked increasingly likely that Armenia would sign an association agreement with the EU, there was an unprecedentedly intense Russian media campaign against the country. The campaign focused on Nagorno-Karabakh, which had proclaimed independence from Azerbaijan in 1991, and has been directly supported by Armenia, and indirectly by Russia, ever since. Media reports proclaimed that Yerevan was "selling out" Nagorno-Karabakh—the most controversial political accusation that could be made in Armenia,[128] and one that the Armenian authorities have continually denied.[129] This was an extremely sensitive issue in Armenian political life and with the Armenian public, given the territory's ethnic Armenian population and its all-out war for independence from Azerbaijan.[130] In July 2013, the recently retired Russian Ambassador Kovalenko proclaimed that "Armenia can only live with Russia or not live at all," and declared that the Russo-Armenian bilateral relationship would suffer if Armenia signed the agreement with the EU, as Moscow would then mind its own interests.[131] Another, simultaneous episode was symptomatic of the efforts of the Russian media to belittle Armenia. In July 2013, when an Armenian migrant worker's truck was involved in a fatal accident in Russia, just hours later the suspect and his nationality were ridiculed in a Russian courtroom and the episode televised by Russia's second largest state-owned television network, *Rossiya-1*.[132]

By early September 2013, under Moscow's pressure Yerevan decided to abandon the association agreement and proclaimed that it would be joining the Eurasian Economic Union. In December 2014 the Armenian parliament ratified the Eurasian Economic Union treaty by a landslide—103 in favor, 7 against, and 1 abstaining.[133] As political scientist Thomas de Waal argued back in 2013, Moscow made Yerevan an offer it could not refuse. With Russia selling weapons to Armenia's arch rival Azerbaijan, it was clear that Armenia had to choose the Economic Union if it wanted to maintain its security.[134] Between 2010 and 2013 Azerbaijan bought $4 billion worth of modern Russian military equipment, an amount that many fear will increase in years to follow.[135] This, together with the failure of a United States–facilitated Armenian-Turkish rapprochement process, significantly deepened Yerevan's dependence on Russia while the propaganda campaign highlighted this vulnerability. Though it would be impossible to conclude that it was Russian information warfare that forced Yerevan to cede, the propaganda regarding Nagorno-Karabakh, the economy, gas prices, and security concerns certainly alarmed the Armenian public and tied Yerevan's hands. Though Armenia had consistently argued that the EU association agreement did not contradict the country's close security cooperation with Russia, and the Armenian public had largely supported both EU and Russia integration tracks for potential economic gain, when the time came, Yerevan's policy options were limited. As de Waal already predicted in 2013, in many ways the pressure on Armenia was just a rehearsal for Ukraine when it contemplated an EU association agreement in the autumn of 2013. For Russia, Ukraine was a much greater prize to lose to Western integration than Armenia as the annexation of Crimea and war in eastern Ukraine demonstrated.[136]

THE FUTURE: PROTECTION AND ANNEXATION?

Belarus and Armenia are unique cases in my proposed reimperialization trajectory, because they are among Russia's closest and most loyal allies out of the former Soviet republics. Both states are members of the Eurasian Economic Union along with Russia's other close allies Kazakhstan and Kyrgyzstan. Both countries are highly homogeneous, with only small numbers of ethnic minorities. The Russian language and culture are respected in both countries, and privileged in the case of Belarus. Lastly, there are no significant historical or contemporary movements for separatism in either country.[137] This seems to leave little for Russia to protect through its compatriot policies. Nonetheless, the case of Sevastopol in Ukraine demonstrated that even a military base might become a target of reimperialization, and both Armenia and Belarus host Russian bases on their territory. Overall, however, this chapter has demonstrated that Russia does not need to formally annex any Belarusian or Armenian territories, because it already strongly influences the foreign policy of these states. One sign of this influence was seen at the Eastern Partnership summit in Riga in May 2015 when a declaration containing a condemnation of Russia's annexation of Crimea had to be redrafted because both Armenia and Belarus refused to sign it.[138] The main task of Moscow's reimperialization policy is to sustain this influence to the maximum without investing too many resources. As the developments in Ukraine show, attempts to acquire larger territories are costly, and perhaps impossible, endeavors.

Belarus

While Belarus has remained Russia's ally since the conflict in Ukraine in 2014, the leadership of Belarus demonstrated some concern regarding the changing regional security context. In his State of the Nation address delivered in April 2014 (shortly after Crimea's annexation), Lukashenko subtly addressed Moscow's nascent propaganda about discrimination against Russians in Belarus: "Today we can hear even more surprising statements about Belarus trying to harass Russians and the Russian language. Of course, it is hard to make up such silliness. . . . As for the statements about Belarus trying to harass Russians, I do not even want to talk about such nonsense. Any talk about Russianness, Belarusianness, pro-Russianness, and pro-Ukrainianness are a step toward the same chaos."[139] Lukashenko reiterated this position in 2015: "Many in Belarus are intermarried and are interrelated with the Russians, Poles, Jews, and other ethnicities. We never paid any attention to this and never will. . . . Why will we pursue a frenzied nationalistic policy? To drive away people who were born here or whose parents were born here? This is nonsense of the highest order!"[140] It appears that Lukashenko has been trying to keep one step ahead of Moscow and defuse any notion of protecting Russian compatriots in Belarus. Even if separatism or annexation of territories inhabited by Russian compatriots is less likely, the future of Belarus may hold other scenarios that would fit into Russia's imperial revival efforts.

In the coming years Belarus is most likely going to continue its economic, political, and military integration with Russia. Belarus is already a member of various Moscow-led groups: the Union State of Belarus and Russia, the CIS, the Collective Security Treaty Organization, and Eurasian Economic Union. Lukashenko proposed the creation of the Union State in the late 1990s with the main goal of becoming president or vice president of the confederation after Yeltsin's term ended.[141] When Putin was slated for the Russian presidency, Lukashenko tried to backpedal. As this important episode suggests, and as Belarusian experts conclude, Lukashenko has largely focused on his personal ambition rather than on the interests of Belarus or Russia.[142] In future he may toy once again with the idea of a closer union with Russia. In 2015, Lukashenko reiterated his loyalty to Moscow in his State of the Nation address in 2015 when he said: "Everyone must be told that we have been together with Russia and will always be. No idle talks about Crimea, deviations and adjustments in Belarus' policy can be allowed."[143]

Future scenarios must also consider the future of Lukashenko's regime. The Belarusian president is sixty years old and has been running Belarus for twenty years, but that still makes him younger than and shorter in office than the Central Asian strongmen. Lukashenko's three sons, and media speculations that the youngest is being groomed for succession, could suggest potential for a dynasty.[144] A prodemocratic uprising in Belarus or in Russia, on the other hand, would threaten Lukashen-ko's regime as well as Belarus's ties to Russia. In the past, popular pro-tests following the 2006 and 2010 presidential elections, as well as the peaceful "silent protests" in the summer of 2011, were either forcibly suppressed or quickly fizzled.[145]

The EU has proposed a future pathway for Lukashenko, including the 2006 "non-paper" offer "What the European Union Could Bring to Belarus," as well as an invitation in 2009 to participate in the Eastern Partnership initiative.[146] However, EU-Belarus dialogue was crushed by Minsk's crackdown on protests during the election night of 19 December 2010.[147] The Ukrainian crisis became an unexpected factor in the EU-Belarusian relationship as Lukashenko hosted two rounds of negotia-tions, first, between Ukraine, Russia, and the separatists in September 2014 (known as Minsk I), and following the cease-fire's collapse, peace talks between Russia, France, Germany and Ukraine in February 2015 (Minsk II).[148] The negotiations in Minsk led to hopes among EU officials about possible positive developments in the relationship with Minsk, but the Eastern Partnership Summit in May 2015 demonstrated that both Belarus and Armenia remain cautious about closer ties with the EU and are not willing to risk their relationship with Russia.

In any future scenario Russia will leverage its gains in Belarus achieved via soft power, compatriot policies, and propaganda. It may then turn to harder means of coercion: blackmail, threats, and a full-fledged information warfare campaign. Moscow has been successful in inciting separatism against all odds in countries like Ukraine, where Ukrainians and Russians have lived peacefully for many decades, and in Moldova's Transnistria, where Russians are a minority. Since 2014, there has been an increase in the activity of pro-Russian Cossack paramilitary groups in Belarus, and more aggressive Russian policies in Belarus cannot be completely excluded in the future.[149] Meanwhile, polls show that a ma-jority of Belarusians feel great ambivalence about their state and are un-likely to fight either for Belarus or for Russia.[150]

Armenia

In Armenia, Russia has always positioned itself as the "sole guarantor" of security in the face of potential threats from Turkey and Azerbaijan.[151] Moscow's decades of support to both sides in the Nagorno-Karabakh conflict enable it to play a game of divide and conquer, and to continue to exert influence over both states. Yet Russia's influence in the region is somewhat tempered: NATO member Turkey unconditionally supports Azerbaijan while Armenia also has a relationship with NATO and the support of its widespread diaspora of some 7–8 million people (largely in Russia, the United States, and France). Also, unlike in other post-Soviet states, Russia has not sought to protect Armenia's tiny Russian minority per se or the local Russian citizens who are mostly ethnic Armenians. Indeed, Armenia is a 98 percent mono-ethnic state with no sizable minority groups and no separatist movements that could require special protection from Russia. Russian annexation of territory is further made improbable by geography. However, protection of the Russian servicemen at the Gyumri base could potentially be a useful pretext if Moscow ever decided to stoke conflict in Armenia as activists on Russian social networks suggested in response to the Armenian protests against the murders allegedly committed by a Russian serviceman.[152] Yet moving in additional Russian troops would be difficult for the same reasons of geography, since the troops would have to move through Georgia, whose border with Russia has been largely closed since the 2000s, or through Azerbaijan, which at this point also seems unlikely.

Overall, Moscow seems inclined to "protect" Armenia and Nagorno-Karabakh more generally from interference by foreign states and interests, regardless of Yerevan's own preferences. The Russian ambassador in Armenia, Ivan Volynkin, addressing a congress of Russian speakers in Yerevan in April 2014, issued a warning to the West and to the Armenian people: "We will thwart any aggressive interference in the internal affairs of friendly states carried out under the pretext of spreading ideas alien to our minds and hearts."[153] Volynkin was speaking of the crisis in Ukraine, and seemingly implying that any pro-West or prodemocracy movements in Armenia will be crushed by Moscow regardless of the actions of Yerevan.

Armenia, like Belarus, is also likely to pursue further political and economic integration with Russia, the Eurasian Economic Union, and the Russian World. All major Armenian political parties, including the ruling Republican Party and opposition parties, supported (albeit with questionable enthusiasm) Armenia's entry into the Eurasian Economic Union in 2015, arguing that it will bring economic advantages with access to a market of 170 million people.[154] Though public support exists for both EU and Eurasian integration, the latter has been even more popular, though its support fell from 67 percent in 2013 to 57 percent in 2014, with respondents citing various reasons, such as Russian policies in the Ukraine crisis.[155] As Armenian political scientist Hovhannes Nikoghosyan concludes, "Today, there is a near consensus in Armenia that if the country were forced to choose sides in a broader Russia-West confrontation, aligning with Russia would be preferred on account of the age-old security dilemma."[156] However, according to the editor of *The Armenian Reporter* Emil Sanamyan, "The 'near consensus' is based on continued Russian security and economic support and if it for some reason flounders, or if a Western alternative finally emerges, this consensus will evaporate."[157] The 2015 tensions over the Russian and Armenian governments' handling of the murders in Gyumri, or similar events in the future, could contribute to a pushback against both Yerevan's conciliatory policies and Moscow's bullying attitude. In the face of the Russian reimperialization trajectory, Armenia still benefits from the country's strong identity, which is distinctly separate from Russia's, and its large and active diaspora in the West.

If Armenia or Belarus were ever to choose Europe and the West over Russia—as their respective neighbors Georgia and Ukraine did before them—it is likely that Moscow would not let them drift away easily. For one, both countries host Russian military bases. Second, over the last decades Moscow has exerted significant soft power, pressure, and coercion, as well as economic and military resources, to maintain them in its orbit. As the experience of both of these Russian allies has shown, there is a thin line between Russia's soft power, partnership, and alliance on one hand and its coercion and blackmail on the other. Former brother nation Ukraine has already experienced how quickly it changed from an ally to a target of Russia's aggressive reimperialization project. The future cannot exclude such a scenario for either Armenia or Belarus—but their resources for resistance would be much more limited.

Conclusion

An Empire founded by war has to maintain itself by war.

—Charles de Montesquieu (1680–1755)

RUSSIA'S TAKEOVER OF CRIMEA in March 2014 and the subsequent war in eastern Ukraine woke up Europe and the United States. Moscow's revisionism seemed undeniable, and talk of neo-imperialism and a new Cold War abounded. However, by mid-2015, in spite of continuing Western sanctions against Russia, rocket attacks against the southern Ukrainian city of Mariupol, and the violations of Minsk I and Minsk II cease-fire agreements, there is already a desire among some European powers to return to business as usual with Russia. There are numerous explanations from Moscow and the business-as-usual-cohorts of why Russia's aggression against Ukraine is a unique case and why we need not worry about Moscow's policies in the other post-Soviet states. First, for some 150 years until 1954 Crimea was part of Russia, thus Moscow had "legitimate" reasons for annexing it. Second, the separatist movements in eastern Ukraine are said to be home-grown movements provoked by a "coup" in Kiev (as Moscow refers to the ousting from power of Ukrainian President Victor Yanukovych in February 2014). Thus Russia's support for separatists is allegedly legitimate rather than an example of a conflict fomented, backed with manpower, and armed by Moscow. On these pretexts, as the world slowly returns to business as usual, as newspapers get tired of the story and feature other headlines, the case of Crimea will be (and largely already has been) cemented as a lost cause. The so-called

people's republics of Luhansk and Donetsk will be perpetuated by frozen conflict—like Georgia's Abkhazia and South Ossetia or Moldova's
Transnistria, which have been forgotten by statesmen and newsmen for
decades.

It is likely that 2014 will be a repeat of 2008 when Russia permanently tore away Georgia's territories in the brief war that rattled the
nerves of both the West and the other former Soviet republics. Then, as
in 2014, the world grumbled, terms like "new Cold War" were tossed
around, and the more aggressive side of Vladimir Putin's regime was
noted. Yet the world soon forgot. Reasonable-sounding arguments were
made that the Russo-Georgian war was an exception. It was easy to point
the finger at Tbilisi and blame it for firing the first shots in its efforts to
regain South Ossetia and Abkhazia from separatist rebels. It was also easy
to forget, or perhaps ignore, more than a decade of Moscow's policies of
wooing, financing, passportizing, and arming the separatist elements of
those territories. In a similar vein, the 1992 war that led to Transnistria's
"independence" from Moldova with the help of Soviet troops and arma-
ments has also been long relegated to the pages of history books.

In fact, however, the seemingly disparate events and Russian policies in Ukraine, Georgia, Moldova, the Baltic States, Armenia, and Central Asia are surprisingly similar and driven by the same underlying
strategy. Whether in "Slavic brother nation" Ukraine with its "Russian"
Crimea, or in the Baltic States with their EU and NATO membership, or
in Russia's allies Kazakhstan and Armenia, Russia has sought to passportize its so-called compatriots while calling for their protection and
waging information warfare campaigns. For more than two decades, and
especially since the mid-2000s, Russia has pursued an increasingly consistent reimperialization policy trajectory toward the post-Soviet states
and particularly toward regions where Russian speakers, ethnic Russians,
and other minority populations reside. At the crux of this reimperialization trajectory has been the political reconstruction of the Russian diaspora of the post-Soviet world as "Russian compatriots." The end goal
of this process is to co-opt the Russian diaspora in order to expand the
territory and the influence of the Russian Federation at the expense of
the former Soviet republics.

Russian compatriot policies often have little to do with improving the
rights or conditions of ethnic Russians or Russian speakers abroad but

rather focus on using them for Russia's own foreign policy and security advantage. Indeed, it took Moscow more than a decade to offer the Russian diaspora an opportunity to return to its motherland—and even then only to populate its most rugged, remote regions like Siberia. Instead, Russian compatriot policies go hand in hand with coercion, disinformation, and use of force against the governments of the target states. These policies at times verge on blackmail to manipulate the compatriots and even allies like Armenia, Belarus, Tajikistan, Kazakhstan, and Kyrgyzstan into participating in the Russian reimperialization project. Moscow offers and extends its protection to compatriots in some cases despite the preferences of the compatriots themselves. Likewise, the persistent propaganda about alleged maltreatment experienced by Russian speakers or other minorities in Ukraine, Georgia, or the Baltics has only fueled societal discord. It has prevented the integration of minorities on terms of peaceful coexistence with majorities in the societies of Russia's neighboring countries. When it did not suit its foreign policy goals, Moscow has ignored pressure on Russian compatriots or ethnic tensions such as in Turkmenistan and Kyrgyzstan. Overall, these policies of trying to co-opt the diaspora fit into the broader goals of Putin's regime, namely to reestablish Russia as a great power on the world stage and resume the trajectory of Russia's history of empire. Many of the countries facing Russian compatriot policies are (and historically have been) attractive targets for Russian economic, energy, military, and security ambitions. The West's insufficient engagement and its tacit acknowledgment that the post-Soviet space (with the exception of the Baltic States) belongs in Russia's sphere of influence have facilitated these Russian policies and even largely left them unnoticed.

RESULTS OF RUSSIAN POLICIES

The Russian reimperialization trajectory has been most successfully implemented in the cases of Ukraine, Georgia, and Moldova. In all three countries, Russia has succeeded in tearing away territories in the name of protecting its citizens and compatriots. The details have differed: in Moldova, it was the Soviet army "protecting" Russian-speaking separatists that played the decisive role; in Georgia, it was Russian peacekeeping and passportization efforts leveraging local ethnic tensions; in Ukraine, it was passportization of Crimea and the arming and manning of separatist-minded militias in the regions of Luhansk and Donetsk. The result has been self-declared "people's republics" in the territories of Transnistria, South Ossetia, Abkhazia, and eastern Ukraine that either have led to frozen conflicts or, as in Ukraine, are likely to do so in the years to come. Only Crimea has been outright incorporated into the Russian Federation. Nonetheless, in the short term, Crimea already resembles the no-man's-lands of frozen conflicts, as its inhabitants are isolated from mainland Ukraine and the rest of the world and non-Russian populations face intimidation and pressure. It is highly likely that following decades of isolation and dire conditions that are inherent in frozen-conflict territories, South Ossetia, Abkhazia, Transnistria, and possibly Luhansk and Donetsk will join the Russian Federation. Processes of closer integration are already on the way in the former. In the end, there are few options left for territories that have broken ties with their home countries, are internationally unrecognized, and receive financial and military support from Moscow other than integration with their protector.

The implications of these developments in Ukraine, Georgia, and Moldova go far beyond the loss of a few territories. The challenge to these countries' territorial integrity (and even indirectly their statehood) will leave a lasting imprint on their future. The fallout from war and loss of territory will forever divide their political systems and societies. Factions will emerge (as seen in Moldova and Georgia) favoring concessions to Russia in hopes that improved relations will enable the countries to regain lost territories, or at a minimum reduce the risk of future territorial conflicts. Other domestic groups will proclaim a nationalist, anti-Moscow, anti-minority line that likewise bodes ill for their states and societies. Because of their disputed borders Ukraine, Georgia, and Moldova will have difficulty gaining EU or NATO membership, which has arguably been among Moscow's primary objectives in stoking conflict. For Moscow, creating frozen conflicts and breakaway territories is a low-cost, high-return strategy that makes life difficult for its recalcitrant neighbor states and for the EU and NATO. Ukraine and Georgia may well follow in the footsteps of Moldova and be stuck in a gray zone of isolation and stagnation between the West and the East. In some respects, the fate of territorially jeopardized states risks not being dramatically different from the frozen-conflict conditions of their lost territories.

In the Baltic States, reimperialization has also made some headway but is far from its final phase of separatism or annexation. The sizable Russian-speaking and minority populations have been targeted by Moscow for decades with various soft power and compatriot policy initiatives. With their large Russian and Russian-speaking populations living on the border with Russia coupled with Moscow's frequent allegations of their maltreatment, Estonia and Latvia have much to be concerned about. Despite a common misperception, Lithuania also faces risk, with its smaller but concentrated pockets of Russian speakers (which together with ethnic Russians also include part of the Polish minority) and its past complacency stemming from the assumption that integration of its minorities has been successful due to its inclusive citizenship policies. In all three states, Moscow's passportization of the Russian minorities has succeeded to various degrees. In Estonia and Latvia, passportization was driven in part by the fact that a number of Russians had not acquired local citizenship and some sought Russian citizenship due to economic considerations. Passportization has reached the most ominous level in Estonia, where in the small town of Narva on the border with Russia approximately 30 percent of the population has acquired Russian citizenship. The conditions are highly reminiscent of the high levels of Russian passportization in Crimea, South Ossetia, and Abkhazia ahead of Moscow's pursuit of more aggressive policies in those regions. While overall passportization in the Baltics has had more limited success, especially with the younger generation of the Russian and Russian-speaking minorities, the three states have already experienced the subsequent phases of the Russian reimperialization trajectory—those of information warfare and calls (though not military actions) for "protection" of the Russian-speaking minorities. The information warfare campaign intensified in 2014 and focused on creating division in Baltic societies and smearing Baltic governments, as well as on rhetorical threats. Beyond rhetoric, the sovereignty of the three states has been challenged with violations of Baltic air space, kidnapping of an Estonian border guard, and a call to prosecute Lithuanians who avoided the Soviet draft following the country's declaration of independence.

Though Russian policies toward the Baltic States may not spell imminent war and land grab as in Ukraine, Georgia, and Moldova, their implications could be in some respects more harmful to the post–Cold War order in Europe because of the Baltics' EU and NATO membership. Their Western integration has not precluded Russia from exerting influence on these states and their Russian and Russian-speaking minorities. As Russian policies in the Baltics escalate to the level of concerted information warfare campaigns, calls for protection, and provision of military training to minority youths, Moscow's pressure on the Baltic States may translate into broader tensions between NATO and Russia. While NATO's Article 5 would most likely preclude Moscow's outright aggression, even indirect challenges to the stability, territory, and sovereignty of member states threaten the integrity of the alliance. NATO has already reacted by beefing up its support and operations in the Baltics, which will likely discourage Russia from trying to score easy gains in this region.

There are also long-term implications from the Russian reimperialization efforts for Baltic domestic political systems. Russia has consistently encouraged the Baltic Russian and other minorities and some minority parties to make political demands (and funded their efforts)— from changes in local language laws to calls for regional autonomy and referendums for separation. The result, however, is that while political parties representing Russian minority interests have had some success (mostly in Latvia) and such interests have been taken into account by broader center-left and minority parties in Estonia and Lithuania, minority interests remain somewhat underrepresented among the mainstream Baltic political forces. Moscow's often nontransparent support for and at times usurpation of control over the Baltic minority parties have made them less trusted in the political mainstream, thus actually working against the minorities' legitimate interests. Meanwhile, mainstream Baltic political parties have neglected the issues of societal integration and minority protection, thus leaving space for the Kremlin to enter.

The five Central Asian states have also been subject to the reimperialization trajectory. The success of Moscow's policies here has varied significantly due to differences in local regimes, in the significance of the compatriot issue, and in the economic and security vulnerability of the states in question. Uzbekistan and Turkmenistan, the most authoritarian and closed regimes, have been able to suppress many Russian initiatives like support for diaspora organizations, compatriot policies, and passportization efforts. In contrast, the weaker, poorer, and more vulnerable states like Tajikistan and more recently Kyrgyzstan have been unable to resist many of Moscow's policies that are carried out with a dose of bribery and coercion. Both of these countries (especially Tajikistan) are dependent on Russian financial support and are arguably constrained by the presence of Russian troops on their soil. The giant of the region, Kazakhstan, falls somewhere in between these two ends of the spectrum, but its large and somewhat disgruntled Russian and Russian-speaking population, concentrated along the northern border with Russia, is susceptible to Russian compatriot policies and potential compatriot-driven territorial takeovers. Over the years Kazakhstan has been a close, and possibly the most reliable, ally of Moscow in Central Asia, and like Tajikistan and Kyrgyzstan, it has permitted some of Russia's softer compatriot policies. However, President Nursultan Nazarbayev's skilled strongman regime has enabled Astana to draw red lines against Russian passportization and to quell separatist movements for now. Like the other Central Asian states and most former Soviet republics, Kazakhstan has been pervaded by the Russian state-owned media, which remain highly popular and influential across most sectors of society since some 75 percent of ethnic Kazakhs speak Russian. At the same time, the five Central Asian states and their leadership do not look at Russia through rose-colored spectacles, but have looked out for their own interests as they have focused on state building ever since independence. They have struck deals with Moscow when it suited them and have tried to protect their security and sovereignty when possible. Only the most vulnerable, like Tajikistan and Kyrgyzstan, have been more constrained in their relationship with Moscow, but are not completely subservient.

The geopolitical implications of the reimperialization trajectory in Central Asia are arguably less worrying than in the case of the Baltic States, but nonetheless cannot be ignored. The region's shared borders with the turbulent states of Afghanistan and Iran, and proximity to Pakistan, imply that any destabilizing effects of Russian-stoked separatism or conflict could be compounded by cross-border extremist movements. Indeed, if frozen-conflict zones that thrive on arms and drug trafficking are created in Central Asia as they were in Georgia and Moldova, they may become hotbeds of terrorism. Such lawless territories would further destabilize a fragile region, creating repercussions for international security and the West's global war on terror. Russia's efforts to maintain a neo-imperial hold on the region may also increasingly come head to head with European and arguably even Chinese interests. The energy-rich states of Turkmenistan, Kazakhstan, and Uzbekistan may in the future play a role in the European nations' efforts to reduce their energy dependence on Russia. China is already a rising consumer of Central Asian energy resources and an increasingly prominent investor in the region. As the Central Asian states have attempted to diversify their allies and economic partners, Russian reimperialization policies could become a hindrance and a source of tensions. In the future, as the aging leadership in Uzbekistan and Kazakhstan eventually leaves the scene, a change of regime and foreign policy, or a turn to less authoritarian leadership, may result in tensions with Moscow or create more opportunities for Russian interference, if not intervention.

The cases of Armenia and Belarus show how even Russia's allies are not immune from its reimperialization efforts. In fact allies may be able to muster less resistance to Moscow's various compatriot-driven policies than other target states. Both countries can be considered never to have left Russia's imperial orbit and certainly not its sphere of influence. Both are unique by virtue of the fact that Russia's wooing efforts are primarily aimed not at Russian or other minority populations (which are small) but rather at the general population, which tends to be open to Russia's cultural and political influence. The Russian media tend to be pervasive in both countries, and in Belarus, the leadership has often embraced or at least not resisted what can be described as Russification policies. However, the story is not simple; neither Armenia nor Belarus meekly accepts all of Moscow's dictates. The two countries also have their differences. In some regards, Armenia shares many similarities with Tajikistan and Kyrgyzstan. As a vulnerable state in its region, stuck in the frozen conflict of Nagorno-Karabakh with neighboring Azerbaijan, Yerevan has looked to Moscow for support and protection. Many Armenians, like Tajiks, have found employment opportunities in Russia and welcome Russian citizenships for economic motives. Despite Armenia's strong cultural identity, the popularity of the Russian language persists among the youth of Armenia in contrast to many parts of the post-Soviet space. The country was subjected to Russian information warfare and economic pressure when it sought closer relations with the EU—a project Yerevan subsequently abandoned. While accommodating in many regards, Armenia has drawn its own red line at the passportization and resettlement to Russia of its citizens, while Moscow's heavy-handedness has generated some official and societal opposition.

Like Armenia, Russia's last stronghold in the Caucasus, Belarus remains the last country in Europe that remains squarely in Russia's sphere of influence. While all other European countries of the Soviet bloc have at least tried to turn Westward, Belarus has remained Russia's trusted ally and to a great degree a willing participant in its reimperialization project. Nonetheless, like Kazakhstan's Nazarbayev, Belarus's President Alexander Lukashenko has used his powerful position to limit some of the more aggressive aspects of the reimperialization trajectory including passportization and absurd allegations of maltreatment of Russian speakers in a country where the overwhelming majority speak Russian. However, as seen in Lukashenko's flirtation with the unification project of Belarus and Russia with his aspiration to lead the resulting state, the Belarusian leader has focused more on the consolidation of his power base and the fulfillment of his personal ambitions than on Belarusian state building. After Russia's meddling in neighboring Ukraine since 2014, there are signs of a nascent state-led return to Belarusian identity and language—a trend that some of the Belarusian population already embraced in the 2010s—but optimism should be tempered as Lukashenko's regime has overall been oppressive toward the Belarusian culture. At the same time, while Belarus tried to take a neutral position as the host of the Minsk I and Minsk II agreements, it has remained Russia's staunch supporter through the Ukraine crisis.

The implications of the reimperialization trajectory in Armenia and Belarus are arguably less significant than in the other countries studied here. In many respects neither country needs to be "reimperialized" because they both already belong to Moscow's core sphere of influence. Nonetheless, these countries may one day change their foreign policies. Armenia had already planned to sign an EU association agreement until it was strong-armed by Moscow into choosing the Russia-led Eurasian Economic Union in 2014. For now, the majority of the Armenian population supports this foreign policy path; but if this changes, Moscow is likely to phase in more aggressive policies vis-à-vis Yerevan. The brutal murder committed by a Russian soldier in the Armenian city of Gyumri in January 2015 already showed that social tensions could have political repercussions. A future risk scenario could involve Moscow's undertaking an information warfare campaign, and making use of its existing military base to "protect" its stationed troops, Russian speakers, and the population of ethnic Armenians that have acquired Russian citizenship. In Belarus a change in leadership or foreign policy priorities may likewise elicit a tougher range of policies from Moscow. As in Ukraine, Moscow could potentially stoke societal divisions and target the most vulnerable border regions, military sites, and industrial bases. Overall, Moscow appears to have the same determination to "protect" its ally states from Western integration as to "protect" Russian compatriots, regardless of whether countries like Armenia and Belarus want this protection or not. At the same time, this "protection" of allied states is similar in its cynicism to the "protection" of compatriots. In the past, Moscow has been a fair-weather friend to both, doling out "protection" when it best suited its interests while withholding support from Kyrgyzstan during its ethnic conflicts and ignoring the Russian diaspora in Turkmenistan when trying to secure a gas deal with Ashgabat. Going forward Russia's support for allied states and its compatriot policies will remain highly adaptable tools of its geopolitical ambitions.

LESSONS FOR THE FUTURE

The analyses developed in this book challenge many conventional interpretations of Russia's policies toward its near abroad. They demonstrate that Russia has increasingly followed a policy of reimperialization of the territories that used to form the historic Russian Empire and the Soviet Union utilizing the Russian compatriots as a tool of its ambitions. This policy certainly gained prominence in the 2000s and particularly the late 2000s, coinciding with Vladimir Putin's regime, but it should not be viewed as solely "Putinist." My aim has been to demonstrate the important threads of historical continuity in policy between Putin's era and those of his predecessors going back to the tsarist times of expansionism, Russification, colonization, and sowing of ethnic strife. Though Putin's personal role in the quest to reestablish Russia as a great power and in spearheading compatriot policies to benefit Russia's foreign ambitions could be an interesting topic for future research, I found that it is difficult to disentangle Putin's role from twenty-five years of post-Soviet

Russian compatriot policies or Soviet and tsarist legacies. When Yeltsin and then Putin came to power, they inherited the Russian diaspora as a product of the Soviet Union's dissolution and Stalin's ethnic policies. Likewise, the issue of large numbers of Russian speakers and minorities residing in foreign territories will persist long after Putin leaves power. Indeed, Russian compatriots will remain a significant factor in Europe and Eurasia in the decades to come, regardless of the leadership in the Kremlin.

Furthermore, while it is too often implied or assumed that Russia possesses an inherent right to privileged interests (if not actual territories) in the countries that used to form the Russian or Soviet empires, this book stems from a different point of view. Although I do not focus extensively on the interests and policy responses of the target countries of Russian ambitions, I never assume that these states do not have a right to choose their own paths—whether of allying and integrating with Russia or with the West. Indeed, I challenge the cynical perspective that these states "belong" to Russia's sphere of interest. Surprisingly my viewpoint is somewhat counter to a number of prevalent analyses of the Ukraine crisis and beyond. Many prominent adherents of the theoretical approaches to international relations of realism (including John Mearsheimer) and constructivism (like Andrei Tsygankov), as well as others (like Noam Chomsky) have emphasized Russia's great power status in its region and argued that Moscow's aggressive policies toward Ukraine or Georgia are a result of the West, NATO, and EU's infringement on Russia's interests.[1] However, these approaches of both Western and Kremlin analysts that focus on the clash of Western and Russian interests in the post-Soviet space as a source of conflict or emphasize how EU and NATO expansion challenges Russia's historical and ideological spheres of influence all carry a certain element of "Orientalism" where eastern countries are studied as passive subjects responding to the actions of the West.[2] In the context of the Ukraine crisis, Kiev also has too often been viewed not as an active agent but as passively subject to the interests of the West or Russia.[3] Such an approach inherently denies the voice and the interests of the countries and peoples in question. The approach becomes particularly dangerous when the debate is shifted to the intrinsically misleading question to what extent Crimea, or eastern Ukraine, or Belarus, is "Russian," ignoring not only Ukraine's or Belarus's own historical narrative and national identity but also its present-day foreign policy preferences. Similar flawed approaches can be extended to most of the post-Soviet space, where Moscow's historical, ideological, or security narrative also concludes that these are "Russian" lands. In fact, shifts from softer to more aggressive phases in the reimperialization trajectory have been triggered by a target state's efforts to turn Westward (as in the cases of Ukraine, Georgia, Moldova, and Armenia). Further research on Moscow's systemic responses to the shifting foreign policies of the post-Soviet states would help us move past assumptions that Russia's aggressive policies have been "unique," "inexplicable," or driven by specific conditions (such as Tbilisi firing the first shot), and rather see them as consistent and continuous, as I propose.

I have also sought to move down one level of analysis and give voice, albeit unsystematically, to the different views and preferences of ethnic Russians, Russian speakers, and other minorities who are often forgotten as they are involuntarily politicized, instrumentalized, and securitized both by their home countries and by the Kremlin. A scientific survey of the Russian diaspora across the former Soviet republics, taking into account generational, socio-economic, cultural, and geographical differences would certainly be welcome since it would shed additional light on a group of people who will remain important to the stability of the post–Cold War order. Meanwhile, my analysis and the interviews included in this book offer several findings. Overall, there was no universal understanding of the term "compatriot" among the Russians and Russian speakers interviewed, and views ranged from insistent shunning of the label, to its passive but skeptical acceptance, to (in the rarer cases) enthusiastic embracement. In frozen-conflict regions such as Transnistria, South Ossetia, and Abkhazia, compatriot attitudes have varied from increasing skepticism due to Moscow's undelivered promises, to pragmatic cynicism, to increased identification with Russia and Moscow's policies. Interviews also suggest that there is a generational divide among the post-Soviet Russian and Russian-speaking diaspora. In the Baltic States, the younger generation generally has acquired local citizenship, gained fluency in the titular languages, and is largely integrated into society. In countries like Ukraine, Belarus, Armenia, and Kazakhstan where a large segment of the titular nations and other minorities are often Russian speakers, the attitudes

of the younger generation toward Russia and its efforts to protect compatriots seemed not to be linked to their ethnicity or native language
unlike with the older generation. Young people who identified themselves as ethnic Russians as against Russian-speaking Ukrainians
were as likely to be critical as supportive of Moscow's policies. In the
future, if the Kremlin continues to exploit the so-called compatriots for
its territorial ambitions, it will be up to the leadership of the post-Soviet
states to first understand their Russian minorities in order to successfully engage and integrate them. To date, however, the opposite seems
true. There is a lack of understanding among many post-Soviet governments of their minority populations and in some cases a fear of them as
possible fifth columnists. This perspective closes the opportunities for
engagement and integration of ethnic Russians and Russian speakers in
their home societies and opens the door for co-optation by Moscow.

A troubling by-product of Russian compatriot and reimperialization
efforts has been frozen conflicts. Nearly all such conflicts in the post-
Soviet space (with the exception of Nagorno-Karabakh) were created by
Russia's efforts to protect its compatriots, and all took the form of self-
proclaimed "people's republics." The conditions in these "republics" are
dire. Arms, drugs, human trafficking, terrorism, organized crime, collapsed economies, and warlords have been the norm from Transnistria
to the latest Donetsk and Luhansk "republics." Such conditions certainly
have transnational consequences, and Russian-stoked separatism that
leads to frozen conflicts should matter to the international community
and not only to torn-apart states and their allies. Too often each of the
post-Soviet frozen conflicts has been treated as a singular case and a
product of unique circumstances, with insufficient attention awarded to
their similarities and common origins in Russian policies that I have
sought to demonstrate. This, too is a subject that would benefit from further research.

While the reimperialization trajectory is intended to grow Moscow's
power and bring post-Soviet states back into Russia's embrace or in some
cases to prevent them from escaping it, the outcomes of these policies
could be contradictory. First, Russia's more aggressive policies toward
its compatriots and the territories where they reside have made states
like Ukraine, Georgia, Kazakhstan, Turkmenistan, and Uzbekistan more
wary in their relationship with Moscow and more likely to shift toward

Europe or China. Second, as Russian national identity is increasingly formulated along ethnic lines and tied to the Russian Orthodox Church rather than to a civic definition, this is bound in the long term to alienate non-Russians and Muslims in parts of the Russian Federation such as Chechnya, Dagestan, Tatarstan, and recently annexed Crimea. It may also work against Moscow's inclusion of non–ethnic Russians in its conceptualization of compatriots, as in South Ossetia and Abkhazia. Third, as Russian compatriot policies encroach on the sovereignty of foreign states and result in war as in Ukraine, there is likely to be a backlash from otherwise sympathetic ethnic Russians and Russian speakers abroad. This rising skepticism toward Moscow's agenda is evident among the younger generation of Russian speakers profiled in this book. Many of them generally identify with Russia and its culture but question the intentions of Moscow's "protection" policies vis-à-vis its compatriots. In the years to come, Russia may lose some support for its softer compatriot and humanitarian policies among its diaspora.

Since the Russian diaspora and Moscow's imperial ambitions are unlikely to disappear in the foreseeable future, Russian compatriot-driven reimperialization efforts will most likely persist in some form or another. As a result, it is useful to consider the most effective policy responses for the target states and the West. Certainly, there is no blanket solution to cover the distinct circumstances in the fourteen unique states ranging from the Baltic to the Caucasus to Central Asia. Policymakers need to be ready to tailor multidimensional solutions to each country's specific conditions as Moscow's policies leveraging Russian compatriots unfold.

Here I will briefly offer some suggestions as to what countermeasures can be taken at each stage of the reimperialization trajectory. The initial phase of the trajectory—and one that presently impacts all post-Soviet states—is Russia's soft power. In response, the United States and Europe would do well first to let go of the erroneous assumption that with the end of the Cold War and with the EU's and NATO's enlargement the West has won the soft power and ideological contest with Moscow. On the contrary, Russia devotes considerable efforts and resources to its soft power efforts in the post-Soviet states and further afield. Moscow's influence is more effective because it is coupled with more coercive measures. The United States and the EU should continue to consistently engage the countries of the post-Soviet space and demonstrate the appeal of liberal democracy and the values it represents. Cultural, educational, and professional exchanges are possible programs to pursue. The post-Soviet states should also consider their own soft power efforts to win over the "hearts and minds" of their Russian and Russian-speaking minority and seek assistance in these efforts from their allies.

Second, recognizing that a number of targeted countries and especially the frozen-conflict zones depend on humanitarian aid from Moscow, the West could consider its own aid programs for those regions. States like Moldova, Georgia, and Ukraine could provide economic, educational, and cultural support to whatever extent possible for their estranged separatist regions rather than leave them in Moscow's pocket. One way to hinder Russian compatriot and passportization policies would be leg-islation by target states as in Central Asia. However, it would be more effective for these governments to pursue policies to integrate their mi-norities, including even policies of cultural support for them, and re-ceive assistance from their allies in that effort. Above all, it is essential to be aware of the potential outcomes of leaving Russia's compatriot poli-cies and passportization efforts unchecked.

Addressing the stage of Russian information warfare is one of the most important policy responses, as propaganda starts as a form of soft power and progresses to become a tool of war. Some positive steps in that direction have already been taken in response to Russia's escalating infor-mation campaign following Crimea's annexation. In January 2015, Britain, Denmark, Estonia, and Lithuania called on the EU to create information alternatives to the Russian propaganda. Also, in 2015 Esto-nia and Latvia have announced plans to develop Russian-language TV channels, and Ukraine launched an English-language channel, Ukraine Today, in 2014. Other initiatives are needed not only on the European continent but also in the Caucasus and Central Asia. The United States-funded Cold War–era creation Radio Free Europe/Radio Liberty would do well to further enhance its role in providing an alternative source of news and information in the Russian language and the languages of the former Soviet states. In October 2014, FRE/RL and Voice of America launched a thirty-minute Russian-language televised news program. Still it is no match for even the single Russian state-funded English-language round-the-clock news channel Russia Today, with a reported annual budget in 2015 of $236 million and an audience exceeding 700 million in more than a hundred countries. In the years to come, the information campaign to counter Russian propaganda would benefit from better funding, organization, and coordination between the target states, the EU, and the United States.

Once Russian reimperialization policies reach the final phases of protection and annexation much of the trajectory will have been completed and implemented. At such stages, policy responses need be even more case-specific, and their analysis lies largely beyond the scope of this book. Some of the post-Soviet states have already taken small steps that may better prepare them if Russian policies move toward their final and most aggressive phases. In January 2015, Lithuania issued a public information manual, *How to Act in Extreme Situations or Instances of War,* so as to better prepare the population for outbreaks of traditional and hybrid warfare. Additional policy responses to consider must include (among others) preparing for Russia's hybrid warfare, riot response, and countering transnational paramilitary groups, as well as engaging separatist territories and frozen-conflict zones. Policymakers in the target states and their allies, as well as the broader international community, should be prepared to offer responses and address Russia's reimperialization activities in the short, medium, and long terms. Returning to business as usual with Moscow will not eliminate the local, regional, and international fallout from Russia's expansionist policies, which take the form of frozen conflicts, broken states, and their stunted future development.

NOTES

CHAPTER 1. THE RETURN TO EMPIRE

1. Leigh Michael, "Transatlantic Relations, Economic Crisis, and the Future of the European Union," *Bologna Center Journal of International Affairs* 16, (2013): 48–53; Joerg Forbrig, quoted in Simon Shuster, "Putin's Latest Moves Tip the Balance of Power Toward Russia," *Time*, 21 December 2013, http://world.time .com/2013/12/21/putins-latest-moves-tip-the-balance-of-power-toward-russia/; Michal Baranowski, quoted in Ian Traynor, "Russia 'Blackmailed Ukraine to Ditch EU pact,'" *The Guardian*, 22 November 2013, http://www.theguardian .com/world/2013/nov/22/russia-ukraine-eu-pact-lithuania.

2. "Mogherini: Russia Is No Longer the EU's Strategic Partner," EurActiv, 3 September 2014, http://www.euractiv.com/sections/global-europe/mogherini -russia-no-longer-eus-strategic-partner-308152; Simon Tisdall, "The New Cold War: Are We Going Back to the Bad Old Days?" *The Guardian*, 19 November 2014, http://www.theguardian.com/world/2014/nov/19/new-cold-war-back-to -bad-old-days-russia-west-putin-ukraine; Alasdair MacDonald and Jan Strupczewski, "EU Leaders Prepare for Long Confrontation with Russia," Reuters, 19 December 2014, http://www.reuters.com/article/2014/12/19/us-russia -crisis-eu-idUSKBN0JX04M20141219.

3. Theodore R. Weeks, *Nation and State in Late Imperial Russia: Nationalism and Russification on the Western Frontier, 1863–1914* (DeKalb: Northern Illinois University Press, 2008); Edward C. Thaden, *Russification in the Baltic Provinces and Finland, 1855–1914* (Princeton, NJ: Princeton University Press, 1981); Darius Staliunas, *Making Russians: Meaning and Practice of Russification in Lithuania and Belarus after 1863* (Amsterdam: Rodopi, 2007).

4. Gatis Pelnēns, ed., *The "Humanitarian Dimension" of Russian Foreign Policy Toward Georgia, Moldova, Ukraine, and the Baltic States* (Riga: Centre for East European Policy Studies, 2009), pp. 9–10.

5. Alexander Motyl, *Imperial Ends* (New York: Columbia University Press, 2001), p. 110.

6. Francis Fukuyama, "The End of History?" *The National Interest,* Summer 1989, http://ps321.community.uaf.edu/files/2012/10/Fukuyama-End-of -history-article.pdf.

7. Motyl, *Imperial Ends,* p. 4.

8. Daniel Litvin, "Oil, Gas and Imperialism," *The Guardian,* 4 January 2006, http://www.theguardian.com/world/2006/jan/04/russia.ukraine2.

9. One of the most-heard voices urging to restore the "humiliated" Russian state and nation is that of Alexander Dugin—former professor at Moscow State University, known for his nationalistic views. Anton Barbashin and Hannah Thoburn, "Putin's Brain: Alexander Dugin and the Philosophy Behind Putin's Invasion of Crimea," *Foreign Affairs,* 31 March 2014, http://www.foreignaffairs .com/articles/141080/anton-barbashin-and-hannah-thoburn/putins-brain.

10. Daniel Treisman, "Vladimir Putin's Remarkable Comeback," CNN, 3 February 2014, http://www.cnn.com/2014/02/03/opinion/treisman-putin-comeback -sochi/index.html.

11. Leon Aron, ed., *Putin's Russia: How It Rose, How It Is Maintained, and How It Might End* (Washington, DC: American Enterprise Institute, 2015).

12. Jeffrey Mankoff, *Russian Foreign Policy: The Return of Great Power Politics* (Lanham, MD: Rowman & Littlefield, 2009); Stephen Sestanovich, "Russia's Foreign Policy is a Near-Complete Failure," *Financial Times,* 3 November 2013, http://www.ft.com/cms/s/0/73d58caa-4258-11e3-8350-00144feabdc0 .html#axzz3KJbA2onB.

13. Dmitri Trenin, "What Russian Empire?" *New York Times,* 23 August 2011, http://www.nytimes.com/2011/08/24/opinion/24iht-edtrenin24.html?_r=0.

14. Johan Galtung, "Geopolitics after the Cold War: An Essay in Agenda Theory," in *The International System After the Collapse of the East-West Order,* ed. Armand Clesse, Richard Cooper, and Yoshikazu Sakamoto (Dordrecht: Martinus Nijhoff, 1994), p. 202, cited in Motyl, *Imperial Ends,* p. 113.

15. Motyl, *Imperial Ends,* p. 103.

16. Edward Lucas, *The New Cold War: Putin's Russia and the Threat to the West* (New York: Palgrave Macmillan), 2014.

17. Emil Pain, "Russia Between Empire and Nation," *Russian Politics and Law* 47, no. 2 (2009): 60–86.

18. Agnia Grigas, "How Putin Carries Out Power Grab," CNN, 4 March 2014, http://www.cnn.com/2014/03/02/opinion/grigas-putin-compatriot-policy -crimea/index.html.

19. "US Lawmakers Call for Arming Ukraine Government," Business Insider, 31 August 2014, http://www.businessinsider.com/us-lawmakers-call-for -arming-ukraine-government-2014-8#ixzz3LuJc2WjD.

20. Indira Lakshmanan, "Congress Passes Tougher Russia Sanctions But Gives Obama Leeway," *Bloomberg.com*, 12 December 2014, http://www.bloomberg .com/politics/articles/2014-12-12/congress-passes-tougher-russia-sanctions -but-gives-obama-leeway.

21. Alexander Motyl, "The Sources of Russian Conduct: The New Case for Containment," *Foreign Affairs*, 16 November 2014, http://www.foreignaffairs.com /articles/142366/alexander-j-motyl/the-sources-of-russian-conduct.

22. Shaun Walker and Harriet Salem, "Russian Parliament Approves Troop Deployment in Ukraine," *The Guardian*, 1 March 2014, http://www.theguardian .com/world/2014/mar/02/russia-parliament-approves-military-ukraine -vladimir-putin.

23. On the "winning hearts and minds" concept see Elizabeth Dickinson, "A Bright Shining Slogan," *Foreign Policy*, 22 August 2009, http://foreignpolicy .com/2009/08/22/a-bright-shining-slogan/.

24. Motyl, *Imperial Ends*, p. 5.

25. Michael W. Doyle, *Empires* (Ithaca, NY: Cornell University Press, 1986), p. 45.

26. Motyl, *Imperial Ends*, p. 4.

27. Richard Pipes, *Russia Under the Old Regime*, Great Britain: Penguin, 1995, p. 163.

28. Motyl, *Imperial Ends*, p. 3.

29. Hélène Carrère d'Encausse, *Decline of an Empire: The Soviet Socialist Republics in Revolt* (New York: Newsweek Books, 1979), cited in Motyl, *Imperial Ends*, p. 3.

30. Motyl, *Imperial Ends*, p. 3.

31. Ibid, p. 99.

32. Daniel Treisman, "Beyond Horror and Mystery," IWMpost, no. 105 (September–December 2010), http://www.sscnet.ucla.edu/polisci/faculty /treisman/PAPERS_NEW/Beyond%20Horror%20and%20Mystery.pdf.

33. Vera Tolz, *Russia* (New York: Oxford University Press, 2001), pp. 235–60; Charles Ziegler, "The Russian Diaspora in Central Asia: Russian Compatriots and Moscow's Foreign Policy," *Demokratizatsiya* 14, no. 1 (2006): 103.

34. "Full Text of Putin's Speech on Crimea," PraguePost, 19 March 2014, http://praguepost.com/eu-news/37854-full-text-of-putin-s-speech-on -crimea.

35. George Friedman, "The Medvedev Doctrine and American Strategy," Stratfor, 2 September 2008, http://www.stratfor.com/weekly/medvedev_doctrine_and _american_strategy. See also "Medvedev Outlines the Five Main Points of Future Foreign Policy," Sputnik International, 31 August 2008, http:// sputniknews.com/world/20080831/116422749.html?id=?id.

36. Ivan Egorov and Nikolai Patrushev, "Ukraine Crisis—The View from Russia," *The Guardian*, 24 October 2014, http://www.theguardian.com/world /2014/oct/24/sp-ukraine-russia-cold-war.

37. Motyl, *Imperial Ends*, p. 3.

38. "National Security Concept of the Russian Federation," Federation of American Scientists, 18 January 2000, https://fas.org/nuke/guide/russia/doctrine /gazeta012400.htm.

39. Levada-Center, http://www.levada.ru/eng/.

40. Robert Coalson, "Russian Nationalists March On, Under Kremlin's Wary Gaze," Radio Free Europe/Radio Liberty, http://www.rferl.org/content/russia -nationalist-march/26672137.html.

41. "Russian Public Opinion 2012–2013," The Analytical Centre of Yury Levada, Moscow, 2013, p. 107, http://www.levada.ru/sites/default/files/2012_eng.pdf.

42. Marek Menkiszak, "The Putin Doctrine: The Formation of a Conceptual Framework for Russian Dominance in the Post-Soviet Area," *OSW Commentary*, no. 131 (28 March 2014): 4.

43. Doyle, *Empires*, p. 45.

44. Menkiszak, "The Putin Doctrine," p. 4.

45. "Indeksy," Levada-Tsentr, http://www.levada.ru/indeksy.

46. Tomas Jivanda, "Vladimir Putin's Approval Rating Hits Three Year High as Russians Back President over Ukraine," *The Independent*, 14 March 2014, http://www.independent.co.uk/news/world/europe/vladimir-putins-approval -rating-hits-three-year-high-as-russians-back-putin-over-ukraine-9192170.html.

47. Brian C. Black, *Crude Reality—Petroleum in World History* (Lanham, MD: Rowman & Littlefield, 2012), p. 145.

48. Agnia Grigas, *The Politics of Energy and Memory Between the Baltic States and Russia* (Farnham, UK: Ashgate, 2013); Margarita M. Balmaceda, *Politics of Energy Dependency: Ukraine, Belarus, and Lithuania Between Domestic Oligarchs and Russian Pressure* (Toronto: Toronto University Press, 2013).

49. Anne Applebaum, "Russia's Corrupt Chokehold on Europe," Slate, 25 July 2014, http://www.slate.com/articles/news_and_politics/foreigners/2014/07 /russia_s_corrupt_control_of_europe_how_vladimir_putin_keeps_the _continent.html; Joshua Keating, "From Russia With Cash," ibid., 26 November 2014, http://www.slate.com/blogs/the_world_/2014/11/26/from_russia _with_cash.html.

50. Ambrose Evans-Pritchard and Peter Spence, "Russian Crisis Turns Systemic as Rouble Crashes 13pc," *The Telegraph*, 15 December 2014, http://www .telegraph.co.uk/finance/economics/11295402/Russian-crisis-turns-systemic -as-rouble-crashes-13pc.html; Peter Spence, "Russian Economic Crisis: As It Happened 16 December 2014," ibid., 16 December 2014, http://www .telegraph.co.uk/finance/economics/11296233/Russian-economic-crisis-live .html.

51. Olga Tanas, "Russia Sees $140 Billion Annual Loss From Oil, Sanctions," BloombergBusiness, 24 November 2014, http://www.bloomberg.com/news /2014-11-24/russia-sees-140-billion-annual-loss-from-oil-sanctions.html.

52. "Medvedev: We're 'Not Afraid' of a New Cold War," Nbcnews.com, 26 August 2008, http://www.nbcnews.com/id/26403580/ns/world_news-europe/t /medvedev-were-not-afraid-new-cold-war/#.VGEZlYfq9Ro.

53. Oliver Bullough, "Former Aide Says Putin Has No Strategic Plans," *Time*, 5 November 2014, http://time.com/3547935/putin-pugachev-oligarchs/.

54. Thomas Frear, Łukasz Kulesa, and Ian Kearns, "Dangerous Brinkmanship: Close Military Encounters between Russia and the West in 2014," European Leadership Network, Policy Brief, November 2014, http://www.european leadershipnetwork.org/medialibrary/2014/11/09/6375e3da/Dangerous %20Brinkmanship.pdf.

55. Ibid.

CHAPTER 2. RUSSIAN REIMPERIALIZATION

Epigraph: Michał Kacewicz, "A Final Interview With Boris Nemtsov," *Newsweek*, 28 February 2015, http://www.newsweek.com/final-interview-boris -nemtsov-310392.

1. In 1989 the crude oil price was $23.73 per barrel and by 1997 it fell to $12.72.

2. "Putin on 'Self-Determination of the Russian People,'" Den'.kiev.ua, 26 January 2014, http://www.day.kiev.ua/en/article/day-after-day/putin-self -determination-russian-people.

3. Nadia Diuk, "Euromaidan: Ukraine's Self-Organizing Revolution," *World Affairs*, March/April 2014, http://www.worldaffairsjournal.org/article/euro maidan-ukraine%E2%80%99s-self-organizing-revolution.

4. Joseph S. Nye Jr., *Soft Power: The Means to Success in World Politics* (New York: Public Affairs, 2004), pp. 6, 8, 11–15.

5. James Sherr, *Hard Diplomacy and Soft Coercion: Russia's Influence Abroad* (London: Chatham House, 2013), p. 2.

6. James Sherr, "Russian Soft Power in the 'New' and 'Old' Europe," Conference on Russian Soft Power, Arlington, VA, 13 January 2011.

7. Agnia Grigas, "Legacies, Coercion and Soft Power: Russian Influence in the Baltic States," Chatham House Briefing Paper, August 2012, http://www .chathamhouse.org/sites/files/chathamhouse/public/Research/Russia%20 and%20Eurasia/0812bp_grigas.pdf.

8. Vladimir Rukavishnikov, "Russia's 'Soft Power' in the Putin Epoch," in *Russian Foreign Policy in the 21st Century*, ed. Roget Kanet (Houndmills, UK: Palgrave Macmillan, 2010), pp. 76–97.

9. Russia, Ministry of Foreign Affairs, "A Survey of Russian Federation Foreign policy," http://www.mid.ru/brp_4.nsf/e78a48070f128a7b43256999005bcbb3 /89a30b3a6b65b4f2c32572d700292f74.

10. "The National Question," cited in James Sherr, *Hard Diplomacy and Soft Coercion*, p. 73.

11. Gatis Pelnēns, ed., *The "Humanitarian Dimension" of Russian Foreign Policy Toward Georgia, Moldova, Ukraine, and the Baltic States* (Riga: Centre for East European Policy Studies, 2009), p. 39.

12. Sherr, *Hard Diplomacy and Soft Coercion*, p. 87.

13. *Almanaque Mundial* 1996 (Mexico City: Editorial América/Televisa, 1995), pp. 548–52.

14. Hilary Pilkington, *Migration, Displacement, and Identity in Post-Soviet Russia* (London: Routledge, 1998), p. 3.
15. Fiona Hill, "Russia's Newly Found 'Soft Power,'" Brookings, 26 August 2004, http://www.brookings.edu/research/articles/2004/08/26russia-hill.
16. Sherr, *Hard Diplomacy and Soft Coercion*, p. 90.
17. Marek Menkiszak, "The Putin Doctrine: The Formation of a Conceptual Framework for Russian Dominance in the Post-Soviet Area," *OSW Commentary*, no. 131 (28 March 2014): 2, http://www.osw.waw.pl/sites/default/files /commentary_131.pdf.
18. Evgeny Verlin, "An Enormous Amount of Work Lies Ahead of Us . . . ," *Russkiy Mir Journal* (January 2010); Lada Korotun, "Russia to Help Its Compatriots with Words and Deeds," The Voice of Russia, http://sputniknews.com /voiceofrussia/2011/04/21/49267112/.
19. "Russkiy yazyk ukreplyaet svoi pozitsii v Gruzii," MSRS, 18 February 2014, http://www.msrs.ru/ournews/2014-02-11; Valeri Bukhalov and Yakov Pliner, "My blagodarny fondu 'Russkiy Mir,'" Delfi, 23 March 2012, http://rus.delfi .lv/news/daily/versions/valerij-buhvalov-yakov-pliner-my-blagodarny-fondu -russkij-mir.d?id=42229746.
20. See Michael Gorham, "Virtual Russophobia: Language Policy as 'Soft Power' in the New Media Age," *Digital Icons: Studies in Russian, Eurasian and Central European New Media*, no. 5 (2011): 30–31; Ilya Azar, "Yazyk Kremlya," Gazeta.ru, 25 June 2007, www.gazeta.ru/2007/06/25/oa_242691 .shtml.
21. Heather A. Conley and Theodore P. Gerber, *Russian Soft Power in the 21st Century: An Examination of Russian Compatriot Policy in Estonia* (Washington, DC: Center for Strategic and International Studies, 2011), p. 13.
22. Tony Halpin, "Russian Orthodox Church Chooses Between 'Ex-KGB Candidates' as Patriarch," *The Times* (London), 26 January 2009, http://www .thetimes.co.uk/tto/faith/article2100100.ece.
23. "Russian Patriarch Calls Putin Era 'Miracle of God,'" Reuters, 8 February 2012, http://uk.reuters.com/article/2012/02/08/uk-russia-putin-religion -idUKTRE81722Y20120208.
24. "Patriarch Kirill: Russian World—A Special Civilization, Which Should Be Protected," newschurch.name, 9 September 2014, http://www.newschurch .name/news/christian-churhes-eastern-europe/patriarch-kirill-russian-world -a-special-civilization-which-should-be-protected/.
25. "Russia's Patriarch Kirill Given Toy Fighter Jet by Factory Workers," *Moscow Times*, 17 September 2014, http://www.themoscowtimes.com/news/article /russia-s-patriarch-kirill-given-fighter-jet-by-factory-workers/507270.html.
26. Thomas de Waal, "Spring for the Patriarchs," *The National Interest*, 27 January 2011, cited in Sherr, *Hard Diplomacy and Soft Coercion*, p. 89.
27. According to a new Pew Research Center analysis of three sets of data (1991, 1998, and 2008) from the International Social Survey Programme (ISSP), "Russians Return to Religion, But Not to Church," Pew Research Center,

http://www.pewforum.org/2014/02/10/russians-return-to-religion-but-not-to -church/.

28. "Russkaya tserkov' ob'edinyaet svyshe 150 mln. veruyushchikh v bolee chem 60 stranah—mitropolit Illarion," Interfax Religiya, 2 March 2011, http:// www.interfax-religion.ru/?act=news&div=39729.

29. Russia, Ministry of Foreign Affairs, "A Survey of Russian Federation Foreign Policy," http://www.mid.ru/brp_4.nsf/e78a48070f128a7b43256999005bcbb3 /89a30b3a6b65b4f2c32572d700292f74?OpenDocument; and "Osnovnye napravleniya politiki Rossiyskoy Federatsii v sfere mezhdunarodnogo kul'turno-gumanitarnogo sotrudnichestva," http://www.mid.ru/bdomp/ns -osndoc.nsf/e2f289bea62097f9c325787a0034c255/fd3aa5ccb0c5f96b442579e c004ec849%21OpenDocument.

30. Pelnēns, The "Humanitarian Dimension" of Russian Foreign Policy, p. 19.

31. Ibid, pp. 22–23; Devon Curtis, "Politics and Humanitarian Aid: Debates, Dilemmas and Dissension," HPG Report 10 (April 2001), http://www.odi.org /sites/odi.org.uk/files/odi-assets/publications-opinion-files/295.pdf.

32. Jonathan Daniel Weiler, Human Rights in Russia—A Darker Side of Reform (Boulder: Lynne Rienner, 2004), pp. 3–22.

33. Pelnēns, The "Humanitarian Dimension" of Russian Foreign Policy, p. 22.

34. Ibid.

35. Ibid, p. 23.

36. Menkiszak, "The Putin Doctrine," pp. 5–6.

37. Ibid, p. 22.

38. Mitchell A. Orenstein, "Putin's Western Allies: Why Europe's Far Right Is on the Kremlin's Side," Foreign Affairs, 25 March 2014, http://www.foreignaffairs .com/articles/141067/mitchell-a-orenstein/putins-western-allies.

39. "Putin: Ukrainian Soldiers Like Nazis in Leningrad," Times of Israel, 29 August 2014, http://www.timesofisrael.com/putin-ukrainian-soldiers-like-nazis -in-leningrad/.

40. "Ukraine Run by 'Miserable' Jews: Rebel Chief," Yahoo! News, 2 February 2015, http://news.yahoo.com/ukraine-run-miserable-jews-rebel-chief -202600090.html.

41. Agnia Grigas and Marcel van Herpen, "The Media Has Swallowed Five Russian Myths That Have Helped Putin Win In Ukraine," Forbes.com, 17 September 2014, http://www.forbes.com/sites/realspin/2014/09/17/the -media-has-swallowed-five-russian-myths-that-have-helped-putin-win-in -ukraine/.

42. Sinikukka Saari, Promoting Democracy and Human Rights in Russia (London: Routledge, 2004), pp. 21–32.

43. "Russian Minorities in the Former Soviet Union," http://folk.uio.no/palk /PRIO%20Diaspora.htm; Olga Zurjari-Ossipova, "Human Rights As the Political-Juridical Issues of the Estonian-Russian Inter-State Relations" (NATO Research Fellowships Programme paper, June 1997), http://www .nato.int/acad/fellow/95-97/zurjari.pdf, pp. 18–22.

44. Ibid.
45. Natalya Kanevskaya, "How The Kremlin Wields Its Soft Power In France," Radio Free Europe/Radio Liberty, 3 November 2014, http://www.rferl.org /content/russia-soft-power-france/25433946.html.
46. Institute For Democracy and Cooperation, http://www.indemco.org/index .php?id=2&language=2.
47. Institut de la Démocratie et de la Coopération, http://www.idc-europe.org/en /The-Institute-of-Democracy-and-Cooperation.
48. Ibid.
49. Pelnēns, The "Humanitarian Dimension" of Russian Foreign Policy, p. 20.
50. "Rossotrudnichestvo to Open Offices in Over 100 Countries—Kosachev," Tass, 24 April 2012, http://tass.com/en/archive/674112.
51. "New Agreement with Rossotrudnichestvo to Strengthen HSE's Presence in Europe," Higher School of Economics (HSE), 7 November 2014, http://www .hse.ru/en/news/edu/136894039.html; "Russia Wants 'Unbiased Attitude'— Agency Head," Sputnik International, 3 September 2012, http://sputniknews .com/politics/20120903/175734669.html.
52. "Russia's Soft-Power Agency Is Allocated More Funds," Sputnik, 24 July 2013, http://sputniknews.com/russia/20130724/182398836/Russias-Soft -Power-Agency-Is-Allocated-More-Funds.html.
53. Clifford J. Levy, "Moscow's Mayor Exports Russia's New Nationalism," New York Times, 25 October 2008, http://www.nytimes.com/2008/10/26/world /europe/26mayor.html?pagewanted=all.
54. Moscow City Government, Department for Foreign Economic Activity and International Relations, http://www.mos.ru/en/authority/mir/.
55. Jackie Gower and Graham Timmins, eds., Russia and Europe in the Twenty- First Century—An Uneasy Partnership (London: Anthem Press, 2007), pp. 80–81.
56. Tatyana Kiilo and Yelena Vladimirova, "Compatriots," Russian Federation 2011: Short Term Prognosis, ed. Karmo Tüür (Tartu: Tartu University Press, 2011), p. 181.
57. Heather A. Conley and Theodore P. Gerber, "Russian Soft Power in the 21st Century. An Examination of Russian Compatriot Policy in Estonia," A Re- port of the CSIS Europe Program (New York: Center for Strategic and Inter- national Studies, 2011), p. 13.
58. "Medvedev Approves New Fund to Protect Rights of Russian Compatriots," rt.com, 25 May 2011, http://rt.com/politics/medvedev-decree-fund -compatriots/.
59. "Moscow creates fund to protect Russian compatriots abroad," RT, 18 April 2011, http://rt.com/politics/russia-compatriots-fund-protection/.
60. "Sud podtverdil, chto fond Vitrenko s pomoshiu rossiyskikh deneg, finansi- roval terrorizm na Donbasse," Tsenzor.net, 11 July 2014, http://censor.net.ua /news/293495/sud_podtverdil_chto_fond_vitrenko_s_pomoschyu_rossiyiskih _deneg_finansiroval_terrorizm_na_donbasse.

61. Conley and Gerber, "Russian Soft Power in the 21st Century," p. 14.
62. Heather Conley and Theodore Gerber, "Russian Soft Power: The Evolution of a Strategy," panel transcript, Carnegie Europe, 8 September 2011, http://carnegieendowment.org/files/2011-9-08-Russian_Soft%20Power.pdf.
63. Valeriy Dzutsev, "Cossacks In North Caucasus Demand Increased Support from Moscow," Central Asia–Caucasus Analyst, 9 August 2013, http://cacianalyst.org/publications/analytical-articles/item/12783-cossacks-in-north-caucasus-demand-increased-support-from-moscow.html; "Armed Cossacks Pour In to Fight Georgians," The Guardian, 9 August 2008, http://www.theguardian.com/world/2008/aug/09/russia.georgia1; Igor Rotar, "The Cossack Factor in Ukrainian War," Eurasia Daily Monitor 11, no. 149 (13 August 2014), http://www.jamestown.org/single/?tx_ttnews%5Btt_news%5D=42747&no_cache=1#.VNacwvmsXxU.
64. Conley and Gerber, "Russian Soft Power in the 21st Century," p. 13.
65. "Third International" entry, Encyclopedia Britannica, http://www.britannica.com/EBchecked/topic/290606/Third-International.
66. Kiilo and Vladimirova, "Compatriots," p. 180.
67. Paul Goble, "Moscow Seeking To Make Russian Diaspora a Soviet-Style Political Weapon Against West," interpretermag.com, 3 February 2015, http://www.interpretermag.com/moscow-seeking-to-make-russian-diaspora-a-soviet-style-political-weapon-against-west/.
68. Eleonora Tafuro, "Fatal Attraction? Russia's Soft Power in Its Neighbourhood—Analysis," FRIDE Policy Brief, no. 181 (May 2014), http://fride.org/download/PB_181_Russia_soft_power_in_its_neighbourhood.pdf; "World Russian Congress Kicks Off in Moscow," Radio Free Europe/Radio Liberty, 1 December 2009, http://www.rferl.org/content/World_Russian_Congress_Kicks_Off_In_Moscow/1892547.html.
69. Igor Zevelev, "Russia's Policy toward Compatriots in the Former Soviet Union," Russia in Global Affairs, no. 1 (January–March 2008), http://eng.globalaffairs.ru/number/n_10351.
70. "Rossiya zaschitit sootechestvennikov v Abkhazii i Yuzhnoi Osetii voyennymi metodami," Delfi, 25 April 2008, http://rus.delfi.ee/daily/abroad/rossiya-zaschitit-sootechestvennikov-v-abhazii-i-yuzhnoj-osetii-voennymi-metodami?id=18762901.
71. Pelnēns, The "Humanitarian Dimension" of Russian Foreign Policy, p. 96.
72. Ibid, p. 24.
73. Florian Mühlfried, "Citizenship at War: Passports and Nationality in the 2008 Russian-Georgian Conflict," Anthropology Today 26, no. 2 (2010): 9.
74. Ibid, p. 13.
75. Pelnēns, The "Humanitarian Dimension" of Russian Foreign Policy, p. 120.
76. Ibid, p. 111.
77. Robert Coalson, "Pro-Russian Separatism Rises in Crimea as Ukraine's Crisis Unfolds," Radio Free Europe/Radio Liberty, http://www.rferl.org/content/ukraine-crimea-rising-separatism/25268303.html.

78. Gary Peach and Maria Danilova, "Russian Passport Handout Stirs Fears," *Moscow Times*, 25 February 2009, http://www.themoscowtimes.com/sitemap /free/2009/2/article/russian-passport-handout-stirs-fears/374765.html.
79. "Compliance of the Russian Federation with the Convention on the Elimination of All Forms of Racial Discrimination," *Russian NGOs' Alternative Report*, March 2008, http://www.memo.ru/hr/discrim/ver1/Report-ICERD-eng -site.html.
80. "Thousands of Moldovans Receive Pensions from Foreign Countries," Teleradio Moldova, 16 August 2013, http://trm.md/en/social/mii-de-moldoveni -primesc-pensii-de-sute-de-euro-de-la-state-straiiiine/; Kamil Calus, "An Aided Economy: The Characteristics of the Transnistrian Economic Model," *OSW Commentary*, no. 108 (14 May 2013), http://www.osw.waw.pl/sites /default/files/commentary_108.pdf.
81. Pelnēns, *The "Humanitarian Dimension" of Russian Foreign Policy*, p. 26.
82. Aleksandr Selivanov, "How Our Land Can Become Foreign Land: On the Architecture of the 'Information War' Against Russia," *Voyenno-Promyshlennyi Kur'er*, March 21, 2007.
83. Allison Quinn, "State Media Giant Rossiya Segodnya to Launch New Agency in 45 Languages—Report," *Moscow Times*, 5 November 2014, http://www .themoscowtimes.com/news/article/state-media-giant-rossiya-segodnya-to -launch-new-agency-in-45-languages-report-/510693.html; Paul Coyer, "The Media Battle for Hearts and Minds in Russia and Central Asia," Forbes.com, 31 December 2014, http://www.forbes.com/sites/paulcoyer/2014/12/31/does -public-opinion-matter-to-authoritarian-leaders/.
84. Delphine D'Amora, "RT, TASS Face Huge Budget Cuts, Layoffs," Russia Insider, 26 January 2015, http://russia-insider.com/en/2015/01/26/2740.
85. "Minkomsvyazi: Finansirovaniye RT i MIA "Rossiya segodnya" v valyute sokratitsya bolee chem v dva raza," *Vedomosti*, 16 January 2015, http://www .vedomosti.ru/politics/news/2015/01/16/minkomsvyazi-finansirovanie.
86. Tina Burrett, *Television and Presidential Power in Putin's Russia* (New York: Routledge, 2011), p. 49; Laura Belin, "Politics and the Mass Media under Putin," in *Russian Politics Under Putin*, ed. Cameron Ross (Manchester: Manchester University Press, 2004), pp. 136–37.
87. "Information Security Doctrine of the Russian Federation," *Rossiiskaya gazeta*, http://www.rg.ru/oficial/doc/min_and_vedom/mim_bezop/doctr.shtm.
88. Ulrich Clauss, "Deutsches Meinungsbild im Visier von Putins Agenten," *Die Welt*, 12 June 2014, http://www.welt.de/politik/deutschland/article128985210 /Deutsches-Meinungsbild-im-Visier-von-Putins-Agenten.html; Luminita Kohalmi, "Motorul geopolitic al războiului informațional rusesc în Crimeea," *Universe Strategic: Revistă Universitară de Studii Strategice Interdisciplinare* 5, no. 4, (October–December 2014): 247.
89. Jolanta Darczewska, "The Anatomy of Russian Information Warfare: The Crimean Operation, a Case Study," *Point of View* (Centre For Eastern Studies, Warsaw), no. 42 (May 2014): 9.

90. Ibid, p. 10.

91. Dmitry Rogozin, ed., *Voina i mir v terminakh i opredeleniyakh* (Moscow: Veche, 2011), p. 32.

92. Ibid.

93. Timothy L. Thomas, "Russia's Reflexive Control Theory and the Military," *Journal of Slavic Military Studies*, no. 17 (2004): 237.

94. Ibid, p. 242.

95. "Yle Kioski Traces the Origins of Russian Social Media Propaganda—Never-before-seen Material from the Troll Factory," Yle Kioski, 20 February 2015, http://kioski.yle.fi/omat/at-the-origins-of-russian-propaganda.

96. Anton Butsenko, "The Sad Life of Putin's 'Troll Army,'" Euromaidan Press, 2 November 2014, http://euromaidanpress.com/2014/11/02/the-sad-life-of-putins-troll-army/.

97. Ibid.

98. Mikle1, "Ukrainian Neo-Nazi," 16 May 2014, http://mikle1.livejournal.com/4181696.html; Mikle1, "Who Are the Real Terrorists in Ukraine?" 23 May 2014, http://mikle1.livejournal.com/4229360.html.

99. David Hollis, "Cyberwar Case Study: Georgia 2008," *Small Wars Journal*, 6 January 2011, http://smallwarsjournal.com/blog/journal/docs-temp/639-hollis.pdf.

100. John Markoff, "Before the Gunfire, Cyberattacks," *New York Times*, 12 August 2008, http://www.nytimes.com/2008/08/13/technology/13cyber.html.

101. Ellen Nakashima, "Russian Hackers Use 'Zero-day' to Hack NATO, Ukraine in Cyber-spy Campaign," *Washington Post*, 14 October 2014, http://www.washingtonpost.com/world/national-security/russian-hackers-use-zero-day-to-hack-nato-ukraine-in-cyber-spy-campaign/2014/10/13/f2452976-52f9-11e4-892e-602188e70e9c_story.html.

102. Miriam Elder, "'Nothing Is True and Everything Is Possible,' by Peter Pomerantsev," *New York Times*, 25 November 2014, http://www.nytimes.com/2014/11/30/books/review/nothing-is-true-and-everything-is-possible-by-peter-pomerantsev.html.

103. Alexander Podrabinek, "The Price of Freedom," Institute of Modern Russia, 7 January 2015, http://imrussia.org/en/opinions/2148-the-price-of-freedom.

104. Karin Deutsch Karlekar and Jennifer Dunham, "Overview Essay. Press Freedom In 2013: Media Freedom Hits Decade Low," in *Freedom of the Press 2014*, http://freedomhouse.org/report/freedom-press-2014/overview-essay#.VFFID77q9Rp.

105. Elder, "'Nothing Is True and Everything Is Possible.'"

106. "Kasparov: Russia May Not Live to See Putin's Death," Euromaidan Press, 21 October 2014, http://euromaidanpress.com/2014/10/21/kasparov-russia-may-not-live-to-see-putins-death/.

107. Damien Sharkov, "Russian Actor Fires at Ukrainian Forces, Wearing Press Helmet," *Newsweek*, 31 September 2014, http://www.newsweek.com/russian-actor-fires-at-ukrainian-forces-wearing-press-helmet-281465.

108. "Latvia Bans Russian Actor Who Donned 'Press' Helmet to Fire at Ukrainian Troops," Ukraine Today, 3 November 2014, http://uatoday.tv/politics/latvia-bans-russian-actor-who-donned-lsquo-press-rsquo-helmet-to-fire-at-ukrainian-troops-389737.html.
109. Pelnēns, The "Humanitarian Dimension" of Russian Foreign Policy, p. 25.
110. Tom Parfitt, "Vladimir Putin Says There Was Nothing Wrong with Soviet Union's Pact with Adolf Hitler's Nazi Germany," The Telegraph, 6 November 2014, http://www.telegraph.co.uk/news/worldnews/vladimir-putin/11213255/Vladimir-Putin-says-there-was-nothing-wrong-with-Soviet-Unions-pact-with-Adolf-Hitlers-Nazi-Germany.html.
111. Rayyan Sabet-Parry, "Blacklisted Russian Historian Denied Entry into Lithuania," baltictimes.com, 14 August 2014, http://www.newz.lt/link.php?articleid=19520&source=0.
112. Simon Shuster, "Russians Rewrite History to Slur Ukraine over War," Time, 29 October 2014, http://time.com/3545855/russia-ukraine-war-history/.
113. Nils Muižnieks, Manufacturing Enemy Images? Russian Media Portrayal of Latvia (Riga: Academic Press of the University of Latvia, 2008).
114. Pelnēns, The "Humanitarian Dimension" of Russian Foreign Policy, p. 190.
115. Kadri Liik, "The 'Bronze Year; of Estonia-Russia Relations," Estonia Ministry of Foreign Affairs Yearbook 2007, http://vm.ee/sites/default/files/content-editors/web-static/053/Kadri_Liik.pdf.
116. European Parliament Resolution on 2 April 2009 on European Conscience and Totalitarianism, 2 April 2009.
117. Halya Coynash, "Russia Accuses Ukraine of Committing 'Genocide of Russian Speakers,'" Human Rights in Ukraine, 1 October 2014, http://khpg.org/index.php?id=1412115043.
118. Roy Allison, Russia, the West, and Military Intervention, 2013 (Oxford: Oxford University Press, p. 127).
119. Ibid.
120. Menkiszak, "The Putin Doctrine," p. 6.
121. Ibid.
122. Ibid.
123. "Statement on the Situation in South Ossetia," August 2008, cited in Pelnēns, The "Humanitarian Dimension" of Russian Foreign Policy, p. 218.
124. "Public Opinion Survey Residents of Ukraine, April 3–12, 2014," International Republican Institute, http://www.iri.org/sites/default/files/2014%20April%2024%20Survey%20of%20Residents%20of%20Ukraine,%20April%203-12,%202014.pdf.
125. Vladimir Socor, "Putin Inflates 'Russian World' Identity, Claims Protection Rights," Eurasia Daily Monitor 1, no. 120 (2 July 2014), http://www.jamestown.org/single/?tx_ttnews%5Btt_news%5D=42579&no_cache=1#.VF45WPmsXEg.
126. Marlene Laruelle, "The "Russian World": Russia's Soft Power and Geopolitical Imagination," Centre on Global Interests, May 2015, http://globalinterests

.org/wp-content/uploads/2015/05/FINAL-CGI_Russian-World_Marlene
-Laruelle.pdf.

127. George Friedman, "The Medvedev Doctrine and American Strategy," Stratfor, 2 September 2008, https://www.stratfor.com/weekly/medvedev_doctrine
_and_american_strategy.

128. "Sergei Lavrov: Many Russian 'Volunteers' in Ukraine," BloombergBusiness,
29 September 2014, http://www.bloomberg.com/video/sergei-lavrov-many
-russian-volunteers-in-ukraine-oAnwPNGoRyGVsHU2Poikdg.html; Hunter
Walker, "NATO Releases Satellite Evidence that Russia Is Lying about Invad-
ing Ukraine," Business Insider, 30 August 2014, http://www.businessinsider
.com/nato-satellite-photo-evidence-russia-lying-about-ukraine-2014-8.

129. Michael Kelley and Brett Logiurato, "Ukrainian President: Russian Troops
Are Advancing Into Ukraine," Business Insider, 28 August 2014 http://
www.businessinsider.com/ukrainian-president-russian-troops-are
-advancing-in-ukraine-2014-8#ixzz3J8o1bBHQ; "Russian Mercenaries Return in Coffins from Their 'Deadly Vacation,'" Euromaidan Press, 5 September, 2014, http://euromaidanpress.com/2014/09/05/russian-mercenaries
-return-in-coffins-from-their-deadly-vacation/.

130. Andrew E. Kramer, "Putin Declares Soldiers' Deaths and Wounds Secret, in
War and Peace," New York Times, 28 May 2015, http://www.nytimes.com
/2015/05/29/world/europe/putin-russian-soldiers-ukraine.html.

131. Coalson, "Top Russian General Lays Bare Putin's Plan for Ukraine."

132. Gerard Toal, John O'Loughlin, "How People in South Ossetia, Abkhazia
and Transnistria Feel about Annexation by Russia," Washington Post,
20 March 2014, http://www.washingtonpost.com/blogs/monkey-cage/wp
/2014/03/20/how-people-in-south-ossetia-abkhazia-and-transnistria-feel
-about-annexation-by-russia/.

CHAPTER 3. RUSSIAN COMPATRIOT POLICIES

Epigraph: Vladimir Putin, Annual Address to the Federal Assembly of the
Russian Federation, 25 April 2005, http://archive.kremlin.ru/eng/speeches
/2005/04/25/2031_type70029type82912_87086.shtml.

1. Oxana Shevel, "Russian Nation-building from Yel'tsin to Medvedev: Ethnic,
Civic or Purposefully Ambiguous?" Europe-Asia Studies 63, no. 2 (2011): 186;
Sven Gunnar Simonsen, "Compatriot Games: Explaining the 'Diaspora
Linkage' in Russia's Military Withdrawal from the Baltic States," ibid., 53,
no. 5 (2001): 771–91.

2. Pål Kolstø, "Interstate Integration in the Pot-Soviet States" in Building Security in the New States of Eurasia: Subregional Cooperation in the Former Soviet
Space, ed. Renata Dwan and Oleksandr Pavliuk (Armonk, NY: M. E. Sharpe,
2000), http://folk.uio.no/palk/Interstate_Integration.htm.

3. Calculated by the author using data from Ethnologue: Languages of the
World, 17th ed., 2013, http://archive.ethnologue.com/16/show_language.asp
?code=rus.

4. Calculated by the author including total populations of former Soviet republics (excluding citizens of the Russian Federation) using the latest data from
national statistical services.
5. Neil Melvin, *Russians Beyond Russia: The Politics of National Identity* (London:
Royal Institute of International Affairs, 1995), p. 16.
6. "COMPATRIOT (eng. Compatriot)—*compatriote,* from lat. *cum*—with and
patria—homeland (or fatherland), *sootechestvennik.*" Aleksandr Prokhorov,
ed., *Bolshaya sovetskaya entsiklopediya,* 3d ed., vol. 12 (Moscow: Sovetskaya
entsiklopediya, 1973).
7. Boris Vvedenskiy, ed., *Bolshaya sovetskaya entsiklopediya,* 2d ed., vol. 32 (Moscow: Gosudarstvennoye nauchnoye izdatelstvo "Bolshaya sovetskaya entsiklopediya," 1955), p. 236.
8. Joseph Stalin, Victory Speech, 9 May 1945, https://www.marxists.org
/reference/archive/stalin/works/1945/05/09v.htm.
9. Szabolcs Pogonyi, Mária M. Kovács, and Zsolt Körtvélyesi, "The Politics of
External Kin-State Citizenship in East Central Europe," *EUDO Citizenship
Observatory,* October 2014, http://eudo-citizenship.eu/docs/ECEcompreport
.pdf.
10. Myra A. Waterbury, "Making Citizens Beyond the Borders: Nonresident Ethnic Citizenship in Post-Communist Europe," *Problems of Post-Communism*
61, no. 4 (2014): 36–49.
11. Sarah Ansari, "Subjects or Citizens? India, Pakistan and the 1948 British Nationality Act," *Journal of Imperial and Commonwealth History* 41, no. 2 (2013):
285–312.
12. For review of Russian compatriot policies in the 1990s see Igor Zevelev, *Russia and Its New Diasporas* (Herndon: United States Institute of Peace, 2001).
13. Joseph S. Nye Jr., *Soft Power: The Means to Success in World Politics* (New
York: Public Affairs Books, 2004), pp. 6–8, 11–15.
14. Andy Byford examines how Russia employs compatriots in international
relations, focusing on the case of Russians in Britain. Andy Byford, "The
Russian Diaspora in International Relations: 'Compatriots' in Britain,"
Europe-Asia Studies 64, no. 4 (2012): 715–35. Oxana Shevel notes that the term
"compatriot" serves various Russian political ambitions: "Russian Nation-
building," pp. 179–202. Passportization was analyzed in Florian Mühlfried,
"Citizenship at War: Passports and Nationality in the 2008 Russian-
Georgian Conflict," *Anthropology Today* 26, no. 2 (2010): 8–13.
15. Maria Nozhenko analyzes compatriot policies as a tool for helping solve the
demographic problem: "Motherland Is Calling You! Motives Behind and
Prospects for the New Russian Policy on Compatriots Abroad," *Lithuanian
Foreign Policy Review* 2, no. 18 (2006): 83–99. Tatyana Kiilo and Yelena Vladimirova acknowledge that Russian compatriot policy serves various interests
and goals, but not territorial ambitions: "Russia's Policy Toward Compatriots," in *Russian Federation 2011: Short-term Prognosis,* ed. Karmo Tüür
(Tartu: Tartu University Press, 2011), p. 183. Iskra Kirova sees Russian pass-

portization policy as a public diplomacy and soft power tool: "Public Diplomacy and Conflict Resolution: Russia, Georgia and the EU in Abkhazia and South Ossetia," CPD Perspectives on Public Diplomacy, Paper 7 (Los Angeles: Figueroa Press, 2012). Case studies of compatriot policy in Estonia also focus on its soft power elements. See Heather A. Conley and Theodore P. Gerber, "Russian Soft Power in the 21st Century. An Examination of Russian Compatriot Policy in Estonia," A Report of the CSIS Europe Program (New York: Center for Strategic and International Studies, 2011).

16. On compatriot policy as humanitarian dimension of Russia's foreign policy see Gatis Pelnēns, ed., *The "Humanitarian Dimension" of Russian Foreign Policy Toward Georgia, Moldova, Ukraine, and the Baltic States* (Riga: Centre for East European Policy Studies, 2009); James Sherr, *Hard Diplomacy and Soft Coercion* (London: Royal Institute of International Affairs, 2013).

17. My view contrasts with that of Charles E. Ziegler, who concludes that in Russia traditional political and security considerations prevail for now: "The Russian Diaspora in Central Asia: Russian Compatriots and Moscow's Foreign Policy," *Demokratizatsiya* 14, no. 1 (2006): 103–26.

18. Simon Sebag Montefiore, *Young Stalin* (New York: Knopf, 2007), p. 42.

19. Timothy Snyder, *Bloodlands* (New York: Basic Books, 2010), p. 11.

20. Ronald Grigor Suny and Terry Martin, *A State of Nations* (New York: Oxford University Press, 2001), p. 12.

21. Amy Knight, "The Political Police and the National Question in the Soviet Union," in *The Post-Soviet Nations*, ed. Alexander J. Motyl (New York: Columbia University Press, 1992), p. 171.

22. Snyder, *Bloodlands*, p. 89.

23. Ibid, p. 329.

24. Ibid, p. 330.

25. The nine nationalities included Poles, Germans, Finns, Estonians, Latvians, Koreans, Chinese, Kurds, and Iranians. See Terry Martin, "The Origins of Soviet Ethnic Cleansing," *Journal of Modern History* 70, no. 4 (1998): 813–61, p. 815; Philip Boobbyer, *The Stalin Era* (London: Routledge, 2001), p. 130.

26. Steven Rosefielde, *Red Holocaust* (London: Routledge, 2010), p. 80.

27. Robert Conquest, *The Harvest of Sorrow: Soviet Collectivization and the Terror-Famine* (New York: Oxford University Press, 1986), p. 306; Rafał Lemkin cited in Snyder, *Bloodlands*, p. 53.

28. Pavel Polian, *Against Their Will: The History and Geography of Forced Migrations in the USSR* (Budapest: Central European University Press, 2004), p. 44.

29. Ibid, p. 152.

30. Around 23 percent of immigrants to Baltic States between 1980 and 1988 were released convicts, prohibited from returning to many cities of the Russian Federation. Melvin, *Russians Beyond Russia*, p. 30.

31. Timothy Heleniak, "Latvia Looks West, But Legacy of Soviets Remains," *Migration Policy Institute*, 1 February 2006, http://www.migrationpolicy.org

/article/latvia-looks-west-legacy-soviets-remains; Estonia.eu, Population by nationality, http://estonia.eu/about-estonia/country/population-by-nationality .html.

32. Lietuvos Statistika (Statistics Lithuania), 2014, http://osp.stat.gov.lt/en/home.

33. Vera Tolz, *Russia* (New York: Oxford University Press, 2001), pp. 235–60.

34. For "Rossiisification" versus Russification see Ammon Cheskin, "Russia's Compatriot Policy: The Consolidation and "Rossiisification" of Russian Speakers Abroad," draft chapter, https://www.academia.edu/9517418/Russia _s_compatriot_policy_The_consolidation_and_Rossiisification_of_Russian _speakers_abroad. According to Ziegler, the term *Russkii* refers to an ethnic Russian; the term *Rossiane* refers to all citizens of the Russian Federation, and the term "compatriots" to culturally Russified persons and those generally regarded as ethnic Russians living in the former Soviet Union. See Ziegler, "The Russian Diaspora in Central Asia," p. 107.

35. Cited in Melvin, *Russians Beyond Russia*, p. 18.

36. Tolz, *Russia*, p. 254.

37. Franklyn Griffiths, "From Positions of Weakness: Foreign Policy of the New Russia," *International Journal* 49 (1994) 699, cited in Simonsen, "Compatriot Games," p. 772.

38. In November 1992 Yeltsin issued a decree "On the Protection of the Rights and Interests of Russian Citizens Outside the Russian Federation." Charles King, *Extreme Politics: Nationalism, Violence, and the End of Eastern Europe* (New York: Oxford University Press, 2010), p. 140. See Nozhenko, "Motherland Is Calling You!" p. 7.

39. Simonsen, "Compatriot Games," p. 772.

40. Ibid.

41. Cited in Simonsen, "Compatriot Games," p. 775.

42. "Yeltsin Asks U.N. to Help Russians in the Baltics," *New York Times*, 8 November 1992, http://www.nytimes.com/1992/11/08/world/yeltsin-asks-un-to -help-russians-in-the-baltics.html, cited in Simonsen, "Compatriot Games," p. 775.

43. Tolz, *Russia*, p. 260.

44. Melvin, *Russians Beyond Russia*, p. 15.

45. John-Thor Dahlburg, "Stankevich: Fall of a Model Democrat," *Moscow Times*, 9 April 1996, http://www.themoscowtimes.com/news/article/stankevich-fall -of-a-model-democrat/325898.html.

46. Melvin, *Russians Beyond Russia*, p. 15.

47. Cited in Nozhenko, "Motherland Is Calling You!" p. 7.

48. Peter J. S. Duncan, "Contemporary Russian Identity between East and West," *Historical Journal* 48, no. 1 (2005): 285–86.

49. Hilary Pilkington, *Migration, Displacement and Identity in Post-Soviet Russia* (London: Routledge, 1998), p. 58.

50. Nozhenko, "Motherland Is Calling You!" p. 8.

51. Pilkington, *Migration, Displacement and Identity*, p. 56.

52. Leonid Rybakovskiy, *Transformatsiya migratsionnykh protsessov na postsovets-kom prostranstve*, pt. 4: *Migratsionniy obmen Rossii I stran Tsentral'noy Asii* (Moscow: Akademiya, 2008), http://rybakovsky.ru/migracia3d4.html.

53. Agnia Grigas, *The Politics of Energy and Memory between the Baltic States and Russia* (Farnham, UK: Ashgate, 2013).

54. In the spring of the same year the Russian parliament established a Commission on Refugee and Forced Migrant Affairs. Pilkington, *Migration, Displacement and Identity*, p. 54. In June 1995, the Russian Duma Committee on CIS Affairs announced the creation of the Council of Compatriots (an advisory body). Scot Parrish, "Kozyrev: Russians in Baltics Still Suffer Discrimination," *OMRI Daily Digest* 1, No. 115 (14 June 1995), http://www.rferl.org/content/article/1140957.html.

55. Deklaratsiya Gosudarstvennoy Dumy Federal'nogo Sobraniya Rossiyskoy Federatsii "O podderzhke rossiyskoy diaspory i o pokrovitelstve rossiyskim sootechestvennikam," http://igrunov.ru/gdrf/sng/sng-archive/declar_sng.html.

56. Nozhenko, "Motherland Is Calling You!" p. 4.

57. Postanovleniye Pravitelstva Rossiyskoy Federatsii ot 17.05.1996 № 590 "O programme mer po podderzhke sootechestvennikov za rubezhom," http://www.lawmix.ru/pprf/108396/.

58. Ibid.

59. Ibid.

60. Ibid.

61. Oleg Shchedrov, "Yeltsin Cozies Up to Lebed Electorate," *Moscow Times*, 25 June 2005, http://www.themoscowtimes.com/sitemap/free/1996/6/article/yeltsin-cozies-up-to-lebed-electorate/322525.html.

62. Pilkington, *Migration, Displacement and Identity*, p. 54.

63. Igor Zevelev, "Russia's Policy Toward Compatriots in the Former Soviet Union," *Russia in Global Affairs*, no. 1 (January–March 2008), http://eng.globalaffairs.ru/number/n_10351.

64. Interfax, 11/24/93, cited in Fiona Hill and Pamela Jewett, "'Back in the USSR': Russia's Intervention in the Internal Affairs of the Former Soviet Republics and the Implications for United States Policy Toward Russia," p. 37, Brookings, January 1994, http://www.brookings.edu/~/media/research/files/reports/2014/03/back%20in%20the%20ussr%201994%20hill%20jewett/back%20in%20the%20ussr%201994.pdf.

65. Zevelev, "Russia's Policy Toward Compatriots."

66. Federal'nyi zakon ot 24.05.1999 № 99-FZ "O gosudarstvennoy politike Rossiyskoy Federatsii v otnoshenii sootechestvennikov za rubezhom," http://base.consultant.ru/cons/cgi/online.cgi?req=doc;base=LAW;n=150465.

67. Byford, "The Russian Diaspora in International Relations," pp. 718–19.

68. Shevel, "Russian Nation-building," p. 192.

69. Byford, "The Russian Diaspora in International Relations," p. 716.

70. Ibid, p. 718.

71. S. Karaganov personal web-site, http://karaganov.ru/en.

72. "Karaganov Doctrine," Latvian History, 31 March 2012, http://latvianhistory .com/tag/karaganov-doctrine/.

73. Ibid.

74. Mark Mackinnon, "Sergey Karaganov: The Man Behind Putin's Pugnacity," The Globe and Mail, 30 March 2014, http://www.theglobeandmail.com/news /world/sergey-karaganov-the-man-behind-putins-pugnacity/article17734125/.

75. "National Security Concept of the Russian Federation," Federation of American Scientists, 18 January 2000, https://fas.org/nuke/guide/russia/doctrine /gazeta012400.htm.

76. "The Foreign Policy Concept of the Russian Federation," Federation of American Scientists, 28 June 2000, http://www.fas.org/nuke/guide/russia /doctrine/econcept.htm.

77. "Kontseptsiya podderzhki Rossiyskoy Federatsii sootechestvennikov za rubezhom na sovremennom etape," http://www.whiteworld.ru/rubriki/000122 /000/01101302.htm.

78. Ibid.

79. Nicholas Eberstadt, "Russia's Peacetime Demographic Crisis: Dimensions, Causes, Implications," National Bureau of Asian Research Project Report, May 2010, http://nbr.org/downloads/pdfs/psa/Russia_PR_May10.pdf.

80. Vladimir Putin, speech at the opening of the Congress of Compatriots, 11 October 2001, http://eng.kremlin.ru/transcripts/8843.

81. Nozhenko, "Motherland Is Calling You!" p. 13.

82. "Kontseptsiya podderzhki Rossiyskoy Federatsii sootechestvennikov za rubezhom na sovremennom etape."

83. Alexander Salenko, "Country Report: Russia," EUDO Citizenship Observatory, July 2012, p. 1, http://eudo-citizenship.eu/docs/CountryReports/Russia .pdf.

84. Pelnēns, The "Humanitarian Dimension" of Russian Foreign Policy, p. 120.

85. "President Vladimir Putin Gives the Foreign Ministry the Task of Developing Policy Guidelines for Compatriots Living Abroad," President of Russia, 5 May 2012, http://eng.kremlin.ru/news/16719.

86. Nozhenko, "Motherland Is Calling You!" p. 11.

87. Vladimir Putin, "Opening Remarks at a State Council Meeting on Russia's International Affairs," President of Russia, 22 January 2003, http://eng .kremlin.ru/transcripts/7279.

88. Rasporyazheniye Pravitelstva Rossiyskoy Federatsii ot 28.11.2002 № 1663-r. "Osnovnye napravleniya podderzhki Rossiyskoy Federatsiyey sootechestvennikov za rubezhom na 2002–2005 gody."

89. Putin, Annual Address to the Federal Assembly of the Russian Federation, 25 April 2005.

90. Nozhenko, "Motherland Is Calling You!" p. 14.

91. Arkady Dvorkovich, "The Russian Economy Today and Tomorrow," Russia in Global Affairs, 12 July 2006, http://eng.globalaffairs.ru/number/n_6863.

92. Olesya Aldushenko, "Russia Interested in the Russian Diaspora Living Abroad," Russia Beyond the Headlines, 1 October 2012, http://rbth.co.uk /articles/2012/10/01/russia_interested_in_the_russian_diaspora_living _abroad_18739.html.

93. Alexander Zhuravsky and Olga Vykhovanets, "Compatriots: Back to Homeland," Russian International Affairs Council, 31 May 2013, http://russian council.ru/en/inner/?id_4=1908#top.

94. "Po programme pereseleniya iz Estonii v Rossiu za tri goda uekhali 20 chelovek," Delfi, 31 August 2010, http://rus.delfi.ee/daily/estonia/po -programme-pereseleniya-iz-estonii-v-rossiyu-za-tri-goda-uehali-20 -chelovek.d?id=32853011; "Interes k programme pereseleniya bolshoy, no pol'zuyutsya eyu—edinitsy," 17 August 2009, Delfi, http://rus.delfi.ee /archive/interes-k-programme-pereseleniya-bolshoj-no-polzuyutsya-eyu -edinicy.d?id=25149335.

95. Nozhenko, "Motherland Is Calling You!" p. 16; Zhuravsky and Vykhovanets, "Compatriots: Back to Homeland."

96. Pelnēns, The "Humanitarian Dimension" of Russian Foreign Policy, p. 154.

97. Vladimir Putin, Opening Address at the World Congress of Russians Abroad, President of Russia, 24 October 2006, http://eng.kremlin.ru /transcripts/8385.

98. Rasporyazheniye Pravitel'stva RossiyskoyFederatsii ot 13.10.2011 № 1799-r, Programma po rabote s sootechestvennikami za rubezhom na 2012–2014 gody, http://government.consultant.ru/page.aspx?1576773.

99. Ibid.; Alexander Chepurin, "Approaching the Far Away," Russia in Global Affairs, 5 September 2009, http://eng.globalaffairs.ru/number/n_13587.

100. Rasporyazheniye Pravitel'stva Rossiyskoy Federatsii ot 19.11.2014 № 2321-r, Programma raboty s sootechestvennikami, prozhivauschimi za rubezom, na 2015–2017 gody, http://government.ru/media/files/ZXiQGZwhcwc.pdf.

101. Putin, Opening Address at the World Congress of Russians Abroad.

102. Postanovleniye Pravitel'stva Rossiyskoy Federatsii ot 20.06.2011 № 492, "O federal'noy tselevoy programme "Russkiy yazik" na 2011–2015 gody."

103. Ibid.

104. Goethe-Institut Budapest, http://www.mobile-studios.org/?name=Goethe -Institut%20Budapest; Watanabe Yasushi and David L. McConnell, eds., Soft Power Superpowers: Cultural and National Assets of Japan and the United States (Armonk, NY: M. E. Sharpe, 2008), p. 228.

105. Ministerstvo inostrannykh del Rossiyskoy Federatsii, Obzor vneshney politiki Rossiyskoy Federatsii, http://www.mid.ru/brp_4.nsf/sps/3647DA97748 A106BC32572AB002AC4DD#%D0%92%D0%92%D0%95%D0%94%D0 %95%D0%9D%D0%98%D0%95.

106. Ibid.

107. "War in the Caucasus: Russia Marches into South Ossetia," Spiegel Online, 8 August 2008, http://www.spiegel.de/international/world/war-in-the -caucasus-russia-marches-into-south-ossetia-a-570834.html.

108. Interview with Television Channel Euronews, 31 August 2008, President of Russia, http://eng.kremlin.ru/transcripts/9768.

109. Interview with Television Channel Euronews, 2 September 2008, President of Russia, http://eng.kremlin.ru/transcripts/9771.

110. The Russian Government, http://government.ru/en/department/93/.

111. Russia's National Security Strategy to 2020, 12 May 2009, http://rustrans .wikidot.com/russia-s-national-security-strategy-to-2020.

112. The document mentions only "increasing effectiveness of protection of rights and interests of Russian citizens abroad." See Ukaz Presidenta Rossi-yskoy Federatsii ot 12.05.2009 № 537, "O Strategii natsional'noybezopasnosti Rossiyskoy Federatsii do 2020 goda," http://www.rg.ru/2009/05/19/strategia -dok.html.

113. Federal'nyi zakon ot 23.07.2010 № 179-FZ, O vnesenii izmeneniy v Federal'nyi zakon "O gosudarstvennoy politike Rossiyskoy Federatsii v ot-noshenii sootechestvennikov za rubezhom," http://www.rg.ru/2010/07/27 /sootech-dok.html.

114. Shevel, "Russian Nation-building," p. 192.

115. Cited in Byford, "The Russian Diaspora in International Relations," p. 720.

116. Shevel, "Russian Nation-building," p. 195.

117. Ministerstvo inostrannykh del Rossiiskoy Federatsii, "Statya stats-sekretariya–zamestitelya Ministra inostrannykh del Rossii G. B. Karasina," 2010 cited in Shevel, "Russian Nation-building," p. 195.

118. There are two dozen Russian compatriot organizations in Abkhazia and two in South Ossetia. Ministerstvo inostrannykh del Rossiiskoy Federatsii, "Respublika Abkhazia," 22 May 2014, http://www.mid.ru/bdomp/ns-reuro .nsf/348bd0da1d5a7185432569e700419c7a/3cf2977ad9223f11c3257927003d 2f44!OpenDocument, and 22 May 2014, http://www.mid.ru/bdomp/ns -reuro.nsf/348bd0da1d5a7185432569e700419c7a/be2d70933881fb75c325792 70040e8a1!OpenDocument.

119. "Executive Order on Establishing a Foundation for Supporting and Protect-ing the Rights of Compatriots Living Abroad," President of Russia, 25 May 2011, http://eng.kremlin.ru/news/2267.

120. On ruvek.ru see Cheskin, "Russia's Compatriot Policy."

121. Ukaz Presidenta Rossiyskoy Federatsii ot 07.05.2012 № 605, "O merakh po realizatsii vneshnepoliticheskogo kursa Rossiyskoy Federatsii," http:// kremlin.ru/acts/15256.

122. The 1994 commission: Ministerstvo inostrannykh del Rossiiskoy Federat-sii, "O pravitel'stvennoy kommissii po delam sootechestvennikov za ru-bezhom," http://www.mid.ru/bdomp/ns-dgpch.nsf/1f19f2b74cd6969ac325 7249003e53ae/b3e8a5763d064b64c325768900266323!OpenDocument.

123. The Russian Government, "Government Commission on Compatriots Liv-ing Abroad," http://archive.government.ru/eng/gov/agencies/156/.

124. "Vladimir Putin's Address to the Participants of the Fourth World Congress of Compatriots," President of Russia, 26 October 2012, http://eng.kremlin.ru/news/4562.

125. Concept of the Foreign Policy of the Russian Federation, 12 February 2012, http://www.mid.ru/brp_4.nsf/0/76389FEC168189ED44257B2E0039B16D.

126. Vladimir Putin, Address to the Federal Assembly, 12 December 2012, http://eng.kremlin.ru/news/4739.

127. Gosudarstvennoy Dumy Federal'nogo Sobraniya Rossiyskoy Federatsii ot 04.04.2014 № 4077–6 GD, "O Federal'nom zakone 'O vnesenii izmeneniy v stat'i 14 i 27 Federal'nogo zakona "O grazhdanstve Rossiiskoi Federatsii"' (proyekt N 417698–6)."

CHAPTER 4. SEPARATISM AND ANNEXATION

Epigraph: "Direct Line with Vladimir Putin," 17 April 2014, President of Russia, http://eng.kremlin.ru/transcripts/7034.

1. State Statistics Service of Ukraine, 1 January 2015, http://www.ukrstat.gov.ua/.

2. Eastern Partnership Index, http://www.eap-index.eu/.

3. Mikheil Saakashvili, "Mikheil Saakashvili: The West Must Not Appease Putin," *Washington Post,* 6 March 2014, http://www.washingtonpost.com/opinions/mikheil-saakashvili-the-west-must-not-appease-putin/2014/03/06/db9e0c82-a4a9-11e3-8466-d34c451760b9_story.html.

4. Matt Frei, "Ukraine Crisis: Echoes of 2008 Russian Invasion of Georgia?" 4News, 3 September 2014, http://www.channel4.com/news/ukraine-crisis-echoes-of-2008-russian-invasion-of-georgia.

5. Thomas de Waal, *The Caucasus: An Introduction* (New York: Oxford University Press, 2010), p. 135.

6. Frankie Martin, "The Olympics' Forgotten People," CNN, 23 January 2014, http://edition.cnn.com/2014/01/23/opinion/martin-olympics-circassians.

7. De Waal, *The Caucasus,* p. 150.

8. Vicken Cheterian, *War and Peace in the Caucasus: Russia's Troubled Frontier* (New York: Columbia University Press, 2009), p. 189.

9. Charles Upson Clark, *Bessarabia* (New York), 1927, http://depts.washington.edu/cartah/text_archive/clark/bc_10.shtml#bc_10.

10. Comisia prezidenţială pentru analiza dictaturii comuniste din românia, "Raport final" (Bucharest, 2006), pp. 579–96, http://www.presidency.ro/static/ordine/RAPORT_FINAL_CPADCR.pdf; Leonore A. Grenoble, *Language Policy in the Former Soviet Union* (Dordrecht: Kluwer Academic Press, 2003), p. 90.

11. Michael Bruchis, "The Language Policy of the CPSU and the Linguistic Situation in Soviet Moldavia," *Europe-Asia Studies* 36, no. 1 (1984): 119.

12. Constitutional Court of the Republic of Moldova, "The Text of the Declaration of Independence Prevails over the Text of the Constitution," 5 December

2013, http://www.constcourt.md/libview.php?l=en&id=512&idc=7&t= /Overview/Press-Service/News/The-text-of-the-Declaration-of -Independence-prevails-over-the-text-of-the-Constitution/; Bertil Nygren, *The Rebuilding of Greater Russia: Putin's Foreign Policy Towards the CIS Countries* (New York: Routledge, 2008), p. 82.

13. Dmytro Levus, "Ukraina i Rossiya: Raznitsa v podkhodakh k Pridnestrovskomu uregulirovaniyu," 27 April 2014, http://www.ut.ee/ABVKeskus/sisu /kohtumised/2012.04.27/Levus_PMR.doc.

14. Vladislav Grosul, ed., *Istoriya Pridnestrovskoy Moldavskoy Respubliki*, vol. 2/2 (Tiraspol: Riopgu, 2001), p. 108; Anna Volkova, *Referendumy v Pridnestrovskoy Moldavskoy Respublike 1989–2003* (Tiraspol: Tipar, 2005).

15. Aleksandru Boldur, *Istoria Basarabiei* (Bucharest: Editura Victor Frunză), 1992.

16. Agnia Grigas and Marcel Van Herpen, "The Media Has Swallowed Five Russian Myths That Have Helped Putin Win In Ukraine," *Forbes*, 17 September 2014, http://www.forbes.com/sites/realspin/2014/09/17/the-media-has -swallowed-five-russian-myths-that-have-helped-putin-win-in-ukraine/.

17. Grigoriy Pivtorak, *Proiskhozhdeniye ukraintsev, russkikh, belorussov i ikh yazykov: Mify i pravda o trekh bratiakh slovianskikh iz obshei kolibeli* (Kiev: Akademiia, 2001), pp. 79–89.

18. Mihaylo Hrushevs'kiy, *Istoriia Ukrainy-Rusi*, vol. 1, sec. 4, p. 4; Natalia Yusova, "Oleksiy Shakhmatov yak fundator kontseptsii davn'orus'koy narodnosti," http://history.org.ua/JournALL/graf/18/12.pdf; Volodimir Bilinski, *Kraina Moksel, abo Moskoviia* (Kiev: Vidavnitstvo imeni Oleni Teligi 2009), p. 376.

19. Robert Payne and Nikita Romanoff, *Ivan the Terrible* (New York: Cooper Square Press), pp. 63–67.

20. Zoia Hizhniak and Valeriy Mankivs'kiy, *Istoriia Kievo-Mohylians'koy Akademii* (Kiev: Akademiia, 2003), pp. 169–70; Aleksey Miller, *Ukrains'kiy Vopros v Rossiiskoi Imperii* (Kiev: Laurus, 2013), pp. 147–49; Pivtorak, *Proiskhozhdeniye ukraintsev, russkikh, belorussov i ikh yazykov*, p. 135.

21. Stanislav V. Kulchitsyi, "Holodomor in Ukraine 1932–1933: An Interpretation of Facts," in *Holodomor and Gorta Mór: Histories, Memories and Representations of Famine*, ed. Christian Noack et al. (London: Anthem Press, 2014), pp. 20–34; Robert Conquest, *The Harvest of Sorrow: Soviet Collectivization and the Terror-Famine* (New York: Oxford University Press, 1986), p. 306.

22. Olga Klinova, " 'Esli vmesto golovy snaryad. . . .': Yak formuvalas' identichnist' Donbasu," *Ukrains'ka pravda, Istorichna pravda*, 11 December 2014, http://www.istpravda.com.ua/articles/2014/12/11/146063/.

23. Ibid.

24. State Statistics Committee of Ukraine, "National Structure of the Population of Ukraine and Its Language Peculiarities" (Kiev, 2003), pp. 130, 137.

25. Vadim Dzhuvaga, "Odna z pershikh deportatsiy imperii: Yak krims'kimi grekami zaselili Dike Pole," *Ukrain'ska pravda, Istorichna pravda*, 17 February 2011, http://www.istpravda.com.ua/articles/2011/02/17/25350/.

26. Oleksandr Paliy, "Chomu naspravdi Stalin deportuvav krims'kikh tatar?" *Ukrain'ska pravda, Istorichna pravda*, 18 May 2012, http://www.istpravda.com .ua/articles/2012/05/18/85876/; "Deportatsiia krims'kikh tatar u travni 1944 r. (do 70-i richnitsy tragedii)," http://territoryterror.org.ua/uk/publications /details/?newsid=405.

27. Interview with Lilia Muslimova, 31 May 2015, Washington, DC.

28. Ibid.

29. State Statistics Committee of Ukraine, "National Structure of the Population of Ukraine and Its Language Peculiarities," p. 244.

30. Muslimova interview.

31. "Sotsopros FBK Khar'kovskoy i Odesskoy oblastyam: Evropa, Rossiya, Novo-rossiya," Naval'niy, 23 September 2014, https://navalny.com/p/3836/.

32. "Direct Line with Vladimir Putin."

33. Interview with Margarita, November 2014, Odessa, Ukraine. Interview conducted by Adam Stahl.

34. Interview with Viktoriya, November 2014, Odessa, Ukraine. Interview conducted by Adam Stahl.

35. Interview with Yelena, November 2014, Kiev, Ukraine. Interview conducted by Adam Stahl.

36. Interview with Deniz, November 2014, Chisinau, Moldova.

37. Interview with Yevgeny, December 2014, Moldova.

38. Interview with Konstantin, December 2014, Moldova.

39. Interview with Yana, December, 2014, Moldova.

40. Interview with Boris, November 2014, Abkhazia, Georgia.

41. Interview with Soslan, December 2014, South Ossetia, Georgia.

42. Dimitri Trenin, "Russia's Spheres of Interest, Not Influence," *Washington Quarterly* (October 2009): 12, http://csis.org/publication/twq-russias-spheres -interest-not-influence-fall-2009.

43. Tunc Aybak, *Politics of the Black Sea: Dynamics of Cooperation and Conflict* (London: I. B. Tauris, 2009), pp. 168–75; George Cioranescu, *Bessarabia: Disputed Land between East and West* (Bucharest: Editura Fundatiei Culturale Române, 1993).

44. Roy Allison, "Russia Resurgent? Moscow's Campaign to 'Coerce Georgia to Peace,'" *International Affairs* 84, no. 6 (2008): 1160–62.

45. "Separatist Passions Heating Up in Russia's North Caucasus," *Deutsche Welle*, 14 September 2008, http://www.dw.de/separatist-passions-heating-up -in-russias-north-caucasus/a-3643886.

46. "Georgia: Detailed Assessment Report on Anti–Money Laundering and Combating the Financing of Terrorism," IMF Country Report No. 13/4 (January 2013), http://www.imf.org/external/pubs/ft/scr/2013/cr1304.pdf; Eric R. Scott, "Uncharted Territory: Russian Business Activity in Abkhazia and South Ossetia," in *Russian Business Power: The Role of Russian Business in Foreign and Security Relations*, ed. Andreas Wenger, Jeronim Perovic, and Robert W. Orttung (New York: Routledge, 2006), p. 231.

47. Jeffrey Mankoff, "The Big Caucasus: Between Fragmentation and Integration," CSIS Report (March 2012), p. 11, http://csis.org/files/publication/120326_Mankoff_BigCaucasus_Web.pdf.

48. Zbigniew Brzezinski, "The Premature Partnership: America and Russia," *Foreign Affairs*, March/April 1994, http://www.foreignaffairs.com/articles/49687/zbigniew-brzezinski/the-premature-partnership.

49. Cited in Marek Menkiszak, "The Putin Doctrine: The Formation of a Conceptual Framework for Russian Dominance in the Post-Soviet Area," *OSW Commentary*, no. 131 (28 March 2014): 1, http://www.osw.waw.pl/sites/default/files/commentary_131.pdf.

50. "Seliger 2014 National Youth Forum," President of Russia, 29 August 2014, http://eng.kremlin.ru/transcripts/22864.

51. Petro Kraliuk, "Mif pro tri 'braters'ki skidnoslov'ians'ki narodi' (Prodovzhenn'a)," *Den'*, 20 February 2014, http://www.day.kiev.ua/uk/article/ukrayina-incognita/mif-pro-tri-braterski-shidnoslovyanski-narodi-prodovzhennya.

52. Victor Yasmann, "Russia: The Fiction and Fact Of Empire," Radio Free Europe/Radio Liberty, 15 May 2015, http://www.rferl.org/content/article/1072489.html.

53. Matthew Kaminski, "Why Putin Fears Ukraine: It's an Alternative Russia," *Wall Street Journal*, 7 March 2014, http://online.wsj.com/articles/SB10001424052702303824204579423450214067982.

54. Maksim Alinov, "Yak im oblashtuvati monopoliiu," ZN,UA, 9 December 2011, http://gazeta.dt.ua/ECONOMICS/yak_yim_oblashtuvati_monopoliyu.html; Mikhail Gonchar, Andrei Tchubik, and Oksana Ishchuk, "Gibridnaya voina Kremlia protiv Ukrainy i ES: Energeticheskiy komponent," ZN,UA, 23 October 2014, http://gazeta.zn.ua/energy_market/gibridnaya-voyna-kremlya-protiv-ukrainy-i-es-energeticheskiy-komponent-_.html.

55. Svetlana Dolinchuk, "Gazovyi zapros: Sekonomit poka ne udaetsya," *Forbes Ukraine*, 19 September 2014, http://forbes.ua/nation/1379339-gazovyj-zapros-sekonomit-poka-ne-udaetsya. Share of Gazprom exports to Ukraine in 2013 was calculated using figures from Gazpromexport, "Statistika postavok," http://www.gazpromexport.ru/statistics/; "Tseny na gas dlya Ukrainy i Evropy: Grafik," *Vedomosti*, 3 April 2014, http://old.vedomosti.ru/special/gaspriceschange.shtml. Share of revenues from exports to Ukraine in 2013 was calculated using figures from "Dokhody Gazproma ot eksporta gaza v 2013 godu uvelichilis' na 7 procentov," neftegaz.ru, 13 February 2014, http://neftegaz.ru/news/view/119861.

56. Gazpromexport, "Statistika postavok," http://www.gazpromexport.ru/statistics/; "V dekabre rossiyskiy gaz oboshelsia Ukraine dorozhe evropeiskogo," Minfin, 21 February 2015, http://minfin.com.ua/2015/02/21/6272146/.

57. Andrew Rettman, "Putin Threatens to Cut Gas to Ukraine, EU Countries," Euobserver, 10 April 2014, https://euobserver.com/economic/123820.

58. Andrey Lipskiy, "Predstavlyaetsya pravil'nym initsiirovat' prisoyediniye vostochnykh oblastey Ukrainy k Rossii," *Novaya Gazeta*, 24 February 2015, http://www.novayagazeta.ru/politics/67389.html.

59. "Ukraine Crisis Sharpens Focus on European Shale Gas," Reuters, 14 March 2015, http://www.reuters.com/article/2014/03/14/europe-shale -ukraine-idUSL6N0MB1WI20140314.

60. State Statistics Service of Ukraine, http://ukrstat.gov.ua/operativ/operativ2008 /vvp/vrp/vrp2008_u.htm.

61. "Vidobutok vuhillia v Ukraini nini vedetsia v 160 shakhtakh: Infografika," Ukrinform, 23 August 2013, http://www.ukrinform.ua/ukr/news/vidobutok _vugillya_v_ukraiini_nini_vedetsya_v_160_shahtah_infografika_1857135.

62. "OSCE: Ukrainian Coal Taken to Russia," UNIAN, 6 November 2014, http://www.unian.info/society/1005904-osce-ukrainian-coal-taken-to -russia.html.

63. Oleksiy Volovich, "Ukrains'ko-rosys'ke spivrobitnitstvo v ekonomichni sferi," pp. 1–2, www.niss.od.ua/p/241.doc; Boghdan Sikora, "Rosiys'ka eko-nomichna ekspansiya v Ukraini," http://universum.lviv.ua/archive/journal /2002/sikora_7.html; "Gazpromu duzhe ne podobaets'ia zaborona na privati-zatsijy ukrains'koi GTS," finance.ua, 22 February 2007, http://news.finance .ua/ua/news/~/93969.

64. "Yuzhmash: Rossii ochen' tyazhelo otkazat'sya ot nashikh komplektuyush-chikh," LIGA, 26 September 2014, http://biz.liga.net/all/all/intervyu /2847399-yuzhmash-rossii-ochen-tyazhelo-otkazatsya-ot-nashikh -komplektuyushchikh.htm; "'Motor Sich' pol'nost'iu prekratila po dvikhat-elei dlia krylatykh raket v RF," 112.ua, 13 November 2014, http://112.ua /ekonomika/motor-sich-polnostyu-prekratila-postavki-dvigateley-dlya -krylatyh-raket-v-rf-145259.html; Viktor Litovkin, "Stroit' avianostsy v Rossii negde," flot.com, http://flot.com/nowadays/concept/reforms/nowhere.htm.

65. S. Marius Gerald, "Crimea—Geostrategic Base Between Balkans and the Caucasus," https://www.academia.edu/676272/Crimea_-_geostrategic_base _between_Balkans_and_the_Caucasus; Michael Peck, "The Battle for Lviv," *Foreign Policy*, 6 March 2014, http://www.foreignpolicy.com/articles/2014/03 /06/the_battle_for_lviv_war_game_orange_crush_ukraine.

66. "Kiev's Blockade of Transnistria a Threat to Regional Security—FM," Sput-nik News, 23 May 2015, http://sputniknews.com/military/20150523 /1022490789.html#ixzz3bXnOYFiz.

67. Serhii Plokhy, "The City of Glory: Sevastopol in Russian Historical Mythol-ogy," *Journal of Contemporary History* 35, no. 3 (2000): 369–83.

68. Vladimir Putin, Presidential Address to the Federal Assembly, President of Russia, 4 December 2014, http://eng.kremlin.ru/news/23341.

69. Paul N. Schwartz, "Crimea's Strategic Value to Russia," CSIS, 18 March 2014, http://csis.org/blog/crimeas-strategic-value-russia.

70. Address by President of the Russian Federation, President of Russia, 18 March 2014, http://eng.kremlin.ru/transcripts/6889.

71. "Rosiys'kiy viys'kovi zahopili korvet 'Ternopil,'" 5 Kanal, 20 March 2014, http://www.5.ua/kijiv/item/374735-rosiiski-viiskovi-zakhopyly-korvet-ternopil.

72. "O komplekse mer po vovlecheniiu Ukrainy v evraziyskiy integratsionnyi protsess," *Dzerkalo Tizhnia. Ukraina*, 16 August 2013, http://gazeta.dt.ua /internal/o-komplekse-mer-po-vovlecheniyu-ukrainy-v-evraziyskiy -integracionnyy-process-_.html.

73. "Noviy front: Energetichna viyna Rosii proti Ukraini i Evropi," UNIAN, 19 September 2014, http://economics.unian.ua/energetics/987144-noviy -front-energetichna-viyna-rosiji-proti-ukrajini-i-evropi.html; "20 rokiv ukraino-rosiys'kikh gazovikh vidnosin: hochesh miru—hotuisia do viyni," BBC Ukraina, 7 February 2013, http://www.bbc.co.uk/ukrainian/multimedia /2013/02/130207_ukraine_russia_gas_history_new_az.shtml.

74. "Rosiya zvodit' svoyu zovnishniu politiku do torgovel'nikh viyn z susidami," Tyzhden'.ua, 12 September 2013, http://tyzhden.ua/News/89104.

75. "Litakobuduvannia yak rozminna moneta," *Dzerkalo tizhnia. Ukraina*, 5 April 2013, http://gazeta.dt.ua/internal/litakobuduvannya-yak-rozminna -moneta-_.html.

76. Gatis Pelnēns, ed., *The "Humanitarian Dimension" of Russian Foreign Policy Toward Georgia, Moldova, Ukraine, and the Baltic States* (Riga: Centre for East European Policy Studies, 2009), p. 275.

77. "Anons meropriyatiy russkiy kulturnyi tsentr ul. Frunze, 8," http://www .ruscultura.info/?id=anons.

78. Oleksandr Afonin, "Bazovi indikatori ukrains'koho knizhkovoho rinku," http://ijimv.knukim.edu.ua/zbirnyk/1_1/afonin_o_v_bazovi_indykatory _ukrainskoho_knyzhkovoho_rynku.pdf; "Ukraina platit sotni milyoniv dol-ariv za pokazi rosiys'koho kino—Illenko," *Vgolos*, 24 October 2014, http:// vgolos.com.ua/news/ukraina_platyt_sotni_milyoniv_dolariv_za_pokazy _rosiyskogo_kino__illenko_161208.html.

79. Pelnēns, *The "Humanitarian Dimension" of Russian Foreign Policy*, pp. 274–82.

80. "Skladeno spisok naibil'shikh rosiyskikh aktiviv v Ukraini," 19 March 2014, LB.ua, http://ukr.lb.ua/news/2014/03/19/259973_sostavlen_spisok _krupneyshih.html.

81. "Na vibori novoho mitropolita UPC MP vitratili 8 mil'yoniv dolariv— dzherela," TSN, 18 August 2014, http://tsn.ua/ukrayina/na-vibori-novogo -mitropolita-upc-mp-vitratili-8-milyoniv-dolariv-dzherela-363590.html.

82. "Vadim Novinskiy sponsiruet vybory novoho mitropolita UPC MP," Ukrrud-prom, 4 August 2014, http://www.ukrrudprom.com/news/Vadim_Novinskiy _sponsiruet_vibori_novogo_mitropolita_UPTS_MP.html.

83. Barometer of Public Opinion, ipp.md, November 2014, http://ipp.md/public /files/Barometru/Brosura_BOP_11.2014_prima_parte-r.pdf.

84. Interview with Iuliana Marcinschi, 10 December 2014, Chisinau, Moldova.

85. Anatol Gudim, "Republic of Moldova: Current Trends of Development," Rus-sian Institute for Strategic Studies, http://cisr-md.org/reports/cont-russint.html.

86. "Dour Grapes: Russia Bans Moldovan Wine, Again," Radio Free Europe/
Radio Liberty 11 September 2013, http://www.rferl.org/content/moldova-wine
-russia-import-ban/25102889.html; "Why Has Russia Banned Moldovan
Wine?" *Economist*, 25 November 2013, http://www.economist.com/blogs
/economist-explains/2013/11/economist-explains-18.
87. "Gagauziya vozobnovila postavki vina v Rossiyu," *REGNUM*, 25 March 2014,
http://www.regnum.ru/news/polit/1782456.html.
88. Irina Pancheva, "Transnistria Is Supplying Militants to Donbass," Odessa
Crisis Media Center, 15 September 2014, http://www.odcrisis.org
/transnistria-is-supplying-militants-to-donbass/.
89. "Voronin: Divizarea datoriilor Chişinăului şi Tiraspolului pentru gaze
înseamnă recunoaşterea Transnistriei," Politik.md, 29 March 2011, http://
www.politik.md/articles/politic/voronin-divizarea-datoriilor-chisinaului-si
-tiraspolului-pentru-gaze-inseamna-recunoasterea-transnistriei/5831/.
90. Charles King, "The Benefits of Ethnic War: Understanding Eurasia's Unrecognized States," *World Politics* 53, no. 4 (2001): 539.
91. Steven Woehrel, "Russian Energy Policy Toward Neighboring Countries,"
CRS Report for Congress, 2 September 2009, http://fas.org/sgp/crs/row
/RL34261.pdf.
92. "Russia Blamed for 'Gas Sabotage,'" BBC, 22 January 2006, http://news.bbc
.co.uk/2/hi/europe/4637034.stm.
93. King, "The Benefits of Ethnic War," pp. 537–46.
94. Ellen Barry, "Georgia Holds 13, Saying They Spied for Russia," *New York
Times*, 5 November 2010, http://www.nytimes.com/2010/11/06/world/europe
/06georgia.html?_r=0.
95. Pavel Felgenhauer, "Russian Policy in Georgia in a State of Flux," The Jamestown Foundation, 4 October 2012, http://www.jamestown.org/programs/edm
/single/?tx_ttnews%5Btt_news%5D=39928&tx_ttnews%5BbackPid%5D
=587&no_cache=1.
96. "Russkaya tserkov' ob'ediniyayet svyshe 150 mln. veruyushchikh v boleye
chem 60 stranah—mitropolit Illarion," Interfaks Religiya, 2 March 2011,
http://www.interfax-religion.ru/?act=news&div=39729.
97. "'Gruzia nikogda ne smiritsya s narusheniyem yeye territorial'noy
tselost'nosti,'" Russkaya narodnaya liniya, 16 October 2013, http://ruskline
.ru/news_rl/2013/10/16/gruziya_nikogda_ne_smiritsya_s_narusheniem
_eyo_territorialnoj_celostnosti/.
98. Vladimir Socor, "Georgia Between Russia and the European Union: Toward the Vilnius Summit and Beyond," The Jamestown Foundation,
25 November 2013, http://www.jamestown.org/programs/edm/single/?tx
_ttnews[tt_news]=41676&tx_ttnews[backPid]=685&no_cache=1#
.VI7SKXtHEXg.
99. Giorgi Menabde, "Kremlin's Followers in Georgia Become Active," ecoi.net,
3 April 2014, http://www.ecoi.net/local_link/273098/388779_en.html.

100. Giorgi Kalatozishvili, "Georgian Opposition Is Going Through a Slight Pro-Russian Shift," *Vestnik Kavkaza*, 12 December 2014, http://vestnikkavkaza .net/analysis/politics/63249.html.

101. Victor Chirila, "Why Do We Need Transnistria?" ipn Archives, 21 December 2011, http://www.ipn.md/en/arhiva/43295.

102. Independent International Fact-Finding Mission on the Conflict in Georgia, "Report," September 2009, http://news.bbc.co.uk/2/shared/bsp/hi/pdfs/30 _09_09_iiffmgc_report.pdf, pp. 11–12.

103. Robert Coalson, "Top Russian General Lays Bare Putin's Plan for Ukraine," TheWorldPost, 2 September 2014, http://www.huffingtonpost.com/robert -coalson/valery-gerasimov-putin-ukraine_b_5748480.html.

104. Independent International Fact-Finding Mission on the Conflict in Georgia, "Report," p. 9.

105. Ibid, p. 14.

106. "Rossiya gotovit pochvu dlya vvedeniya mirotvorcheskikh vojsk na territo-riyu Ukrainy," Obozrevatel, 14 May 2014, http://obozrevatel.com/politics /26195-rossiya-gotovit-pochvu-dlya-vvedeniya-mirotvorcheskih-vojsk-na -territoriyu-urainyi-is.htm; "Lidery DNR poprosili Putina vvesti mirot-vorcheskiye voiska," Novorossia, 21 June 2014, http://novorossia.su/ru/node /2968.

107. Independent International Fact-Finding Mission on the Conflict in Georgia, "Report," p. 247.

108. Pelnēns, *The "Humanitarian Dimension" of Russian Foreign Policy*, p. 249.

109. "Ukraini potribno reformuvati zakonodavstvo tshodo natsional'nykh men-shin," Golos.ua, 5 November 2008, http://www.golosua.com/suspilstvo /2008/11/05/ukrayini-potribno-reformuvati-zakonodavstvo-shodo-/.

110. Pelnēns, *The "Humanitarian Dimension" of Russian Foreign Policy*, p. 251.

111. "Mir ne vyuchil uroki voiny," *pravorf.org*, http://pravorf.org/index.php/news /85-lessons-of-war.

112. King, "The Benefits of Ethnic War," p. 543.

113. Cited in Pelnēns, *The "Humanitarian Dimension" of Russian Foreign Policy*, p. 113.

114. Ibid, pp. 113–17.

115. Ministry of Economic Development of Pridnestrovian Moldovan Republic, "Annual Report 2014," http://www.mepmr.org/pechatnye-izdaniya /statisticheskij-ezhegodnik-pmr.

116. Pelnēns, *The "Humanitarian Dimension" of Russian Foreign Policy*, p. 224.

117. "Gotovimsya uchit'sya v Rossii," Kongress Russkykh Obshchin Respubliki Moldova, 20 December 2013, http://krorm.ru/news/412-gotovimsya -uchitsya-v-rossii.html; "Dvizheniye 'Ravnopraviye' idet na vybory pod lo-zungom 'Za Moldovu v sostave Rossii!'" Kongress Russkykh Obshchin Re-spubliki Moldova, 8 November 2014, http://krorm.ru/news/718-dvizhenie -ravnopravie-idet-na-vybory-pod-lozungom-za-moldovu-v-sostave-rossii .html.

118. "V Moskve proshlo zasedaniye Vsemirnogo koordnatsionnogo soveta rossiyskikh sootechestvennikov," Kongress Russkykh Obshchin Respubliki Moldova, 10 April 2013, http://krorm.ru/news/rossiya/288-zasedanie-vkss.html.

119. Pelnēns, The "Humanitarian Dimension" of Russian Foreign Policy, p. 222.

120. "Gosudarstvennaya politika po zashchite prav natsional'nykh men'shistv," Nezavisimaya Moldova, 1 August 2006, http://www.nm.md/article /gosudarstvennaya-politika-po-zashchite-prav-nacionalnyh-menshinstv.

121. "Zakon o pravakh lits, prinadlezhashchikh k natsional'nym men'shistvam, i pravovom statuse ikh organizatsiy," http://lex.justice.md/viewdoc.php ?action=view&view=doc&id=312817&lang=2.

122. Pelnēns, The "Humanitarian Dimension" of Russian Foreign Policy, pp. 252–59.

123. "Dugin gotovil provozglasheniye DNR pri Yanukoviche," Khartiya '97, 30 July 2014, http://charter97.org/ru/news/2014/7/30/109103/; "SBU zapit do Rosii dlia z'yasuvannia prichetnosti Oleksandra Dugina i Pavla Zarifullina do vandalizmu v Ukraini," TSN, 18 August 2007, http://tsn.ua /ukrayina/sbu-vidpravila-zapit-na-dugina-ta-zarifullina.html.

124. "Donetskiye separatisty gotovilis' k voine s 2009 goda," Sirgis inform, 3 August 2014, http://sirgis.info/2014/08/03/donetsk_separatists_prepeared_to _fight_from_2006/.

125. "Organizatsii sootechestvennikov za rubezhom: Vseukrainskiy koordinatsionnyi sovet organizatsiy rossiyskikh sootechestvennikov Ukrainy," materik.ru, http://www.materik.ru/nationals/database/migrants/detail.php?ID =13524.

126. Independent International Fact-Finding Mission on the Conflict in Georgia, "Report," September 2009, http://news.bbc.co.uk/2/shared/bsp/hi/pdfs/30 _09_09_iiffmgc_report.pdf, p. 18.

127. Tengiz Pkhadze, ed., Soft Power: The New Concept of Russian Foreign Policy toward Georgia (Tbilisi: International Centre for Geopolitical Studies and Konrad Adenauer Stiftung, 2010), pp. 68–71.

128. Pelnēns, The "Humanitarian Dimension" of Russian Foreign Policy, p. 122.

129. Independent International Fact-Finding Mission on the Conflict in Georgia, "Report," p. 18.

130. See Pelnēns, The "Humanitarian Dimension" of Russian Foreign Policy, pp. 119–21.

131. "Ponad 1,5 tisyachi viys'kovich ChF RF nezakonno otrimali pasporti Ukraini," Krimska svitlytsia, 12 September 2008, http://svitlytsia.crimea.ua /?section=article&artID=6311.

132. "Devushka Olia iz biblioteki Sevastopolia zaprosto "vydaet" rossiyskiye pasporta?" UNIAN, 20 August 2008, http://www.unian.net/politics/139055 -devushka-olya-iz-biblioteki-sevastopolya-zaprosto-vyidaet-rossiyskie -pasporta.html.

133. "Rossiya utverzhdayet, chto ne vydayet pasporta v Krimu," 6 September 2008, Newsru.ua, http://rus.newsru.ua/ukraine/06sep2008/passports .html.

134. "National Security and Defense," Ukrainian Centre for Economic and Political Studies, No. 10 (104), 2008, p. 7, http://www.uceps.org/eng/files/category _journal/NSD104_eng.pdf.

135. Muslimova interview.

136. "Frankfurter Allgemeine: Esli my hotim voiti v NATO, to eto iskliuchitel'no nash vybor. Interv'iu Ohryzko," *Korrespondent*, 5 September 2008, http:// korrespondent.net/worldabus/576256.

137. Volodimir Sagaidachniy, "Offitsial'niy Kiyev prihrozil ukraintsam s dvoinym grazhdanstvom," *Pressa Ukrainy*, 6 January 2015, http://uapress .info/ru/news/show/55575.

138. "Russian Passport Holders in Moldova's Transnistria on the Rise," moldova .org, 3 November 2009, http://www.moldova.org/russian-passport-holders -in-moldovas-transnistria-on-the-rise-204295-eng/; State Statistical Service of the Transnistrian Moldavian Republic, "Sotsial'no-ekonomicheskoye razvitiye PMR za 2013 god (okonchatel'niye danniye)," 2014, p. 3, http://www .mepmr.org/gosudarstvennaya-statistika/informacziya/62-o-soczialno -ekonomicheskom-polozhenii-pmr/2051-soczialno-ekonomicheskoe-razvitie -pmr-za-2013-god-okonchatelnye-dannye.

139. Pelnēns, *The "Humanitarian Dimension" of Russian Foreign Policy*, p. 225.

140. Interview with Dmytro Kondratenko, 28 November 2014, Kiev, Ukraine. Interview conducted by Adam Stahl.

141. "Glaz'ev: Ukrainu zhdet defolt, yesli ona podpishet soglasheniye s ES," *RianovostiUkrainia*, 17 October 2013, http://rian.com.ua/analytics/20131017 /338854402.html.

142. "Evromaidan—yeto fashizm," Segodnya.Ru, 18 February 2014, http://www .segodnia.ru/content/135322.

143. "Ukrains'ki filii rosiyskikh radiostantsyi pereviriatime SB," *Pohliad*, 31 July 2014, http://pohlyad.com:8080/news/n/56570.

144. "Kornilov: Yednistvennyi vykhod dlya Ukrainy—federalizatsiya i referendum," *B'lyi Khar'kov'*, 21 December 2013, http://srn.kharkov.ua/uk /journalism/45-novosti/2613-hsrn.html.

145. "Lavrov: Ukraine Should Abandon Unitarity [sic] Position and Ukrainization," UNIAN, 22 April 2015, http://www.unian.info/politics/1070203-lavrov -ukraine-should-abandon-unitarity-position-and-ukrainization.html.

146. "FAKE: Ukraintsy massovo begut v Rossiu," stopfake.org, 2 March 2014, http://www.stopfake.org/fake-ukraintsy-massovo-begut-v-rossiyu/.

147. Slava Taroshchina, "Svoboda, Slava," *Novaya Gazeta*, 27 October 2014, http://www.novayagazeta.ru/columns/65867.html; "Inter predlahaiut lishit' litsenzii za prorossiyskiy novohodniy kontsert," Gordon, 1 January 2015, http://gordonua.com/news/culture/Inter-predlagayut-lishit-licenzii-za -prorossiyskiy-novogodniy-koncert—58946.html.

148. "'Inter' teper' pol'nost'yu prinadlezhit Firtashu i Levochkinu," *Ukrainskaya Pravda*, 3 February 2015, http://www.pravda.com.ua/rus/news/2015/02/3 /7057259/; Slawomir Matuszak, "The Oligarchic Democracy: The Influence

of Business Groups on Ukrainian Politics," OSW Studies No. 42 (Warsaw, September 2012), pp. 17–19, http://www.osw.waw.pl/sites/default/files/prace _42_en.pdf.

149. "Spivrobitniki gazeti 'Vesti' blokuiut' redaktsiu i zavazhaiut' provoditi obshchuk—Mindohodiv (DOPOVNENO)," TeleKritika, 22 May 2014, http:// www.telekritika.ua/pravo/2014-05-22/93916.

150. "Kabel'ni operatori Krimu vidkliuchili ukrains'ki kanali, bo im pogrozhu- vali zbroeiu—dzherela '1+1,'" TSN, 10 March 2014, http://tsn.ua/politika /kabelni-operatori-krimu-vidklyuchili-ukrayinski-kanali-bo-yim -pogrozhuvali-zbroyeyu-dzherela-1-1-338916.html; "U Donets'ku vidkliuchili vsi ukrains'ki kanali," *Ukrains'ka pravda*, 15 July 2014, http://www.pravda .com.ua/news/2014/07/15/7031995/.

151. Vladi Vovchuk, "Crimea Colludes With Russia to Block Ukrainian Web- sites," vocativ, 22 February 2015, http://www.vocativ.com/world/russia /russian-censorship-crimea-ukraine/.

152. Tim Maurer and Scott Janz, "The Russia-Ukraine Conflict: Cyber and Infor- mation Warfare in a Regional Context," ISN ETH Zurich, 17 October 2014, http://www.isn.ethz.ch/Digital-Library/Articles/Detail/?id=184345.

153. Ibid.

154. Randell Suba, "Ukraine Was Bitten by Sophisticated Cyber Virus Snake During Crimea Tension: Did Russia Set It Loose?" Tech Times, 12 March 2014, http://www.techtimes.com/articles/4250/20140312/ukraine -was-bitten-by-sophisticated-cyber-virus-snake-during-crimea-tension-did -russia-set-it-loose.htm.

155. "West accuses Russia of cyber-warfare," IHS Jane's Intelligence Review, 28 December 2014, http://www.janes.com/article/47299/west-accuses -russia-of-cyber-warfare.

156. Institutul de Politici Publice, "Barometer of Public Opinion," ipp.md, October–November 2014, http://ipp.md/public/files/Barometru/Brosura _BOP_11.2014_prima_parte-r.pdf.

157. See "Ioan Strelciuc: Moscow's Geopolitical Interests Jeopardize the Security of Moldova," Centre for East European Policy Studies, 4 December 2009, http://appc.lv/?p=375.

158. Ibid.

159. Pelnēns, *The "Humanitarian Dimension" of Russian Foreign Policy*, p. 135.

160. Ministry of Foreign Affairs of Georgia, "Timeline of Russian Aggression in Georgia," 21 September 2008, http://usa.mfa.gov.ge/index.php?lang_id =ENG&sec_id=595&info_id=79.

161. "Russia's Blunt Warning over Peacekeepers," Civil Georgia, 19 June 2008, http://www.civil.ge/eng/article.php?id=18576%20accessed:%2014/12/2014.

162. Pelnēns, *The "Humanitarian Dimension" of Russian Foreign Policy*, p. 100.

163. Cited in Allison, "Russia Resurgent?" p. 1152; "On the Situation in South Ossetia (Press Review)," Russian Embassy, Turkey, 10 August 2008, http:// www.turkey.mid.ru/hron/press_e_07.html.

164. Independent International Fact-Finding Mission on the Conflict in Georgia, "Report," p. 27.

165. Pkhadze, *Soft Power*, pp. 77–90.

166. David Hollis, "Cyberwar Case Study: Georgia 2008," *Small Wars Journal*, 6 January 2011, http://smallwarsjournal.com/blog/journal/docs-temp/639 -hollis.pdf.

167. John Markoff, "Before the Gunfire, Cyberattacks," *New York Times*, 12 August 2008, http://www.nytimes.com/2008/08/13/technology/13cyber.html.

168. Alexander Melikishvili, "The Cyber Dimension of Russia's Attack on Georgia," *Eurasia Daily Monitor* 5, no. 175 (12 September 2008).

169. Hollis, "Cyberwar Case Study: Georgia 2008."

170. Pelnēns, *The "Humanitarian Dimension" of Russian Foreign Policy*, pp. 252–63.

171. "Aleksandr Dugin: Ukrainskuyu neonazistskuyu kliku nado nakazat,'" http://zerkalov.org.ua/node/2493; "Na referendume krymchane i segodnya progolosovali by za prisoyedineniye k Rossii,—krymskiy deputat," *Novyi Region*, 15 October 2013, http://nr2.com.ua/News/Ukraine_and_Europe/na -referendume-krymchane-i-segodnja-progolosovali-by-za-prisoedinenie-k -rossii-%E2%80%93-krymskij-deputat-46443.html.

172. "'Onotole' Vasserman: Referendum nado bylo provesti ne tol'ko v Krymu, a na vsey Ukraine," Piter.TV, 25 March 2014, http://piter.tv/event/Vasserman _pro_Ukrainu/.

173. "Putin: Voina," Putin: Itogi, http://www.putin-itogi.ru/putin-voina/.

174. "Rosiyski desantniki u formy 'Berkuta' zakhopliuvali Krim, dekhto teper na Donbasi," Ukrains'ka pravda, 3 September 2014, http://www.pravda.com.ua /news/2014/09/3/7036657/.

175. Simon Shuster, "Putin's Man in Crimea Is Ukraine's Worst Nightmare," Time, 10 March 2014, http://time.com/19097/putin-crimea-russia-ukraine -aksyonov/.

176. "Memorandum on Security Assurances in Connection with Ukraine's Accession to the Treaty on the NPT," United Nations Security Council, 19 December 1994, https://www.msz.gov.pl/en/p/wiedenobwe_at_s_en/news /memorandum_on_security_assurances_in_connection_with_ukraine_s _accession_to_the_treaty_on_the_npt.

177. Ilya Somin, "Russian Government Agency Reveals Fraudulent Nature of the Crimean Referendum Results," Washington Post, 6 May 2014, http://www .washingtonpost.com/news/volokh-conspiracy/wp/2014/05/06/russian -government-agency-reveals-fraudulent-nature-of-the-crimean-referendum -results/.

178. "Putin Acknowledges Russian Military Serviceman Were in Crimea," Russia Today, 17 April 2014, http://rt.com/news/crimea-defense-russian -soldiers-108/.

179. "Khronologiia perebihu viyni na Skhodi Ukraini. Kviten' 2014," Kolona, 11 July 2014, http://www.kolona.net/xronologiya-perebigu-vijni-na-sxodi -ukraïni-kviten-2014/.

180. "Separatisti: Posle referenduma v statuse Donetskoy oblasti ne izmenit'sya nichego," *Ukrainskaya Pravda*, 11 May 2014, http://www.pravda.com.ua/rus /news/2014/05/11/7025013/; "DNR provozglasila sebya suverennym gosudarst-vom," RIA.ru, 11 May 2014, http://ria.ru/world/20140512/1007507367.html.

181. Pavel Fel'gengauer, "Malaiziyskiy 'Boing'—oshibka, kotoruyu nikto ne priznayet," *Novaya Gazeta*, 21 July 2014, http://www.novayagazeta.ru /columns/64483.html; "MH17 Crash: Ukraine Releases Alleged Intercepts," BBC News, 18 July 2014, http://www.bbc.com/news/world-asia-28362872; "Flight MH17: Searching for the Truth," CORRECT!V, https://mh17 .correctiv.org/english/.

182. "Tselyu ukrainskoy rakety mog byt' samolet prezidenta Rossii," Teleradio-kompaniya Zvezda, 17 July 2014, http://tvzvezda.ru/news/vstrane_i_mire /content/201407172217-uyse.htm; "Rossiyskaya propaganda vydala v efir sfalsifitsirovanniye 'dokazatel'stva' o sbitom Boinge-777," *Ukrainskaya Pravda*, 15 November 2014, http://www.pravda.com.ua/rus/news/2014/11/15/7044336/.

183. Maria Epifanova, "Ischezayushchiye obyekty," *Novaya Gazeta*, 4 August 2014, http://www.novayagazeta.ru/inquests/64688.html.

184. "Ukraine Forces Brace for Fighting with Pro-Russian Troops at 'Second Front,' " *The Guardian*, 28 August 2014, http://www.theguardian.com/world /2014/aug/28/ukraine-russian-fighting-second-front-mariupol.

185. "Ukraine Crisis: Fighting in Donetsk Despite Ceasefire," *BBC News*, 14 September 2014, http://www.bbc.com/news/world-europe-29195880.

186. "Details of the Ukraine Cease-Fire Negotiated in Minsk," *New York Times*, 12 February 2015, http://www.nytimes.com/2015/02/13/world/europe /ukraine-cease-fire-negotiated-in-minsk.html.

187. Maksymilian Czuperski, John Herbst, et al., "Hiding in Plain Sight: Putin's War in Ukraine," The Atlantic Council, May 2015, https://dl .dropboxusercontent.com/content_link/xFPdCHC7wA7bUFLbvZvzVDzNO ZevSyp9DgImIIoB4ZDh45xXrOidJwuZKoN4dGjC.

188. "Odessity prosyat zashchitit' ikh ot boyevikov 'Pravogo sektora,' " Vesti.ru, 3 March 2014, http://www.vesti.ru/doc.html?id=1343074; "Odesskie separat-isty prosiat Putina o voennoi pomoshchi," 048.ua, 13 April 2014, http://www .048.ua/article/515057.

189. "Direct Line with Vladimir Putin."

190. "Vladimir Putin Answered Journalists' Questions on the Situation in Ukraine," President of Russia, 4 March 2014, http://eng.kremlin.ru /transcripts/6763.

191. Julia Ioffe, "Russia and Georgia, Three Years Later," *New Yorker*, 9 August 2011, http://www.newyorker.com/news/news-desk/russia-and-georgia-three -years-later.

192. "Interview by Minister of Foreign Affairs of the Russian Federation Sergey Lavrov to BBC," The Ministry of Foreign Affairs of the Russian Federation, 9 August 2008, http://www.mid.ru/brp_4.nsf/0/F87A3FB7A7F669EBC325 74A100262597.

193. Ibid; Allison, "Russia Resurgent?" p. 1152.

194. Cited in Allison, "Russia Resurgent?" p. 1153.

195. Independent International Fact-Finding Mission on the Conflict in Georgia, "Report," p. 21; "Georgia and Russia: Clashing over Abkhazia," International Crisis Group, 5 June 2008, http://www.crisisgroup.org/en/publication-type /media-releases/2008/europe/georgia%20and%20russia%20clashing%20 over%20abkhazia.aspx.

196. Allison, "Russia Resurgent?" pp. 1152–53.

197. "Security Council Holds Third Emergency Meeting as South Ossetia Conflict Intensifies, Expands to Other Parts of Georgia," Security Council press release, 10 August 2008, http://www.un.org/press/en/2008/sc9419.doc .htm; Vitaly Churkin's speech in United Nations Security Council Meeting, 14 August 2008, https://www.youtube.com/watch?v=u6TjuPz4xr4.

198. Independent International Fact-Finding Mission on the Conflict in Georgia, "Report," p. 21.

199. Stephen Blank, "Russia and the Black Sea's Frozen Conflicts in Strategic Perspective," *Mediterranean Quarterly* 19, no. 3 (Summer 2008): 23–54.

200. Dumitru Minzarari, "The Gagauz Referendum in Moldova: A Russian Political Weapon?" *The Jamestown Foundation*, 5 February 2014, http://www .jamestown.org/programs/edm/single/?tx_ttnews%5Btt_news%5D=41922 &cHash=8ffd794ad44b029f0b95198c743709d4#.VIkp44vq9Ro.

201. See Radu Pădure, "TERORIST arestat pe Aeroportul din Chișinău. Venea de la MOSCOVA!" evz.ro, 29 October 2014, http://www.evz.ro/terorist-gagauz -arestat-pe-aeroportul-din-chisinau-venea-de-la-moscova.html; "Mama unui demnitar găgăuz: Fiul meu se teme să revină în Moldova," noi.md, 6 November 2014, http://www.noi.md/md/news_id/50586.

202. "Diversioniștii lui Formuzal condamnați la cinci ani de închisoare cu . . . suspendare," Știrimd, 8 March 2014, http://stirimd.net/?p=2014.

203. "Extremists Were Preparing for Violent Riots after the Elections in Moldova," moldova.org, 27 November 2014, http://www.moldova.org/extremists -were-preparing-for-violent-riots-after-the-elections-in-moldova/.

204. "Rusia încearcă să destabilizeze situația din Moldova prin intermediul unor organizații extremiste," *publika.md*, 11 November 2014, http://www.publika .md/rusia-incearca-sa-destabilizeze-situatia-din-moldova-prin-intermediul -unor-organizatii-extremiste_2150831.html.

205. "At Long Last, Ukraine Puts Formal End to Military Cooperation with Russia," UNIAN, 26 May 2015, http://www.unian.info/politics/1081894-at-long -last-ukraine-puts-formal-end-to-military-cooperation-with-russia.html.

206. Inna Vedernikova, "Mezhdu federalizatsiei i blokadoi," ZN,UA, 21 November 2014, http://gazeta.zn.ua/internal/mezhdu-federalizaciey-i-blokadoy-_ .html.

207. "Ukaz Prezidenta Soiuza Sovetskikh Sotsialisticheskikh Respublik o Merakh po Normalizatsii Obstanovki v SSR Moldova," *Sovetskaia Moldova*, no. 295 (17249) (23 December 1990): 1.

208. "Anxiety Grows in Europe as Transnistria Asks for Russian Annexation," EurActiv.com, 20 March 2014, http://www.euractiv.com/europes-east /romanian-president-fears-moldova-news-534219.

209. Ceslav Ciobanu, *Frozen and Forgotten Conflicts in the Post-Soviet States: Genesis, Political Economy, and Prospects for Solution* (New York: Distributed by Columbia University Press, 2009), p. 4.

210. Andrei Sinitsyn, "Russian Cash Hurts Breakaway Republics," *Moscow Times*, 4 June 2014, http://www.themoscowtimes.com/opinion/article/russian-cash -hurts-breakaway-republics/501552.html.

211. "RuseTisa da afxazeTis e.w. xelSekruleba euTos mudmivi sabWos sxdomaze ganixiles," 28 November 2014, http://news.ge/ge/news/story/114454 -rusetisa-da-afkhazetis-e.ts.-khelshekruleba-eutos-mudmivi-sabchos -skhdomaze-ganikhiles; "Russia-Proposed Treaty with Abkhazia on 'Alliance and Integration,'" Civil.ge, 13 October 2014, http://www.civil.ge/eng /article.php?id=27714.

212. "Axali etapi saqarTvelo-ruseTis urTierTobebSi: anti-aneqsiuri strategiis Camoyalibebis aucilebloba," interpressnews.ge, 12 November 2014, http:// www.interpressnews.ge/ge/thvalsazrisi/304688-akhali-etapi-saqarthvelo -rusethis-urthierthobebshi-anti-aneqsiuri-strategiis-chamoyalibebis -aucilebloba.html; "On Crimea Anniversary, Russia Signs South Ossetia Deal," *Deutsche Welle*, 18 March 2015, http://www.dw.de/on-crimea -anniversary-russia-signs-south-ossetia-deal/a-18323719.

213. "Aslan Basaria: U menya takoye ochshushcheniye, chto nad etim dogovorom rabotali lyudi, kotoriye sovershenno ne razbirayutsya v abkhazskoy spetsifike," *Nuzhnaya gazeta*, 16 October 2014, http://abh-n.ru/aslan -basariya-u-menya-takoe-oshhushhenie-chto-nad-etim-dogovorom-rabotali -lyudi-kotorye-sovershenno-ne-razbirayutsya-v-abxazskoj-specifike/.

214. Interview with Elguja (Gia) Gvazava, 13 December 2014, Tbilisi, Georgia.

CHAPTER 5. NATO'S ACHILLES' HEEL

Epigraph: "Putin Calmed the Baltic States: We Will Not Bring In Military Forces," *Lithuania Tribune*, 6 January 2014, http://www.lithuaniatribune .com/60283/putin-calmed-the-baltic-states-we-will-not-bring-in-military -forces-201460283/.

1. Agnia Grigas, *The Politics of Energy and Memory between the Baltic States and Russia* (Farnham, UK: Ashgate, 2013); Jānis Sapiets, "The Baltic Republics," in *The Soviet Union and Eastern Europe*, ed. George Schöpflin (New York: Facts on File, 1986), p. 273.

2. "PHC 2011: 157 Native Languages Spoken in Estonia," Statistics Estonia, 30 August 2012, http://www.stat.ee/64629?parent_id=39113. Final results of the population and housing census 2011 in Latvia: "Gyventojai pagal tautybę ir gimtąją (-ąsias) kalbą (-as)," http://statistics.bookdesign.lt/dalis _04.pdf, p. 164. The total Russian minority population in Lithuania might be as much as 15 percent. Meilutė Ramonienė, ed., "Miestų gyventojai,

gimtąja įvardiję rusų kalbą," Kalbos Lietuvos miestuose, http://www
.kalbuzemelapis.flf.vu.lt/lt/zemelapiai/miestu-gyventoju-gimtoji-kalba
/miestu-gyventojai-gimtaja-ivardije-rusu-kalba/.

3. Interview with Darya, Riga, Latvia, October 2014. (Some names have been changed at the interviewees' request.)

4. Interview with Artyom, Riga, Latvia, October 2014.

5. Interview with Nadia, Riga, Latvia, October 2014.

6. Svetlana Djackova, "Statelessness among Children in Latvia: Current Situation, Challenges and Possible Solutions," European Network on Statelessness, 29 September 2014, http://www.statelessness.eu/blog/statelessness -among-children-latvia-current-situation-challenges-and-possible-solutions.

7. Interview with Anton, Tallinn, Estonia, October 2014.

8. Interview with Yelena, Tallinn, Estonia, October 2014.

9. Interview with Alisa, Vilnius, Lithuania, October 2014.

10. Interview with Yaroslav, Vilnius, Lithuania, October 2014.

11. Interview with Nataliya, Vilnius, Lithuania, October 2014.

12. Interview with Alyona, Tallinn, Estonia, October 2014.

13. Interview with Lidiya, Kohtla-Järve, Estonia, October 2014.

14. Interview with Raivo Vetik, Tallinn, Estonia, February 2015; Raivo Vetik and Jelena Helemäe, eds., *The Russian Second Generation in Tallinn and Kohtla-Järve: The TIES Study in Estonia* (Amsterdam: Amsterdam University Press, 2011), p. 220; Raivo Vetik, ed., *Nation-Building in the Context of Post-Communist Transformation and Globalization: The Case of Estonia* (New York): Peter Lang, 2012, p. 328.

15. Interview with Laurynas Kasčiūnas, Vilnius, Lithuania, September 2014.

16. "Transcript: Putin Says Russia Will Protect the Rights of Russians Abroad," *Washington Post*, 18 March 2014, http://www.washingtonpost.com/world /transcript-putin-says-russia-will-protect-the-rights-of-russians-abroad/2014 /03/18/432a1e60-ae99-11e3-a49e-76adc9210f19_story.html.

17. Hugh Ragsdale, ed., *Imperial Russian Foreign Policy* (New York: Cambridge University Press, 1993), p. 36.

18. Jerzy Lukowski, *The Partitions of Poland: 1772, 1793, 1795* (London: Addison Wesley Longman, 1999), pp. 1–3.

19. Edward C. Thalen, *Russification in the Baltic Provinces and Finland, 1855– 1914* (Princeton, NJ: Princeton University Press), 2014.

20. Romual J. Misiunas, "Soviet Occupation," *Encyclopedia Britannica*, 4 January 2013, http://www.britannica.com/EBchecked/topic/50985/Baltic-states/37263 /Soviet-occupation; Raivo Vetik, "The Cultural and Social Makeup of Estonia," in *National Integration and Violent Conflict in Post-Soviet Societies: The Cases of Estonia and Moldova*, ed. Pål Kolstø (Lanham, MD: Rowman & Littlefield), p. 74.

21. Stéphane Courtois et al., *The Black Book of Communism: Crimes, Terror, Repressions* (Cambridge: Harvard University Press, 1997), pp. 4, 212, 235–36.

22. Mark Kramer, "NATO, the Baltic States and Russia: A Framework for Sustainable Enlargement," *International Affairs* 78, no. 4 (2002): 731–56.

23. "Regions and Territories: Kaliningrad," BBC News, 22 November 2011, http://news.bbc.co.uk/2/hi/europe/country_profiles/6177003.stm; Laura Secorun Palet, "Russia's Strongest Foothold in Europe: It's Not the Ukraine," *USA Today*, 26 April 2014, http://www.usatoday.com/story/news/world/2014/04/26/ozy-russia-kaliningrad/8194403/; "Russia Stations Iskander Missiles in Kaliningrad: NATO Cries Wolf," SputnikNews, 28 May 2015, http://sputniknews.com/us/20150528/1022658842.html.

24. Wayne C. Thompson, *Nordic, Central, and Southeastern Europe 2014* (Lanham, MD: Rowman & Littlefield, 2014), p. 165; Stasys Gudavičius, "Rusijos karinis tranzitas per Lietuvą mažėja," 9 September 2014, http://vz.lt/article/2014/9/9/rusijos-karinis-tranzitas-per-lietuva-mazeja?pageno=1.

25. Janusz Bugajski, *Cold Peace—Russia's New Imperialism* (Westport, CT: Praeger, 2004), p. 129.

26. "The Russian Quest for Warm Water Ports," GlobalSecurity.org, 9 July 2011, http://www.globalsecurity.org/military/world/russia/warm-water-port.htm.

27. Agnia Grigas, "The EU's Unresolved Issue of the Russian Embargo against Lithuania's Oil Refinery," EurActiv.com, 31 October 2014, http://www.euractiv.com/sections/energy/eus-unsolved-issue-russian-embargo-against-lithuanias-oil-refinery-309661.

28. Grigas, *The Politics of Energy and Memory*, p. 45.

29. "Interv'yu Dmitriya Medvedeva telekanalam Rossiya pervomu, NTV," 31 August 2008, http://kremlin.ru/events/president/news/1276.

30. Interview with Andis Kudors, Riga, Latvia, November 2014.

31. Gatis Pelnēns, ed., *The "Humanitarian Dimension" of Russian Foreign Policy Toward Georgia, Moldova, Ukraine, and the Baltic States* (Riga: Centre for East European Policy Studies, 2009), p. 10.

32. Agnia Grigas, "Legacies, Coercion and Soft Power: Russian Influence in the Baltic States," Chatham House Briefing Paper, August 2012, pp. 2–3, http://www.chathamhouse.org/publications/papers/view/185321.

33. Grigas, *The Politics of Energy and Memory*, p. 184.

34. Heather A. Conley and Theodore P Gerber, "Russian Soft Power in the 21st Century: An Examination of Russian Compatriot Policy in Estonia," A Report of the CSIS Europe Program (New York: Center for Strategic and International Studies, 2011), p. 13.

35. Nils Muižnieks, *Latvian-Russian Relations: Dynamics since Latvia's Accession to the EU* (Riga: University of Latvia Academic Press, 2011), pp. 63–64.

36. Embassy of Russia in Estonia, http://rusemb.ee/relations/.

37. "PHC 2011: Over a Quarter of the Population Are Affiliated with a Particular Religion," Statistics Estonia, 29 April 2013, http://www.stat.ee/65352?parent_id=39113; "Latvia 2012 International Religious Freedom Report," U.S. State Department, 2012, http://www.state.gov/documents/organization/208544.pdf.

38. "Svyateishiy Patriarkh Kirill prizval Predstoyateley Pomestnykh Tserkvey vozvysit' golos v zashchitu pravoslavnykh khristian vostoka Ukrainy," 14 August, 2014, https://mospat.ru/ru/2014/08/14/news106782/.

39. Margarita Kornysheva, "Obrashcheniye Russkoy pravoslavnoy tserkvi: Nyet prichiny, pochemu Estoniya dolzhna delat' shag, kotoryi grozit oslabit' nashe gosudarstvo," Delfi, 22 May 2014, http://rus.delfi.ee/daily/estonia /obraschenie-russkoj-pravoslavnoj-cerkvi-net-prichiny-pochemu-estoniya -dolzhna-delat-shag-kotoryj-grozit-oslabit-nashe-gosudarstvo?id=68728737; Kook Urmet, "Kooseluseaduse vastu on enim Keskerakonna valijad," Err.ee, 5 August 2014, http://uudised.err.ee/v/eesti/f0062775-161f-43a1-8ae8 -3cad644e5af6.

40. Dovydas Pancerovas, "Kremliaus propagandos arsenale—ir tradicinės šeimos vertybės," lrytas.lt, 14 December 2013, http://www.lrytas.lt/lietuvos -diena/aktualijos/kremliaus-propagandos-arsenale-ir-tradicines-seimos -vertybes.htm.

41. Laurynas Kasčiūnas, "L. Kasčiūnas: 'Liberalizmas,' kuris naudingas Rusi- jai," Delfi, 10 October 2014, http://www.delfi.lt/news/ringas/lit/l-kasciunas -liberalizmas-kuris-naudingas-rusijai.d?id=66080996.

42. Kasčiūnas interview.

43. Muižnieks, *Latvian-Russian Relations*, pp. 60–61.

44. "Sustabdžius 'Ūkio banko' veiklą, 'Žalgiris' situacijos kol kas nekomentu- oja," basketnews.lt, 12 February 2013, http://www.basketnews.lt/news-58987 -sustabdzius-ukio-banko-veikla-zalgiris-situacijos-kol-kas-nekomentuoja .html#.VGfDD2cqOKw.

45. Muižnieks, *Latvian-Russian Relations*, p. 62.

46. Laurynas Kasčiūnas, Marius Laurinavičius, and Vytautas Keršanskas, "Vlad- imir Putin's Pyramid of Rule: Who Really Governs Russia?" 5 August 2014, http://en.delfi.lt/central-eastern-europe/vladimir-putins-pyramid-of-rule-who -really-governs-russia.d?id=65432116#ixzz3HHZiRbB0.

47. " 'Lietuvos rytas' ir 'Neptūnas' nežais Vieningoje lygoje, į LKL priimti Mažeikiai," *kauno.diena.lt*, http://kauno.diena.lt/naujienos/sportas/krepsinis /lietuvos-rytas-nezais-vieningoje-lygoje-i-lkl-priimti-mazeikiai-641078; "Ge- ography," VTB United League, http://www.vtb-league.com/en/content /geography.htm.

48. Grigas, *The Politics of Energy and Memory*, p. 179.

49. Grigas, "Legacies, Coercion and Soft Power," p. 3.

50. Agnia Grigas, "Klaipeda's LNG Terminal: A Game Changer," EurActiv, 22 September 2014, http://www.euractiv.com/sections/energy/klaipedas-lng -terminal-game-changer-308613.

51. Licia Cianetti, "Granting Local Voting Rights to Non-Citizens in Estonia and Latvia: The Conundrum of Minority Representation in Two Divided Democra- cies," *Journal on Ethnopolitics and Minority Issues in Europe* 13, no. 1, (2014): 86–112; Graham Smith, "Transnational Politics and the Politics of the Russian Diaspora," *Ethnic and Racial Studies* 3, no. 22 (2010): 500–523; Ruta M. Kalvaitis, "Citizenship and National Identity in the Baltic States," *Boston University In- ternational Law Journal* 1, no. 16 (1998): 231–71.

52. Kudors interview.

53. Stephen Shulman, "Challenging the Civic/Ethnic and West/East Dichotomies in the Study of Nationalism," *Comparative Political Studies* 35, no. 5 (2002): 554–85, http://www.columbia.edu/itc/journalism/stille/Politics%20 Fall%202007/readings%20weeks%206-7/Civic%20and%20Ethnic%20 Nations%20and%20Nationalism.pdf.

54. Sven Gunnar Simonsen, "Compatriot Games: Explaining the 'Diaspora Linkage' in Russia's Military Withdrawal from the Baltic States," *Europe-Asia Studies* 53, no. 5 (2001): 771.

55. J. A. S. Grenville and Bernard Wasserstein, eds., *The Major International Treaties of the Twentieth Century* (London: Routledge, 2001), p. 886.

56. Tony Barber, "Fury in Baltics over Yeltsin Troops Decree," *The Independent*, 31 October 1992, http://www.independent.co.uk/news/world/europe/fury-in -baltics-over-yeltsin-troops-decree-1560583.html.

57. "Yeltsin Asks U.N. to Help Russians in the Baltics," *New York Times*, 8 November 1992, http://www.nytimes.com/1992/11/08/world/yeltsin-asks-un-to -help-russians-in-the-baltics.html.

58. "Yeltsin Denounces Latvian Citizenship Law," *Moscow Times*, 5 August, 1994, http://www.themoscowtimes.com/news/article/yeltsin-denounces -latvian-citizenship-law/349704.html.

59. Martin Smith, *Russia and NATO since 1991—From Cold War Through Cold Peace to Partnership?* (London: Routledge, 2006), p. 48.

60. Rita Peters, "Russia Pressures the Baltic States," *Perspective* 4, no. 3 (1994): http://www.bu.edu/iscip/vol4/Peters.html.

61. Ibid.

62. Thomas Ambrosio, *Russian Resistance to Democratization in the Former Soviet Union* (Farnham, UK: Ashgate g, 2009), pp. 92–96.

63. Tony Barber, "Baltic States Fear Kremlin Focus on Ethnic Russians," *Financial Times*, 2 September 2014, http://www.ft.com/cms/s/0/71d9145c-3268 -11e4-a5a2-00144feabdco.html#axzz3JoqsdvIJ; "Latvijas iedzīvotāju sadalījums pēc valstiskās piederības," 1 January 2014, http://www.pmlp.gov .lv/lv/assets/01072013/01.01.2014/ISVP_Latvija_pec_VPD.pdf.

64. Judith Kelley, "International Actors on the Domestic Scene: Membership Conditionality and Socialization by International Institutions," *International Organization* 58, no. 3 (2004): 425–57.

65. Shulman, "Challenging the Civic/Ethnic and West/East Dichotomies in the Study of Nationalism," pp. 554–85.

66. "Katalog 'Ves' Russkiy Mir,'" Russkiy Mir, http://www.russkiymir.ru /catalogue/; Donata Motuzaite, "Moscow, We Have a Problem in Lithuania," re:baltica, 19 March 2012, http://www.rebaltica.lv/en/investigations/money _from_russia/a/603/moscow_we_have_a_problem_in_lithuania.html; "Chto finansiruyet v Latvii fond Putina 'Russkiy Mir,'" TVnet, 22 March 2012, http://rus.tvnet.lv/novosti/kommjentariy/195556-chto_finansirujet_v_latvii _fond_putina_russkiy_mir; Sulev Vedler, "Moscow's Spin Machine in Estonia," re:baltica, 20 March 2012, http://www.rebaltica.lv/en/investigations

/money_from_russia/a/608/moscow%E2%80%99s_spin_machine_in
estonia.html.

67. Embassy of Russia in Estonia, "Sootechestvenniki," rusemb.ee, http://www
.rusemb.ee/relations/compatriots/.

68. Nadezhda Shirinskaya, "Vsemirnyi koordinatsionnyi sovet—unikal'nyi
kanal, kotorym ya imeyu vozhmozhnost' pol'zovat'sya," *vksrs.com*, 21 November 2014, http://vksrs.com/info/2014/11/21/vsemirnyj-koordinaczionnyj
-sovet-unikaln.

69. Embassy of Russia in Lithuania, "O konferentsii rossiyskikh sootechestvennikov, prozhivayushchikh v Litve," 5 October 2011, http://www.lithuania.mid
.ru/doc/konf_rs.htm.

70. Interview with Vytis Jurkonis, Vilnius, Lithuania, October 2014.

71. Pelnēns, The *"Humanitarian Dimension" of Russian Foreign Policy*, p. 11.

72. Sergei Gurkin, "Zhizn russkikh obshchin Pribaltiki posle ukrainskikh so-
bytiy," *vksrs.com*, 5 August 2014, http://vksrs.com/info/2014/08/05/zhizn
-russkix-obshhin-pribaltiki-posle-u.

73. Ibid.

74. "Komandy-uchastniki," http://soldatru.ru/game8/docs/comands.htm.

75. Dovydas Pancerovas, "Vilniaus S. Kovalevskajos mokyklos mokiniai ren-
giami tapti Rusijos desantininkais," 15min.lt, 8 October 2014, http://www
.15min.lt/naujiena/aktualu/lietuva/vilniaus-s-kovalevskajos-mokyklos
-mokiniai-rengiami-tapti-rusijos-desantininkais-56-458524#ixzz3FkD6hb22.

76. "Interes k pereseleniyu iz Latvii v Rossiu s kazhdym godom rastet," Newsbalt, 4 April 2014, http://www.newsbalt.ru/detail/?ID=26261.

77. Jevgenijus Bradauskas et al., "Koks tikrasis Rusijos tėvynainių programos
tikslas?" Delfi, 22 June 2014, http://www.delfi.lt/news/daily/lithuania/koks
-tikrasis-rusijos-tevynainiu-programos-tikslas.d?id=65107565.

78. "Po programme pereseleniya iz Estonii v Rossiyu za tri goda uyehali 20 chelovek," 31 August, 2010, http://rus.delfi.ee/daily/estonia/po-programme
-pereseleniya-iz-estonii-v-rossiyu-za-tri-goda-uehali-20-chelovek.d?id
=32853011; "Interes k programme pereseleniya bol'shoy, no pol'zuyutsya
yeyu—yedinitsy," 17 August 2009, http://rus.delfi.ee/archive/interes-k
-programme-pereseleniya-bolshoj-no-polzuyutsya-eyu-edinicy.d?id
=25149335.

79. Statistics Estonia, 2014, http://pub.stat.ee/px-web.2001/I_Databas
/Population/01Population_indicators_and_composition/04Population
_figure_and_composition/04Population_figure_and_composition.asp.

80. Tallinn City Government, *Statistical Yearbook of Tallinn 2013*, 2013, p. 21,
http://www.tallinn.ee/g2677s70004.

81. "Keskerakond on mitte-eestlaste seas jätkuvalt populaarseim partei," Posti-
mees, 23 September 2012, http://www.postimees.ee/982022/keskerakond-on
-mitte-eestlaste-seas-jatkuvalt-populaarseim-partei.

82. Koorits Vahur, "LOE kapo kirjeldust, kuidas Savisaar 2010 aastal Keskerakonna jaoks Venemaalt raha küsis," 3 January 2014, http://www.delfi.ee

/news/paevauudised/eesti/loe-kapo-kirjeldust-kuidas-savisaar-2010-aastal
-keskerakonna-jaoks-venemaalt-raha-kusis?id=67547848.
83. "Erakonnad," e-äriregister, https://ariregister.rik.ee/erakonnad.py?sess=50
1226692292588759466426287322509960030385220784204536892083 6635
&lang=est; "Riigikogu valimised," http://www.vvk.ee/arhiiv/riigikogu
-valimised/.
84. "Vene Erakond Eestis (VEE)," erakonnad.info, 2012, http://www.erakonnad
.info/erakond/reg/vana/vee.html.
85. "Population by Sex, Ethnic Nationality and County," January, 2014, http://
pub.stat.ee/px-web.2001/Dialog/varval.asp?ma=PO0222&lang=1.
86. "Narva in Figures 2012," http://web.narva.ee/files/5620.pdf, p. 9; Gordon F.
Sander, "Could Estonia Be the Next Target of Russian Annexation?" *Christian Science Monitor*, 3 April 2014, http://www.csmonitor.com/World/Europe
/2014/0403/Could-Estonia-be-the-next-target-of-Russian-annexation.
87. "Omavalitsusüksuste võrdlus," 20 October 2014, http://www.stat.ee/ppe
-46953; "Linda Clinic Campaign Goes to Court," Baseline Hiv, 19 February
2014, http://www.baseline-hiv.co.uk/hiv-articles/2014/2/19/linda-clinic
-campaign-goes-to-court.
88. Katri Raik, *Minu Narva* (Tallinn: Petroni Print, 2013).
89. "Narva in Figures 2012," p. 9.
90. Matt Withers, " 'Narva Is Not Another South Ossetia' Russia Says," *Baltic
Times*, 1 October 2008, http://www.baltictimes.com/news/articles/21444/#
.U6MkKPmSxZk.
91. Robert Anderson, "Estonia's Russian Passport Holders Show Little Sign of
Being 5th Column," bneIntellinews, 22 August 2014, http://www.bne.eu
/content/estonias-russian-passport-holders-show-little-sign-being-5th
-column.
92. Ott Omelas, "Putin's 21 Year Quest to Be Russian Guardian Began in Estonia," BloombergBusiness, 13 April 2014, http://www.bloomberg.com/news
/2014-04-13/putin-21-year-quest-to-be-guardian-of-russians-began-in-estonia
.html.
93. Interview with Ivan Lavrentjev, Tallinn, Estonia, October 2014.
94. Final results of the population and housing census of 2011; Agnia Grigas,
"Compatriot Games: Russian-Speaking Minorities in the Baltic States,"
World Politics Review, 11 October 2014, http://www.worldpoliticsreview.com
/articles/14240/compatriot-games-russian-speaking-minorities-in-the-baltic
-states.
95. Kristīne Bērziņa, "Latvia: EU Presidency at a Time of Geopolitical Crisis," in
A Region Disunited? Central European Responses to the Russia-Ukraine Crisis,
ed. Joerg Forbrig, German Marshall Fund Europe Policy Paper, February
2015, http://www.gmfus.org/file/4250/download.
96. Steven Musch, "Russian Speakers Protest in Riga for Preservation of Their
Language," Euroviews, 13 April 2014, http://www.euroviews.eu/2014/04/13
/russian-speakers-protest-in-riga-for-preservation-of-their-language/; Steven

Lee Myers, "World Briefing: Europe: Latvia: Students Protest Language Law," *New York Times*, 6 February 2004, http://www.nytimes.com/2004/02 /06/world/world-briefing-europe-latvia-students-protest-language-law.html.

97. Grigas, *The Politics of Energy and Memory*, pp. 49–77.

98. Final results of the Population and Housing Census 2011 in Latvia, http:// data.csb.gov.lv/pxweb/lv/?rxid=319dd78d-d7bb-4814-bc18-9c81e3357a89.

99. Ibid.

100. Ibid.

101. Ibid.

102. Ludmila Vessel, "Zhiteli Latgalii stabil'no poluchayut rossiyskoye grazhdan- stvo," Grani.lv, 10 January 2013, http://www.grani.lv/latvia/31800-zhiteli -latgalii-stabilno-poluchayut-rossiyskoe-grazhdanstvo.html.

103. Evgeniy Pavlov, "Zhiteli Latgalii perekhodyat granitsu s Rossiyey," Vesti.lv, 10 December 2009, http://telegraf.vesti.lv/news/zhiteli-latgalii-perehodyat -granicu-s-rossiei.

104. Andrew Higgins, "Latvian Region Has Distinct Identity, and Allure for Rus- sia," *New York Times*, 20 May 2015, http://www.nytimes.com/2015/05/21 /world/europe/latvian-region-has-distinct-identity-and-allure-for-russia .html?_r=0.

105. Jurga Andriejauskaitė, "Latvians Celebrate Referendum Results and Claim They Voted against Foreign Language, Not against Nation," 15min.lt, 19 Feb- ruary 2012, http://www.15min.lt/en/article/world/latvians-celebrate -referendum-results-and-claim-they-voted-against-foreign-language-not -against-nation-529-197310#ixzz3LQJhHYCw.

106. "Antros valstybinės kalbos Latvijoje nebus," Delfi, 18 February 2012, http:// www.delfi.lt/news/daily/world/antros-valstybines-kalbos-latvijoje-nebus.d ?id=55645739; "Latvijoje surinkta pakankamai parašų už referendumą dėl rusų kalbos paskelbimo antrąja valstybine," Bernardinai.lt, 20 December 2011, http://www.bernardinai.lt/straipsnis/2011-12-20-latvijoje-surinkta -pakankamai-parasu-uz-referenduma-del-rusu-kalbos-paskelbimo-antraja -valstybine/74055.

107. Aleksandr Nosovich, "Russkiye v politicheskom protsesse Latvii: Kruglyi stol v Kaliningrade," Rubaltic.ru, 5 December 2013, http://www.rubaltic.ru /article/politika-i-obshchestvo/russkie-v-politicheskom-protsesse-latvii -kruglyy-stol-v-kaliningrade05122013/.

108. "Opros: V Krymskom voprose u russkikh Latvii net edinodushiya," *mixnews. lv*, 11 April 2014, http://www.mixnews.lv/ru/society/news/2014-04-11/148108.

109. Vitaliy Portnikov, "Russkiye Baltii i ukrainskiy krizis," svoboda.org, 21 Feb- ruary 2015, http://www.svoboda.org/content/transcript/26852885.html.

110. Kudors interview.

111. Inga Spriņģe, Donata Motuzaite, and Gunita Gailāne, "Spreading Democ- racy in Latvia, Kremlin Style," re:baltica, 19 March 2012, http://www .rebaltica.lv/en/investigations/money_from_russia/a/606/spreading _democracy_in_latvia_kremlin_style.html.

112. Vita Petrušauskaitė and Vilana Pilinkaitė Sotirovič, "Rusai Lietuvoje: Etninės grupės raida ir socialinės integracijos iššūkiai 2001-2011 m.," LSTC, 2012, http://www.ces.lt/wp-content/uploads/2013/01/EtSt _Petru%C5%A1auskait%C4%97_Pilinkait%C4%97-Sotirovi%C4%8D _2012.pdf.

113. "Lithuanian 2011 Population Census in Brief," 2012, p. 23, http://www1 .unece.org/stat/platform/download/attachments/64881183/Lithuanian%20 2011%20Population%20Census%20in%20Brief%20rev.pdf?version=1 &modificationDate=1350633816572&api=v2; Ramonienė, "Miestų gyvento- jai, gimtąja įvardiję rusų kalbą."

114. "Lithuanian 2011 Population Census in Brief," p. 23; Ramonienė, "Miestų gyventojų gimtoji kalba."

115. Ramonienė, "Miestų gyventojų gimtoji kalba."

116. Lietuvos Statistikos Departamentas, "Gyventojai pagal tautybę, gimąją kalbą ir tikybą," 15 March 2013, p. 2, https://osp.stat.gov.lt/documents/10180 /217110/Gyv_kalba_tikyba.pdf/1d9dac9a-3d45-4798-93f5-941fed00503f; Ramonienė, "Miestų gyventojai, gimtąja įvardiję rusų kalbą."

117. Vytenė Stašaitytė, "Mitų griovimas Visagine: ar tai lietuviškasis Krymas?" 23 May 2014, Delfi, http://www.delfi.lt/news/daily/lithuania/mitu -griovimas-visagine-ar-tai-lietuviskasis-krymas.d?id=64856511.

118. Kasčiūnas interview.

119. Tomas Janeliūnas, "Politinė nekrofilija," IQ, 18 October 2010, http://iq.lt /lietuva/politine-nekrofilija; Steven Lee Myers, "Lithuanian Parliament Re- moves Country's President after Casting Votes on Three Charges," New York Times, 7 April 2004, http://www.nytimes.com/2004/04/07/world/lithuanian -parliament-removes-country-s-president-after-casting-votes-three.html.

120. Pelnēns, The "Humanitarian Dimension" of Russian Foreign Policy, p. 19.

121. Grigas, The Politics of Energy and Memory, pp. 127–73; Nerijus Aleksiejūnas, Didžiųjų ir mažųjų valstybių santykių teorijų taikymas: Lietuvos ir Rusijos santykių analizė (Vilnius: Vilniaus universiteto leidykla, 2003), pp. 30–31.

122. Grigas, The Politics of Energy and Memory, pp. 127–73.

123. Aivars Stranga, "Russia and the Security of the Baltic States: 1991–1996," in The Baltic States: Search for Security, ed. Atis Lejiņš and Daina Bleiere (Riga: Latvian Institute of International Affairs, 1996), p. 144.

124. Grigas, The Politics of Energy and Memory, pp. 131–32; Kadri Liik, "The 'Bronze Year' of Estonia-Russia Relations," 2007, http://vm.ee/sites/default /files/content-editors/web-static/053/Kadri_Liik.pdf.

125. "Bush Denounces Soviet Domination," BBC News, 7 May 2005, http://news .bbc.co.uk/2/hi/europe/4521663.stm.

126. Aleksiejūnas, Didžiųjų ir mažųjų valstybių santykių teorijų taikymas, p. 34; Liik, "The 'Bronze Year' of Estonia-Russia Relations."

127. "Kremlin Denies Soviet 'Occupation' of Baltics," Daily Times, 6 May 2005, http://archives.dailytimes.com.pk/foreign/06-May-2005/kremlin-denies -soviet-occupation-of-baltics.

128. Interview with Nerijus Maliukevičius, Vilnius, Lithuania, October 2014.

129. Pelnēns, *The "Humanitarian Dimension" of Russian Foreign Policy.*

130. TNS media research cited in Mantas Martišius, "Nori stabdyti Kremliaus melą—reikia drąsos," 15min.lt, 27 October 2014, http://www.15min.lt /naujiena/ziniosgyvai/komentarai/mantas-martisius-nori-stabdyti -kremliaus-mela-reikia-drasos-500-462599#ixzz3HTl6kIzf.

131. Milda Seputyte, "Snoras Bank Likely Over-Reported 300 Million Euros in Assets," BloombergBusiness, 18 November 2011, http://www.bloomberg.com /news/articles/2011-11-18/snoras-bank-likely-over-reported-300-million-euros -in-assets; "Snoras UK High Court Appeal Scheduled for 22 July," *Lithuania Tribune*, 14 March 2014, http://www.lithuaniatribune.com/65147/snoras-uk -high-court-appeal-scheduled-for-22-july-201465147/.

132. Maliukevičius interview.

133. Grigas, "Legacies, Coercion and Soft Power," pp. 2–3.

134. Ibid.

135. Lavrentjev interview.

136. Grigas, "Legacies, Coercion and Soft Power," pp. 3–5; Ian Traynor, "Russia Accused of Unleashing Cyberwar to Disable Estonia," *The Guardian*, 17 May 2007, http://www.theguardian.com/world/2007/may/17/topstories3.russia; "Estonia Hit by 'Moscow Cyber War,'" BBC News, 17 May 2007, http://news .bbc.co.uk/2/hi/europe/6665145.stm.

137. Przemysław Żurawski vel Grajewski, "The Military Aspect of the National Security Strategy of the Republic of Poland of 2007 and the Programme of Professionalization of the Polish Armed forces of 2008 in the Context of NATO," in *NATO Towards the Challenges of a Contemporary World 2013*, ed. Robert Czulda and Robert Łoś (Warsaw: International Relations Research Institute, 2013), p. 106.

138. Anda Rožkalne, "Slēptā reklāma nogalina maigi," Providus, 12 October 2010, http://new.politika.lv/article/slepta-reklama-nogalina-maigi.

139. "Too Russian to Have Rights? Latvia to Vote on 'Alien' Language," RT, 6 February 2012, http://rt.com/news/russian-latvia-language-referendum -559/.

140. "Language Inquisition: Estonia Bans Speaking Russian," RT, 3 December 2012, https://www.youtube.com/watch?v=oYgwAyac7Iw.

141. "Estonian, Latvian Russian-language TV Channels Plan Cooperation," news.err.ee, 31 March 2015, http://news.err.ee/v/politics/cd4f475b-2c59-4721 -8087-583ba9dd92d7.

142. "Rossiiskoe TV o Evromaidane: 'Mest' shvedov za Poltavu,'" *podrobnosti.ua*, 2 December, 2013, http://podrobnosti.ua/945652-rossijskoe-tv-o-evromajdane -mest-shvedov-za-poltavu.html.

143. "Prigovorennye: Kapkan dlya gruppy Al'fa," NTV, http://www.ntv.ru /peredacha/Prigovorennye/last23589540/.

144. The channels were NTV Mir, First Baltic Channel PBK, and RTR Planeta; "Temporal [*sic*] Suspension of NTV Mir Lithuania Programme Parts,"

19 March 2014, http://www.rtk.lt/en/news/news/temporal_suspension_of
_ntv_mir_lithuania_programme_parts.

145. "VSD: šalyje kurstoma etninė nesantaika," lzinios.lt, 4 September 2014,
http://lzinios.lt/lzinios/Lietuvoje/vsd-salyje-kurstoma-etnine-nesantaika
/186781.

146. Lietuvos Respublikos valstybės saugumo departamentas, "2014 metų veik-
los ataskaita," March 2015, http://www.vsd.lt/Files/Documents
/635645217977365000.pdf.

147. Dalia Grybauskaitė, "Privalome ginti Lietuvos informacinę erdvę," 12 December 2014, http://www.president.lt/lt/spaudos_centras_392/pranesimai
_spaudai/privalome_ginti_lietuvos_informacine_erdve.html.

148. "Vilniuje, Kaune, Klaipėdoje—kratos: Rusiją šlovino ne šiaip sau," Delfi,
19 March 2015, http://www.delfi.lt/news/daily/lithuania/vilniuje-kaune
-klaipedoje-kratos-rusija-slovino-ne-siaip-sau.d?id=67477918.

149. Lavrentjev interview.

150. "Putin Calmed the Baltic States: We Will Not Bring In Military Forces."

151. "Kremliaus provokacija: Prijunkime Klaipėdos kraštą prie Rusijos," lrytas.
lt, 12 March 2014, http://www.lrytas.lt/lietuvos-diena/aktualijos/kremliaus
-provokacija-prijunkime-klaipedos-krasta-prie-rusijos.htm.

152. Vytenė Stašaitytė, "Mitų griovimas Visagine: Ar tai lietuviškasis Krymas?"
Delfi, 23 May 2014, http://www.delfi.lt/news/daily/lithuania/mitu
-griovimas-visagine-ar-tai-lietuviskasis-krymas.d?id=64856511.

153. "Sulaikė Latvijos gyventoją, rinkusį parašus už šalies prisijungimą prie
Rusijos," Delfi, 27 February 2015, http://www.delfi.lt/news/daily/world
/sulaike-latvijos-gyventoja-rinkusi-parasus-uz-salies-prisijungima-prie
-rusijos.d?id=67300506#ixzz3T4KlJ8jA.

154. Edgars Skvarik, "Rally at Latvian Embassy in Russia Propagates Latgale as
Part of Russia," LETA, 17 April 2014, http://www.leta.lv/eng/home
/important/6E450BC2-FB58-4FDA-860C-EEBA83F9BB6C/.

155. Neil Melvin, Russians Beyond Russia: The Politics of National Identity (London: Royal Institute of International Affairs, 1995), p. 49.

156. Liis Kangsepp and Juhana Rossi, "Estonia Says Officer Abducted Near Russian Border," Wall Street Journal, 5 September 2014, http://www.wsj.com
/articles/estonian-officer-abducted-near-border-with-russia-1409928475.

157. "Russia Reopens Criminal Cases against Lithuanians Who Refused to
Serve in Soviet Army," 8 September 2014, http://en.delfi.lt/lithuania
/foreign-affairs/russia-reopens-criminal-cases-against-lithuanians-who
-refused-to-serve-in-sovietarmy.d?id=65776132#ixzz3JohouZbh; Edmundas
Jakilaitis, "Lithuanian Defence Minister: We Are Doing All to Protect Our
Citizens against Prosecution in Russia," 9 September 2014, http://en.delfi.lt
/lithuania/defence/lithuanian-defence-minister-we-are-doing-all-to-protect
-our-citizens-against-prosecution-in-russia.d?id=65786158#ixzz3JoiizYd.

158. "J.Olekas apie skandalingą Rusijos užmojį: Reaguoti būtina," Delfi, 9 September 2014, http://www.delfi.lt/news/daily/lithuania/j-olekas-apie

-skandalinga-rusijos-uzmoji-reaguoti-butina.d?id=65785428; "Going after Tomas," *Economist*, 13 January 2015, http://www.economist.com/news /europe/21638345-russia-wants-prosecute-former-deserters-army-country -no-longer-exists-going-after.

159. Artūras Jančys, "Seimas grąžino šauktinių kariuomenę," Lietuvos Rytas, 19 March 2015, http://www.lrytas.lt/lietuvos-diena/aktualijos/seimas -grazino-sauktiniu-kariuomene.htm.

160. Lauryna Vireliūnaitė, "Seimas apsisprendė—šauktinių kariuomenė bus," 19 March 2015, http://www.15min.lt/naujiena/aktualu/lietuva/seimas -apsisprende-sauktiniu-kariuomene-bus-56-491729.

161. "Estonia: Defense Leagues on the Rise," Deutsche Welle, 15 April 2015, http://www.dw.de/estonia-defense-leagues-on-the-rise/av-18386445.

162. "Russian Air Incursions Rattle Baltic States," *Financial Times*, 24 September 2014, http://www.ft.com/cms/s/0/9d016276-43c3-11e4-baa7-00144feabdc0 .html#axzz3ZqjkLD00.

163. "Baltic Fleet Holds Exercises in Framework of Surprise Inspection," Tass, 3 March 2014, http://en.itar-tass.com/russia/721751.

164. "Secretary General Announces North Atlantic Council to Meet Following Poland's Request for Article 4 Consultations," NATO/OTAN, 3 March 2014, http://www.nato.int/cps/en/natolive/news_107711.htm?selected Locale=en.

165. "U.S. Troops Head to the Baltics," *Baltic Times*, 23 April 2014, http://www .baltictimes.com/news/articles/34750/#.U4K_a3aWm8s.

166. "Russia Sends 24 Warships, Bombers to Baltic Drills as NATO Stages War Games," RT, 12 June 2014, http://rt.com/news/165464-russia-baltic-drills -nato/.

167. "Iron Sword 2014: NATO Stages Massive Military Drill in Lithuania," RT, 3 November 2014, http://rt.com/news/201771-lithuania-iron-sword-wargame/.

168. "NATO Foreign Ministers Announce Interim Spearhead Force," NATO/ OTAN. 2 December 2014, http://www.nato.int/cps/en/natohq/news_115552 .htm; Julian Borger, "Nato Will Establish Rapid Reaction Force to Counter Perceived Threat of Russian Aggression," *The Guardian*, 5 February 2015, http://www.theguardian.com/world/2015/feb/05/nato-rapid-reaction-force -counter-russia-ukraine.

169. Agnia Grigas, "The Media Has Swallowed Five Russian Myths that Have Helped Putin Win in Ukraine," *forbes.com*, 17 September 2014, http://www .forbes.com/sites/realspin/2014/09/17/the-media-has-swallowed-five-russian -myths-that-have-helped-putin-win-in-ukraine/; Anne Applebaum, "Nationalism Is Exactly What Ukraine Needs," *newrepublic.com*, 12 May 2014, http:// www.newrepublic.com/article/117505/ukraines-only-hope-nationalism.

CHAPTER 6. STATE BUILDING AND SHIFTING LOYALTIES

Epigraph: Cited in Fiona Hill and Pamela Jewett, "Back in the USSR: Russia's Intervention in the Internal Affairs of the Former Soviet Republics and the Implications for United States Policy Toward Russia" (Cambridge, Mass.: Harvard University Ethnic Conflict Project, January 1994), p. 37, http://www.brookings.edu/~/media/research/files/reports/2014/03/back in the ussr 1994 hill jewett/back in the ussr 1994.pdf.

1. Martha Brill Olcott, "Central Asia's Catapult to Independence," *Foreign Affairs*, Summer 1992, http://www.foreignaffairs.com/articles/47979/martha-brill-olcott/central-asias-catapult-to-independence.

2. Marlene Laruelle, "Russia in Central Asia: Old History, New Challenges," EUCAM Working Paper No. 3, September 2009, http://www.ceps.eu/publications/russia-central-asia-old-history-new-challenges.

3. "GDP Per Capita 2013," *worldbank.org*, http://data.worldbank.org/indicator/NY.GDP.PCAP.CD.

4. Edward Schatz and Elena Maltseva, "Kazakhstan's Authoritarian 'Persuasion,'" *Post-Soviet Affairs* 28, no. 1 (2012): 45–65.

5. "N. Nazarbayev: Poka my byli koloniyey Rossii—yedva ne lishilis' svoikh," TsentrAsia, 14 October 2012, http://www.centrasia.ru/newsA.php?st=1350219540.

6. "Zayavleniye dlya pressy po itogam foruma mezhregional'nogo sotrudnichestva mezhdu Rossiyey i Kazakhstanom," Informatsionno-Analiticheskiy Tsentr, 12 November 2013, http://www.ia-centr.ru/publications/16960/.

7. Marlene Laruelle and Sebastien Peyrouse, *Globalizing Central Asia: Geopolitics and the Challenges of Economic Development* (Armonk, NY: M. E. Sharpe, 2013), pp. 128–30.

8. Neil J. Melvin, *Uzbekistan: Transition to Authoritarianism on the Silk Road* (Amsterdam: Harwood Academic Publishers, 2000), p. 43.

9. Alexey Malashenko, "Uzbekistan: What Changes Can Be Expected," *Carnegie Moscow Center Briefing* 14, no. 5 (December 2012): http://carnegieendowment.org/files/MalashenkoBriefing_14-5-12_eng_uz.pdf; Wojciech Ostrowski, "Rentierism, Dependency and Sovereignty in Central Asia" in *Sovereignty After Empire: Comparing the Middle East and Central Asia*, ed. Sally N. Cummings and Raymond Hinnebusch (Edinburgh: Edinburgh University Press, 2011), p. 298.

10. Andrei Kolesnikov, "Vyvod fanatizma iz regiona," *Kommersant*, 16 April 2013, http://www.kommersant.ru/doc/2171124; Andrei Kolesnikov, "S chuvstvom vycherknutogo dolga," *Kommersant*, 11 December 2014, http://www.kommersant.ru/doc/2630128.

11. "Uzbekistan prizval uchityvat' interesy RF v ukrainskom konflikte," RIA, 12 September 2014, http://ria.ru/politics/20140912/1023791209.html.

12. "Rossiya yavlyaetsya osnovnym strategicheskim partnerom Kyrgyzstana—Almazbek Atambayev," Trend, 1 December 2011, http://www.trend.az/casia/kyrgyzstan/1963950.html.

13. Annette Bohr, "Revolution in Kyrgyzstan—Again," REP Programme Paper 03/10 Chatham House, April 2010, p. 4, http://www.chathamhouse.org/publications/papers/view/109326.

14. Sebastien Peyrouse, *Turkmenistan: Strategies of Power, Dilemmas of Development* (Armonk, NY: M. E. Sharpe, 2012), p. 222.

15. Alexander Cooley, *Great Games, Local Rules: The New Great Power Contest in Central Asia* (Oxford: Oxford University Press, 2012), p. 204.

16. "Berdymukhamedov: Rossiya i Kitay—strategicheskiye partnery Turkmenistana," Vestnik Kavkaza, 12 December 2014, http://www.vestikavkaza.ru /news/Berdymukhamedov-Rossiya-i-Kitay-strategicheskie-partnery -Turkmenistana.html.

17. Barbara A. West, *Encyclopedia of the Peoples of Asia and Oceania*, vol. 2/2 (New York: Facts on File, 2009), p. 770.

18. Jim Nichol, "Tajikistan: Recent Developments and U.S. Interests," Congressional Research Service, 25 September 2013, https://www.fas.org/sgp/crs /row/98-594.pdf.

19. Embassy of the Republic of Tajikistan in the Kyrgyz Republic, "Rakhmon: Rossiya—glavnyi strategicheski partner Tadzhikistana," 17 April 2012, http://www.tajikemb.kg/index.php?option=com_content&task=view&id =1314&Itemid=67.

20. See Sebastien Peyrouse, "The Russian Minority in Central Asia: Migration, Politics, and Language," Kennan Institute Occasional Paper 297, Washington, DC, 2008, pp. 3–5, http://www.wilsoncenter.org/sites/default/files /OP297_russian_minority_central_asia_peyrouse_2008.pdf.

21. Interview with Sebastian Peyrouse, Washington D.C., February 2015.

22. Olga Altynbekova, "Migratsia v Kazakhstane: Novyi status russkogo yazyka," Demoscop Weekly, 19 June 2006, http://www.demoscope.ru/weekly/2006 /0251/analit05.php.

23. Peyrouse interview; Rachel van Horn, "Central Asia: Russian Language Experiencing Rapid Decline," Eurasianet.org, 15 December 2011, http://www .eurasianet.org/node/64711.

24. Interview with Anya, December 2014, Almaty, Kazakhstan.

25. Interview with Stanislav, December 2014, Almaty, Kazakhstan.

26. Interview with Viktoriya, December 2014, Almaty, Kazakhstan.

27. Interview with Oleg, December 2014, Almaty, Kazakhstan.

28. Interview with Yolbars, December 2014, Turkmenistan.

29. Interview with Berdi, December 2014, Turkmenistan.

30. Interview with Artur, December 2014, Kyrgyzstan.

31. Interview with Yusuf, December 2014, Tajikistan.

32. Interview with Katerina, December 2014, Tajikistan.

33. Interview with Anatoly, December 2014, Tajikistan.

34. Interview with Gash, January 2015, Uzbekistan.

35. Interview with Karina, January 2015, Uzbekistan.

36. Alexei Malashenko, "Interesy i shansy Rossii v Tsentral'noy Azii," *Pro et Contra*, January–April 2013, p. 21, http://carnegieendowment.org/files /ProEtContra_58_21-34.pdf. For Russia-Chinese developments see "Russia,

China Agree to Integrate Eurasian Union, Silk Road, Sign Deals," RT, 8 May 2015, http://rt.com/business/256877-russia-china-deals-cooperation/.

37. Cooley, *Great Games, Local Rules*, p. 7.

38. Frank Shanty, *The Nexus: International Terrorism and Drug Trafficking from Afghanistan* (Santa Barbara: Greenwood, 2011), pp. 37–41.

39. Rossiiskiy Sovet po Mezhdunarodnym Delam, "Interesy Rossii v Tsentral'noy Azii," Rossiiskiy Sovet po Mezhdunarodnym Delam, 2013, pp. 6–7, http://russiancouncil.ru/common/upload/RIAC_Central_Asia.pdf.

40. Malashenko, "Interesy i shansy Rossii v Tsentral'noy Azii," p. 21.

41. "Vserossiiskiy molodyozhnyi forum 'Seliger-2014,'" *kremlin.ru*, 29 August 2014, http://kremlin.ru/events/president/news/46507.

42. Nuria Kutnayeva, "Inostrannye voyennye bazy na territorii post-sovetskoy Tsentral'noy Azii," *Tsentral'naya Azia i Kavkaz* 13, no. 2 (2010): 85–86.

43. See "Governing Uranium," http://uranium.csis.org/production/; "Uranium and Nuclear Power in Kazakhstan," World Nuclear Association, December 2014, http://www.world-nuclear.org/info/Country-Profiles/Countries-G-N/Kazakhstan/.

44. Isabel Gorst, "Former Kazakh Nuclear Chief Given Jail Term," *Financial Times*, 12 March 2010, http://www.ft.com/cms/s/0/965ba1f2-2dfc-11df-b85c-00144feabdco.html.

45. World Nuclear Association, "Uranium and Nuclear Power in Kazakhstan."

46. Anna Matveeva, "Selective Engagement: Russia's Future Role in Central Asia," Central Asia Policy Brief No. 3, Elliott School of International Affairs, July 2012, p. 3, http://037eabf.netsolhost.com/wordpress/wp-content/uploads/2013/10/Policy_Brief_3_July_2012.pdf.

47. Kutnayeva, "Inostrannye voyennye bazy na territorii post-sovetskoy Tsentral'noi Azii," pp. 85–86.

48. Viktor Baranets, "Vo chto nam obkhodyatsya voyennye bazy za granitsey," *Komsomol'skaya pravda*, 14 June 2012, http://www.kp.ru/daily/25899.4/2856991/.

49. Rustem Falyakhov, "Rossiya zaplatit za soyuznikov," Gazeta.ru, 23 December 2014, http://www.gazeta.ru/business/2014/12/23/6356133.shtml.

50. Andrei Kolesnikov, "Integratsioznye processy," *Kommersant*, 25 October 2013, http://kommersant.ru/doc/2327907; Nargis Kassenova, "Kazakhstan and Eurasian Economic Integration: Quick Start, Mixed Results and Uncertain Future," Russei.Nei.Reports n14, Centre Russie/NEI, November 2012, p. 24.

51. Sergei Strokan, "Nursultan Nazarbayev vstupilsya za nezavisimost," *Kommersant*, 1 September 2014, http://www.kommersant.ru/doc/2557170.

52. Rossiiskiy Sovet po Mezhdunarodnym Delam, "Interesy Rossii v Tsentral'noy Azii," p. 12.

53. "Uzbekistan Will Never Join Any Union That Resembles Soviet Union: Islam Karimov," Tengri News, 16 January 2015, http://en.tengrinews.kz/politics

_sub/Uzbekistan-will-never-join-any-union-that-resembles-Soviet-Union
-Islam-Karimov-258399/.

54. Rossiyskiy Sovet po Mezhdunarodnym Delam, "Interesy Rossii v Tsentral'noy
Azii," p. 15.

55. "BP Statistical Review of World Energy June 2013," p. 20, https://www.bp
.com/content/dam/bp/pdf/statistical-review/statistical_review_of_world
_energy_2013.pdf. For alternative figures see "International Energy Outlook
2010," Washington, DC: U.S. Energy Information Administration, July 2010,
p. 57, http://www.eia.gov/forecasts/archive/ieo10/pdf/0484%282010%29.pdf.

56. "BP Statistical Review of World Energy June 2013," p. 6.

57. Jim Nichol, "Central Asia: Regional Developments and Implications for U.S.
Interests," Congressional Research Service, 21 March 2014, p. 53, http://
www.fas.org/sgp/crs/row/RL33458.pdf.

58. Roy Allison and Lena Jonson, *Central Asian Security: The New International
Context* (Tehran: Institute of Political and International Studies, 2003).

59. Adnan Vatansever, *Russia's Oil Exports: Economic Rationale Vs. Strategic
Gains* (Washington: Carnegie Endowment for International Peace, 2010),
pp. 18–19.

60. Nichol, "Central Asia: Regional Developments and Implications for U.S. Interests," p. 52.

61. Alexander Vershinin, "China Loans Turkmens $4bln in Exchange for Gas,"
BloombergBusiness, 26 April 2011, http://www.businessweek.com/ap
/financialnews/D9MRG3C0o.htm.

62. Chris Rickleton, "Is Turkmenistan's Gas Flowing Toward a One-Country
Policy?" Eurasianet.org, 18 August 2014, http://www.eurasianet.org/node
/69591.

63. "Is Turkmenistan Losing Iran as a Gas Customer?" Radio Free Europe/Radio
Liberty, 14 August 2014, http://www.rferl.org/content/qishloq-ovozi-turk
menistan-iran-gas/26530894.html.

64. U.S. Energy Information Administration, "Turkmenistan," January 2012,
http://www.eia.gov/countries/country-data.cfm?fips=TX.

65. Boris Barkanov, "The Geo-Economics of Eurasian Gas: The Evolution of
Russia-Turkmen Relations in Natural Gas (1992–2010)," in *Export Pipelines
from the CIS Region*, ed. Andreas Heinrich and Heiko Pleines (Stuttgart:
Ibidem Press, 2014), pp. 165–67.

66. Alexandros Petersen and Katinka Barysch, *Russia, China and the Geopolitics
of Energy in Central Asia* (London: Centre for European Reform, 2011), p. 52.

67. World Bank, Migration and Remittances: Recent Developments and Outlook,
Migration and Development Brief 22, 1 April 2014, p. 4, http://siteresources
.worldbank.org/INTPROSPECTS/Resources/334934-1288990760745
/MigrationandDevelopmentBrief22.pdf.

68. Malashenko, "Interesy i shansy Rossii v Tsentral'noy Azii," p. 25.

69. Alexei Malashenko, "Turning Away From Russia: New Directions For Central Asia," in *Commonwealth and Independence in Post-Soviet Eurasia*,

ed. Bruno Coppieters, Alexei Zverev, and Dmitri Trenin (London: Frank Cass, 1998), p. 158.

70. Aleksandr Solzhenitsyn, *Kak nam obustroit' Rossiyu? Posil'nye soobrzheniya* (Leningrad: Sovetskiy pisatel,' 1990), p. 110, http://www.solzhenitsyn.ru /proizvedeniya/publizistika/stati_i_rechi/v_izgnanii/kak_nam_obustroit _rossiyu.pdf.

71. "Putin zayavil, chto Kazakhstan nikogda ne byl gosudarstvom," TSN, 29 August 2014, http://ru.tsn.ua/svit/putin-zayavil-chto-kazahstan-nikogda-ne-byl -gosudarstvom-383871.html.

72. "Kazakhstan Celebrating 500 Years of Statehood," neurope.eu, 18 January 2015, http://www.neurope.eu/article/kazakhstan-celebrating-500-years -statehood.

73. "The Constitution of the Republic of Kazakhstan," President of Kazakhstan, http://www.akorda.kz/en/category/konstituciya; "The Constitution of the Kyrgyz Republic," Government of the Kyrgyz Republic, http://www.gov.kg/ ?page_id=263.

74. "The Constitution of the Republic of Tajikistan," President of the Republic of Tajikistan, http://www.prezident.tj/ru/taxonomy/term/5/112.

75. Peyrouse, "The Russian Minority in Central Asia," pp. 16–18.

76. Kamoludin Abdullaev and Shahram Akbarzaheh, *Historical Dictionary of Tajikistan* (Lanham, MD: Scarecrow Press, 2010), p. 218; Zarina Ergasheva and Bilol Shams, "Uzbeks Face Obstacles in Increasingly Tajik State," Institute for War & Peace Reporting, 28 July 2014, https://iwpr.net/global-voices /uzbeks-face-obstacles-increasingly-tajik-state.

77. Peyrouse, "The Russian Minority in Central Asia," pp. 4–5, 17–18.

78. Sebastien Peyrouse, "Christian Minorities on the Central Asian Silk Road," in *The Oxford Handbook of Christianity in Asia*, ed. Felix Wilfred (Oxford: Oxford University Press, 2014), p. 60.

79. Didar Kassymova, Zhanat Kundakbayevaa, and Ustina Markus, *Historical Dictionary of Kazakhstan* (Lanham, MD: Scarecrow Press, 2012), p. 206.

80. Martha Brill Olcott, *Kazakhstan: Unfulfilled Promise* (Washington, DC: Carnegie Endowment for International Peace, 2010), p. 208.

81. "Nazarbayev budet nagrazhden odnim iz vyzshikh ordenov russkoy pravoslavnoy tserkvi," Novosti Kazakhstan, 17 January 2010, http://newskaz.ru /society/20100117/418536.html.

82. "Nazarbayev: Islam i pravoslaviye yavlyayutsya stolpami nashey dukhovnosti," Novosti Kazakhstan, 5 May 2013, http://newskaz.ru/society /20130505/5061581.html.

83. Peyrouse, "Christian Minorities on the Central Asian Silk Road," pp. 57–60.

84. Maureen S. Crandall, *Energy, Economics, and Politics in the Caspian Region: Dreams and Realities* (London: Praeger Security International, 2006), pp. 122–26.

85. *Kazakhstan: Oil & Gas Report 2013* (London: Business Monitor International, 2013), pp. 72–75.

86. "XI Forum Mezhregional'nogo Sotrudnichestva Rossii i Kazakhstana," President of Russia, 30 September 2014, http://www.kremlin.ru/transcripts /46700/work.

87. Muriel Atkin, "Tajikistan: From De Facto Colony to Sovereign Dependency," in *Sovereignty after Empire: Comparing the Middle East and Central Asia*, ed. Sally N. Cummings and Raymond Hinnebusch (Edinburgh: Edinburgh University Press, 2011), p. 318.

88. "Prezident Rakhmon otkazal RUSALu," Newsru.com, 29 August 2007, http://www.newsru.com/finance/29aug2007/rusal.html.

89. Donnacha Ó Beacháin and Rob Kevlihan, "State-building, Identity and Nationalism in Kazakhstan: Some Preliminary Thoughts," Working Paper in International Studies No. 1, Centre for International Studies, Dublin City University, 2011, p. 4, http://doras.dcu.ie/16243/1/1101.pdf.

90. Kelly M. McMann, "Central Asians and the State: Nostalgia for the Soviet Era," National Council for Eurasian and East European Research, Washington, DC, 16 February 2005, pp. 3–10, http://www.ucis.pitt.edu/nceeer/2005 _818_09_McMann.pdf.

91. John Heathershaw, "New Great Game or Same Old Ideas? Neo-Sovietism and the International Politics of Imagining Central Asia," in *The CIS: Form or Substance?* ed. David Dusseault (Helsinki: Aleksanteri, 2007), pp. 237–68.

92. "V Kazakhstane nostal'giruyut po SSSR," Respublika, 16 March 2013, http:// www.respublika-kaz.info/news/society/29282/.

93. Peyrouse interview.

94. Ministry of Foreign Affairs of the Russian Federation, *Kommentariy departamenta informatsii i pechati MID*, 21 April 2014, http://www.mid.ru/brp_4 .nsf/newsline/3FFD899DE26AB99044257CC100337622.

95. Lena Johnson, *Tajikistan in the New Central Asia: Geopolitics, Great Power Rivalry and Radical Islam* (London: I. B. Tauris, 2006), p. 42.

96. Muriel Atkin, "Tajikistan: Reform, Reaction and Civil War," in *New States, New Politics: Building the Post-Soviet Nations*, ed. Ian Bremmer and Ray Taras (Cambridge: Cambridge University Press, 1997), pp. 619–20.

97. Anuradha M. Chenoy, *The Making of New Russia* (New Delhi: Har-Anand Publications, 2001), p. 155.

98. Andres Smith Serrano, "CIS Peacekeeping in Tajikistan," in *Regional Peacekeepers: The Paradox of Russian Peacekeeping*, ed. John Mackinlay and Peter Cross (Tokyo: UN University Press, 2003), pp. 178–79.

99. Catherine Poujol, "The Tajik Conflict and the Wider World," in *Tajikistan: The Trials of Independence*, ed. Mohammad-Reza Djalibi, Frederic Grare, and Shirin Akiner (London: Routledge, 1998), p. 115.

100. Chenoy, *The Making of New Russia*, p. 155.

101. Nichol, "Tajikistan: Recent Developments and U.S. Interests," p. 14.

102. Miriam Elder, "Kyrgyzstan Tests Russia's Regional Commitments," globalpost, 15 June 2010, http://www.globalpost.com/dispatch/russia/100614 /kyrgyzstan-ethnic-violence.

103. Brian Whitmore, "Sphere of Reluctance: Russia Hesitant About Kyrgyz Intervention," Radio Free Europe/Radio Liberty, 15 June 2010, http://www.rferl.org/content/Sphere_Reluctance_Russia_Hesitant_Kyrgyz_Intervention/2072776.html.

104. The Russian minority in Eastern Kazakhstan region makes up 14 percent of the total Russian population in Kazakhstan, that in Karaganda (central Kazakhstan) also makes up 14 percent, in Almaty (south Kazakhstan) 12 percent, and in Kostanay region (north Kazakhstan) (north Kazakhstan) 10 percent. Kazakhstan Statistics, "Ethnic Composition of the Population of Kazakhstan at the Beginning of 2014," Agency of Statistics, Almaty, 2014.

105. Assambleya Naroda Kazakhstana, "Deyatel'nost' Assambley Naroda Kazakhstana," http://www.assembly.kz/ru/deyatelnost-assamblei-naroda-kazahastana.

106. Peyrouse, "The Russian Minority in Central Asia," pp. 10–12.

107. According to 2014 data of the Russian federal agency Rossotrudnichestvo, Predstavitel'stvo Rossotrudnichestva v Respublike Kazakhstan, "organizatsii rossiyskikh sootchestvennikov v Respublike Kazakhstan," http://kaz.rs.gov.ru/node/16.

108. Ibid.

109. The main purpose is defined as the provision of "resources and all other kinds of support to the teaching of Russian language, literature, culture, and history" in Kazakhstan. "Katalog russkikh tsentrov," Russkiy Mir, http://www.russkiymir.ru/rucenter/catalogue.php.

110. Yekaterina Shcherbakova, "Dolya titul'noy natsional'nosti vozrastayet vo vsekh stranakh SNG krome Rossii," Demoskop, June 2013, http://www.demoscope.ru/weekly/2013/0559/barom02.php; Nikita Mkrtchyan and Bulat Sarygulov, "Izmeneniyr etnicheskogo sostava naseleniya," in *Naseleniye Kyrgyzstana v nachale XXI veka*, ed. Mikhail Denisenko (Bishkek: Fond OON, 2011), pp. 82–92.

111. Koordinatsionnyi Sovet Rossiskikh Sootechestvennikov Respubliki Tadjikistan, http://www.russ.tj.

112. KSPSK, http://www.korsovet.kg.

113. Charles Ziegler, "The Russian Diaspora in Central Asia: Russian Compatriots and Moscow's Foreign Policy," *Demokratizatsiya* 13, no. 5 (2006): 119.

114. Peyrouse, "The Russian Minority in Central Asia," p. 11.

115. "Soyuz" (Union), and the name "Victory's Heirs" refer to the Soviet Union's victory in the Second World War.

116. "Komandy-uchastniki," http://www.soldatru.ru/game8/docs/comands.htm.

117. "Soyuz 2014—Nasledniki Pobedy," http://soldatru.ru/game8/game.php.

118. "Organizatsionnyi plan," 18 August 2014, http://soldatru.ru/game8/game.php.

119. "Polozheniye o provedenii Pervogo Mezhdunarodnogo sbora 'Soyuz-2007—Issyk-Kul,'" http://www.soldatru.ru/game1/polojenie.htm.

120. Šarūnas Černiauskas, "Chemu v rossiyskom voyennom lagere uchili 'kadetov' iz Litvy," ru.delfi.lt, 9 September 2014, http://ru.delfi.lt/news/live

/chemu-v-rossijskom-voennom-lagere-uchili-kadetov-iz-litvy.d?id
=65786078.

121. "Voyenno-patrioticheskiye sbory naslednikov Pobedy napugali natselitu
Litvy," Newsbalt, 9 October 2014, http://www.newsbalt.ru/detail/?ID=43605.

122. Peyrouse, "The Russian Minority in Central Asia," pp. 4–10.

123. Mikhail Boyarintsev, "'Dobrososedstvo' i 'vzaimovygodnoye sotrudnichestvo' mezhdu Rossiey i Turkmenistanom: Igra v odni vorota," Vremya
Vostoka, 19 August 2010, http://www.easttime.ru/analitic/1/4/840.html.

124. "Rossiyskiye sootechestvenniki v Turkmenistane proveli vstrechu v
posol'stve RF," asgabat.net, 4 November 2011, http://www.asgabat.net
/novosti/rosiiskie-sotechestveniki-v-turkmenistane-proveli-vstrechu-v
-posolstve-rf.html.

125. Peyrouse, "The Russian Minority in Central Asia," p. 4.

126. "Rossiskiye sootechestvenniki v Respublike Uzbekistan," Russian Embassy,
Uzbekistan, 16 August 2009, http://www.russia.uz/index.php/2009-08-16
-10-30-58/2009-08-16-10-34-21/692-dekada2009.

127. Polina Nikol'skaya, "My nikogo ne zastavlyayem vozvrashat'sya," Kommersant, 3 February 2014, http://www.kommersant.ru/doc/2394915.

128. "Kolichestvo uyezhayushchikh russkikh iz Kazakhstana udvoilos," yk.kz,
23 September 2011, http://www.yk.kz/news/show/11692.

129. "Tadzhiki khotyat uyekhat' v Rossiyu kak 'sootechestvenniki,'" BBC Russian Service, 18 November 2012, http://www.bbc.co.uk/russian/russia/2012
/11/121118_tajik_compatriots.

130. "75 tysyach grazhdan Tajikistana imeyut rossiskoye grazhdanstvo," Khovar,
15 July 2008, http://khovar.tj/rus/archive/12157-m.-shabozov-75-tysyach
-grazhdan-tadzhikistana-imeyut-rossiyskoe-grazhdanstvo.html.

131. Peyrouse, "The Russian Minority in Central Asia," p. 13.

132. Igor Zevelev, "Russia's Policy Toward Compatriots in the Former Soviet
Union," Russia in Global Affairs, no. 1 (January–March 2008), http://eng
.globalaffairs.ru/number/n_10351.

133. Bertil Nygren, The Rebuilding of Greater Russia: Putin's Foreign Policy Towards the CIS Countries (London: Routledge, 2008), p. 203.

134. Jennet Nazarova, "The Question of Turkmen-Russian Dual Nationality,"
News Central Asia, 31 March 2013, http://www.newscentralasia.net/2013/03
/31/the-question-of-turkmen-russian-dual-nationality/; Rein Mullerson,
Central Asia: A Chessboard and Player in the New Great Game (London: Routledge, 2007), p. 177.

135. Peyrouse, Turkmenistan: Strategies of Power, Dilemmas of Development,
pp. 91–92.

136. "Kak reshayetsya 'russki vopros' v Turkmenii," Russkiy Mir, 9 April 2013,
http://russkiymir.ru/publications/86154/.

137. "Chego stoit zastupnichestvo Kremlya v Turkmenii?" BBC Russian Service, 4 April 2013, http://www.bbc.co.uk/russian/russia/2013/04/130404
_russia_turkmenistan_compatriots.

138. Ibid.

139. Olcott, *Kazakhstan: Unfulfilled Promise*, pp. 56–57.

140. Mikhail Alexandrov, *Uneasy Alliance: Relations Between Russia and Kazakhstan in the post-Soviet Era* (Westport: Greenwood Press, 1999), pp. 125–29.

141. *Azia* newspaper, 13 April 1994, cited in Sally Cummings, *Kazakhstan: Power and the Elite* (London: I. B. Tauris, 2005), p. 82.

142. "Treaty on the Legal Status of Russian Federation Citizens Residing Permanently on the Territory of the Republic of Kazakhstan, and of Citizens of the Republic of Kazakhstan Residing Permanently on the Territory of Russian Federation" and "Agreement between the Republic of Kazakhstan and Russian Federation on Simplifying the Procedure for Obtaining Citizenship by Citizens of the Russian Federation Arriving for Permanent Residence in Kazakhstan, and Citizens of the Republic of Kazakhstan Arriving for Permanent Residence in Russian Federation," in Alexandrov, *Uneasy Alliance*, p. 129.

143. Alexandrov, *Uneasy Alliance*, pp. 131–35.

144. "Obshchego grazhdanstva u Rossii, Kazakhstana i Belorussii ne budyet," RBK, 26 May 2014, http://top.rbc.ru/economics/26/05/2014/926214.shtml.

145. "Kazakhstantsy nezakonno poluchayut dvoinoye grazhdanstvo," *Kazakhstanskaya Pravda*, 7 August 2014, http://www.kazpravda.kz/news/view /23830.

146. Zakon Respubliki Uzbekistan o Grazhdanstve Respubliki Uzbekistan, http://www1.umn.edu/humanrts/asylum/Ruzbek4.1.12.html.

147. Deistvuyushchiy zakon Kyrgyzskoi Respubliki "O Grazhdanstve KR," http://russkg.ru/index.php?option=com_content&view=article&id=5153:— -q—q&catid=96:2013-05-24-22-55-30&Itemid=71.

148. "Rossiiskaya propaganda gluboko zapustila svoy shchupal'tsa v obshchestvo Kazakhstana," Uainfo, 31 October 2014, http://uainfo.org/blognews/428005 -rossiyskaya-propaganda-gluboko-zapustila-svoi-schupalca-v-obschestvo -kazahstana.html.

149. See above, Chapter 2, note 83.

150. "On December 10, Sputnik Launches Its Multimedia Hub in Kyrgyzstan," Sputnik International, 10 December 2014, http://sputniknews.com/agency _news/20141210/1015685102.html.

151. Chris Rickleton, "Kyrgyzstan: Russian 'Information Wars' Heating Up," Eurasianet.org, 16 April 2014, http://www.eurasianet.org/node/68280.

152. "Modernizatsiya trendov i razvitiye kontenta," *Delovoy Kazakhstan*, 29 February 2013, http://dknews.kz/modernizaciya-trendov-i-razvitie-kontentov/.

153. "Rossiiskaya propaganda gluboko zapustila svoy shchupal'tsa v obshchestvo Kazakhstana," Uainfo, 31 October 2014, http://uainfo.org/blognews/428005 -rossiyskaya-propaganda-gluboko-zapustila-svoi-schupalca-v-obschestvo -kazahstana.html.

154. J'Son & Partners Consulting, "Obzor rynka televizionnogo kontenta v Respublike Kazakhstan," Json.tv, 27 June 2014, http://json.tv/ict_telecom

_analytics_view/obzor-rynka-televizionnogo-kontenta-v-respublike
-kazahstan.

155. "Kazakhstantsy ob Ukraine, Rossii i integratsii," Nomad, 25 April 2014, http://www.nomad.su/?a=10-201404250025.

156. Rickleton, "Kyrgyzstan: Russian 'Information Wars' Heating Up."

157. "Russkiye v Tadzhikistane," Radio Ekho Moskvy, 3 April 2013, http://www.echo.msk.ru/programs/linguafranca/1044568-echo/.

158. "Zhizn' russkikh v Uzbekistane," Radio Ekho Moskvy, 23 July 2013, http://echo.msk.ru/programs/linguafranca/1120730-echo/.

159. "V Uzbekistane otklyuchili rossiyskiy telekanal RBK i telekanal SNG 'MIR,'" Newsru.com, 20 October 2014, http://www.newsru.com/world/20oct2014/uz.html.

160. "V Uzbekistane prekrasno osvedomleny o tom, chto proiskhodit v Ukraine," 12news.uz, 13 October 2014, http://www.12news.uz/news/2014/10/в-узбекистане-прекрасно-осведомлены/.

161. Olcott, Kazakhstan: Unfulfilled Promise, p. 78.

162. "Tsentral'no-Aziatskoye napavleniye TsATU," Tsatu, 17 August 2012, http://catu.su/index.php?option=com_content&view=category&layout=blog&id=39&Itemid=28; David Timerman, "NPO v Tsentral'noy Azii—taktika 'serogo kardinala,'" 12news.uz, 18 August 2014, http://www.12news.uz/news/2014/08/нпо-в-центральной-азии-тактика-сер/.

163. Ilya Azar, "Ust-Kamenogorskaya Narodnaya Respublika," Meduza, 20 October 2014, https://www.meduza.io/news/2014/10/20/ust-kamenogorskaya-narodnaya-respublika.

164. Jeffrey Mankoff, Russian Foreign Policy: The Return of Great Power Politics (Lanham, MD: Rowman & Littlefield, 2012), p. 252.

165. Bohr, "Revolution in Kyrgyzstan—Again," p. 4.

166. Mankoff, Russian Foreign Policy, p. 252.

167. Erica Marat, "Russian Mass Media Attack Bakiyev," Eurasia Daily Monitor 7, no. 63 (1 April 2010), http://www.jamestown.org/programs/edm/single/?tx_ttnews%5Btt_news%5D=36226&tx_ttnews%5BbackPid%5D=484&no_cache=1#.VYgqnGqD67o.

168. Bohr, "Revolution in Kyrgyzstan—Again," p. 4.

169. Roy Allison, Russia, the West, and Military Intervention (Oxford: Oxford University Press, 2013), p. 37.

170. Alexandrov, Uneasy Alliance, p. 122.

171. Izvestiya, 16 November 1993, cited ibid, p. 123.

172. Hill and Jewett, "Back in the USSR," p. 37.

173. "President Nazarbayev Visits Maastricht Conference," BBC Monitoring Service: Former USSR, 4 December 1993, cited in Alexandrov, Uneasy Alliance, p. 124.

174. Ibid.

175. Ibid.

176. Ziegler, "The Russian Diaspora in Central Asia," p. 118.

177. "Putin vstretilsya s rukovoditelyami assotsiatsiy rossiyskikh sootechestven-nikov v Kazakhstane," Newsru.com, 10 October 2000, http://www.newsru .com/russia/10oct2000/russ.html.

178. Lev Gudkov, *Russkiye v Kazakhstane* (Moscow: Nauka, 1995), table 16.

179. Cited in Olcott, *Unfulfilled Promise*, p. 277.

180. Ibid, pp. 76–79.

181. Dmitri Trenin, *The End of Eurasia: Russia on the Border Between Geopolitics and Globalization* (Washington, DC: Carnegie Endowment for International Peace, 2002), pp. 189–90.

182. Olcott, *Kazakhstan: Unfulfilled Promise*, p. 79.

183. Dmitriy Starostin, "Viktor Kazimirchuk: Nas khoteli pokazatel'no udavit,'" *Moskovskiye novosti* 47 (8 December 2006): 12–13, http://www.arba.ru/news /870/.

184. "Kazakhstanskiye kazaki khotyat borot'sya za Krym?" Kursivkz, 28 Febru-ary 2014, http://www.kursiv.kz/news/details/obshestvo/Kazahstanskie -kazaki-hotyat-borotsya-za-Krym/.

185. Joanna Lillis, "Kazakhstan: Russians Blend Loyalty to Nazarbayev with Pro-Kremlin Sentiments," Eurasianet.org, 14 April 2014, http://www.eurasianet .org/node/68270.

186. "Kazakhstan uzhestochayet nakazaniye za separatizm," Newsru.ua, 9 April 2014, http://rus.newsru.ua/world/09apr2014/kazasepar.html.

187. Elena Korotrkova, "Eduard Limonov prizyvayet Rossiyu k okkupatsii severa Kazakhstana," News-Asia, 20 February 2014, http://www.news-asia.ru/view /5948.

188. "Posol RF: zayavleniye o vozmozhnosti prisoyedineniya severa RK k Rossii—bespochvenno," inform.kz, 24 February 2014, http://www.inform .kz/rus/article/2633733.

189. "V Rossii zagovorili o prisoyedinenii Vostochnogo Kazakhstana. Astana obespokoyena," Newsru.ua, 11 April 2014, http://rus.newsru.ua/world /11apr2014/vostokazahstan.html.

190. "MID Respubliki Kazakhstan otreagiroval na rech' Shtygasheva," Kapital, 11 April 2014, http://kapital.kz/gosudarstvo/28852/mid-rk-otreagirovalo-na -rech-shtygasheva.html.

191. "V MID Rossii nazvali bezotvetsvennymi vyskazyvaniya regionalnykh poli-tikov o Kazakhstane," Tengri News, 11 April 2014, http://tengrinews.kz /kazakhstan_news/mid-rossii-nazvali-bezotvetstvennyimi-vyiskazyivaniya -253494/.

192. "Vladimir Zhirinovskiy: 'Posle Ukrainy my zakhvatim Kazakhstan,'" Haqqin.az, 29 August 2014, http://haqqin.az/news/29045.

193. Interview with Nargis Kassenova, 1 January 2015, Almaty, Kazakhstan.

194. Kathleen Collins, *Clan Politics and Regime Transition in Central Asia* (Cam-bridge: Cambridge University Press, 2009); Edward Schatz, *Modern Clan Politics: The Power of "Blood" in Kazakhstan and Beyond* (Seattle: University of Washington Press, 2004); Eric McGlinchey, *Chaos, Violence, Dynasty:*

Politics and Islam in Central Asia (Pittsburgh: University of Pittsburgh Press, 2011).

195. Olcott, *Kazakhstan: Unfulfilled Promise*, pp. 186–87; Bhavna Dave, *Kazakhstan: Ethnicity, Language and Power* (London: Routledge, 2007).

CHAPTER 7. ALLIES OR TARGETS?

Epigraphs: Interview with *Frankfurter Allgemeine Zeitung*, cited in Robin Sheperd, "The United States and Europe's Last Dictatorship," in *Prospects for Democracy in Belarus*, ed. Joerg Forbrig et al. (Washington: GMF, 2006), p. 74; Emil Danielyan, "Ex–Russian Envoy Warns Armenia Over European Integration Drive," Azatutyun.am, 8 July 2013, http://www.azatutyun.am /content/article/25040228.html.

1. Pyotr Kravchenko, *Belarus na Rasputiye, ili Pravda o belovezhskom soglashenii: Zapiski diplomata i politika* (Moscow: Vremiya, 2006), pp. 297, 305.
2. Laure Delcour, "Faithful But Constrained? Armenia's Half-Hearted Support for Russia's Regional Integration Policies in the Post-Soviet Space," London School of Economics Ideas: Geopolitics of Eurasian Integration, 2014, http://ssrn.com/abstract=2460335.
3. Interview with Vytis Jurkonis, 13 December 2014, Vilnius, Lithuania.
4. Andrew Wilson, *Belarus: The Last European Dictatorship* (New Haven, CT: Yale University Press, 2011), p. 51; Jovita Pranevičiūtė-Neliupšienė et al., *Belarusian Regime Longevity: Happily Ever After* (Vilnius: Vilnius University Press, 2014), p. 67.
5. Vytis Jurkonis, "Fate and Role of the Belarusian Language" in Pranevičiūtė-Neliupšienė et al., *Belarusian Regime Longevity*, pp. 81–84.
6. Kathleen J. Mihalisko, "Belarus: Retreat to Authoritarianism," in *Democratic Changes and Authoritarian Reactions in Russia, Ukraine, Belarus, and Moldova*, ed. Karen Dawisha and Bruce Parrott (Cambridge: Cambridge University Press, 1997), p. 233.
7. Jurkonis interview.
8. Valiancin Akudovič, *Nesaties kodas* (Vilnius: Versus Aureus, 2008).
9. Alexander Lukashenko, State of the Nation Address to the Belarusian people and the National Assembly, 22 April 2014, http://president.gov.by/en /news_en/view/alexander-lukashenko-to-deliver-state-of-the-nation-address -on-22-april-8550/.
10. More information at http://budzma.by.
11. Interview with Roman Yakovlevsky, January 2015, Minsk, Belarus.
12. Interview with Hovhannes Nikoghosyan, 10 December 2014, Yerevan, Armenia.
13. Rossiyskiy tsentr nauki i kultury v Yerevane, "Armyano-rossiyskiye otnosheniya," http://arm.rs.gov.ru/node/406.
14. Ohannes Geukjian, *Ethnicity, Nationalism and Conflict in the South Caucasus: Nagorno-Karabakh and the Legacy of Soviet Nationalities Policy* (Farnham, UK: Ashgate, 2012).

15. Thomas de Waal, *Black Garden* (New York: New York University Press, 2003), pp. 116–18.

16. Ibid, p. 162.

17. Nikoghosyan interview.

18. Peter Pry, *War Scare: Russia and America on the Nuclear Brink* (Westport: Greenwood, 1999), pp. 122–25.

19. "Dogovor mezhdu Rossiyskoy Federatsiyey i Respublikoy Armeniya o rossiyskoy voyennoy baze na territorii Respubliki Armeniya," 16 March 1995, http://docs.cntd.ru/document/901933348.

20. Interview with Emil Sanamyan, January 2015, Washington, DC.

21. De Waal, *Black Garden*, p. 202.

22. Thomas de Waal, *The Caucasus: An Introduction* (Oxford: Oxford University Press, 2010), p. 116.

23. National Statistical Committee of the Republic of Belarus, Population Census 2009, http://belstat.gov.by/en/perepis-naseleniya/perepis-naseleniya -2009-goda/.

24. Oleg Manaev, ed., *The Future of Belarus: The Perspective of Independent Experts* (St. Petersburg: Nevskii prostor, 2012), p. 36.

25. National Statistical Service of the Republic of Armenia, 2011 Armenian Nationwide Census, http://armstat.am/file/doc/99478358.pdf.

26. Interview with Artyom, November 2014, Yerevan, Armenia.

27. Interview with Araxya, November 2014, Yerevan, Armenia.

28. Interview with Valentina, November 2014, Yerevan, Armenia.

29. Interview with Kristina, November 2014, Yerevan, Armenia.

30. Interview with Ivan, December 2014, Minsk, Belarus.

31. See more at Zapadnaya Rus', http://zapadrus.su/.

32. Interview with Nastya, December 2014, Minsk, Belarus.

33. *Vatniki* is a derogatory term used to denote Russian patriots. In the original meaning, it is a quilted jacket, but since 2012 it has been used on the Russian-speaking internet to symbolize Russian rednecks.

34. Interview with Pavel Usov, January 2015, Minsk, Belarus.

35. Interview with Tatsiana, December 2014, Minsk, Belarus.

36. Interview with Olga, December 2014, Minsk, Belarus.

37. Jurkonis interview.

38. "Boris Gryzlov: Armeniya yavlyayetsya forpostom Rossii na Yuzhnom Kavkaze," Regnum, 15 December 2004, http://www.regnum.ru/news/polit /376296.html.

39. "Armenian, Russian Presidents Sign New Cooperation Agreement," Radio Free Europe/Radio Liberty, 27 September 2000, http://www.rferl.org/content /article/1142248.html.

40. "Russia Extends Lease on Military Base in Armenia Through 2044," Sputnik International, 20 August 2010, http://sputniknews.com/military/20100820 /160276128.html.

41. Delcour, "Faithful But Constrained?"

42. Anna Dolgov, "Russian Activists Ask Putin to Send Troops Into Armenia," *Moscow Times*, 19 January 2015, http://www.themoscowtimes.com/news /article/russian-activists-ask-putin-to-send-troops-into-armenia-/514546.html.

43. Emil Sanamyan, "Gruesome Killings Threaten Russian-Armenian Rapport," *Jane's Defence Weekly*, 4 February 2015.

44. Sergey Markedonov, "Russia and Armenia in the South Caucasus Security Context: Basic Trends and Hidden Contradictions," in *Armenia's Foreign And Domestic Politics: Development Trends*, ed. Mikko Palonkorpi and Alexander Iskandaryan (Yerevan: Caucasus Institute and Aleksanteri Institute, 2013), p. 30.

45. Sargis Arutyunyan, "V sluchaye napadeniya Azerbaidzhana na Karabakh 'v konflikt mozhet byt vovlechena' rossiyskaya baza v Armenii," Azatutyun.am, 31 October 2013, http://rus.azatutyun.am/content/article/25153651.html.

46. Vadim Dubnov, "Kak polkovnik Ruzinskiy possoril Rossiyu i Azerbaidzhan," RIANovosti, 7 November 2013, http://ria.ru/analytics/20131107/975370885 .html.

47. "Rusakan razmabazayi tsaxseri kesy Hayastani aghqatik byujei userin e," azatutyun.am, 6 November 2014, http://www.azatutyun.am/content/article /26678066.html.

48. Heritage Foundation, 2014 Index of Economic Freedom: Armenia, http:// www.heritage.org/index/country/armenia.

49. Sergey Minasyan, "Russia and Armenia," in *Russian Federation 2013: Short-term Prognosis*, ed. Karmo Tüür and Viacheslav Morozov (Tartu: Tartu University Press, 2013), http://www.ut.ee/ABVKeskus/sisu/prognoosid/2013/en /pdf/VF2013.pdf.

50. European Commission Directorate General for Trade, "European Union, Trade in Goods with Armenia," http://trade.ec.europa.eu/doclib/docs/2006 /september/tradoc_113345.pdf.

51. Armen Sahakyan, "Threading the Needle: Armenia's Policy towards the EU and the EAU," The European Institute, April 2013, http://www .europeaninstitute.org/index.php/173-european-affairs/ea-april-2013/1722 -threading-the-needle-armenias-policy-towards-the-eu-and-the-eau.

52. "Vaghe storagrvelu e 'Guyk' partk'i dimats' hamadzaynagire," azatutyun.am, 16 July 2002, http://www.azatutyun.am/content/article/1569922.html; Ian McGinnity, "Selling Its Future for Short: Armenia's Economic and Security Relations with Russia" (Senior thesis, Claremont McKenna College, 2010), pp. 7–8, http://scholarship.claremont.edu/cgi/viewcontent.cgi?article=1059 &context=cmc_theses.

53. Vladimir Socor, "Armenia's Giveaways to Russia: From Property-For-Debt to Property-For-Gas," *Eurasia Daily Monitor* 3, no. 7 (19 April 2006), http://www .jamestown.org/single/?no_cache=1&tx_ttnews[tt_news]=31599.

54. Vitali Silitski, "Belarus in an International Context," in *Belarus and the EU: From Isolation Towards Cooperation*, ed. Hans Georg Wieck and Stephan Malerius (Berlin: Konrad Adenauer Stiftung, 2011), p. 15.

55. Ben Judah et al., *Dealing With a Post-BRIC Russia* (Brussels: ECFR, 2011), http://www.ecfr.eu/page/-/ECFR44_POST-BRIC_RUSSIA.pdf; "Antey i Volga: Rossiyskiye voyennye bazy na territorii Belarusi," 19 October 2014, http://1863x.com/antei-volga/; Živilė Dambrauskaitė et al., *Belarusian Challenge to the New EU Policy: Ignorance Equals Legitimation* (Vilnius: EESC, 2010), http://www.eesc.lt/uploads/news/id452/Belarusian%20Challenge%20to%20the%20New%20EU%20Policy-Ignorance%20Equals%20Legitimation_EN.pdf.
56. "V belorusskom Bobruiske raspolozhitsya rossiyskaya voyennaya baza," Pravda.ru, 15 October 2014, http://www.pravda.ru/news/world/formerussr/belorussia/15-10-2014/1231181-baza-0/.
57. Belarusian Optical & Mechanical Association, http://www.belomo.by/en/; BalTechExport, http://www.bte.by/en/o-kompanii/; Joint Stock Company, "140th Repair Plant," http://www.140zavod.org/en.
58. Anna Maria Dyner, "Prospects and Consequences of Military Cooperation between Belarus and Russia," PISM Bulletin, no. 61 (514) (4 June 2013), http://www.pism.pl/files/?id_plik=13796.
59. Vytis Jurkonis and Tadas Pikčiūnas, "(In)dependent Economy of Belarus Through the Lenses of International Trade and FDI," in Pranevičiūtė-Neliupšienė et al., *Belarusian Regime Longevity*, pp. 254–56.
60. Laurynas Jonavičius, "From Russia with Love: Internal Balance of Power in Russia and the Survival of Lukashenko's Regime," in Pranevičiūtė-Neliupšienė et al., *Belarusian Regime Longevity*, p. 238.
61. "Beltransgaz Returns to Gazprom Family," Gazprom, 4 April 2014, http://www.gazprom.com/press/reports/2012/beltransgaz-photo-reportage/.
62. Silitski, "Belarus in an International Context," pp. 14–17.
63. Jurkonis interview; "Belorusskiye kompanii nevol'no 'otmyli' milliardy rossiyskikh dollarov," Myfin.by, 12 June 2013, http://myfin.by/stati/view/1711-belorusskie-banki-nevolno-otmyli-milliardy-rossijskih-dollarov.
64. Robin Sheperd, "The United States and Europe's Last Dictatorship," in Forbrig et al., *Prospects for Democracy in Belarus*, p. 74.
65. Vytis Jurkonis, "Kremlin Is Forcing Belarus to Be Part of the Russian World," svaboda.org, 20 June 2014, http://www.svaboda.org/content/article/25429862.html.
66. Usov interview.
67. Jurkonis, "Kremlin Is Forcing Belarus to Be Part of the Russian World."
68. Laurynas Jonavičius, "Epilogue," in Pranevičiūtė-Neliupšienė et al., *Belarusian Regime Longevity*, p. 318.
69. "Lukashenko dal ukazaniye snizhat' vliyaniye russkogo yazyka i ukreplyat' 'belorusskuyu natsiyu,'" Novorossiya, 25 November 2014, http://novorus.info/news_don/policy_don/30642-lukashenko-dal-ukazanie-snizhat-vliyanie-russkogo-yazyka-i-ukreplyat-belorusskuyu-naciyu.html.
70. Alexander Lukashenko, State of the Nation Address to the Belarusian people and the National Assembly, 22 April 2014.

71. "Belarus' nachinayet derussifikatsiyu shkol," Belnovosti, 24 January 2015, http://belnovosti.by/society/34845-belarus-nachinaet-derusifikaciju-shkol .html; "After Decades of Russian Dominance, Belarus Begins to Reclaim Its Language," The Guardian, 28 January 2015, http://www.theguardian.com /world/2015/jan/28/-sp-russian-belarus-reclaims-language-belarusian.
72. Jurkonis interview.
73. "Negativnaya dinamika doveriya institutam," http://iiseps.org/old/12-13-05 .html.
74. "Veruyushchikh v Belarusi men'she, chem . . . pravoslavnykah," 31 December 2011, http://naviny.by/rubrics/society/2011/12/23/ic_articles_116_176268 /.
75. " 'Chernyi internatsional': Kak Moskva kormit pravye partii po vsemu miru," The Insider, 27 November 2014, http://theins.ru/politika/2113/.
76. "Svyataya Rus,'" http://www.holyrussia.com/; "Kazaki v Respubliki Belarus,'" http://www.kazaki.by/; "Zapadnaya Rus,'" http://zapadrus.su/; "Ustav ROO 'Belorusskoye kazachestvo,'" http://belkazak.by/org/ustav.html.
77. Nezavisimyi institut sotsial'no-ekonomicheskikh i politicheskikh issledovanii, "Pobeda kak ob'edinyaushchiy simvol raskolotogo obshchestva," http:// iiseps.org/old/03-12-08.html.
78. See Pavel Shekhtman, "Plamya davnikh pozharov," Armenian House, 1992, http://www.armenianhouse.org/shekhtman/docs-ru/contents.html.
79. "Hogevor arrachnordnere koch en anum het k'ashel dipukaharnerin," azatutyun.am, 29 November 2011, http://www.azatutyun.am/content/article /24404406.html; "Armenian, Azeri Faith Leaders Make Karabakh Pledge," Today's Zaman, 27 April 2010, http://www.todayszaman.com/world _armenian-azeri-faith-leaders-make-karabakh-pledge_208622.html.
80. "Fond 'Russkiy mir' otkryvayet v Erevane 'Russkiy tsentr,'" Russkiy Mir, 5 February 2008, http://russkiymir.ru/news/12911/; "Naira Airapetyan: russkiy yazyk v Armenii ne dolzhen byt' inostrannym," Russkiy Mir, 29 August 2014, http://www.russkiymir.ru/publications/149085/.
81. "Russkiy yazyk v Armenii ne chuzhoy—predstavitel' Rossotrudnichestva," 12 November 2010, http://newsarmenia.ru/arm1/20101112/42341498.html.
82. "Russia's Chief Propagandist," Economist, 10 December 2013, http://www .economist.com/blogs/easternapproaches/2013/12/Ukraine; "Nel'zya kul'turno integrirovat'sya v odnom napravlenii, a bezopasnost' iskat' v drugom—Kiselev ob Armenii," Regnum, 12 June 2014, http://regnum.ru /news/fd-abroad/armenia/1813489.html/.
83. "Russkiy yazyk yavlyaetsya opredelennym tegom armyano-rossiyskikh otnoshenii—Ashotyan," 26 August 2014, http://newsarmenia.ru/society /20140826/43094546.html; "Ministr obrazovaniya Armenii: Armyanskaya molodezh' nuzhdayetsya v russkom yazyke," Fond Gorchakova, 13 November 2014, http://gorchakovfund.ru/news/9059/; "K'arravarut'yune rrusats lezvin petakan kark'avidjak shnorhelu anhrajeshtut'yun chi tesnum," azatutyun. am, 12 June 2014, http://www.azatutyun.am/content/article/25419398.html;

"Armen Arzumanyan: 'HH nahagahe drakan e verabervum michazgayin chapanishnerov dprots himnadrelun,'" panorama.am, 9 June 2010, http://www.panorama.am/am/education/2010/06/09/armen-arzumanyan/.

84. "Soglasheniye mezhdu Pravitel'stvom Rossiyskoy Federatsii i Pravitel'stvom Respubliki Armeniya ob usloviyakh uchrezhdeniya i deyatel'nosti v gorode Erevane Rossiysko-Armyanskogo universiteta," http://rau.am/uploads/blocks/0/6/650/files/650_1_soglashenie_old.pdf.

85. "Raskhody na filial MGU v Erevane voz'met na seba Armeniya," rus.azatutyun.am, 27 August 2014, http://rus.azatutyun.am/content/article/26552713.html.

86. "Dos'e: Rossiysko-armyanskiye otnosheniya," Tass, 2 December 2013, http://itar-tass.com/info/803765.

87. Sahakyan, "Threading the Needle: Armenia's Policy towards the EU and the EAU."

88. Laure Delcour and Hrant Kostanyan, "Towards a Fragmented Neighbourhood: Policies of the EU and Russia and Their Consequences for the Area That Lies In Between," CEPS Essays No. 17, 17 October 2014, http://ssrn.com/abstract=2513712; Sergey Minasyan, "Russian-Armenian Relations: Affection or Pragmatism?" PONARS Eurasia Policy Memo No. 269, July 2013, http://www.ponarseurasia.org/memo/russian-armenian-relations-affection-or-pragmatism.

89. Sergey Markedonov, "Russia and Armenia in the South Caucasus Security Context: Basic Trends and Hidden Contradictions," in Palonkorpi and Iskandaryan, *Armenia's Foreign and Domestic Politics*, pp. 29–36.

90. "Nevstupleniye Armenii v EAES moglo by privesti k kollapsu i potere $3–4 mlrd. za pyat' let—ekonomist," 29 November 2014, http://www.newsarmenia.ru/politics/20141129/43132272.html.

91. Sergey Glazyev, "Who Stands to Win?" *Russia in Global Affairs*, 27 December 2013, http://eng.globalaffairs.ru/number/Who-Stands-to-Win-16288; "Vyacheslav Kovalenko: Vstupleniye Armenii v Evraziyskiy soyuz stalo by dlya nee bol'shim blagom," PanArmenian.net, 4 December 2011, http://www.panarmenian.net/rus/interviews/85626/.

92. Delcour and Kostanyan, "Towards a Fragmented Neighbourhood."

93. "Nuclear Power in Armenia," http://www.world-nuclear.org/info/Country-Profiles/Countries-A-F/Armenia/.

94. Natalya Oganova, "Rossiysko-armyanskiye otnosheniya nakhoditsya na bespretsedentno vysokom urovne," *NoyevKovcheg*, no 8 (May 2014), http://www.noev-kovcheg.ru/mag/2014-08/4466.html.

95. Sargis Arutyunyan, "Posol RF predlagayet 'neitrolizovat'' NPO, 'vbivayushchiye klin' v rossiysko-armyanskiye otnosheniya," rus.azatutyun.am, 7 May 2014, http://rus.azatutyun.am/content/article/25376316.html.

96. Tigran Avetisian, "Russian Senator Slams Pro-EU NGOs in Armenia," azatutyun.am, 27 February 2015, http://www.azatutyun.mobi/a/26872870.html.

97. Interview with *Frankfurter Allgemeine Zeitung*, cited in Sheperd, "The United States and Europe's Last Dictatorship," p. 74.

98. "Lukashenko pro zapret na postavki belorusskoy produktsii: My fakticheski odna strana. Zachem vy eto delayete?" Tut.by, 27 November 2014, http://news.tut.by/economics/425473.html.

99. Manaev, *The Future of Belarus*, p. 56.

100. "'Russkiy Mir' otkroyet tsentr v Breste," Regnum, 2 December 2014, http://www.regnum.ru/news/fd-abroad/belarus/1872496.html.

101. Usov interview.

102. Predstavitel'stvo Rossotrudnichestva v Respublike Belarus', "O predstavitel'stve," http://blr.rs.gov.ru/node/1.

103. The *Pahonia* (or *Vytis*) was the coat of arms of the Grand Duchy of Lithuania, of which Belarus was an important part.

104. Jurkonis interview.

105. Kravchenko, *Belarus na Rasputiye*, pp. 303–7.

106. Oksana Yanovskaya, "Inostrantsy budut zhit' v Belarusi po novym pravilam," Naviny.by, 6 April 2010, http://naviny.by/rubrics/society/2010/04/06/ic_articles_116_167351/.

107. "Portret belorusskogo gastarbaytera," *Delovaya gazeta*, 16 December 2014, http://bdg.by/news/society/31946.html; Andrei Yeliseyeu, "Response to the Research Report 'The Impact of Labour Migration on Belarus: A Demographic Perspective,'" CARIM-East Analytic and Synthetic Notes 2012/13, 2012, http://www.carim-east.eu/media/CARIM-East-AS2012-13.pdf.

108. Vladimir Stupishin, *Moya missiya v Armeniyu. 1992–94* (Moscow: Academia, 2001), http://armenianhouse.org/stupishin/docs-ru/mission/48.html.

109. Ovannes Nikogosyan, "Armeniya mezhdu dvumya Evro: Evro-pa ili Evr-azia," *The Analitikon*, November 2011, http://theanalyticon.com/?p=1127&lang=ru.

110. "End of 'Compatriots'? Government says Russian Immigration Program Unacceptable for Armenia," ArmeniaNow.com, 4 October 2012, http://www.armenianow.com/society/40234/russian_program_compatriots_concerns_armenia_labor_migration.

111. "Yeritasardakan nakhadzerrnut'yune pahanjum e p'akel 'Hamyerkratsiner' ts'ragire," azatutyun.am, 2 August 2011, http://www.azatutyun.am/content/article/24284913.html; "Mtavorakannere ahatsang en hnchetsnum," azatutyun.am, 1 July 2007, http://www.azatutyun.am/content/article/24252709.html.

112. "Hayastane 'k'aghak'akan makardakum' klutsi 'Hamyerkratsiner' tsragri khndire," azatutyun.am, 22 July 2011, http://www.azatutyun.am/content/article/24273494.html.

113. "'Hamyerkratsiner' tsragrov HH marzerits Rusastan e meknel 600 entanik', nor tsragir," news.am, 11 August 2011, http://news.am/arm/news/70646.html.

114. The USAID-supported Eurasia Partnership Foundation was among the most visible.

115. "'Hamyerkratsiner'—i vtange tegh hasav (tesanyut)," a1+, 12 October 2012, http://www.a1plus.am/64516.html.

116. "Hayastani karravarut'yune dimakayum e rrusakan 'Hamyerkratsi' tsragrin," panorama.am, 3 October 2012, http://www.panorama.am/am /politics/2012/10/03/government/.

117. "End of 'Compatriots'?"

118. "Derr dimum chen endunum," armtimes.com, 24 May 2013, http://www .armtimes.com/hy/6500; "Hayastanits Rusastan ugharkoh rusakan 'Hamy-erkratsiner' tsragir sarretsvel e," news.am, 22 January 2014, http://news.am /arm/news/190319.html.

119. "Hayastani bnakchut'yun 10 tokose Rusastani q'akha'qatsiut'yun uni," azat-utyun.am, 21 March 2014, http://www.azatutyun.am/content/article /25305438.html.

120. "End of 'Compatriots'?"

121. "Hayastani bnakchut'yun 10 tokose Rusastani q'akha'qatsiut'yun uni."

122. Dmitry Travin, "Belarusian 'Godfather' Falls Out with His Masters," Open-Democracy, 12 July 2010, https://www.opendemocracy.net/dmitry-travin /belarusian-godfather-falls-out-with-his-masters.

123. "TV-Propaganda and Life," IISEPS, 10 October 2014, http://iiseps.org /analitica/812/lang/en.

124. "Negativnaya dinamika doveriya institutam"; "TV-Propaganda and Life."

125. Jurkonis interview.

126. Konstantin Amelyushkin, "Belorusskiy oppozitsioner: Lukashenko nabi-rayet ochki ne bez pomoshchi ES," 25 November 2014, http://ru.delfi.lt /news/politics/belorusskij-oppozicioner-lukashenko-nabiraet-ochki-ne-bez -pomoschi-es.d?id=66491042#ixzz3MFcBNLce.

127. Edward S. Herman and Noam Chomsky, *Manufacturing Consent: The Political Economy of the Mass Media* (New York: Pantheon Books, 1988).

128. "Gerakshorgh kartsik': Hayastan-Gharabagh sahmanin (irakan) mak'saket chi lini," ArmeniaNow.com, 3 June 2014, https://www.armenianow.com/hy /economy/54888/armenia_karabakh_eurasian_union_customs_border; "Maksayin mtahozut'yunner: Gharabaghi het sahmanin hnaravor maksa-keti," ArmeniaNow.com, 6 October 2014, http://armenianow.com/hy /karabakh/57358/armenia_karabakh_customs_border_eurasian_union.

129. "Gharabaghi yev Hayastani michev maksaket chi divelu: Ekonomikayi na-harar," henaran.am, 15 October 2014, http://henaran.am/news_view.php ?post_id=48778.

130. "Enddimadirnere tsankanum en gharabaghi hantsnel," October 2013, http://www.iravunk.com/index.php?option=com_content&view=article&id =10567:2013-10-16-16-02-48; "Rus portsaget: Hayastani yev Gharabaghi sah-manin maksaket, t'ekuzev dzevakan, bayts klini," azatutyun.am, 29 Septem-ber 2014, http://www.azatutyun.am/content/article/26611093.html;

"Khmagrakan: Gharabaghi prkutyune Gharabaghe 'Gharabaghi prkoghne-rits' prklene," ilur.am, 19 October 2013, http://www.ilur.am/news/view /19934.html.

131. "Ex-Russian Envoy Warns Armenia Over European Integration Drive," azatutyun.am, 8 August 2013, http://www.azatutyun.am/content/article /25040228.html.

132. Hayk Hovhannisyan, "Russia Tightens Grip as Armenia Moves Closer to Europe," *asbarez.com*, 1 August 2013, http://asbarez.com/112324/russia -tightens-grip-as-armenia-moves-closer-to-europe/.

133. "Armenian Parliament Ratifies Treaty on Joining Eurasian Economic Union," Tass, 4 December 2014, http://itar-tass.com/en/economy/765194.

134. Thomas de Waal, "An Offer Sargsyan Could Not Refuse," Eurasia Outlook, Carnegie Moscow Center, 4 September 2013, http://carnegie.ru /eurasiaoutlook/?fa=52841.

135. Zulfugar Agayev, "Azeri-Russian Arms Trade $4 Billion Amid Tension With Armenia," BloombergBusiness, 13 August 2013, http://www .bloomberg.com/news/articles/2013-08-13/azeri-russian-arms-trade-4 -billion-amid-tension-with-armenia.

136. Ibid.

137. In the past, Lukashenko has expressed concern about separatism only regarding the Grodno region, but the potential instigator here was perceived to be Poland, not Russia. "Lukashenko zanyalsya poiskami proyavleniy separatizma v Belarusi," ua-ru.info, 16 November 2014, http://www.ua-ru.info /news/37017-lukashenko-zanyalsya-poiskami-proyavleniy-separatizma-v -belarusi.html.

138. "Reuters: Armenia, Belarus Refuse to Sign up EaP Declaration over Crimea Reference," ArmeniaNow, 21 May 2015, http://armenianow.com/news /63646/armenia_riga_summit_eu_eastern_partnership_crimea.

139. Alexander Lukashenko, State of the Nation Address to the Belarusian people and the National Assembly, 22 April 2014.

140. Alexander Lukashenko, Address of the President to the Belarusian People and the National Assembly, 29 April 2015, http://president.gov.by/en/news _en/view/belarus-president-to-address-nation-parliament-on-29-april-11303/.

141. Jonavičius, "From Russia with Love," p. 229; Petr Kravchenko, *Belarus na Rasputiye*, p. 305.

142. Jonavičius, "Epilogue," p. 208; Vytis Jurkonis, "Vitis Jurkonis: Partnerstvo s Kremlem—eto igra so spichkami u benzokolonki," *belaruspartisan.org*, 31 May 2014, http://www.belaruspartisan.org/politic/268531/.

143. Alexander Lukashenko, Address of the President to the Belarusian people and the National Assembly, 29 April 2015, http://president.gov.by/en/news _en/view/belarus-president-to-address-nation-parliament-on-29-april-11303/.

144. Shaun Walker, "Who's That Boy in the Grey Suit? It's Kolya Lukashenko— the Next Dictator of Belarus . . . ," *The Independent*, 29 June 2012, http:// www.independent.co.uk/news/world/europe/whos-that-boy-in-the-grey-suit

-its-kolya-lukashenko—the-next-dictator-of-belarus-7897089.html; "Belarus' Leader Denies Building Dynasty," Sputnik International, 2 July 2012, http://sputniknews.com/world/20120702/174366944.html.

145. "Belarus: 'Silent Protests' Outlawed," *New York Times*, 5 October 2011, http://www.nytimes.com/2011/10/06/world/europe/belarus-silent-protests-outlawed.html?_r=0.

146. European Union External Action, "What the European Union Could Bring to Belarus," http://eeas.europa.eu/delegations/belarus/documents/eu_belarus/non_paper_1106.pdf.

147. "Belarus: Presidential Election Day Ends in Protests and Crackdown," GlobalVoices, 19 December 2010, http://globalvoicesonline.org/2010/12/19/belarus-presidential-election-day-ends-in-protests-and-crackdown/.

148. Paul Roderick, "Putin Comes Out On Top In New Minsk Agreement," *Forbes*, 13 February 2015, http://www.forbes.com/sites/paulroderickgregory/2015/02/13/putin-comes-out-on-top-in-new-minsk-agreement/.

149. See "Ustav ROO 'Belarusskoye Kazachestvo,'" Belorusskoye Kazachestvo, http://belkazak.by/org/ustav.html; "Kazaki v Respublike Belarus'," http://www.kazaki.by/.

150. "Ukrainian Compass for Geopolitical Poles of Belarus," IISEPS, 4 October 2010, http://iiseps.org/analitica/808/lang/en; "Attitude to Separatism in Belarus: 'Doves' and 'Hawks,'" IIPS, 6 October 2014, http://iiseps.org/analitica/809/lang/en.

151. Delcour, "Faithful But Constrained?"

152. Dolgov, "Russian Activists Ask Putin to Send Troops Into Armenia."

153. Irina Hovhannisyan, "Yerevan Silent after Russian 'Threat,'" azatutyun.am, 18 April 2014, http://www.azatutyun.mobi/a/25354760.html.

154. "Mitinguyushchiye v Armenii posovetovali Putinu 'idti domoy,'" BBC Russian Service, 2 December 2013, http://www.bbc.co.uk/russian/international/2013/12/131202_russia_armenia_rally.

155. Sargis Arutyunyan, "V Armenii znachitel'no sokratilos' chislo storonnikov Evraziyskogo soyuza," azatutyun.am, 10 September 2014, http://rus.azatutyun.am/content/article/26576404.html.

156. Nikoghosyan interview.

157. Sanamyan interview.

CONCLUSION

Epigraph: R. J. W. Evans and Hartmut Pogge von Strandmann, eds., *The Coming of the First World War* (Oxford: Clarendon Press, 2001), p. 120.

1. Alexander J. Motyl, "The Surrealism of Realism: Misreading the War in Ukraine," *World Affairs* (January–February 2015), http://www.worldaffairsjournal.org/article/surrealism-realism-misreading-war-ukraine; John J. Mearsheimer, "Why the Ukraine Crisis Is the West's Fault: The Liberal Delusions That Provoked Putin," *Foreign Affairs*, September–October 2014, http://www.foreignaffairs.com/articles/141769/john-j-mearsheimer

/why-the-ukraine-crisis-is-the-wests-fault; Noam Chomsky, "Ossetia-Russia-Georgia," chomsky.info, 9 September 2008, http://www.chomsky.info/articles/200809—2.htm; Andrei Tsygankov, "The High Cost of Ignoring Russia in Ukraine," *Moscow Times*, 28 February 2014, http://www.themoscowtimes.com/opinion/article/the-high-cost-of-ignoring-russia-in-ukraine/495336.html.

2. Edward W. Said, *Orientalism* (New York: Vintage, 1978).

3. Fabio Belafatti, "Orientalism Reanimated: Colonial Thinking in Western Analysts' Comments on Ukraine," EuroMaidan, 27 October 2014, http://euromaidanpress.com/2014/10/27/western-commentators-should-rid-themselves-of-old-prejudices-dating-back-from-the-age-of-colonialism-before-commenting-on-eastern-european-affairs/.

INDEX

Abkhazia, 28, 53–55, 107, 114, 133–34,
244, 252, 254; compatriot policies,
90, 116–17; energy policy, 113;
information warfare, 124–26;
passportization, 43, 83, 119–20;
peacekeeping in, 115–16; protection,
129–31; Russian speakers, 105
Akayev, Askar, 175
annexation, 9, 27, 53–56, 97–98,
132–33, 256; of Crimea, 92, 123–24,
127, 129, 160; threat in Abhkazia
and South Ossetia, 133–34; threat
in Baltic States, 162; threat in
Northern Kazakhstan, 207; threat
in Transnistria, 133
Armenia, 18–19, 23, 108, 197, 211–12,
242–43, 248–50; history of, 211–12,
214; information warfare, 234–36;
passportization, 41, 231–33; protection, 238–39; and Russian interests,
220–22; Russian speakers, 215–18;
soft power, 226–29
Armenian Apostolic Church, 33, 226
ArmRosGasProm, 222
Assembly of the People of Kazakhstan,
194

Association Agreement with the EU,
19; of Armenia, 234–35, 249; of
Moldova, 113; of Ukraine, 108,
236
Atambayev, Almazbek, 175, 186
Atasu-Alashankou pipeline, 187
Atyrau-Samara pipeline, 187
Azerbaijan, 10, 113, 175, 187, 224; and
Armenia, 211–12, 214–15, 221, 227,
234–35, 238–39

Baikonur Cosmodrome, 185
Bakiyev, Kurmanbek, 175, 203–4
Baku-Tbilisi-Ceyhan pipeline, 20, 107,
187
Baltic Pipeline System-2, 223
Baltic States, 10, 20, 23, 31, 56, 63,
245–46; citizenship policies of, 42;
compatriot policies, 69, 71, 73, 93;
history of, 49, 66, 213; information
warfare, 245; passportization, 42,
199; provocations, 22; and Russian
interests, 17, 19, 35, 50; Russian
speakers, 252. *See also* Estonia,
Latvia, Lithuania
Baranovichi radar system, 222